VIOLENT OFFENDERS

Theory, Research, Public Policy, and Practice

Matt DeLisi, PhD
Department of Sociology
Iowa State University
Ames, IA

Peter J. Conis, PhD
Department of Sociology
Iowa State University
Ames, IA

JONES AND BARTLETT PUBLISHERS

Sudbury, Massachusetts

BOSTON   TORONTO   LONDON   SINGAPORE

World Headquarters

Jones and Bartlett Publishers
40 Tall Pine Drive
Sudbury, MA 01776
978-443-5000
info@jbpub.com
www.jbpub.com

Jones and Bartlett Publishers
Canada
6339 Ormindale Way
Mississauga, Ontario L5V 1J2
CANADA

Jones and Bartlett Publishers
International
Barb House, Barb Mews
London W6 7PA
UK

Jones and Bartlett's books and products are available through most bookstores and online booksellers. To contact Jones and Bartlett Publishers directly, call 800-832-0034, fax 978-443-8000, or visit our website, www.jbpub.com.

Substantial discounts on bulk quantities of Jones and Bartlett's publications are available to corporations, professional associations, and other qualified organizations. For details and specific discount information, contact the special sales department at Jones and Bartlett via the above contact information or send an email to specialsales@jbpub.com.

Production Credits

Acquisitions Editor: Jeremy Spiegel
Production Director: Amy Rose
Editorial Assistant: Lisa Gordon
Associate Production Editor: Mike Boblitt
Marketing Manager: Wendy Thayer
Cover Design: Kristin E. Ohlin
Manufacturing Buyer: Amy Bacus
Composition: Publishers' Design and Production Services, Inc.
Cover Image: © Evon Lim Seo Ling/ShutterStock, Inc.
Chapter Opener Image: © Masterfile
Printing and Binding: Malloy, Inc.
Cover Printing: Malloy, Inc.

Library of Congress Cataloging-in-Publication Data

DeLisi, Matt.
    Violent offenders : theory, research, public policy, and practice / Matthew DeLisi and Peter Conis. — 1st ed.
        p. cm.
    Includes bibliographical references and index.
    ISBN-13: 978-0-7637-5479-2
    ISBN-10: 0-7637-5479-X
    1. Violent offenders. 2. Violent crimes—Research. 3. Criminal psychology. 4. Criminology. I. Conis, Peter. II. Title.
    HV6133.D45 2008
    364.15—dc22

                                                                                        2007024848

6048

Printed in the United States of America
11 10 09 08 07   10 9 8 7 6 5 4 3 2 1

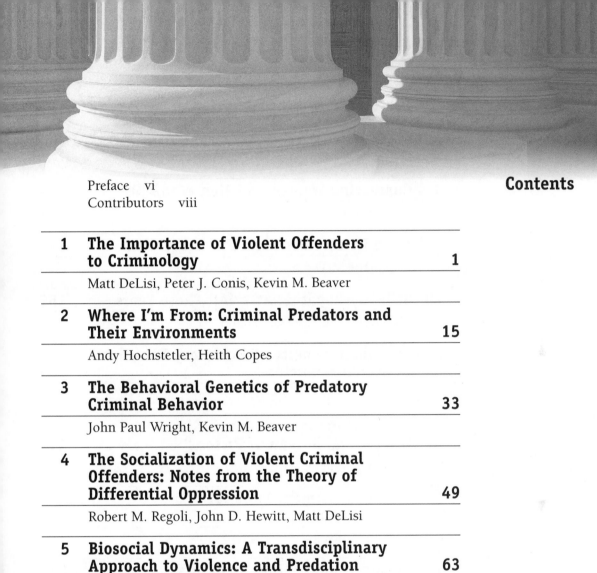

Contents

Contents

Preface

What is it about "bad guys" (i.e., violent offenders) that gets people so interested in criminal justice? Why is it that the more extreme, the more reprehensible, and the more dramatic the antisocial behavior, the more likely it will spawn a television series, movie, or book? Why are our criminology and criminal justice undergraduates so eager to become forensic psychologists, criminal profilers, FBI Special Agents, or crime scene investigators? The answer is easy: They want to catch the "bad guys."

For some, the interest in criminal justice—especially the interest in the most serious and violent offenders—is simply intrigue. Others view an emphasis on violent criminals as a fad, or entertainment, or sensationalistic fodder for unrefined minds. Still others view violent offenders as a diversion from the real menace to society: white-collar criminals. There is no one, clear-cut, explanation for this phenomenon.

That we are so fascinated by the "bad guys" speaks to the fundamental goodness of people. Violent criminal offenders aggravate our sense of morality. We are appalled by those who murder, rape, rob, and molest because they violate basic fundamental codes of conduct. Violent offenders serve as a sort of measuring stick to evaluate our own conduct and to try to understand the reasons why some people commit grievous forms of antisocial behavior. With violent offenders, we are at once interested and unnerved, fascinated and repulsed, outraged and sympathetic.

"Bad guys" get a lot of attention for another important reason: They commit the bulk of bad acts that occur in society. This is an important scientific point. The most active 10 percent of criminals account for easily more than half of all crime, and even higher proportions of crimes, such as murder, rape, robbery, assault, kidnapping, etc. Increasingly, understanding the "bad guys" is what criminology is about.

We have created a text that presents the state-of-the-art on violent offenders to help students understand the breadth of violent offenders, including gangs, serial killers, sex offenders, and career criminals. The book is divided into three sections. Part one covers the theoretical and disciplinary foundations of the study of violent behavior, spanning the disciplines of sociology, psychology, biology, and neuroscience. Part two discusses empirical and topical linkages to criminological subjects, in-

cluding homicide offenders and victims, sex offenders, and gang members. Part three explores public policy and practical applications, describing the various ways that criminal justice systems respond to violent offenders from the insightful perspectives of people who work among them on a daily basis.

As former criminal justice practitioners, we are stridently prejudiced toward applied, practitioner expertise and scholarly perspectives that stem from hands-on research experience with real offenders. *Violent Offenders: Theory, Research, Public Policy, and Practice* offers a list of contributors who are international experts on violent offenders. Some are academics, some are practitioners, and some are both. This collaboration provides students with a realistic and cutting-edge view of why people commit violent crimes and how our criminal justice system, as a whole, responds to these offenders and these violent acts.

Matt DeLisi
Peter J. Conis

Contributors

Joanne Archambault
Sexual Assault and Training Investigations, Inc.
Addy, WA

Eric Beauregard, PhD
Assistant Professor
Simon Fraser University
Burnaby, British Columbia

Kevin M. Beaver, PhD
Assistant Professor
Florida State University
Tallahassee, FL

Heith Copes, PhD
Associate Professor
University of Alabama at Birmingham
Birmingham, AL

Mark D. Cunningham, PhD, ABPP
Clinical and Forensic Psychologist
Private-Practice Forensic Psychologist
Lewisville, TX

Kirsten Faisal
State Trainer
Iowa Coalition Against Domestic Violence
Des Moines, IA

David P. Farrington
Professor
University of Cambridge
Cambridge, United Kingdom

Jay Healey, PhD candidate
Simon Fraser University
Burnaby, British Columbia

John D. Hewitt, PhD
Professor
Grand Valley State University
Grand Rapids, MI

Andy Hochstetler, PhD
Associate Professor
Iowa State University
Ames, IA

Doni Lynn Homish
University of Pittsburgh Medical Center
Western Psychiatric Institute and Clinic
Pittsburgh, PA

Frank Kardasz, EdD
Project Director
Arizona Internet Crimes Against Children Task Force
Phoenix Police Department
Phoenix, AZ

Benoit Leclerc, PhD
Assistant Professor
University of Montreal
Philippe Pinel Institute of Montreal
Montreal, Canada

Rolf Loeber, PhD
Distinguished University Professor
University of Pittsburgh
Pittsburgh, PA

Patrick Lussier, PhD
Assistant Professor
Simon Fraser University
Burnaby, Canada

Contributors

Jean Marie McGloin, PhD
Assistant Professor
University of Maryland
College Park, MD

Jean Proulx, PhD
Professor
University of Montreal
Philippe Pinel Institute of Montreal
Montreal, Canada

Shelley L. Reese MSA
Dallas County Sheriff Department
Waukee, IA

Robert M. Regoli, PhD
Professor
University of Colorado, Boulder
Boulder, CO

Roxann M. Ryan, JD, PhD
Iowa Department of Public Safety
Des Moines, IA

Laurie Schipper
Executive Director
Iowa Coalition Against Domestic Violence
Des Moines, IA

Jennifer Schwartz
Assistant Professor
Washington State University
Pullman, WA

Rebecca Stallings
University of Pittsburgh Medical Center
Pittsburgh, PA

Denise Timmins, JD
Assistant Attorney General
Iowa Attorney General's Office
Des Moines, IA

Michael G. Vaughn, PhD
Assistant Professor
University of Pittsburgh
Pittsburgh, PA

Glenn D. Walters, PhD
Federal Correctional Institution
Schuylkill, PA

John Paul Wright
Associate Professor
University of Cincinnati
Cincinnati, OH

The Importance of Violent Offenders to Criminology

1

Matt DeLisi
Iowa State University

Peter J. Conis
Iowa State University

Kevin M. Beaver
Florida State University

"There exists, it is true, a group of criminals, born for evil, against whom all social cures break as against rock."

—*Cesare Lombroso*[1]

"For some, the term career criminal is a label that will serve to further stigmatize and exacerbate the risk factors that chronic offenders experience. For others, this moniker is the mark of Cain."

—*Matt DeLisi*[2]

For most of the twentieth century, criminology floundered because it focused on normal processes and situations that were purported to cause people to be delinquent. Strain, anomie, stress, poverty, living in a bad neighborhood, discrimination, and hanging out with friends that enjoy breaking the law were some of the dominant explanations of crime. Over time, especially during the 1960s and 1970s, the causes of crime were even attributed to functional institutions of society. For instance, the criminal justice system was blamed for causing crime or enabling recidivism because the police, judicial, and correctional systems negatively intervened in the lives of criminals. Sociological, specious, and liberal, criminology had a credibility problem because its major theories of crime lacked the ring of truth. They were too academic.

Then, between 1985 and 1993, three major works appeared that saved criminology.[a] These were James Q. Wilson and Richard Herrnstein's *Crime and Human Nature* (1985),[3] Michael Gottfredson and Travis Hirschi's *A General Theory of Crime* (1990),[4] and Terrie Moffitt's developmental taxonomy theory (1993).[5] Individually and collectively, these works have made a towering impact on the study of criminal behavior. Wilson and Herrnstein's work is probably known as much for the star-power of the authors as its substantive impact. Both are best-selling authors, both are distinguished academics who crossed over into the role of public intellectual (as least in terms of the media coverage of their works), and both are viewed as conservative, which in academic circles is controversial.[6] More than anything else, *Crime and Human Nature* wrestled the study of crime from the stranglehold of sociology by incorporating ideas from economics, psychology, and biology. Borrowing from economics, Wilson and Herrnstein articulated the idea that crime is fundamentally a matter of choice. As such, rational choice theory and the thought processes of individual actors are essential in understanding why some people use violence against others. Wilson and Herrnstein expanded this idea using psychological theories to show that choosing to commit crime is not simply the outcome of rational calculus but is molded and influenced by an array of factors, such as family background, social class, environmental influences, and prior experience and education. From biology, Wilson and Herrnstein drew the idea of "the existence of biological predispositions means that circumstances that activate behavior in one person will not do so in another, that social forces cannot deter criminal behavior in 100% of the population, and that the distribution of crime within and across societies may, to some extent, reflect underlying distributions of constitutional factors. Crime cannot be understood without taking into account predispositions and their biological roots."[3] With its insistence on the individual and its friendliness to biology, *Crime and Human Nature* shook the discipline.

Gottfredson and Hirschi's *A General Theory of Crime*, which advanced the idea that low self-control is the indispensable predictor of crime and violence,[4] received a similar reception because it occupied a similar niche. Like Wilson and Herrnstein, Gottfredson and Hirschi are very accomplished and influential academics who,

---

[a]Of course, other valuable criminological works appeared during this time period; however, the works by Wilson and Herrnstein, Gottfredson and Hirschi, and Moffitt were truly paradigm-changing as ways to understand individual-level criminality.

because they focused on individual-level factors to explain crime, went against the grain of the discipline. *A General Theory of Crime* has single-handedly dominated criminological journals as a source since 1990, racking up more than 1,300 citations. By comparison, Hirschi's other classic work, *Causes of Delinquency*, published in 1969, has a comparable number of citations.

Terrie Moffitt's developmental taxonomy theory appeared as an article published in *Psychological Review* in 1993.[5] It has been massively influential, as evidenced by over 1,300 citations! Her theory advances two offender prototypes. The first is a normative group (adolescence-limited) of offenders who tend to engage in low levels of crime consisting of benign offenses during adolescence. Their antisocial behavior is the result of the growing pains experienced during the uneven and often tumultuous transitions from childhood to adulthood. The second is a pathological group (life-course persistent) of offenders whose antisocial behavior is chronic, frequent, serious, and violent. Their antisocial behavior is the product of interactions between neuropsychological deficits and adverse home environments. Biological factors—specifically neurological and genetic factors—are also implicated in the behavior of life-course persistent offenders. Perhaps the scholar who conducts the most purely scientific criminological research, Moffitt has advanced understanding of the interaction between nature and nurture in explaining crime and violence.[7–9]

■ Current Focus

This chapter explores three general contributions of the works described above. First, as a result of the popularity, appeal, and empirical strength of these researchers, there has been a renewed emphasis on the individual as the correct locus or place to explain criminal and violent behavior. Second, there has been increased recognition of criminality as an important way, perhaps *the* important way, to understand violent criminal behavior. Third, there has been an increased appreciation for the diversity of criminals from an array of disciplinary perspectives. With these new reformulations, criminology has become a more believable and scientifically confident discipline because it disproportionately focuses scholarly attention on the most serious offenders, namely the violent offenders that pose the greatest threat to society.

■ Reductionism and Violence

Individuals—not communities, regions, nations, or cultures—commit murder, rape, robbery, and assault. So to understand violent offenders, it is imperative to understand individual-level factors, such as personality, temperament, self-control, temper, or psychopathy, that influence behavior. To boil scientific explanations down to a more fundamental unit of analysis is known as reductionism. Thus, to understand violent offenders, it is necessary to understand the characteristics that appear to typify violent offenders, not just the statuses they might occupy. Of course, environmental or sociological factors matter also, but they matter indirectly because they are processed by individuals. This is an important distinction. Many phenomena presumed to correlate with crime and violent behavior, such as poverty, employment status, neighborhood of residency, and ethnicity, really owe their "relationship" to crime to individual-level factors. As Gottfredson and Hirschi suggested, "[it] is hard to overstate the magnitude of this problem in criminology because of the tendency of people with low self-control to avoid attachment to or involvement in all social institutions—a tendency that produces a negative correlation between institutional experience and delinquency. This gives all institutions credit for negative effects on crime, credit they may not deserve."[4]

An interest in individuals as *the* unit of analysis to explain crime was a major contribution of Wilson and Herrnstein. The very title of their work, *Crime and Human Nature*, speaks to the pressing need to acknowledge constitutional features of people that powerfully affect how they choose to behave. According to Wilson and Herrnstein, "whatever factors contribute to crime . . . must all affect the behavior of individuals, if they are to affect crime. If people differ in their tendency to commit crime, we must express those differences in terms of how some array of factors affects their individual decisions."[3]

What are the characteristics of violent individuals? Numerous profiles emerge from the criminological literature. Even as children and adolescents, violent offenders are noteworthy for their callousness and emotional traits that reflect low empathetic concern for others, little guilt or anxiety over misdeeds, and limited emotional range.[10] Kathleen Heide studied adolescent patricide offenders (children who murder their parents) and found that many had been severely abused, some were severely mentally disturbed or psychotic, and some were dangerously antisocial or sociopathic.[11] Donald Lynam, Alex Piquero, and Terrie Moffitt examined the case histories of violent offenders from a New Zealand birth cohort and found that they were suspicious, alienated, callous, cruel, unempathetic, and prone to overreact to stress. Violent offenders were also different in constraint, which included levels of reflectivity, caution, ability to plan, and excitement-seeking.[12] Margo Watt and her colleagues reported that incarcerated violent offenders have low moral intelligence evidenced by low empathy for others, low self-control, self-centeredness, poor moral reasoning, and weak socialization.[13] Finally, in a review of the predictors of recidivism, Wagdy Loza documented a laundry list of personality characteristics of violent offenders, such as incapacity to feel sympathy, inability to learn from experience, narcissistic traits, inner rage, paranoia, external locus of control, self-indulgence, and globally irresponsible.[14]

Although this is but a small sampling of perspectives, criminologists have copiously documented the individual-level characteristics of violent offenders and core personality traits that recurrently appear. First and foremost, violent offenders are often unmoved by normal human emotions and exhibit little connectedness to others. Their lack of empathy facilitates their ability to harm others. As a quick illustration, children in the Pittsburgh Youth Study who were evaluated as lacking a sense of guilt about antisocial behavior were between 480 and 630% more than normal children likely to present with multiple behavioral problems![15] A smattering of other traits, such as impulsiveness, irresponsibility, external locus of control, and narcissism, similarly compromise the ability of violent offenders to fit in well with others in traditional social settings. Moreover, these constitutional factors are present throughout the life-course, even in early childhood. When criminogenic traits are so apparent early in life, and when they accompany violent or antisocial behaviors, it is likely that their etiology stems from the offenders themselves.

■ Criminality: The Mark of Cain

The scale items below are used to measure psychopathic traits in children.

- Does not show feelings or emotions
- Helpful if someone is hurt, upset, or feeling ill
- Feels bad or guilty when he/she does something wrong
- Has at least one good friend
- Considerate of other people's feelings
- Kind to younger children
- Is concerned about how well he/she does at school
- Often has temper tantrums or hot temper
- Generally obedient, usually does what adults request
- Often fights with other children or bullies them
- Often lies or cheats
- Steals from home, school, or elsewhere

A recent study conducted by Essi Viding, James Blair, Terrie Moffitt, and Robert Plomin found significant genetic risk for psychopathy in 7-year-olds.[16] The data are staggering. Among children with psychopathic tendencies, 81% of extreme antisocial behavior was explained by genetics, and 0% was explained by shared environmental factors. Among identical twins, nearly 70% of extreme callous-unemotional traits were explained by genes.[16] These findings offer two frightening implications. First, extremely violent behavior develops in some as very young children; second, it strikes from within.

This speaks to criminality, a negative form of personality. Personality is the relatively enduring, distinctive, integrated, and functional set of psychological characteristics that result from people's temperaments interacting with their cultural and developmental experiences.[17] Criminality can be understood as the raw material or potential to engage in crime and violence that every person has within. It ranges on a continuum from very low to very high. Criminality is not normally distributed; most people have low criminality, whereas a small number of people have very high criminality. Criminality is a global characteristic in that it affects more than just criminal behavior. The elemental components of criminality, for example, also affect school performance, sociability, work performance, and "bad habits," such as smoking, gambling, drinking, and other risky activities. These are consequences of criminality, but what constitutes it?

Arguably the most popular example of criminality is the low self-control construct developed by Gottfredson and Hirschi. They suggest that "people who lack self-control will tend to be impulsive, insensitive, physical (as opposed to mental), risk-taking, short-sighted, and nonverbal, and they will tend therefore to engage in criminal, and analogous acts. Since these traits can be identified prior to the age of responsibility for crime, since there is considerable tendency for these traits to come together in the same people, and since the traits tend to persist through life, it seems reasonable to consider them as comprising a stable construct useful in the explanation of crime."[4] In other words, theories of criminality attempt to identify the characteristics and behaviors that describe the "types of people" most likely to commit crime and violence. For example, temper is the dimension that has the most obvious connection to violence and is useful in understanding how core components of a person's being influence their behavior. While everyone has a temper to some degree, most people are able to stifle their tempers and muffle their impulses or desires to respond negatively or aggressively to another person. Most people stifle not only the physical urges but also the verbal urges that are aroused by our tempers. Instead of violently attacking someone who has made us angry, we turn the other cheek, ignore, or otherwise defuse the situation. Those with hair-trigger tempers, such as violent offenders, do not behave similarly. They are unable and unwilling to check themselves, and as a result, even seemingly trivial affronts or confrontations are grounds for an argument, fight, or worse. Everyone has known a person with a bad temper. And everyone knows that such a person is significantly more likely to get into trouble because of a single, perhaps innate, personality trait.[18,19] This is the logic of self-control theory.

The self-control approach to criminality has enjoyed tremendous research support.[20] Alex Piquero and his colleagues examined the link between self-control and criminal careers using a large sample of youths from a New Zealand birth cohort. They found that those with the lowest self-control were also the most frequent, serious, and persistent criminals.[21] Using data from a Dutch sample of 1,531 persons involved in traffic accidents, Marianne Junger and her colleagues found that persons who displayed risky traffic behavior (a component of low self-control) that resulted in an accident were also likely to engage in various forms of criminal behavior.[22] Specifically, they were 160% more likely to have an arrest for a violent crime, 150% more likely to have an arrest for property crime, and 430% more likely to have an arrest for additional traffic crimes.[22] Using a sample of extreme offenders with a minimum of 30 arrests, Matt DeLisi and his colleagues found that offenders with low self-control are likely to accumulate many arrests for the most serious forms of violence.[23] In addition, poorly controlled offenders continue to engage in violence while incarcerated and continually run afoul of the criminal justice system.[23–25] Irrespective of context, low self-control increases the likelihood for trouble, violence, and other deleterious outcomes.

Although self-control is a compelling basis for understanding criminality, it lacks the scientific punch of Terrie Moffitt's description of the processes that give rise to the most serious, violent offenders (known as life-course persistent offenders and discussed later in this chapter). Briefly, according to Moffitt, two types of neuropsychological defects—defects affecting verbal and executive functions—give rise to an assortment of antisocial behaviors. Verbal functions include reading ability, receptive listening, problem-solving skill, memory, speech articulation, and writing; in short, they comprise our verbal intelligence. Executive functions relate to behavioral and personality characteristics, such as inattention, hyperactivity, and impulsivity. Children with these neuropsychological deficits are restless, fidgety, destructive, non-compliant, and can be violent. They are also exceedingly difficult to parent. Children with neuropsychological deficits coupled with adverse home environments are especially at risk.[26] Indeed, neurodevelopmental and family risk factors at age 3 predict life-course persistent offending in adulthood.[27] Whereas Gottfredson and Hirschi invoke sociology to describe the etiology of crime and violence, Moffitt uses a multidisciplinary perspective that spans psychology and neuroscience. Irrespective of one's theoretical orientation, criminology only recently paid close attention to the criminality that likely distinguishes mundane from deeply problematic offenders.

■ The Diversity of Violent Criminals

Visualize the following two offenders. Offender 1 raped and murdered an adult female who was a stranger. Offender 2 raped and murdered his own mother. It is more than the victimology in these cases that is different. While the first offender is obviously a violent person, he pales in comparison to the second offender. The second offender's conduct is considerably more reprehensible, taboo, and repellent than the first offender's because it violates social relationships between offender and victim that don't exist in the first case. It is likely that different theoretical explanations are utilized to create a profile of them. Again, while one is simply violent, the other is not only violent but also draped in psychopathology. Similarly, criminal justice practitioners can appreciate the diversity of violent offenders. For instance, domestic assaulters, bar fighters, and gang bangers often pose a different "feel" because their violence is contextually different or even contextually-driven. Whether a murderer kills by firearm, knife, or manual strangulation matters because there are likely compelling differences in the offender's psychology to lend insight into their behavior.

A psychological phenomenon that has historically been helpful in understanding violent offenders is psychopathy. The "modern" understanding of psychopathy was realized in 1941 with the publication of Hervey Cleckley's *The Mask of Sanity*.[28] Cleckley's work was the most systematic clinical study of psychopathy of its day, and it laid the groundwork for contemporary research. Cleckley's work is helpful in discerning subtle but important differences among even the most violent offenders:

> *In repetitive delinquent behavior, the subject often seems to be going a certain distance along the course that a full psychopath follows to the end. In the less severe disorder, antisocial or self-defeating activities are frequently more circumscribed and may stand out against a larger background of successful adaptation. The borderlines between chronic delinquency and what we have called the psychopath merge in this area. Although anxiety, remorse, shame, and other consciously painful subjective responses to undesirable consequences are deficient in both as compared with the normal, this callousness or apathy is far deeper in the psychopath.*[28]

Focusing on the individual-level characteristics of the most serious criminals has also led to strides in understanding crime from general and more specific theoretical perspectives. As the examples above indicate, serious criminals are not a monolithic group. While there are great commonalities in the lives of serious offenders, there are also important distinctions between them. In some areas of research, these distinctions necessitate typologies with specific offender types. In a way, Wilson and Herrnstein, Gottfredson and Hirschi, and Moffitt have started somewhat of a theoretical paradox where similarities and appreciable differences among violent offenders beg for parsimonious general theories that are flexible enough to explain the great diversity of violence. What do the violent criminals look like descriptively and why are they meaningful to criminology? We explore these questions next.

Because murder and rape are the most serious forms of violence, much scholarly attention is devoted toward the offender and offense characteristics of murderers and various types of sexual offenders. Easily the most serious example of violence is sexual homicide, which occurs in less than 1% of homicides annually and is the primary motivation of serial killers. Sexual homicides are classified as two general types: organized and disorganized. According to Robert Ressler, Ann Burgess, and John Douglas, organized sexual homicides are planned, target strangers, and reflect control.[29] The perpetrator demands submission, uses restraints, is aggressive before the murder, does not use a weapon, and transports and hides the body. Disorganized sexual homicides are spontaneous attacks of a known but depersonalized victim. These attacks are random and sloppy, involve post-mortem sexual acts, have weapons at the scene, and the victim is left at the death scene.[29] J. Reid Meloy developed a clinical typology that builds upon the organized/disorganized distinction.[30] According to Meloy, organized killers are compulsive sexual sadists with antisocial and narcissistic personality disorders. They are chronically emotionally detached, often primary psychopaths, are autonomically hyporeactive (e.g., low resting heart rate), and most did not experience early trauma or abuse in childhood. Disorganized killers are described as catathymic, and perpetrators are men with mood disorders and avoidant traits. They desire attachment, are moderately psychopathic, are autonomically hyperactive, and have histories of physical and/or sexual trauma.[30] How dangerous are these characteristics? A recent study by Jill Levenson and John Morin examined the factors that predicted selection of sexually violent predators for civil commitment in Florida[31] (civil commitment is the involuntary confinement of violent criminals in treatment facilities following their completion of a prison sentence). Persons with a diagnosis for pedophilia were 4,656% more likely to be civilly committed than those without the diagnosis. For sexual sadists, there was a staggering 85,562% increased likelihood of civil commitment. For those diagnosed with paraphilias not otherwise specified, the liability was 10,580%.[31]

In terms of psychopathology and risk for violence, those who commit sexual homicides are the most dangerous and disturbed offenders in society; however, they are but one type of sexual offender. There are other types of sexual offenders that are distinguished primarily by the characteristics of their victims, such as rapists, pedophiles, etc. Importantly, all criminals are prone to be versatile in their offending behavior and most do not specialize in narrow or discrete criminal behaviors. What is clear is that persons who commit the most serious crimes are at risk to commit the "other" serious crimes. For example, Brian Francis and Keith Soothill conducted a 21-year retrospective study of more than 7,400 sex offenders in the United Kingdom and found that about 3% of sex offenders ultimately commit murder.[32] While this seems low, the rate of murder among sex offenders was one homicide for every 400 sex offenders compared to a general population ratio of one homicide per 3,000 individuals.[32] Lisa Sample found that nearly 8% of child molesters ultimately commit murder using a large database of offenders in Illinois.[33] Leonore Simon compared 142 child molesters, 51 rapists, and 290 other violent offenders in terms of their offending characteristics.[34] Regardless of an offender's current conviction status, sex offenders also commit a range of criminal activity spanning violent, property, drug, white-collar, nuisance, and noncompliance offenses.[34]

Generalized criminal involvement is not limited to sex offenders or murderers. Even groups that are considered to be comparatively innocuous offenders, such as non-violent drug offenders, include individuals who behave violently. A recent study found that inmates currently incarcerated for non-violent drug possession or trafficking charges were also significantly likely to have arrest for serious violent crimes, such as murder, rape, robbery, aggravated assault, or kidnapping.[35] Students introduced to criminology often gravitate to the most extreme types of offenders, and there is often the misperception that offender types are just that—narrow categories of offenders who only commit single offenses. Empirically, this does not hold. All criminals dabble in an assortment of antisocial behaviors. The same applies to those who commit the most serious crimes—they just happen to murder, rape, kidnap, and molest in conjunction with robbery, burglary, auto theft, fraud, and drugs.

■ Conclusion

Why are violent offenders meaningful to criminology? We offer a handful of broad answers to this question. First, violent offenders pose a great public health threat to societies in terms of mortality, victimization, lost and diminished productivity, fear of crime, lower quality of life, and untold costs required to manage and supervise them in the criminal justice system. With all apologies to corporate crime, which results in far greater financial losses, violent crime is a direct affront to the social and moral order of society. For this reason, violent offenders are those whom the general public entrusts criminal justice practitioners to apprehend, prosecute, and detain.

Second, violent offenders have forced criminologists to sharpen their theoretical ideas. No longer can banal social processes be cited to explain serious interpersonal violence (although the media still does this). It is doubtful that offenders disarm and kill police officers, or construct a dungeon to facilitate the kidnapping and rape of runaways, or murder 48 people because of the unemployment rate, general strain, or poverty. These things might matter, but they are small pieces of the puzzle of violent behavior. And the need to understand violence is much broader now, borrowing concepts from across the social and behavioral sciences, medical sciences, and beyond.

Third, the landmark works described in this chapter afforded criminology greater credibility and authenticity. Not too long ago, it was dubious to suggest that personality traits were related to crime, that family processes were not just risk factors but causes of crime, and that criminality not only exists but is stable, contributes to heinous forms of violence, and is poorly mollified by punishment. After Wilson and Herrnstein, Gottfredson and Hirschi, and Moffitt, criminology confidently knows that individual-level factors are paramount and the pathology of the most violent and serious offenders is largely attributable to biological factors and the complex interplay between nature and nurture.

Finally, violent offenders hold the most promise for criminology to achieve its most noteworthy scientific goals, including a specific account of criminality. Increasingly, the sociological processes of criminological theories will be recast as biosocial, in fact, this is already being done. To illustrate, Kevin Beaver and his colleagues recently extended Gottfredson and Hirschi's work and provided evidence showing that self-control should be viewed as an executive function that is housed in the prefrontal cortex of the brain.[36] Using data from Early Childhood Longitudinal Study-Kindergarten Class of 1998–1999 (the largest nationally representative sample of children), Beaver and his colleagues found that deficits to neuropsychological functioning were related to levels of self-control in kindergarten and first grade students. These results held for both genders even after partitioning out the effects of parental and neighborhood influences, and even after controlling for prior levels of low self-control. Contrary to self-control theory, they revealed that most of the parenting measures had relatively small and inconsistent effects on self-control. Overall, the neuropsychological measures were among the most consistent predictors of childhood levels of self-control.[36] Over time, many similar advances will occur in criminology, and a scientifically curious eye on the most antisocial and violent offenders will lead the way.

References

1. Lombroso, C. (1911). *Crime: Its Causes and Remedies*. Boston: Little, Brown & Co, p. 447.
2. DeLisi, M. (2005). *Career Criminals in Society*. Thousand Oaks, CA: Sage, p. 118.
3. Wilson, J. Q., Herrnstein, R. J. (1985). *Crime and Human Nature: The Definitive Study of the Causes of Crime*. New York: Simon and Schuster.
4. Gottfredson, M. R., Hirschi, T. (1990). *A General Theory of Crime*. Stanford, CA: Stanford University Press.
5. Moffitt, T. E. (1993). Adolescence-limited and life-course persistent antisocial behavior: A developmental taxonomy. *Psychol Rev* 100:674–701.
6. DeLisi, M. (2003). Conservatism and common sense: The criminological career of James Q. Wilson. *Justice Q* 20:661–674.
7. Caspi, A., Moffitt, T. E. (2006). Gene-environment interactions in psychiatry: Joining forces with neuroscience. *Nat Rev* 7:583–590.
8. Moffitt, T. E. (2005). The new look of behavioral genetics in developmental psychopathology. *Psychol Bull* 131:533–554.
9. Moffitt, T. E., Caspi, A., Rutter, M. (2005). Strategy for investigating interactions between measured genes and measured environments. *Arch Gen Psychiatr* 62:473–481.
10. Frick, P. J., Hare, R. D. (2002). *The Antisocial Process Screening Device*. Toronto, Canada: Multi-Health Systems.
11. Heide, K. M. (1995). Dangerously antisocial youths who kill their parents. *J Police Crim Psychol* 10:10–14.
12. Lynam, D. R., Piquero, A. R., Moffitt, T. E. (2004). Specialization and the propensity to violence. *J Contemp Crim Justice* 20:215–228.
13. Watt, M. C., Frausin, S., Dixon, J., Nimmo, S. (2000). Moral intelligence in a sample of incarcerated females. *Crim Justice Behav* 27:330–355.
14. Loza, W. (2003). Predicting violent and nonviolent recidivism of incarcerated male offenders. *Aggress Violent Behav* 8:175–203.
15. Loeber, R., Farrington, D. P., Stouthamer-Loeber, M., et al. (2002). Male mental health problems, psychopathy, and personality traits: Key findings from the first 14 years of the Pittsburgh Youth Study. *Clin Child Family Psychol Rev* 4:273–297.
16. Viding, E., Blair, R. J. R., Moffitt, T. E., Plomin, R. (2005). Evidence for substantial genetic risk for psychopathy in 7-year-olds. *J Child Psychol Psychiatr* 46:592–597.
17. Walsh, A., Ellis, L. (2007). *Criminology: An Interdisciplinary Approach*. Thousand Oaks, CA: Sage.
18. Wright, J. P., Beaver, K. M. (2005). Do parents matter in creating self-control in their children? A genetically informed test of Gottfredson and Hirschi's theory of low self-control. *Criminology* 43:1169–1202.
19. Beaver, K. M., Wright, J. P. (2005). Evaluating the effects of birth complications on low self-control in a sample of twins. *Int J Offender Ther Compar Criminol* 49:450–471.

20. Gottfredson, M. R. (2006). The empirical status of control theory in criminology. Pp. 77–100 in F. T. Cullen, J. P. Wright, K. R. Blevins (Eds.), *Taking Stock: The Status of Criminological Theory* (Advances in Criminological Theory, Vol. 15). New Brunswick, NJ: Transaction.

21. Piquero, A. R., Moffitt, T. E., Wright, B. E. (2007). Self-control and criminal career dimensions. *J Contemp Crim Justice* 23:1–18.

22. Junger, M., West, R., Timman, R. (2001). Crime and risky behavior in traffic: An example of cross-situational consistency. *J Res Crime Delinq* 38: 439–459.

23. DeLisi, M. (2001). Designed to fail: Self-control and involvement in the criminal justice system. *Am J Crim Justice* 26:131–148.

24. DeLisi, M. (2001). It's all in the record: Assessing self-control theory with an offender sample. *Crim Justice Rev* 26:1–16.

25. DeLisi, M., Berg, M. T. (2006). Exploring theoretical linkages between self-control theory and criminal justice processing. *J Crim Justice* 34:153–163.

26. Moffitt, T. E. (1990). Juvenile delinquency and attention deficit disorder: Boys' development trajectories from age 3 to age 15. *Child Dev* 61:893–910.

27. Moffitt, T. E., Caspi, A. (2001). Childhood predictors differentiate life-course persistent and adolescence-limited pathways among males and females. *Dev Psychopathol* 13:355–375.

28. Cleckley, H. (1941). *The Mask of Sanity*. St. Louis: C. V. Mosby.

29. Ressler, R. K., Burgess, A. W., Douglas, J. E. (1988). *Sexual Homicide: Patterns and Motives*. Lexington, MA: DC Heath.

30. Meloy, J. R. (2000). The nature and dynamics of sexual homicide: An integrative review. *Aggression Violent Behav* 5:1–22.

31. Levenson, J. S., Morin, J. W. (2006). Factors predicting selection of sexually violent predators for civil commitment. *Int J Offender Ther Compar Crim* 50: 609–629.

32. Francis, B., Soothill, K. (2000). Does sex offending lead to homicide? *J Forensic Psychiatr* 11:49–61.

33. Sample, L. L. (2006). An examination of the degree to which sex offenders kill. *Crim Justice Review*, 31, 230–250.

34. Simon, L. M. J. (2000). An examination of the assumptions of specialization, mental disorders, and dangerousness in sex offenders. *Behav Sci Law* 18: 275–308.

35. DeLisi, M. (2003). The imprisoned nonviolent drug offender: Specialized martyr or versatile career criminal? *Am J Crim Justice* 27:167–182.

36. Beaver, K. M., Wright, J. P., DeLisi, M. (2007). Self-control as an executive function: Reformulating Gottfredson and Hirschi's parental socialization thesis. *Crim Justice Behav*, in press.

References

Where I'm From: Criminal Predators and Their Environments

Andy Hochstetler
Iowa State University

Heith Copes
University of Alabama at Birmingham

"In the favellas [of Rio De Janeiro], buildings are pock-marked with bullet holes, and youths with military-style small arms patrol the streets at night. Incursions by police or rival factions can happen at any time. Jefferson is an 18-year-old former drug trafficker. Where he lives, gangs have dragged concrete pillars across the streets to stop police, and murals of Osama Bin Laden are painted on the walls. Many people there have lost several relatives to the violence. Jefferson says the gun battles affect everyone in the favellas, including the children. 'They can't play in the street. Half their childhood is spoilt. Everytime the fireworks go off [let off by child lookouts to warn of incursions] their mothers yell at them to get inside,' he says. 'People can't stand at the bar and have a drink normally—fireworks go off and they have to find shelter' . . . Jefferson says he took part in the execution of a 15-year-old friend who passed information to the police, 'Other informers are frightened and the community knows not to grass.'

—*BBC News, 2005.*[1]

Although it talks about only one dimension of ghetto life, even the most casual observers of conditions in impoverished nations and neighborhoods of the world will find nothing surprising in the quote above. Jefferson's story is familiar, if only from the cinema and occasional forays of the news media into the rows of ramshackle cardboard and corrugated tin residences in South American and African cities. It elicits the same sympathies as stories of the AK-47 wielding children of the Congo, the child soldiers of Sierra Leone, and similarly situated persons that appear, if infrequently, on our television screens. Typically, we frame the lives of such young persons living in the worst ghettos of the world as devoid of attractive options. Social and geographic distance, as well as the prominent features of abject poverty, allows us to interpret their actions as products of environments. We do not begrudge or condemn Jefferson or others like him for their unusually hardened criminal acts. Abject poverty in some places focuses our critical aim at community or national leaders, and we also are likely to look to the economic roots of the trouble. We are not inclined to wonder precisely when a criminal resident's trajectory slipped in an unfortunate direction or how variables interacted and sequenced between the ages of five and fifteen to culminate in criminal choices. Such questions seem academic, akin to focusing on whether seized pistons or cracked heads are the mediating causes of engine failures in motors without oil.

Yet, we often do not view crime by hardened, youthful offenders here in the United States with the same understanding eyes. Instead, we are apt to point to personal failure, faulty decision-making, or moral ineptitude when explaining why those closer to us choose crime. But if we are so willing to sympathize with Jefferson and his kin, why do we have such a hard time doing so for those predators in our own ghettos? Aren't the forces that push and pull people to crime in *favellas* also at work elsewhere? In this chapter, we explore how people incorporate neighborhood characteristics into identity and rely on these areas to provide opportunities and help construct excuses for their own brutal actions. That is, we examine how sane offenders in criminogenic environments interpret their world and how the locations contribute to people choosing crime.

Drawing on the perspectives of persistent and serious street offenders from the United States, predominantly in pre-Hurricane Katrina New Orleans, we raise questions about the degree to which contemporary criminology and its complex concerns obscure some links between the environment and violent offending. The psychology and conditions linking place to crime are real and are more likely to occur in the most impoverished communities. Environmental and social conditions are shown to affect thinking as street offenders make sense of emergent opportunities that fit patterns they have seen before in the larger context of their lifestyles.

We will not slow the reader with a thorough description of the methodology. Simply stated, we arrived at our conclusions through intuition gained from previously published interview-based research, offender biographies, and our own research involving in-depth interviews with dozens of violent offenders. We thought about interviews that we had done before, but drew mainly on interviews with 30 people who had committed at least one carjacking in Louisiana. Carjacking is a crime that almost always is associated with violent career criminals who spend much of their leisure time in impoverished neighborhoods with open-air drug markets.[2] Here we interpret what these offenders said about the environmental contexts of their crimes. At times, common sense leads us to be skeptical of some details in offenders' accounts, and we expect the reader may be as well—but this is not court, and these are admitted thieves and robbers. Some degree of dishonesty is expected and assumed.[3] Distorted facts and tall stories impart meaning. Indeed, exaggerations and fictions may reveal more about a person than fact, especially when one is discussing how places shape their identity and behavior.

We argue that it is the outlooks of congregations of the disaffected, violent young persons, mainly men, hustling on street corners, usually in drug neighborhoods (and sometimes engaged in ongoing street warfare) that lead to a great many violent criminal incidents. Their criminal decisions are made in an instant, yet they are congruous with a path through life marked by few legitimate successes and fit easily into what the offenders think they are meant to do based upon their social surroundings. We are not arguing, of course, that structural and economic arrangements are insignificant in explanations of crime's distributions. To the contrary, we are attempting to show that characteristics of place have real consequences for how offenders think about crime, evaluate opportunity, identify with a place and make sense of environments to justify criminal choices.

■ Peopled Streets

Most analysts of the spatial distribution of crime accept the premise that criminals choose to offend based on evaluation of the costs and benefits of crime.[4] For example, this belief underlies routine activity theory, which examines patterned convergences of motivated offenders, suitable targets, and an absence of capable guardianship as explanation of crime rates. In their introductory discussion from the most famous statement of the theory, and probably of predatory crime's distribution, Lawrence Cohen and Marcus Felson state:

> [I]n the context of [direct predatory violations], people, gaining and losing sustenance, struggle among themselves for property, safety, territory, hegemony, sexual outlet, physical control and sometimes for survival itself. The interdependence between offenders and victims can be viewed as a relationship between functionally dissimilar groups . . . violations can only be sustained by feeding upon other activities.

> *As offenders cooperatively increase their efficiency at predatory violations and as potential victims organize their resistance to such violations, both groups apply the symbiotic principle to improve their sustenance position.*[5]

Those interested in the spatial and temporal distribution of crime typically set aside agency and the mental mechanisms (or motivations) whereby arrangements of opportunities and objects lead to greater or lesser rates of offending. Little is said, therefore, of *how* offenders make crime more attractive by cooperatively increasing their efficiency at predatory violations. All investigators know, however, that efforts by some offenders to reshape and frame their world make crime more likely for others. Through more-or-less intentional, incremental actions and interactions, offenders cultivate suitable local and cultural environments for monetary success by criminals and improve their chances of success in interpersonal evaluations.

There are innumerable studies of the effects of limited legitimate opportunities and the availability of illicit ones on rates of offending.[6] There also has been considerable speculation (and some study) of how signs of incivility or disorder and the widespread perception that a place is disorderly figures in the decision to commit crime.[7] What is missing from most of this discussion is the likely offender's perspective on their surroundings, including how criminal opportunities are interpreted, created, and viewed. Exceptions to the neglect of the environmental psychology of crime are works that attempt to look to places where crime is common and the outlooks associated with it in these places. These typically appear in ethnographies like *The Social Order of the Slum, In Search of Respect, Ain't No Making It*, and *A Place on the Corner*.[8-11] All are exceptional in that they give due theoretical attention to cultural/geographic space. All show that inhabitants understand intuitively more about place than what the costs and benefits of various actions in immediate circumstances are.

Places have deeper meanings and serve as locales for passing these meanings along. Sometimes places make things seem rational that would not seem rational elsewhere and bend preferences and expectations accordingly; think about aberrant behavior occurring at Spring Break on Mexico's beaches, during Mardi Gras in New Orleans, or on the Strip in Las Vegas, where advertising confirms that shameful behavior is expected. These expectations may be readily available and can have salient associations with what a place means, such as a crack-dealing set. All of us have some idea of what the expectations would be there, although we might have doubts about whether we would fit in; most of us have no intention of finding out. We describe the things that predatory street offenders say about the environmental context of behavioral expectancies and argue that their understandings of opportunities in the impoverished community occur through a cognitive lens provided partially by an intuitive understanding of places and personal relations to them.

■ Open Drug Dealing, Related Activities, and Opportunities for Crime

Crime is extremely concentrated by place.[12] New students of the spatial distribution of crime almost always open their eyes when they realize that crime hot spots are characterized by tight concentrations of dots on a map that signify impoverished, urban geographies. Sometimes criminal events that are exceedingly rare in general pile one atop the other in certain cul-de-sacs and street corners. When looking at crime maps of impoverished areas in large cities, it is preposterous to pretend that the spatial concentration of crime is exclusively the result of economic variables when there are other obvious and direct reasons; namely, crime repeatedly occurs in places where many known offenders live and tends to occur disproportionately among people who trade in drugs and frequent drug corners. To ignore this leaves unspoken the volatile and violent scenes that drug dealers, their customers, prostitutes, and pimps create; this oversight could lead to faulty assumptions about connections between neighborhood characteristics and crime. By comparison, how important is it that in poor neighborhoods people living in cramped apartments would rather be outside? This idea has been postulated as a reason for concentrated crime.[13] Does this explanation justify why persons would go to the crack corner at unusual hours or why some might smack strangers in the head with a pistol? Statistical analysis of spatial antecedents of open-air drug markets and crime without mention of or attention to the markets' presence obscures the impact of dangerous activities on offending opportunities, criminal opportunism, and most importantly, the outlaw spirit that develops in places where drugs are distributed in this way.

Neighborhoods infested with illicit drug markets create opportunities not only for those few offenders who make money exclusively by dealing, but also for criminals including fences, small con artists, and street robbers. By the street criminal's standards, opportunities arising from constant cash transactions in drug markets are tremendous even if the risks are sometimes high. For example, drug markets are one place where there is an almost certain way to get otherwise scarce cash for those who would hazard it. A robber explains his consideration of options:

> *You go to a [convenience store] and they got a little drop box in it and the [clerk] can't get in there. When you hit the register, they got $40. You would be pretty mad. But, you know a big dope dealer, he got a lot of dope and usually money goes along with dope. He might have some nice jewelry. So, usually it works out better when you hit dope dealers.*

Drug corners and drug neighborhoods, especially those that appear to be beyond authorities' control, lead to attitudes toward violence that may seem incredible to all but those who have stayed there long enough to know that violence erupts frequently and can be sparked by a large variety of incidents. It may occur simply because someone nearby is perceived by one or more to have wronged or insulted someone else.

Inhabitants of drug corners are prepared for violence always. In the worst neighborhoods, in addition to incidental violence, there are battles between those who possess drugs, drug money, or convenient access to customers and those who want their assets. A robber of drug dealers recounts the brutality among his cadre when it came to taking their piece of the local drug economy.

> *I don't want to kill. I don't want to go in nobody's house. If it comes down to it, I'll do it, but I'm not going to go in there and shoot babies and children and women and shit. [My partner] will go in there and a woman flinch he gonna down her, you dig. Whoever move gonna get killed in an instant. [If someone's] like "man I ain't got no dope in here. Ain't nothing in here bro." Then [he'll] threaten him with a gun. Hitting him with pistol. It took an O.G. from the hood to tell me how to do it right bro. Take a stick pin and put it press it right up under their fingernails and they will show you where the dope is at. A stick pin get their mind all the way right. They gonna tell you everything. Stick pins, that's some painful shit . . . I've had cases where I have to pull out the stick pin.*

Such men know well the surest and easiest way to make a robbery worthwhile, as well as the extreme risks that such worthwhile crimes pose:

> *Might have ten thousand dollars in the house, some guns and shit and we don't like him. He can be somebody we fuck with, you dig, but he got it and he don't break bread so we gonna hit him, you dig. Go kicking in doors, doing what we got to take it. But, there's a lot you gotta worry about. You don't know who's upstairs. [They] maybe, going to shoot at you, you know.*

A dealer confirms that this thinking is prevalent in recognizing himself as a high profile target and pointing to the importance of mental preparation and readiness for violence.

> *See, I am going to put it in the aspects of the game I was in. I'm gonna put it in those aspects. You know what I worried about more than anything? Robbers! Dudes that would come kidnap you because you were doing your thing and had money. And if you have a name . . . If you are really doing it, then you are going to have a name. See a name comes with the game. If you are really doing it, then your name*

going to have a rank and the police are going to get to know your
name and try to bust you. They gonna harass you, but that is noth-
ing. When the people come, the robbers and the jackers . . . I mean
the consequences is different. They gonna kill you to get what you got.

Only a few have sufficient "heart," as reckless brutality can be called, to rob
reputable dealers but the events are not rare.[14] There are of course, easier and more
convenient targets in neighborhoods where drug trafficking is part of daily life than
to attempt to extort or rob dope dealers. Where there are drug dealers, there are
also addicts and other hangers-on. These peripheral players offer low hanging fruit.
Still, many of these require putting familiarity with violence to use. A man who
targeted them remembers his hunting grounds, "They had this certain place where
a lot of drug activity . . . you know, drug dealers would hang out." Another explains,
"People would ride through there all through the day wanting to buy drugs."
Lines of drug users flowing in and out of places where they may or may not be wel-
comed as insiders are perfect marks for the many awaiting opportunists known to
them only by street monikers, if at all.

I go to the car and as he stopped . . . It was like, it was the thing
where if you coming through in your car and you come to buy drugs,
you have to put your car in park or cut your keys off because deal-
ers knew they would take drugs and pull off. So, I say yeah I got
something, put your car in park. They were used to that. I grab the
door and I am about to show him something and I grabbed him and
I throw the gun at him.

I didn't have to like go around and sit on a corner at wee hours of
the night or nothing [for victims]. They come through. The neighbor-
hood was that kind of neighborhood. Hey man, that's what happens—
that's all.

[The victims] were three or four places back [in a row of cars].
Already had four cars in front of it. You got people selling drugs
out there . . . And it just seemed like the opportunity when the light
didn't turn. It was like it had already turned, it was red and it didn't
turn back green. And I just, pow! Just something went off. Boom! And
the guy just went straight down and we jerked him out. It was on
from there.

The flow of drug customers is a significant source of opportunity for the prepared, but other parts of the informal economy also open doors. Heavy traffic and
anonymity of impoverished city life allow offenders convenience and mechanisms
for getting close to victims.[15]

In New Orleans we got a lot of people, you know, asking, begging
for money and stuff. What I'm saying is that you more or less act like

> *you selling something. You see the people are out there with food*
> *stamps; people selling flowers; people with big ole cans of change and*
> *stuff. [I] got a nice little can and be acting like I'm begging for change*
> *or something like that and walk up to them. Some people ain't gonna*
> *let they window down, but some people will let they window down to*
> *put change. [That's when I] put a gun at they throat.*

These robberies and other crimes are enabled by a neighborhood context, where offenders assume that they can operate with impunity based on their past ability to do so as well as by their read of what neighborhood residents will tolerate or be able to stop. The fact that drug markets exist in the open or are only slightly hidden imparts a message clearer than that communicated by other signs of neighborhood deterioration. Several offenders explained that normal activities in their neighborhood created a situation where any who knew about crime were unlikely to report it. Some thought that it should be understood that to be on certain streets was tacit entry into the world of the street hustler and acceptance of the risks of street life; their view was confirmed when victims rarely called police or when nothing changed as a result of these calls.

> *Nah, they wouldn't call the police because they knew they was doing*
> *dirty anyway. Some of them have warrants. They don't want to turn*
> *themselves in. Some of them be the ones that be like ducking their*
> *own people [their own dealers or fellow gang members]. They look-*
> *ing for them. I know I got a chance in jacking them because I know*
> *they ain't gonna call people.*
>
> *We moved mainly in the neighborhoods where. . . . See, in our*
> *neighborhood ain't no such thing as a police patrolling. Everybody is*
> *black and everybody is young and thugging. Ain't no cops over there.*

The practiced behaviors that some offenders continually engage in firmly establishes in their minds that they exist in places where crime is safe and where everyone understands this to be the case. Cut off socially, geographically, and economically from the conventional world, high on powerful drugs, and familiar with the nighttime streets, one can mistakenly assume that all others recognize dangers and are part of the game. Witnessed crimes where no one is arrested or prosecuted also lead to the immediate perception that the police and law are distant, even if officers are always on patrol nearby. Offenders know well how dangerous and crime ridden their locales are. Several interviewed here described their friends dying or being shot themselves very near places where they committed their own crimes; others used more mundane accounts to show how unusually dangerous were the places where they offended.

> *David and Danny always carried nine millimeters. They brag about*
> *how they have it and point it toward me and my mother when we*

get out of the car. They always carried that. Danny always had that big twelve gauge shotgun. It's night time in the little area we live in. There's not too much traffic. And there's not cops. I'm talking about they don't come in that area. You know the school, the church, everything is closed down. It's not the first time something like this happened on the street. They've had other killings and everything on this street. So, you don't travel it much at night.

Places perceived to be crime laden provide those living in these places with excuses and anonymity.

■ Our Place

People interpret their spaces. This is at the heart of the Defensible Space approach to crime.[16] Behaviors, movements, and mood are shaped by a shared understanding not only of how places look, but also of what places mean—ask any landscape or structural architect. Abstract understandings of place include degrees of ownership, attachment, and allegiance to them. Needless to say, most street offenders are not metropolitan, as many are tethered to the spots they know best. They often have a special affinity for their neighborhoods and attribute strong meanings to them. They are familiar and relatively comfortable with their places and the rules of conduct there.

Binding oneself to and living in an area brings a familiarity with the people and routines of the territory, which affords opportunities and protections and contributes to a sense of ownership and place. As previously mentioned, targets are easy to find for local offenders, and unusual incidents and opportunities are noticed. As in all communities, access to the grapevine is important and adds to confidence, security, and opportunity: as one man put it, "if you live in a town you hear everything, [like] that this person has got money. So, I thought, well look if he's got money then I am going to get him for everything he has got." Several mentioned that specific information about targets could be gained by listening to storied events of wealthy street characters and tales of recent big scores. In addition to information they provide, friends can diminish some of the risks of street-life and crime. Ideally this is true of retaliation from stranger victims,

You not really gonna come back there and try to find somebody that done you wrong. Even though I was on drugs, a lot of people would still be there for me, you know. As far as if you come shooting at me, they gonna shoot at you. If you try to kill me . . . you know I'm saying it was just a raggedy rough life. That's kinda how I could carjack people. You know, that was my setting in the drug area.

The distinction between outsiders and insiders sometimes is maintained stringently and severely affirming that place is salient in some neighborhoods.

> *There have been times when we'll go jump on somebody or something. See somebody we don't like or from another city, we go jump on them and everything. You know some are ready to kill and everything.*

A recurring theme was to point out that strangers who have the markings of successful but locally unknown street players are in particular danger.

> *If he's not cool with us or is someone we can trust, then we gonna get the fellow. But, that's the only thing that make them stand out. You know, people flashing jewel or people flashing money. That's why we would get an individual person. But, if they just puttering along on about their business, we don't usually even pay them no attention.*

One of the most obvious ways that people lay claim to territory is with the assertion that people like or close to them literally control its economy and events. An offender neatly articulates an obvious reason for feeling safe as a criminal in his neighborhood (i.e., murderous retaliation):

> *You would find out if somebody . . . see them people don't say nothing. They see people get their head busted in broad daylight on main corners and . . . People come out and they don't know nothing. If they call the police when we doing something then we gonna . . . see, we don't have to worry about no police. We knew nobody gonna tell the police.*

Because localities have rules of conduct, they can become linked intimately with identities of inhabitants. To be from a place is understood by some to mean that one was part of its character and could get along under its code. Moreover, it is in the interest of those who claim to be at the center of constructing the norms and business of a place to ensure that their attributes are continually appreciated. Many of the challenges, playful and serious confrontations, as well as instances of criminal victimization designed to show street-corner dominance, can be interpreted not only as claims based on maintaining the integrity of personal criminal identities but also on claims to place and belonging. In sustaining the rules of criminal places through action, offenders sustain worlds and places where others appreciate their attributes. Many come to believe that because of qualities that make them suitable for street life, they prevail—or at least do acceptably well—in criminal areas. Those that share their approaches to life and spend considerable time with them "on the streets" struggle for place by keeping local codes true and real.

■ Geographic Excuses

One of the most important elements in the decision to commit crime is the psychological process of sanitizing the conscience so that it can be accomplished. For this reason, there is a great deal of paper in criminal social psychology devoted to the ways that offenders make sense of or account for their criminal acts and related behaviors.[17] Offenders' enabling accounts are designed to explain or make excuses for behavior that the culturally distant or otherwise ignorant outsider might assess as aberrant or inexplicable and distasteful. The best possible pitch is made, although usually it is unconvincing. Criminologists have long thought that offenders mentally justify their acts before deciding to commit crime, although all acknowledge that these explanations might be rough, ill-conceived and only partially articulated in the offenders' conscience before the act.[18]

Before proceeding with a discussion of space and rationalization, it is important to recognize that for an excuse to work for oneself and others, it must be viable to the offenders' imagined and somewhat conventional audience. The offender explains why he does it in a way that *normal people*, as he imagines them, might accept. Therefore, rationalizations often have at least a chime of truth, however muted and dull. For example, in the abstract we understand that oppressive work places and poverty tempt some to pilfer products from work. While considering the act, pilferers know that social audiences will generally understand their decisions, and this helps them carry out the task. For many of the offenders in this sample, environments serve to provide nearly perfect excuses. (We usually mean the drug markets in their neighborhoods and the troublesome activities these bring by environment.)

Ordinary Business

Offenders are often keen to acknowledge that crime is seen as ordinary business in their neighborhoods and hangouts. Recognition of this fact led to two significant recurrences in their accounts for understanding how they view crime and its appeal. First, violent acts and callous disregard for others are viewed with a morally neutral stance because others are portrayed as having consented to play within the brutal rules of the street game. Crime can be approached with a surprising moral neutrality, already seen in some of the quotes above, because recognition that crime is business signifies that offenders bear neither ill will towards their victims nor guilt for acting senselessly or against innocents when it is done.

> *Everything revolves around money and business. It's business. When we go to war with people over there, if we go to war with them, that shit's just business. They got to do it. They gonna kill beaucoup people, but it's just business.*

Being in criminal places or involved in criminal transactions means that one has recognized the risks and decided to take part, or at least wandered too near to an extremely dangerous place where risks are known. The assumption is that all who occupy this space do so knowing the risks, and spoils, of doing so. The expectation is that at some point, even the most virulent aggressors will be victimized. Offenders embedded in these areas recognize that they are not alone in their mindset. Many have a surprisingly fatalistic and cavalier attitude about what they see as inevitable consequences of life and competition in their neighborhoods and on the streets. As they see it, one of the unwritten rules or ethics of their places is that the strong survive and the weak perish. Of the possibility of others robbing or killing him, an offender contends:

> *If they ever catch me down bad, I got to respect it. Because all of this dirt that I have done, and that is the type of life I've lived. I got to respect it, because it come with it.*

The second form of rationalization that occurs when crime is ordinary business in a neighborhood is the belief that crime is appropriate behavior there. This appears in offender statements that point to the unlikely contention that *everyone* in the place is doing it. We heard that *everyone* in their neighborhood was directly involved in the drug world from four of the thirty that we interviewed, and this belief was implied by several more. A more specific and temporally circumscribed example of the same rationalization follows in a carjacker's description of the immediate period preceding a city street party:

> *See, everybody in the hood was hitting cars on the regular during the Essence Festival and Bayou Classic to go to the French Quarter, [which is] packed with females. Everybody just jumping shop to go to that park.*

Sources of rationalizations also are found in potentially exaggerated references to the fact that signs indicating that a place is criminal are so apparent that no one could ignore them. In unquestionably criminal places, what else could happen? An example follows.

> *You know that's where they dump. It's by the Mississippi River. It is right by the Mississippi River. They dump the bodies there. I mean they will dump kills and bodies. Mostly drug dealers. So, we go right back there.*

Another offender remembers,

> *On the backway, you got a street only go down so far and it got a deadend. That's where everybody go that steal cars. Take them to get what they want out and burn them. So, like that whole street full of cars like a junkyard.*

Local Knowledge

Many individuals we spoke with had long histories of crime and had begun offending early. Some had worked from an early age in drug distribution networks or gangs, but more often, as youths they had spent considerable time in proximity to offenders and observing their activities from nearby. Of course, early exposure to criminal influences brings with it not only the objective conditions and opportunities that make crime more likely, but also the mindset that allows one to quickly and conveniently rationalize participation when confronted with potential sources of criminal opportunity. One young man put it succinctly, "See, when you are young, you watch a lot of drugs done and see how to get money and cars and stuff like that." Another offender claims that choice of crime is contingent on what the older men in the neighborhood do: "If they robbers, then the younger ones is gonna be robbers; if they dealers, then they gonna be dealers, and if they jackers, then they gonna be jackers." In the following passage, an offender recognizes explicitly how his place in the world, locally and writ large, figured in his preparation for crime and recognition of criminal opportunity that led to a "spontaneous" carjacking.

> *It was a spur of the moment thing, because that morning I went to the store. I went to Winn-Dixie to be exact, and I was like, man, how am I going to get home? When I walked out of the store, I had a little pocket knife and a Glock on me, so I was like, all these cars, and all I got to do is get me a brand new one. I'll be straight with you, I grew up doing that and watching the older kids in New Orleans. So, I already knew it was easy. I'm in the parking lot, and I just did it.*

Being from certain places brings with it expectations of how one should respond in specific situations. These environmental expectations make choosing crime more palatable. After all, this is what people like them in places like these do.

Passing Through

As important as their acknowledgment that their place led them to be socialized into understanding how to get by *in the streets*, which can be shown on maps but are also metaphorical avenues, is the ready recognition by many offenders that they are but players in a long-running drama or game. They may make their temporary mark and hoodlum reputation on street scenes, but the game will inevitably outlast them. In fact, there will be characters almost indistinguishable from themselves occupying neighborhood roles when they abandon them. These understandings approach very nearly to one of the most frequently heard rationalizations among all who bend or break rules: "If I don't do it, someone else will." In environments where crime has proliferated for years, it is easy to sustain this view. Actors and actions created by the continuing environment are replaceable cogs caught in a system. Structural conditions and local histories have, in these portrayals, so constrained personal choices as to make them almost irrelevant for the occurrence of discrete events. Most street actors are quick to point out that they chose their life, but also remind the listener that they simply fill a niche and step into ongoing social circles of neighborhood criminals. When they opt out or go away, nothing changes. One offender makes an obvious, and useful, comparison about conditions in his neighborhood and the prospect for continued violence in a more formal sort of behavior system.

> *Any person, you back them against a wall and you never know what they are going to do. You know people you never believe go and join the Army or the Air Force or the Marines, and next thing you know, they're in Afghanistan killing Arabs and Muslims. People you've never think of doing something like that. They are out there just doing what they are trained to do.*

Another man refers to the inevitability of crime in a drug neighborhood. He notes that criminal activity has persisted while he has been in prison, and accepts that it will persist and be "popular" no matter what one says or does.

> *The drugs just bringing them down. Killing them slowly now, you know what I'm saying. It still goes on. Like in the middle of New Orleans, that is where this goes on. Carjacking is still going to be popular there—I don't care what you say.*

No Way Out

Rationalization based on neighborhood conditions or familiarity with space would not be very convincing if offenders thought that they could be physically or socially mobile. But many believed that their early mastery of the street environment precluded, or at least made more difficult to obtain, outlooks that would lead to success in other places. The streets provided them with the self-perpetuating logic that plays a small part in their long histories of criminal choices. Although on many levels they are not, the lived conditions of the streets seem inescapable.[10] Curiously, admitting to simply not paying heed to conventional morality or claiming to have never been taught any better can rationalize the most abhorrent acts, even if one claims to be an inherently valuable and good person. Purported or real ignorance of what law-abiding life is like is a perfect excuse.

> *If the streets raise you, or if you raised up in the streets, this is going to seem all right to you. It doesn't matter what the point is behind it or if the cops is behind. Everything just seems right. Most people do it for the fame, the cars, the big rides or whatever. But, as we start*

getting independent, we start saying, man, now you got to make it on your own. Sleeping on the streets ain't no fun thing. Eating out of garbage cans ain't no fun thing. So, we like, man, this is just our life. You know it seems right for us to do.

Another offender points to the difficulty of overcoming the pull of the streets in answering a question about his post-release plans. His response reveals a dilemma for the released offender, who will in all likelihood return to an environment very like that known before prison. More frightening is that this territory and its rules are familiar, and in some cases most other ways are somewhat foreign. The quoted offender begins the journey knowing not only that returning to crime is possible, but also that it can seem like a legitimate course of action given his background and likely place. He explains, "I'm trying very hard—very, very hard. It would be easy for me to go back to doing what I was doing. That's easy *there*, you know what I'm saying? The hard part is trying not to do it."

■ Conclusion

Admittedly, the places that produce high rates of violent criminal offenders in the United States are rosy by comparison to those in economically peripheral nations. The most apparent explanations of place and crime intrude nearly as obviously in parts of the United States as they do in Brazil's *favellas*, however. Concentrated poverty and all the conditions associated with it makes it difficult— nearly impossible—to precisely pinpoint the factors in these places that cause crime. While identifying discrete criminogenic factors and placing them in neat succession to discover mediators and moderators is a lovely armchair dream, it is important to remember that the professors' penchants for precise, neat, and sophisticated explanation sometimes obscures reality. Where many serious and persistent offenders grow up and live, it requires little imagination and modest inferences to make a few connections between places and criminal mindsets, but this may be difficult to model formally. Young men on the streets and in drug-ravaged, impoverished communities think differently about the prospects of crime and individual criminal acts than outsiders. Places provide opportunities and transform thoughts. Inhabitants may not give it a great deal of mental attention, but they have an understanding of place based on history and experience; they have also estimated their prospects in the larger world. Offenders predict what they can hope to accomplish according to where they are and how they live, and predictions are often bleak. In many places in the United States, the "internal peripheries" as they are fashionably called, the causes of crime are not mild incivilities found in environments or intricacies of child rearing and development. A little trash on the streets, scratched up school lockers, a few discarded needles, or cantankerous neighbors are not messengers for the idea that shooting someone is a feasible and reasonable solution in some circumstances. These environmental conditions in combination may play a small role in supporting such thinking by making despair seem suitable, but it is more important that gunfire in the area is common. The violent view comes from an understanding of brutal environments and its expectations, often gained in the lifelong experiences of street children.

When discussing place and cultures of place, it is tempting to discount offenders' ability to construct meanings and identity. We should remember that offenders seldom shirk from danger or street success. Although most learn the ways of the streets before the age of legal emancipation, they also actively place themselves in situations where they can show what they have learned and further expand their "street" identity. At some deeper psychological level, all may be in a defensive mode hoping to ward off future attacks and insults by trying to look hard and bad until this stance becomes habit. Their views on how to behave in the streets might result from past confrontations and victimization at the hands of other hard men. But they are predators nonetheless and may be unsympathetic to those who do not stand up well under the code of the streets; many look constantly for opportunities to assert their criminal selves and are especially dangerous in their familiar environ.[19] There may not be options about where one lives, but there are always alternative models for how one lives. It may seem unrealistic to stay in the house, end bad habits, withdraw from drugs, or work all day for low wages, but generally such decisions are possible and are the better choices among unpleasant options.

Neighborhoods do not produce homicides like randomizing shufflers at casinos produce aces; they do it by providing twisted logics among a few residents who prey upon others and for whom committing a robbery or pulling a trigger seems to make sense in certain circumstances. These persons pass the logics along. If asked in private, the neighbors in impoverished neighborhoods can point out such hostile, dangerous persons and can also identify those that will likely inherit their worldview, if not with perfect predictive accuracy. Given few perceived avenues for reaching better places, no small number of persons will find that they can thrive in another way—and in doing so, they strengthen the particular dictates right where they are.

We realize that the depiction of offenders in this essay will seem harsh to some. It is difficult to avoid the potential for condemnation when typifying subcultures that lead to violent street crime. But conclusions need not be as harsh as the depiction of street life. To say that offenders will find opportunities, identities, and excuses linked to places is not to say that nothing can be done. Emphasis on agency says nothing about how we can help potential offenders reach different conclusions. Indeed, we see no reason more compelling for efforts to improve conditions and standards of living in deteriorated neighborhoods than that it removes convenient rationalizations for failure and misbehavior. Modest improvements may make horrible behaviors seem out of a place's character.[20] Gangster posses are almost laughable among youth from middle class and affluent neighborhoods (except in the rare cases where they lead to authentic tragedy) because they are based upon different cultural understandings of place and class and what they are likely to produce. No young person should be able to cast himself as a societal refugee and endanger others easily, but the responsibility to change this behavior is found only in part in offenders' freely formed and subculturally shared perceptions. Those with resources to do something share responsibility for the objective conditions and ease of excuses in chaotic neighborhoods.[11]

The offender, like the rest of us, knows that he is part of a predictable environment. It will outlast him. It will produce successes and failures according to particular environmental dictates. It provides reassurances that personal mistakes and victories are irrelevant in the big picture. It is comforting to think that life's contingencies can be viewed as so structured that choices are incidental. Because the fundamental rules and outcomes of the practiced game do not change, it is justifiable to play it reasonably and to conclusion despite the likely potential for unfortunate outcomes. Even if one must walk away from a gambling table busted, it is comforting to know that other players with a chance of winning remain; those familiar with the tables also like knowing that there is a place where they know their way around and fit in easily, even when the odds are stacked and almost everyone loses eventually. Just as the compulsive gambler is comforted by the casino and knows that walking away from any single event victorious or busted will not change long run prospects for self or similar others, the street player finds comfort in the ongoing and familiar game. Pursuits for local acclaim continue because an intrinsic value is placed on established personal patterns of behavior, subcultural dictates, and appropriate thrills. Understandings of place transcend the spatial and occupy thoughts about how to behave. They contain the same metaphorical meaning found in the phrases "living on the streets" or "living on skid row," which can mean spending considerable time on certain streets or, perhaps more importantly, living life according to the dictates of one or another form of street culture. The streets become part of who one is and *responsible* for decisions. The mind carries place. Recently, after a riot in London's Heathrow airport that injured several people, a big-talking member of a music star's entourage who helped start the fight taunted proudly as he was led away by police: "This is how it goes down in L.A." What a curious thing to say.

References

1. BBC News. (2005). Rio slums blighted by gun crime. October 21. http://news.bbc.co.uk/1/hi/world/americas/4338652.stm. Accessed December 15, 2006.
2. Jacobs, B., Topalli, V., Wright, R. (2003). Carjacking, streetlife and offender motivation. *Br J Criminol* 43:673–688.
3. Jacobs, B., Wright, R. (2006). *Street Justice: Retaliation in the Criminal Underworld.* Cambridge: Cambridge University Press.
4. Brantingham, P., Brantingham, P. (1984). *Patterns in Crime.* New York: Macmillan.
5. Cohen, L. E., Felson, M. (1979). Social change and crime rate trends. *Am Sociol Rev* 44:588–605.
6. Cloward, R., Ohlin, L. E. (1960). *Delinquency and Opportunity: A Theory of Delinquent Gangs.* New York: Free Press.
7. Sampson, R. J., Raudenbush, S. (1999). Systematic social observation of public spaces: A new look at disorder in urban neighborhoods. *Am J Sociol*, 105: 603–651.
8. Suttles, G. (1968). *The Social Order of the Slum: Ethnicity and Territory in the Inner City.* Chicago: University of Chicago Press.
9. Bourgois, P. (2002). *In Search of Respect: Selling Crack in El Barrio*, 2nd edition. Cambridge: Cambridge University Press.
10. MacLeod, J. (1995). *Ain't No Making It: Aspirations and Attainment in a Low-Income Neighborhood.* Boulder, CO: Westview.
11. Anderson, E. (2003). *A Place on the Corner*, 2nd edition. Chicago: University of Chicago Press.
12. Sherman, L. W., Gartin, P. R., Buerger, M. E. (1989). Hot spots of predatory crime: Routine activities and the criminology of place. *Criminology* 27:27–56.
13. Stark, R. (1987). Deviant places: A theory of the ecology of crime. *Criminology* 25:893–910.
14. Jacobs, B. (2000). *Robbing Drug Dealers: Violence Beyond the Law.* Somerset, NJ: Aldine.
15. Wright, R., Decker, S. (1997). *Armed Robbers in Action.* Boston: Northeastern University Press.
16. Newman, O. (1972). *Defensible Space: Crime Prevention Through Urban Design.* New York: Macmillan.
17. Maruna, S., Copes, H. (2005). What have we learned from five decades of neutralization research? *Crime Justice Rev Res* 32:221–320.
18. Sykes, G., Matza, D. (1957). Techniques of neutralization: A theory of delinquency. *Am Sociol Rev* 22:664–670.
19. Anderson, E. (1999). *Code of the Street: Decency, Violence and the Moral Life of the Inner City.* New York: W.W. Norton.
20. Jacobs, J. (1961). *The Death and Life of Great American Cities.* New York: Random House.

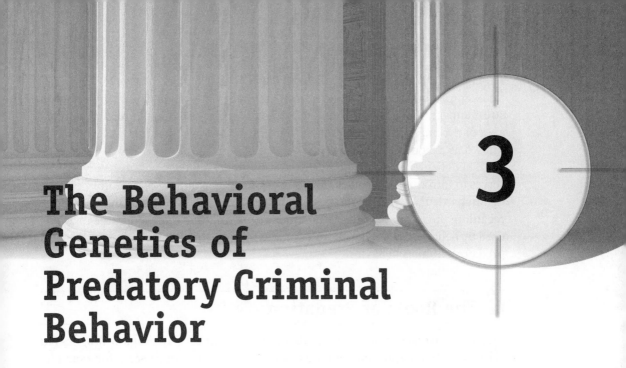

The Behavioral Genetics of Predatory Criminal Behavior

John Paul Wright
University of Cincinnati

Kevin M. Beaver
Florida State University

Even the most casual observer of science must be struck by the rate at which new findings on human development and maladjustment are published. Hardly a day passes in which the media do not report startling results linking brain function to criminal behavior, or report new linkages between specific genes and criminal traits. The individuals who have led the way into this exciting, uncharted territory, however, have not been sociologically trained criminologists. Unfortunately, most criminologists remain on the disciplinary sidelines, or worse, remain wedded to an ideology that rejects genetic influences in any form. This may be why "the biological sciences have made more progress in our understanding of criminal behavior in the last ten years than sociology has made over the past 50 years."[1]

While some criminologists may bristle at this declaration, there can be little doubt that an explosion of knowledge on the development of criminal conduct has occurred, especially knowledge about serious predatory conduct, and that the results have been published in journals that feature studies on genetics and biology. Not a single path-breaking study on criminal behavior has been published in any leading criminology or sociology journal. Even more telling is the fact that the leading criminological theories—that is, social learning theory, strain theory, and self-control theory—all *require* biological and genetic factors to be valid. Learning, for example, occurs when connections are made between synapses in the brain; stress and strain have been found to impinge on hippocampus–pituitary–adrenal axes of the brain; while self-control reflects a broader set of brain-based abilities known as executive functions.

This chapter seeks to demystify the influence genes have on behavior and serves to introduce the reader to a "biosocial" understanding of predatory offending. In particular, we provide the reader a brief introduction to current knowledge regarding predatory offending, the fundamentals of human genetics, the methods used by behavioral geneticists, and the way this information is used to understand predatory human behavior.

■ The Roots of Predation

Predation involves an intention to do harm to another, or at least a willingness to actively seek out and injure another person. Predation can be seen, for example, when armed robbers make a choice to "hold up" an individual or commercial establishment, or when a rapist takes his time to stalk his victim and then, when the risk of being identified or caught is the lowest, he commits his crime. Predation can also be seen when a child molester seeks out and abducts a child.[2]

Even among criminals, predation in criminal conduct is unusual. Only the most serious and habitual offenders are predatory. Other offenders tend to be opportunistic or influenced by situational contingencies, such as the presence of criminal others or the use of drugs and alcohol. This is not to say that predatory offenders are not also opportunists or that they do not commit crimes when under the influence; the difference is that predatory offenders do not require or are not driven by these concerns. To be direct, predatory offenders are the truly criminal.

Research on the development of serious criminal conduct has shown three important factors. First, the warning signs for serious predation are visible in infancy and childhood. Infants who are fussy, irritable, difficult to soothe, and who react negatively to novel situations are significantly more likely to grow into children who have conduct disorders and into adults with antisocial personality disorder.[3–6]

Second, traits related to later criminal conduct are also visible in infancy and early childhood. While these traits have been labeled in a variety of ways, they generally focus on the ability of the infant and child to increasingly regulate his own behavior and to conform to the social expectations found in varied environments. Impulse control, self-regulation, self-control, emotional regulation, and hyperactivity generally fall under this broad umbrella of traits. Third, and more important, studies into the development of aggression have found that its onset occurs around the time when children gain mobility—that is, when they start walking and interacting socially with other children. Richard Tremblay's studies of very young Canadian children, for example, found the peak age for aggression was around 27 months, but he also found that over 90% of young children had engaged in acts of aggression, such as hitting, kicking, and biting, before 36 months of age.[7–9]

Physical aggression is a nearly universal human capacity and is "normal" early in life, but it becomes more uncommon in children over time.[7] Indeed, children who fail to "age out" of the use of physical aggression by age 4 are significantly more likely to continue using physical aggression over long swaths of their life-course. Perhaps not surprisingly, an early age of onset is one of the strongest predictors of future adult predatory offending. Reviews by Marvin Krohn and his colleagues found that early onset offenders committed 40 to 700% more crimes than individuals who had an onset of problem behaviors later in life. Moreover, virtually every predatory offender has experienced an early age of onset.[10]

In summary, children who exhibit a variety of criminogenic traits, who fail to gain sufficient self-regulatory capacities by age 4, and whose behavior remains consistent across time and situation are at substantial risk of developing into predatory adults. That this risk trajectory materializes at such an early point in the life-course necessarily hints at the likelihood that genetic factors are at play.

■ A Behavioral Genetic Understanding of Predatory Offending

How do we understand this set of empirical facts? With a few exceptions, such as Moffitt's developmental taxonomy, traditional criminological theories remain silent, largely because these theories of crime locate the causes of misconduct in adolescence. Even if we broaden their theoretical lens and take a leap of faith, criminologists would likely point to parental rearing environments as the putative source of variation in young children's behaviors. But would they be correct?

Before we answer that question, let's first examine how a behavioral geneticist would understand this issue. Behavioral genetics is the field of study that examines how much variance in any given trait or behavior is accounted for by genetic *and* environmental influences. Behavioral genetic studies estimate this variance by analyzing samples of monozygotic and dizygotic twins, relying on the laws of genetics, and using sophisticated statistical models. At the heart of the field, however, is the estimation of genetic and environmental influences.

Figure 3.1 shows the hypothetical results of a behavioral genetic analysis of some trait, such as impulsivity. As you can see from the pie chart, genetic influences account for most of the variance in impulsivity (65%), while non-shared environmental influences account for 25% and shared environmental influences only 10%. Estimates of genetic influences are denoted by h^2, which stands for the degree to which a trait, characteristic, or behavior is heritable. The term "heritable"

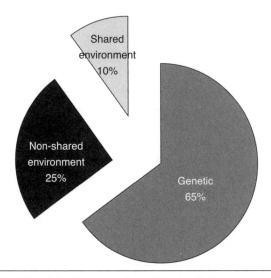

Figure 3.1 How Behavioral Geneticists Decompose the Variance in a Trait.

should not be confused with "inherited." Individuals "inherit" DNA that will ultimately code for the creation of the brain, nervous system, and arms and legs. Heritability reflects the degree to which a complex trait can be influenced by genes. This distinction is critical to understanding behavioral genetics because one may be endowed with a specific genetic propensity, such as alcoholism or drug dependency, but the propensity may never be realized. Alcoholism in traditional Muslim countries, for example, is very low because of the cultural prohibitions against alcohol use. Of course, this does not mean that certain Muslims do not have a propensity for addiction.

Behavioral geneticists also specify two types of environmental influences. Non-shared environments are those unique experiences that make individuals more different than alike. Siblings, even twins, often have different peer groups, for example. Different peer groups represent a unique (non-shared) environment. Conversely, environments shared by individuals are thought to make people more alike. Children born to the same parents are exposed to similar broad parental management strategies.

Findings from hundreds of studies now show that virtually every human trait and characteristic is genetically influenced. For certain characteristics, such as vocational interests or religious orientations, the influence of genes is very low. For other characteristics, especially those associated with predatory offending, genetic influences dominate.[11] For example, IQ, impulsivity, and self-control appear to be primarily genetic in origin.[12] These same studies, however, also reveal that unique environmental experiences usually outweigh the influences of shared environmental influences—that is, shared experiences do not appear to make individuals more similar, but instead highlight their differences.[13–16]

Would criminologists be correct in predicting that parenting practices early in life produced adult predatory behavior? The behavioral genetic studies typically show that shared environments, or the ways in which parents establish an overall home environment, have little to no effect on the adult offspring.[17] Does this mean that parenting has nothing to do with adult predation? Not exactly. The processes that link parenting practices to human development likely operate through biological mechanisms. When rats lick their pups, for instance, the stimulation releases oxytocin and prolactin, which are hormones that aid in the creation of feelings of safety and love. Studies of Romanian orphans brought up in horrific conditions show reduced levels of these hormones. Nurturance may thus help build a healthy brain—at least for certain kids. Some children may respond well to nurturance; others may have no response at all. This is part of the reason that it may be difficult to detect parental socialization effects. The genetic propensities of the child may interfere with or not respond to parenting efforts.

A Brief Note on Human Genetics

Humans inherit 23 pairs of chromosomes from each parent, one of which is the sex differentiating chromosome. Males receive a Y chromosome from the father and an X chromosome from the mother (XY); females receive an X chromosome from both parents (XX). Chromosomes are made of deoxyribonucleic acid (DNA). DNA, in turn, is composed of two elongated sections bonded to chemical bases—the now-familiar double helix. The chemical bases are adenine (A), thymine (T), guanine (G), and cytosine (C). Due to their molecular structure, A can only bond with T, and G can only bond with C to form what are known as "base pairs." Genes, which are embedded in chromosomes, are merely stretches of DNA with a known arrangement of base pairs.

Current estimates place the number of genes in the human genome between 19,000 and 25,000. This number is far below other "lower level" life forms, including some plants. Nonetheless, Mendelian theory tells us that we inherit two copies of each gene, one from the father and one from the mother. At one level, Mendelian theory is correct: we do inherit our genes from our parents. However, research has recently found evidence that for some genes, we may inherit more than just two copies; that is, one or both parents may pass down more than one copy of particular genes. Three international research projects found that at least 10% of all human genes, or roughly 2,900 genes, can vary in their number of copies within an individual. Estimates that used to indicate that humans were 99.9% genetically similar have to be revised to about 99% genetically similar. This translates from a 3 million base-pair difference between humans to at least a 30 million base-pair difference. This also means that it is even more likely that genes play a significant role in serious, predatory behavior.

Even if multiple copies of some genes are present, they are not all turned "on" or "off" at one time. The process whereby our genes are made active or inactive is called *genetic imprinting*. Genes, moreover, come in different varieties. Differences in genes are called *alleles*. Allelic variation occurs when mutations, genetic drift, cultural selection, evolution, or any combination of factors alters a gene. For example, the dopamine transporter gene DRD4 comes in several allelic varieties, with some of these varieties linked to an increased transmission of impulsivity and attention deficit hyperactivity disorder (ADHD).[18,19] Genes with various alleles are referred to as *polymorphic*.

Individuals can differ substantially, even at the genetic level. Understanding the role of genes in complex human phenotypes, however, is made even more complicated by the fact that humans do not always follow Mendelian genetic principles. According to these principles, human genetic expression should follow a dominant and recessive form. Under most conditions, dominant genes should be expressed. At one level, some of our genes follow the dominant/recessive framework, such as the genes for eye color. For complex traits, however, human genes do not appear to follow this principle. Instead, functional human genes appear to follow a pattern of incomplete dominance in their relationship to traits and behaviors. *Incomplete dominance* refers to a situation where the effects of dominant and recessive alleles are blended and then expressed in a phenotype.

How Do Genes Work to Influence Predation?

Complex traits and behaviors are usually not produced by single genes. It is typically the case that multiple genes act in concert to bring about specific genetic potentials.[20] We use the term *genetic potentials* because genes create general behavioral tendencies, or propensities, that can sometimes be contingent on the environment for their activation. Earlier, we used the example of the low alcoholism rate in traditional Muslim countries. Clearly, some Muslims will have a genetic potential to become addicted to alcohol, but that propensity will not materialize if the individual never drinks. Single gene influences are also typically rather small, usually explaining less than 5% of the variance in any complex behavior, such as violence. Research by Comings and his colleagues has shown that genes have an additive influence on ADHD, oppositional defiant disorder (ODD), conduct disorder, and various personality dimensions. It appears that input from many genes working in concert is required to produce traits and behaviors.[21–23]

How does this knowledge contribute to an understanding of serious, predatory criminal behavior? **Figure 3.2** provides an overview of the respective influences genotypes have on predation. Since our focus is on genetic influences, we leave out the influence of environmental variables. We do this for brevity and be-

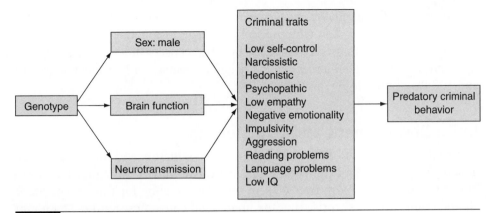

Figure 3.2 How the Genotype Influences Predatory Criminal Conduct.

cause theory indicates that high-risk genotypes will experience "faulty" development regardless of their environmental setting—that is, for the types of individuals we are concerned with, serious predatory offenders, it is likely that their genotype confers so much risk that environmental mediators and moderators will be rendered ineffectual. Again, we are dealing with the truly criminal.

The first arrow in Figure 3.2 leads from the genotype to sex. In studying predatory offenders, there is one overriding, consistent, and obvious fact: predatory offenders are almost universally male. At one level, being male is one of the best known risk factors to criminal involvement overall, but in terms of serious predation, males have the market cornered. Of course, being a male is caused by the father passing along Y chromosome to his offspring. The Y chromosome contains the SRY gene, which causes the testes to form and drop in the developing male fetus. It has only 78 genes, which code for 27 proteins. All other chromosomes contain more genes than the Y chromosome.

Once activated, the SRY gene signals the developing testes to flood the brain with androgens, the most commonly known of which is testosterone. Testosterone appears to "masculinize" the developing male brain. This has several effects. The first is that it creates what has been termed the "male brain." The male brain tends to excel in tests of spatial skills, the ability to focus on an issue or problem, map reading, and mathematics and sciences; it also shows a greater desire to seek risks and has 10% more area dedicated to aggression.[24] Females, in contrast, are more religious, score higher in tests of empathy and emotional recognition, score better on tests of verbal skills, and are 60 to 70% better in memory for "locations and landmarks."[25]

The second effect can be seen in the social behavior of males. Men are generally more status oriented than women and ascribe to status hierarchies more than women. Status hierarchies are also known as dominance hierarchies. Dominance can be achieved through a variety of methods, but the most efficient method—one employed more frequently by males than females—is violence. Dominance fueled by testosterone may explain why overt physical aggression and predatory behavior in men appears to fully materialize during adolescence, a time when testosterone levels are 10 times higher and when males add an average of 1 to 2 feet in growth and 100 lbs of muscle.[26]

Brain Development and Functioning

The next arrow leads from the genotype to brain structure and functioning. The genotype spends a significant amount of nuclear resources coding for the development of the brain. With over 60% of our genes coding for this one organ, it should come as little surprise that the brain itself consumes significant amount of resources. Weighing in at 3 lbs, or about 2% of total body weight, the brain consumes roughly 10 times the amount of glucose as the rest of the organs, and roughly 20% of the body's oxygen intake.[1]

In terms of development, the human brain develops in a linear fashion: from the simplest parts that control life-sustaining non-reflexive activities, such as breathing, to the most complex and most recently evolved systems. The brain stem and lower brain are the first part to develop. Controlling all necessary functions, the brain stem and lower brain are important for the regulation of sleep and appetite.

Sitting on top of the brain stem is the limbic system. The limbic system is composed of various structures in the brain that regulate hormones, control memory, and create emotions. Fear, anxiety, jealousy, anger, lust, and sadness are biochemical responses to environmental stimuli, the origin of which can be located in the limbic system. Of particular interest to the study of predatory criminal behavior is the amygdala. The amygdala is the "seat of emotions and emotional memory." It provides humans with the ability to match an event to a specific emotion and thereby gives us the ability to recall the experiences along with the feelings associated with the experience.

As we mentioned earlier, predation involves the willingness, if not desire, to bring harm to another individual. For most individuals, the thought of hurting an innocent person brings about feelings of guilt, shame, and anxiety. But what if these internal constraints are missing? What if the thought of hurting another person brings instead feelings of joy, excitement, or even worse, apathy? Several studies show that the lack of empathy, a primary controlling emotion, is absent in psychopaths, and that its absence is due to problems associated with amygdala responses. Moreover, several studies, including studies of active offenders, have found that committing crime can be fun or emotionally rewarding, and that it can build a positive social reputation among other criminals.

The last part of the brain to develop is the neocortex, or the "thinking part" of the brain. The cortex sits atop the limbic system and is responsible for the human abilities of planning, delaying gratification, impulse control, and rational thought. The speech and language parts of the brain, known as Wernike's and Broca's areas, are also located in the neocortex.

Taking over 20 years to fully mature, the cortex houses the "executive functions" of the human brain, such as self-control and emotional regulation. Numerous studies have shown that the cortex, especially the orbital-frontal cortex (OFC), is critical to prosocial human behavior. Certain individuals appear to lack self-control because of deficits in the ventrolateral prefrontal cortex, especially deficits in the left hemisphere. This pattern of findings is particularly striking for males who have more problems with impulse control.

All sensory input is channeled first to the limbic system. Under constant monitoring by the cortex, the limbic system may send some of this information to the motor cortex, to the language centers, or to the neocortex—or to all necessary parts of the brain. The cortex has the ability to override the initial limbic impulses, given that the cortex is intimately "wired" into the limbic system. When strong emotions are encountered, the initial limbic impulse may be to act with violence, or to act aggressively. The cortex, however, may intervene to curtail or modify the initial limbic impulse. Obviously, deficits in the cortex will allow those impulses to materialize in the form of behavior.

Neurotransmission

The last arrow leads from the genotype to the box labeled neurotransmission. With 100 billion neurons, and even more glia cells, the human brain is a masterpiece of complexity. Even more astonishing is the fact that each neuron can connect to between 1 and 10,000 other neurons. Neurons communicate to each other by channeling an electric charge down an axon. As the electric charge reaches the end of the axon it forces the release of neurotransmitters from the synaptic cleft. These neurotransmitters then pass across synaptic space, which is about 1/600th the width of a human hair, and bond to receptors located on the dendrite of the receiving neuron.

Neurotransmitters come in two types, excitory and inhibitory. Excitory neurotransmitters, such as dopamine, instigate movement, while inhibitory neurotransmitters, such as serotonin, reduce motivation. Neurotransmission occurs in response to environmental input, but it is under substantial genetic control.[27] The genotype, for example, codes for the number of neurotransmitter receptors located on dendrites.

Neurotransmission is also related to brain functioning. Since many genes are expressed in the brain, scientists have recently undertaken efforts to examine how certain functional genetic variants are related to the overall brain–behavior response. One of the most fascinating studies genotyped subjects to ascertain which form of a gene the subjects inherited. The gene codes for monoamine oxidase A (MAOA), an enzyme in the brain that breaks down excess serotonin. Molecular research has shown that there is an "efficient" allele and an "inefficient" allele of the MAOA gene. Those with the inefficient allele were thought to have excess serotonin, which theoretically would decrease impulsivity. With this information at hand, researchers then used 3-D magnetic resonance imaging to compare those with the efficient and less efficient alleles.[28]

Compared to individuals with the efficient MAOA allele, individuals with inefficient allele showed substantial reductions in brain volume (measured by gray matter) in areas of the brain that control attention (anterior cingulated cortex) and emotions (amygdala). For males only, however, researchers also found a 14% reduction in the OFC. Further evaluation found that the OFC was less active and less connected to the amygdala in men with the inefficient allele. Recall that the OFC is deeply implicated in self-control and emotional regulation.

To summarize the information thus far, human genetics is related to predatory offending through three primary variables: sex, brain structure and functioning, and neurotransmission. How the genotype codes for these biological factors plays a large role in the resulting expression of criminogenic traits. It is worth noting again that the genotype is also influenced by environmental variables, such as the induction of neurotoxins and constant stress and anxiety. However, it is not clear that serious offenders would behave differently even if presented with entirely prosocial environmental stimuli.[29,30]

■ Criminality

By way of Figure 3.2, it should be clear that the genome may not influence behavior directly—that is, genes do not cause behavior. Instead, genes create the conditions for various human traits to be expressed in terms of personality, thinking patterns, and ultimately behavior. The concentration of these traits within an individual elevates the likelihood that he will engage in predatory conduct for much of his life. Several dimensions distinguish predatory offenders from non-offenders, and even from minor offenders. Predatory offenders often have problems with self-control, in that they act impulsively and sometimes without accurately assessing the immediate situation. They tend to be narcissistic, thinking primarily of themselves and their needs and wants, and they appear unable to relate to the pain and anguish they cause others. Moreover, they also tend to be below average in measures of IQ, especially on measures of verbal IQ. Finally, they tend to view the world negatively, with open hostility towards others, and they tend to act aggressively without provocation. Theirs is also a lifestyle of drug-use, partying, and general irresponsibility.

Criminality—the propensity to commit crime and other destructive behaviors—manifests itself from the confluence of these traits. A behavioral genetic understanding of these traits highlights three interrelated points: First, all of these traits have high levels of heritability, especially IQ, impulsiveness, and self-control.[31–35] This is part of the reason that all of these traits have been linked to sex, brain functioning, and neurotransmission.

Second, many individuals with relatively low levels of self-control, high levels of impulsivity, and non-empathetic personalities are *not* criminal. A behavioral genetic understanding would point out that it is not only the confluence of these multiple heritable traits working in conjunction with each other, but it is also the degree to which these heritable traits dominate one's personality and behavior. Psychologists use the term *clinical* to indicate that an individual's score on a measured personality characteristic, such as narcissism, is significantly different from the average score in the population. This term also indicates that the characteristic is associated with problems in that person's life or that it has interfered with or delayed their development. Serious, predatory offenders are likely to score in the "clinical" range on all, or at least most, of these criminal traits and characteristics.

■ Conclusions

We agree with Robinson that behavioral geneticists have provided more insights into the origins of serious predatory conduct in the last 10 years than sociology has in the last 50 years. These insights, however, have yet to fully penetrate criminology. While the reasons for this are numerous, one reason is that many criminologists fear that recognizing genetic influences will leave them with nothing left to study. Understanding predation from a behavioral genetic viewpoint, however, does not obviate the importance of environmental factors. Indeed, just the opposite is true—a behavioral genetic viewpoint helps to clarify how environmental stimuli operate on the human organism and it helps to specify more precisely which stimuli sponsor criminality and which do not.

As we hope we have made clear, genetic influences on criminality are complex and multifaceted. It is simply not the case that "bad" genes create bad people. Any over-simplification of genetic influences does a disservice to the science of human behavior and gives a misleading and incomplete picture of the operation of the human genome on evolved behavioral patterns. While we have endeavored to provide the reader with a basic understanding of the behavioral genetics of serious criminality, we caution against any further simplification.

The astute reader will likely ask about policy consequences associated with a behavioral genetic understanding of pathology. Just as behavioral genetics shed light on the operation of genes and environmental factors, it also supports various policies. We cannot make an exhaustive listing of potential policies, but there are three that are at the forefront. First, there is good evidence that ADHD can be effectively treated and managed through a combination of medications and individual and family counseling. Given the overlap between characteristics of impulsivity and criminality, there is ample reason to also believe that serious misbehavior may also respond well to this combination of intervention efforts.

Second, the earlier the age of onset of problem behaviors the more likely those problems are to become resistant to change. Unfortunately, criminal behavioral patterns are relatively stable for long periods of time.[36–39] This evidence points to the need for early intervention with high-risk children and their families. Given the incredible personal and social costs associated with a life-time of personal pathology, the earlier and more frequent the intervention efforts, the better.

It is unreasonable to expect that even our best efforts to habilitate or rehabilitate a criminal individual will be successful in all cases. For those individuals who demonstrate an inability to effectively manage and regulate their antisocial tendencies, then nothing else is left but incarceration for lengthy periods of time. As we mentioned earlier, even among offenders, serious predation is not common. The crimes these men commit are typically the most serious and the most brutal. Protective social efforts are thus necessary. Moreover, the gravity of their crimes will dictate retribution.

Behavioral genetics is a fascinating, integrative field of study and has much to offer to students of criminal behavior. Perhaps its most important contribution is its focus on consilience. No single field has the capacity to completely unravel the complexities of human behavior. Interdisciplinary efforts are necessary to integrate findings from various disciplines that study the same topic. As an overarching perspective, the field of behavior genetics offers invaluable insights into the origins of predatory criminal conduct.

References

1. Robinson, M. B. (2004). *Why Crime? An Integrated Systems Theory of Antisocial Behavior.* Upper Saddle River, NJ: Prentice Hall, pp. ix–x.
2. Wright, R. T., Decker, S. H. (1997). *Armed Robbers in Action: Stickups and Street Culture.* Boston, MA: Northeastern University Press.
3. Caspi, A., Roberts, B. W., Shiner, R. (2005). Personality development: Stability and change. *Ann Rev Psychol* 56:453–484.
4. Moffitt, T., Caspi, A., Dickson, N., et al. (1996). Childhood-onset versus adolescent-onset antisocial conduct problems in males: Natural history from ages 3 to 18 years. *Dev Psychopathol* 8:399–424.

5. Schmitz, S., Fulker, D. W., Plomin, R., et al. (1999). Temperament and problem behavior during early childhood. *Int J Behav Dev* 23:333–355.

6. Shiner, R. L., Masten, A. S., Roberts, J. M. (2003). Childhood personality foreshadows adult personality and life outcomes two decades later. *J Personality* 71:1145–1170.

7. Tremblay, R. E., Nagin, D. S., Séguin, J. R., et al. (2004). Physical aggression during early childhood: Trajectories and predictors. *Pediatrics* 114:e43–e50.

8. Vitaro, F., Brendgen, M., Tremblay, R. E. (2002). Reactively and proactively aggressive children: Antecedent and subsequent characteristics. *J Child Psychol Psychiatr Allied Discipl* 43:495–505.

9. Tremblay, R. E. (2006). Prevention of Youth Violence: Why not start at the beginning? *J Abnorm Child Psychol* 34:480–486.

10. Krohn, M., Thornberry, T., Rivera, C., LeBlanc, M. (2001). Later delinquency careers. Pp. 67–93 in Rolf Loeber and David P. Farrington (Eds.), *Child Delinquents: Development, Intervention, and Service Needs*. Thousand Oaks, CA: Sage.

11. Plomin, R., Chipuer, H. M., Neiderhiser, J. M. (1994). Behavioral genetic evidence for the importance of non-shared environment. In M. Hetherington, D. Reiss, R. Plomin (Eds.), *Separate Social Worlds of Siblings: The Impact of the Non-Shared Environment on Development*. Hillsdale, NJ: Lawrence Erlbaum.

12. Barkley, R. A. (1997). *ADHD and the Nature of Self-Control*. New York: The Guilford Press.

13. Plomin, R., Daniels, D. (1987). Why are children in the same family so different from one another? *Behav Brain Sci* 10:1–60.

14. Plomin, R., DeFries, J. C., McClearn, G. E., Rutter, M. (1997). *Behavioral Genetics*, 3rd edition. New York: W. H. Freeman.

15. Plomin, R., Owen, M. J., McGuffin, P. (1994). The genetic basis of complex human behaviors. *Science*, 264, 1733–1739.

16. Rowe, D. C., Plomin, R. (1981). The importance of non-shared (E1) environmental influences in behavioral development. *Dev Psychol* 17: 517–531.

17. Wright, J. P., Beaver, K. M. (2005). Do parents matter in creating self-control in their children? A genetically informed test of Gottfredson and Hirschi's theory of low self-control. *Criminology* 43:1169–1202.

18. Arcos-Burgos, M., Castellanos, F. X., Konecki, D., et al. (2004). Pedigree disequilibrium test (PDT) replicates association and linkage between DRD4 and ADHD in multigenerational and extended pedigrees from a genetic isolate. *Molec Psychiatr* 9:252–259.

19. Mill, J. S., Caspi, A., McClay, J., et al. (2002). The dopamine D4 receptor and the hyperactivity phenotype: A developmental-epidemiological study. *Molec Psychiatr*, 7:383–391.

References

References

20. Comings, D. E., Gade-Andavolu, R., Gonzalez, N., et al. (2001). The additive effect of neurotransmitter genes in pathological gambling. *Clinical Genetics*, 60:107–116.

21. Comings, D. E., Gade-Andavolu, R., Gonzalez, N., et al. (2000). Comparison of the role of dopamine, serotonin, and noradrenaline genes in ADHD, ODD and conduct disorder: Multivariate regression analysis of 20 genes. *Clinical Genetics*, 57:178–196.

22. Comings, D. E., Gade-Andavolu, R., Gonzales, N., et al. (2000). Multivariate analysis of associations of 42 genes in ADHD, ODD, and conduct disorder. *Clinical Genetics*, 58:31–40.

23. Comings, D. E., Gade-Andavolu, R., Gonzalez, N., et al. (2000). A multivariate analysis of 59 candidate genes in personality traits: The temperament and character inventory. *Clinical Genetics* 58:375–385.

24. Baron-Cohen, S. (2002). The extreme male brain theory of autism. *Trends Cognitive Sci* 6:248.

25. Craig, I. W., Harper, E., Loat, C. S. (2004). The genetic basis for sex differences in human behavior: Role of the sex chromosomes. *Ann Human Genet* 68:269–284.

26. Booth, A., Granger, D. A., Mazur, A., Kivlighan, K. T. (2006). Testosterone and social behavior. *Social Forces* 85:167–191.

27. Fishbein, D. (2001). *Biobehavioral Perspectives in Criminology*. Belmont, Calif.: Wadsworth.

28. Meyer-Lindenberg, A., Buckhoitz, J. W., Kolachana, B., et al. (2006). Neural mechanisms of genetic risk for impulsivity and violence in humans. *Proc Natl Acad Sci* 103:6269–6274.

29. Caspi, A., Moffitt, T. E. (2006). Gene–environment interactions in psychiatry: Joining forces with neuroscience. *Nat Revs Neurosci* 7:583–590.

30. Rutter, M. (2006). *Genes and Behavior: Nature-Nurture Interplay Explained*. Malden, MA: Blackwell Publishing.

31. Cadoret, R. J., Cain, C. A., Crowe, R. R. (1983). Evidence for gene-environment interaction in the development of antisocial behavior. *Behav Genet* 13:301–310.

32. DiLalla, L. F. (2002). Behavior genetics of aggression in children: Review and future directions. *Dev Rev* 22:593–622.

33. Koenen, K. C., Caspi, A., Moffitt, T. E., et al. (2006). Genetic influences on the overlap between low IQ and antisocial behavior in young children. *J Abnorm Psychol* 115:787–797.

34. Moffitt, T. E. (2005). The new look of behavioral genetics in developmental psychopathology: Gene-environment interplay in antisocial behaviors. *Psychol Bull* 131:533–554.

35. Rietveld, M. J. H., Hudziak, J. J., Bartels, M., et al. (2003). Heritability of attention problems in children: Cross-sectional results from a study of twins, age 3 to 12 years. *Neuropsychiatr Genet* 1176:102–113.

36. Farrington, D., Gallagher, B., Morley, L., et al. (1986). Unemployment, school leaving and crime. *Br J Criminol* 26:335–356.

37. Loeber, R. (1982). The stability of antisocial and delinquent child behavior: A review. *Child Dev* 53:1431–1446.

38. Olweus, D. (1979). Stability of aggressive reaction patterns in males: A review. *Psychol Bull* 86:852–875.

39. Robins, L. W., Caspi, A., Moffitt, T. E. (2002). It's not just who you're with, it's who you are: Personality and relationship experiences across multiple relationships. *J Personality* 70:925–964.

References

The Socialization of Violent Criminal Offenders: Notes from the Theory of Differential Oppression

4

Robert M. Regoli
University of Colorado, Boulder

John D. Hewitt
Grand Valley State University

Matt DeLisi
Iowa State University

"Man is human and the small amount of intelligence one may possess counts little or nothing against the rage of passion and the limits of human nature pressing upon him."

—*Goethe*[1]

Serious, violent criminal offenders rarely just emerge in adulthood and commit predatory crime. Rather, their lives are typically characterized by recurrent participation in problem behaviors throughout adulthood, adolescence, and childhood. Many times, today's violent felon was yesterday's juvenile delinquent, and in the more distant past, the "problem child." This link between antisocial behaviors occurring during different life stages has been the focus of developmental or life-course criminology.

Related to this process of moving from problem child to adult criminal is the finding from research that many violent offenders were maltreated by their parents or adult caretakers. A study that directly speaks to this was conducted by Carolyn Smith and David Farrington.[2] Using data from the Cambridge Study in Delinquent Development, they explored the extent to which antisocial behavior in parents predicted antisocial behavior in children in two successive generations. They also examined the degree to which a man's childhood antisocial behavior predicted antisocial behavior in his own children, the ways that parenting problems were related to delinquency in two successive generations, and the extent to which intergenerational continuities in antisocial behavior were mediated by parenting. The findings were interesting: Between generations, antisocial parents in the first generation predicted conduct problems among children in the next two generations. Within generations, second generation child conduct problems predicted adult antisocial behavior and antisocial partnerships, which in turn predicted conduct problems among their children (the third generation). Parental conflict and authoritarian parenting resulted in early childhood conduct problems in two successive generations. Second generation boys who were poorly supervised by their parents were themselves poor supervisors as fathers. Both first and second generations displayed assortative mating, which means that antisocial males tended to marry antisocial females.[2]

In this way, parents specifically, and adults generally, cultivate delinquency, violence, and other maladaptive behaviors directly as a consequence of the way they treat children. This thesis is the basis of Regoli and Hewitt's *theory of differential oppression*. This paper reviews differential oppression theory and provides linkages between it and developmental criminological explanations of violent criminal behavior.

■ The Theory of Differential Oppression

In 1991, Robert M. Regoli and John D. Hewitt developed the *theory of differential oppression*, a micro-conflict explanation of delinquency that is rooted in the social relationships between adults and children. They contend that from conception, children have little to no power to influence their social world. Children make few choices regarding who they associate with, and they have limited resources or social capital available to influence others or to support themselves independently of adults. Therefore, they have the least access to resources that could allow them to negotiate changes in their environment. In comparison to parents, teachers, and other adults, children are relatively powerless and are expected—often required—to submit to the power and control of adults. When this power is used to deny children self-determination and impede them from developing a sense of competence and self-efficacy, it becomes oppression.[3]

Regoli and Hewitt believe that *all* children are oppressed. Oppression is a matter of degree and falls on a continuum, ranging from simple demands for obedience to rules designed for the convenience of adults to the physical, sexual, and emotional abuse of children. The problem behaviors of children, including crime and delinquency, drug and alcohol abuse, and mental disorders may be understood as adaptive reactions to oppressive social situations created by adults. While many children grow up under oppressive conditions that neglect their developmental needs, the psychological, emotional, or physical consequences a child suffers depends on the duration, frequency, intensity, and priority of the oppression, and on the child's stage of development. The theory of differential oppression is organized around the following four principles:

1. Children lack power due to their age, size, and lack of resources and are easy targets for adult oppression.

2. Adult oppression of children occurs in multiple social contexts and falls on a series of continua ranging from benign neglect to malignant abuse.

3. Oppression leads to adaptive reactions by children. The oppression of children produces four adaptations: passive acceptance; exercise of illegitimate coercive power; manipulation of one's peers; and retaliation.

4. Children's adaptations to oppression create and reinforce adults' views of children as inferior, subordinate, and being troublemakers. This view enables adults to justify their role as oppressor and further reinforces children's powerlessness.

Forms of Oppression

The term *oppression* is a summation of the abusive, neglectful, and disrespectful relations children confront. This oppression occurs in multiple social contexts (i.e., at home, at school, and in church) and falls on continua of frequency and severity. Some children infrequently experience oppressive acts, while other children face them daily. Oppressive acts also range from benign neglect to malignant abuse; they occur whenever adults act in ways that belittle or trivialize children as being something less than authentic and feeling human beings. Children are exposed to different levels and types of oppression that vary depending on their age, their level of development, and the beliefs and perceptions of their parents. While there are occasions when adults exercise power over children out of sincere concerns for the child's welfare, Regoli and Hewitt focus on the times when an adult's use of power over children is about the needs and interests of the adult, rather than the child. In fact, much of the oppression children suffer stems from the parents' inability to meet the needs of their children, either because adults are uninformed about what these needs are at various stages of development, because they are not capable of responding to those needs, or because they are egoistically focused on meeting their own needs.

Oppressive structural forces, such as poverty, social isolation, and residing in a disadvantaged neighborhood, also negatively influence parenting practices. For instance, Rolf Loeber and his colleagues found that boys raised by drug-using parents and living in impoverished neighborhoods were much more likely to be diagnosed with conduct disorder (CD), oppositional defiant disorder (ODD), and attention-deficit hyperactivity disorder (ADHD). Other researchers similarly found that boys raised in poor neighborhoods with high levels of parental conflict display the highest levels of antisocial behavior during childhood.[4,5] However, the underlying source of adult oppression may be found in the mistreatment they received as children and continue to experience as adults. Therefore, the oppression adults inflict on children is likely a part of a chain of coercion and abuse that is transmitted from one generation to the next.

Healthy development requires that social contexts provide opportunities for children to fulfill their physical, intellectual, psychological, and social developmental needs. Unfortunately, for many children, their social contexts are oppressive and damaging rather than supportive and nurturing. Using a developmental-ecological perspective provides a means for understanding how the oppression of children is likely to occur within multiple social contexts that may interact to produce harmful outcomes for children. These contexts include both micro-level relationships with family and friends and macro-level structural elements, such as race, class, neighborhood, and age, which expose individuals to more or less oppression of different types.[6]

Micro-level Oppression

The most severe and damaging oppression adults inflict upon children is officially defined as child maltreatment. The major forms of child maltreatment include physical abuse, sexual abuse, neglect, and emotional abuse. Child maltreatment produces $24 billion in direct costs related to the criminal justice and social service responses to child maltreatment cases each year. The indirect, long-term economic consequences are estimated at $69 billion annually. In other words, each year the United States pays nearly $100 billion in costs to respond to child maltreatment. The actual pain and suffering to child victims is in many ways incalculable. About three million cases of child maltreatment involving over five million children are reported to state protective services each year. Sixty percent of these cases were referred for investigation, and slightly less than one-third of the investigated cases resulted in a disposition of either substantiated or indicated child maltreatment. About 60% of the victims suffered neglect, while nearly 20% suggested physical abuse, and another 10% were sexually abused.[7]

Certain parenting styles are more likely than others to oppress children. For example, Kenneth Dodge and his colleagues found that among preschoolers with behavioral problems, the children whose parents were most passive and inattentive with them had the most severe behavioral problems.[8] Some parents oppress children as they attempt to impose and maintain adult conceptions of social order. Such parents may view their children as extensions of themselves and not as individuals and therefore feel free to impose their will on their children. In any case, the children are required to obey rules designed to reinforce adult notions of right and wrong behavior. In an attempt to exert greater control over their children, parents and other adults often use coercion or force. For instance, a self-report study based on a national sample of 3,346 adults indicated that 63% of parents reported they had used at least one form of psychological aggression on their children in the previous year.[9] According to Murray Straus and Richard Gelles, American cultural norms regarding violence in families teaches that it is acceptable to hit a child if he or she is doing something wrong and "won't listen to reason." Such coercion may become excessive, lead to physical harm and long-term psychological damage, and is a mechanism for transmitting an ageist ideology that diminishes the value of children in relation to adults across society.[10]

Other parents oppress children through neglectful parenting that fails to meet their children's physical, emotional, and educational needs. Examples of physical neglect include the refusal of or delay in seeking health care, abandonment, expulsion from the home or refusal to allow a runaway to return home, and woefully inadequate supervision. Emotional neglect includes inattention to the child's needs for affection, refusal of or failure to provide needed psychological care, and spousal abuse in the child's presence. Allowing chronic truancy, failing to enroll a child of mandatory school age in school, and failing to attend to special educational needs are all examples of educational neglect. Generally, neglect occurs *any* time a caretaker permits a child to experience suffering or fails to provide one of the basic ingredients essential for developing a child into a physically, intellectually, emotionally, and psychologically healthy person. Although single incidents of neglect may have no noticeable harmful effects, in some cases, they can result in death. Chronic patterns of neglect also may result in developmental delays or emotional disabilities.

Macro-level Oppression

Macro-level social forces, such as poverty, also oppress children. Children living in poverty are more likely to experience oppression than children living in more affluent conditions. This oppression can be viewed developmentally and is likely to be cumulative as children continue to grow and develop in destitute conditions.

During the early years, socioeconomic disadvantage oppresses children by impairing their physical health status at birth and providing less access to resources that could moderate the negative consequences of those problems. For healthy development, young children need exposure to stimulating materials or experiences. Unfortunately, children living in poverty are less likely than their wealthier counterparts to have access to these materials or experiences. Often their homes are unsafe and lack heat, adequate plumbing, and other basic amenities. In addition, they have increased exposure to chemical toxins, such as lead, which are associated with cognitive deficits, lower school achievement, and long-term impairment of neurological function. Rather than receiving cognitively stimulating experiences, many young children living in disadvantaged neighborhoods rarely leave their homes. Environmental and work-related conditions often limit their access to the outdoors. Poor children are more likely than non-poor children to live in housing located in commercial and industrial areas, which often lack safe outdoor places for children to play and limit opportunities for social interaction and cognitive development.

Poverty and economic disadvantage also have oppressive influences on school age and adolescent children. During middle childhood and adolescence, children increasingly come into direct contact with their neighborhoods through involvement in school, youth-serving organizations, and informal neighborhood groups. For young people, the physical features of their neighborhood establish the boundaries of their social universe. Some neighborhoods offer youth a variety of supervised instruction and structured activities, while others send the majority of the children out on the street. Due to the restricted tax base in poor distressed neighborhoods, limited public resources are available to support the education, recreation, and health needs of youth and their families. In contrast, youth living in wealthy neighborhoods have opportunities and resources that poor children do not, such as summer camp, music lessons, sports training, home computers, IPods, and special tutoring. Instead, adolescents in dilapidated inner-city neighborhoods have much higher exposure to physical and environmental danger, criminal activity, and drug use.[11]

Because successful adaptation at each stage of youth development is influenced by earlier developmental histories, long-term exposure to oppressive living conditions typically results in significantly worse developmental outcomes for children. African American and Hispanic children are more likely than white children to experience persistent poverty and to live in areas of concentrated poverty.[12] For instance, concentrated poverty is so segregated by race that virtually *no* white children live in the worst neighborhoods, whereas many African American and Hispanic children do.[13,14] High-risk contexts such as poverty, chronic stress, and child maltreatment may have lasting effects when they damage or impair crucial adaptive systems, such as adult-child attachment, intelligence, and self-regulation of emotions and behavior. Persistent poverty is consistently found to have more adverse effects than transitory poverty on children's cognitive development and school achievement. Children living for long periods in impoverished conditions experience more negative life events and adverse conditions that frequently place demands on their coping resources well beyond what they can handle. One reason for this circumstance is that living in violent environments actually alters the neuron connectors in the child's brain, thus permanently changing how the child processes information. Consequently, exposure to chronic adversity exacts a toll on a child's mental, physical, and emotional health. This likely triggers a cycle of lifelong deficiencies encompassing many contexts of their lives. Since many social problems are significantly clustered and correlated with concentrated poverty, cumulative oppression and its ensuing pathways to long-term developmental problems are much more frequent for children who endure lifelong exposure to impoverished social environments.[15]

Adaptations to Oppression

Most children adapt to oppression through *passive acceptance* and subsequent obedience. This obedience is built upon fear and derives from implied threats and intimidation. This adaptation is characterized by the child's passive acceptance of their subordinate and inferior status. It is more common among females, reflecting the higher status generally afforded males and generally lower female involvement in delinquency. It also is true that females are *doubly oppressed*; first as children, and second because they are girls. Since children are inundated by adult domination, they quickly learn that obedience is expected. Such adaptations among children are similar to the passive acceptance of the slave role, adaptations of prison inmates, and immersion in the cycle of violence for battered women. These children outwardly accept their inferior positions but develop a repressed hatred for their oppressors, adapting to the structures of domination in which they are immersed. Once a situation of violence and oppression has been established, it engenders an entire way of life and behavior for those caught up in it, oppressors and oppressed alike. Both are submerged in this situation and both bear marks of oppression. The oppressed are likely to believe they have no purpose in life except those the oppressor prescribes for them. Passive children do not fully explore personal autonomy; they never become the "authors of their own lives," so to speak. This repression results in negative self-perceptions that may become manifest in a wide range of problem behaviors including alcoholism, drug addiction, eating disorders, low self-esteem, and psychiatric disorders.[16]

A second adaptation to oppression is the *exercise of illegitimate coercive power*. Many adolescents are attracted to delinquency; it makes it possible for them to establish a sense of autonomy and control in their lives. This *anticipatory* delinquency is a yearning for adult status. Delinquent acts can immediately and demonstratively make things happen and provide the child with a sense of restored potency denied him or her by adults and parents. Sexual misbehavior, illicit use of drugs or alcohol, and violations of the criminal law derive greater symbolic importance for the child to the extent they demonstrate resistance to adult attempts to exert control over his or her behavior.

A third adaptation is the *manipulation of one's peers*. This is an attempt by the child to become empowered. Through the manipulation of others within the peer group, a child who has experienced oppression at the hands of adults may acquire a sense of strength and control or a degree of empowerment not otherwise felt. Gerald Marwell suggests "at any given point of time this potential [for social power] lies primarily in the opinions of the actor held by those with whom one interacts. If one is thought strong, one, by and large, is strong, or at least, may use 'strength' to manipulate others."[17] The school bully is an example; so is the child who spreads gossip in hopes of gaining status and prestige in the eyes of others. Unfortunately, the mere involvement of a child with his or her peers leads many adults to view the involvement as problematic in itself. Adults may then react by exercising even greater control over the child's interaction with others.

The fourth adaptation is *retaliation*, which may include delinquent acts ranging from property crimes to violent offenses. It is the most severe and least common of the adaptations to oppression. Retaliation is more common among males than females. Children may engage in retaliation to get back at the people or the institutions they believe are the source of their oppression. School vandalism sometimes occurs because a student is angry with a teacher or principal. Some children may strike directly at their parents or peers by assaulting or killing them. Others try to hurt their parents by turning inward, becoming chronically depressed and contemplating or committing suicide. For instance, Janna Haapasalo and Marjo Kankkonen compared the childhood abuse experiences of 16 sex offenders and 16 violent offenders. They found that sex offenders reported significantly more psychological abuse, especially verbal abuse, and also experienced slightly more physical and sexual abuse than the violent offenders. In general, the sex offenders remembered their parents in a more negative light than the comparison group. The offender groups did not differ from each other in the total amount of self-reported early conduct disorder symptoms. In sum, the sex offenders appeared to come from more abusive childhood family environments.[18]

Confronted by oppressive forces, children, to put it simply, adapt. Adults individually or collectively affect children and children react. Intuitively, this should make sense. The theory of differential oppression contends that "people first interpret, then people proceed," or, to put it differently, "people interpret something (e.g., who children are in relation to them), then people see *them* (children) as they interpreted *them*." And while children *as a group* are oppressed, the impact is most significantly experienced at the individual level. Oppression is differentially experienced, both in its application and impact. Children adapt differentially and the individual reasons for how particular children adapt are generally unknown. Even children growing up in the same family, in the same neighborhood, and experiencing similar oppressive situations will often exhibit different adaptations.

The long-term ramifications of the oppression of children are severe and facilitate a host of social problems. Unfortunately, once a child is an object of oppression, it is difficult to surmount it. For example, Jean McGloin and Cathy Widom interviewed more than 600 adults who had been abused or neglected as children to assess their ability to be resilient in the face of their victimization. They looked at eight domains of functioning, such as employment, homelessness, education, social activity, psychiatric disorder, substance use, self-reported violence, and official criminal record. To qualify as resilient, the respondents had to achieve success in at least six of these domains. Only 22% of the sample demonstrated resilience—more than 20 years after being the victim of childhood abuse and neglect.[19] Or, in other words, nearly 80% of abused (or oppressed) children demonstrate multiple antisocial behaviors decades later.

■ Current Focus

The theory of differential oppression is the only criminological theory that gives attention to the potential contextual effects of all developmental stages, from conception, to pregnancy, infancy, childhood, and adolescence, and, identifies for us the ways that adults create oppression in the lives of children. Differential oppression theory is an active, dynamic theory that attributes the causal blame for maladaptive behaviors to adults. Conversely, other theories of crime are typically passive in that etiological sources are described but not always implicated for their predictive power. For example, many theories point to the family as a socializing force that produces both positive and negative outcomes. But it is not enough to state that various family factors constitute risks for violent criminal behavior. Here is where differential oppression theory is able to empower extant developmental theories of crime, by showing that assorted family risk factors are in fact examples of oppression that produce delinquency, maladaptive behaviors, and violence and by teaching traditional life-course theorists that oppression "begins in the beginning," not at some later stage in life. To be blunt, delinquents do not parachute to earth when they are 10, 11, or 12 years old.

■ Violent Offenders, Developmental Criminology, and Oppression

The theory of differential oppression is compatible with some of the primary concepts in developmental criminology. Self-control theory, arguably the most popular and widely-tested theoretical perspective posits that parental socialization in the first decade of life instills self-control so that children can co-exist with others, delay gratification, and modulate their urges sufficiently well to function in society. When parents do not effectively socialize their children, children are at risk for a variety of maladaptive behaviors because they fundamentally lack the ability to control themselves.[20] To illustrate, Shayne Jones and his colleagues studied a sample of incarcerated adolescent offenders and found that most delinquents had parents who weakly supported them. In turn, poor parenting contributed to several negative outcomes among their children, including antisocial behavior, low impulse control, and low consideration of others.[21] In other words, parents unwittingly, passively, negligently, and, at times, purposely fail to socialize their children, and in doing so make them susceptible to crime. Although Gottfredson and Hirschi did not invoke the term "oppression," the socialization processes that engender self-control (or fail to) are clearly reconcilable with the theory of differential oppression. A lack of personal self-control is likely one of many deficits that children have when they are oppressed.[22]

The theory of differential oppression is also consistent with Terrie Moffitt's developmental taxonomy.[23] For instance, the second adaptation to oppression, the exercise of illegitimate coercive power, reflects a yearning for adult status, autonomy, and control and encompasses delinquent acts relating to alcohol use, drug experimentation, and sexual behavior. These are essentially acts of rebellion against the adult social order and are similar to the delinquencies of the adolescence-limited offender in Moffitt's developmental taxonomy. The other offender prototype in Moffitt's theory is the life-course persistent offender, a person who habitually engages in antisocial conduct across the life-course. This profile meshes with Regoli and Hewitt's fourth adaptation to oppression, retaliation. Youths responding to oppression in this way commit a range of antisocial behaviors including serious violent crime. Retaliation is the most severe and rarest adaptation to oppression and is overwhelmingly more common among males than females. As the most severe adaptation, it is probable that youths who retaliate against oppression are likely to have endured the most malignant forms of abuse and neglect. Indeed, in theorizing the development of life-course persistent offenders, Moffitt claimed "vulnerable infants are disproportionately found in environments that will not be ameliorative because many of the sources of neural maldevelopment co-occur with family disadvantage or deviance."[23]

The evidence that violent offenders have pronounced histories of victimization at the hands of their family is extensive. According to Carolyn Smith and Susan Stern, "We know that children who grow up in homes characterized by lack of warmth and support, whose parents lack behavior management skills, and whose lives are characterized by conflict or maltreatment will more likely be delinquent, whereas a supportive family can protect children even in a very hostile and damaging external environment."[24] Janna Haapasalo and Elina Pokela examined several major longitudinal studies of delinquency, such as the Cambridge Study in Delinquent Development, Christchurch Health and Development Study, Dunedin Multidisciplinary Health and Development Study, and the Oregon Youth

Study. They found that chronic adult criminals who experienced harsh, punitive, overly lax, and neglectful types of parenting styles were significantly more likely to be rejected by their parents, and to have suffered more severe forms of child abuse.[25]

The linkages between abuse, neglect, oppression, and violence are more glaring among female offenders whose lives are characterized by greater and more severe forms of victimization.[26] For instance, Chad Trulson and his colleagues studied the life histories of 2,436 serious, violent, and chronic youthful offenders released from the Texas juvenile correctional system. Among female offenders, there was significant evidence of family dysfunction and abuse. Nearly 40% had divorced parents, 61% were born into poverty, 27% had been physically abused, 39% had been sexually abused, 37% had been emotionally abused, 10% had been abandoned by their parents, and 15% had been neglected.[27]

Similar findings emerge from the study of sex offenders. Susan Smith and her colleagues found that chaotic home lives were the norm in a sample of adolescent sex offenders. Fully 80% of offenders were raised in homes with caregiver instability, 40% lived in homes with domestic violence, and nearly 60% lived with a single parent. Moreover, the most violent adolescent sex offenders had the most dysfunctional home lives.[28] Joseph Lee and his colleagues examined the childhood adversity affecting nearly 100 criminal offenders that had been diagnosed with various paraphilias. They found that offenders who had been sexually abused by their parents were nearly 300% more likely to be diagnosed sexual offenders. Offenders whose childhoods were characterized by emotional abuse and family dysfunction were about 230% more likely to be sex offenders. The effects of early parental abuse, especially sexual abuse, were most pronounced among pedophiles.[29,30]

Michael Rutter noted that "[e]nvironments are not randomly distributed, and through their behavior people shape and select their own environments and those of their children."[31] In the same way, oppression is not randomly distributed. In some contexts, oppression is normative and unintentional, and its effects on child development are relatively mild. In others, the oppression is severe and encompasses neglect, physical abuse, mental abuse, emotional abuse, and sexual abuse. In these cases, the effects are likely to be more severe resulting in a retaliatory response to adult oppression.

■ Conclusion

There is ample evidence that serious, violent offenders develop and evolve from birth through childhood and adolescence. Much of this oppression pertains to family strife and overt forms of abuse. But the cycle of oppression begins even earlier than the time periods covered by *all* developmental theories of crime. For instance, Kate Keenan and Daniel Shaw summarized the literature on parental socialization and behavioral problems during infancy and toddlerhood. Again, the main findings are entirely consistent with the theory of differential oppression. For example, mothers who have low rates of positive involvement with their newborns during the first months of life predict disruptive behaviors at age 4. Parental hostility toward toddlers predicts aggression levels into the elementary school years. Toddlers of parents who were observed as rejecting during a clean-up task demonstrate an increased risk for conduct problems later. When parents demonstrate rejecting forms of parenting toward children at ages 1 and 2, the children have significantly higher conduct problems at ages 5 and 8. In other words, "how parents respond to negative emotions and behaviors during the toddler period significantly appears to affect the continuity of such problems even after controlling for variation in toddler behavior."[32]

To return to where we started, serious, violent offenders rarely just emerge in adulthood to engage in crime. Instead, their pathology is the product of nature and nurture interacting over the developmental stages of life. In this way, the early family experiences and parental socialization are vital to understanding the etiology of violent criminal behavior. Most theories cover this. What sets the theory of differential oppression apart from other theoretical perspectives is the honesty with which abuse, neglect, and oppression are afforded. When parents treat their children as lesser beings or possessions, they fundamentally demean their humanity. Perhaps—thankfully—most of the time children respond to oppression passively by accepting the social order as it is. Most of the time, the oppression is done without malicious intent and the behavioral consequences for children are benign. But when oppression is described as parental neglect, parental rejection, and any form of parental abuse, the consequences are more severe and the behavioral consequences for children are often predictable: violence.

1. Goethe, J. W. (1774/1993). *The Sorrows of Young Werther*. New York: Modern Library Classics, p. 62.

2. Smith, C. A., Farrington, D. P. (2004). Continuities in antisocial behavior and parenting across three generations. *J Child Psychol Psychiatr* 45:230–247.

3. Regoli, R. M., Hewitt, J. D. (2006). *Delinquency in Society*, 6th edition. New York: McGraw-Hill.

4. Loeber, R., Green, S. M., Keenan, K., Lahey, B. B. (1995). Which boys will fare worse? Early predictors of the onset of conduct disorder in a six-year longitudinal study. *J Am Acad Child Adolesc Psychiatr* 34:499–509.

5. Fonagy, P. (2004). Early-life trauma and the psychogenesis and prevention of violence. *Ann NY Acad Sci* 1036:181–200.

6. Kingston, B., Regoli, B., Hewitt, J. D. (2003). The theory of differential oppression: A developmental-ecological explanation of adolescent problem behavior. *Crit Criminol* 11:237–260.

7. Centers for Disease Control and Prevention. (2006). *Child Maltreatment: Fact Sheet*. Atlanta: National Center for Injury Prevention and Control.

8. Bates, J. E., Pettit, G. S., Dodge, K. A., Ridge, B. (1998). Interaction of temperamental resistance to control and restrictive parenting in the development of externalizing behavior. *Dev Psychopathol* 34:1–14.

9. Vissing, Y., Straus, M., Gelles, R., Harrop, J. (1991). Verbal aggression by parents and psychosocial problems of children. *Child Abuse Neglect* 15:223–228.

10. Straus, M., Gelles, R. (1989). *Physical Violence in American Families: Risk Factors and Adaptations to Violence in 8,145 Families*. New Brunswick, NJ: Transaction.

11. Wilson, W. J. (1987). *The Truly Disadvantaged*. Chicago: University of Chicago Press.

12. Duncan, G., Brooks-Gunn, J. (1997). *Consequences of Growing Up Poor*. New York: Russell Sage Foundation.

13. McNulty, T. (2001). Assessing the race-violence relationship at the macro level: The assumption of racial invariance and the problem of restricted distributions. *Criminology* 39:467–490.

14. McNulty, T., Bellair, P. (2003). Explaining racial and ethnic differences in adolescent violence: Structural disadvantage, family well-being, and social capital. *Justice Q* 20:1–31.

15. DeLisi, M. (2003). Self-control pathology: The elephant in the living room. In M. R. Gottfredson, C. L. Britt (Eds.), *Control Theories of Crime and Delinquency*. Advances in Criminological Theory Volume 12. New Brunswick, NJ: Transaction, pp. 21–38.

16. Kingston, B., Regoli, B., Hewitt, J. D. (2003). The theory of differential oppression: A developmental-ecological explanation of adolescent problem behavior. *Crit Criminol* 11:237–260.

References

17. Marwell, G. (1966). Adolescent powerlessness and delinquent behavior. *Social Probl* 14:35–47, p. 36.
18. Haapasalo, J., Kankkonen, M. (1997). Self-reported childhood abuse among sex and violent offenders. *Arch Sexual Behav* 26:421–431.
19. McGloin, J. M., Widom, C. S. (2001). Resilience among abused and neglected children grown up. *Dev Psychopathol* 13:1021–1038.
20. Gottfredson, M. R., Hirschi, T. (1990). *A General Theory of Crime*. Stanford, CA: Stanford University Press.
21. Jones, S., Cauffman, E., Piquero, A. R. (2007). The influence of parental support among incarcerated adolescent offenders: The moderating effects of self-control. *Crim Justice Behav* 34:229–245.
22. DeLisi, M. (2001). It's all in the record: Assessing self-control theory with an offender sample. *Crim Justice Rev* 26:1–16.
23. Moffitt, T. E. (1993). 'Life-course persistent' and 'adolescence-limited' antisocial behavior: A developmental taxonomy. *Psychol Rev* 100:674–701, p. 681.
24. Smith, C. A., Stern, S. B. (1997). Delinquency and antisocial behavior: A review of family processes and intervention research. *Social Serv Rev* 71: 382–420, p. 383.
25. Haapasalo, J., Pokela, E. (1999). Child-rearing and child abuse antecedents of criminality. *Aggress Violent Behav* 4:107–127.
26. DeLisi, M. (2002). Not just a boy's club: An empirical assessment of female career criminals. *Women Crim Justice* 13:27–46.
27. Trulson, C. R., Marquart, J. W., Mullings, J. L., Caeti, T. J. (2005). In between adolescence and adulthood: Recidivism outcomes of a cohort of state delinquents. *Youth Violence Juvenile Justice* 3:355–387.
28. Smith, S., Wampler, R., Jones, J., Reifman, A. (2005). Differences in self-report measures by adolescent sex offender risk group. *Int J Offender Therap Compar Criminol* 49:82–106.
29. Lee, J. K. P., Jackson, H. J., Pattison, P., Ward, T. (2002). Developmental risk factors for sexual offending. *Child Abuse Neglect* 26:73–92.
30. Lussier, P., Beauregard, E., Proulx, J., Nicole, A. (2005). Developmental factors related to deviant sexual preferences in child molesters. *J Interpers Violence* 20:999–1017.
31. Rutter, M. (2003). Crucial paths from risk indicator to causal mechanism. In B. B. Lahey, T. E. Moffitt, A. Caspi (Eds.), *Causes of Conduct Disorder and Juvenile Delinquency* (Pp. 3–24). New York: The Guilford Press, p. 7.
32. Keenan, K., Shaw, D. S. (2003). Starting at the beginning: Exploring the etiology of antisocial behavior in the first years of life. In B. B. Lahey, T. E. Moffitt, A. Caspi (Eds.), *Causes of Conduct Disorder and Juvenile Delinquency* (Pp. 153–181). New York: The Guilford Press, p. 165.

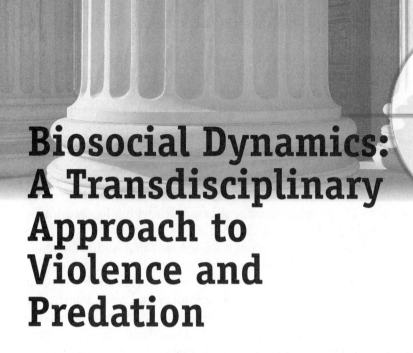

Biosocial Dynamics: A Transdisciplinary Approach to Violence and Predation

Michael G. Vaughn, Ph.D.
University of Pittsburgh

"Nothing in nature is quite so separate as two mounds of expertise."
—*M. Harris*[1]

Violent behavior involves processes influenced by genetic, physiological, psychological, and environmental factors. Literally volumes of research findings and theoretical musings have been produced on various aspects of the study of violence. Summaries of research forays on specific topics within the violence research literature strongly support the notion of an existence of factors that occur at multiple levels of analysis, such as genetic, cellular, hormonal, individual, family, and community. Because violence is multidimensional in nature, its understanding necessarily will involve a host of disciplines (e.g., genetics, neuroscience, endocrinology, psychology, sociology). This joining together of disciplines toward a common understanding of a complex problem can be termed a *transdisciplinary approach*.

Transdisciplinary approaches are gaining ascendancy across scientific fields because of their potential ability to solve problems that cut across multiple domains. Indeed, the Office of Behavioral and Social Sciences Research (OBSSR) has the mission of integrating behavioral and social science research across the many institutes of the National Institutes of Health (NIH), which is the largest source of funding for scientific research in the United States. The OBSSR uses a framework that organizes well-being across a continuum of biological and social factors that occur over the life course. Levels of organization range from the genomic to the global economic and geopolitical, with such domains as organ level and work-group level in between. An example of collaborative transdisciplinary research on a large scale is the funding of 17 mind-body centers in health. This effort involves the National Cancer Institute (NCI), National Institute on Aging (NIA), National Institute of Drug Abuse (NIDA), and several other national institutes with research centers at Columbia University, University of California at Berkeley, University of Utah, University of Pittsburgh and many others, each with a focused investigative topic and ongoing information sharing.

When transdisciplinary reasoning is not used, the resulting studies fail to integrate the individual with the environment. Moreover, these studies are isolated, as they do not link to other research, leading to myopic conclusions that explain violence strictly in terms of a singular disciplinary focus and make limited use of new methodologies and theories arising from related fields. An example of this is in the field of criminology, where suspicion of biological and personality variables seems widespread. This perspective is largely due to the professional membership being historically comprised of sociologists; as a result, poor socialization is given primacy in criminological theories.

Although the necessity for transdisciplinary approaches in comprehending and intervening in complex human problems is often acknowledged by scholars, the effective execution of transdisciplinary knowledge gathering is often hampered by the narrow disciplinary training and indoctrination which in turn inhibits theory building and research design.[2,3] With regard to violence and predatory behavior, several basic ingredients are necessary to begin to develop a conceptual framework that can guide and organize research. First, a theoretical framework is needed that is capable of accounting for the organismic structure and dynamics of the individual actor within a socio-behavioral system of successive levels of context. Second, this framework must be capable of incorporating specific theories across disciplines. Third, the static architecture of the components and variables need to be detailed in order to assess future change and offer points of intervention.

In this chapter, I argue that, by virtue of the multidimensional nature of violence and predation, a general synthesis that incorporates biology and sociocultural science in a coherent fashion may be of particular utility. To this end, this chapter will focus on *biosocial dynamics*, a conceptual strategy designed to integrate cutting-edge developments from multiple disciplines within an evolutionary (both biological and cultural) framework. As a synthesis, biosocial dynamics is ultimately based on seminal research and numerous empirical studies drawn and synthesized from such diverse fields as anthropology, neurobiology, cultural geography, psychology, primatology, and macro-sociology. Constructs and their attendant variables were fashioned into an overall paradigm that incorporates recent developments from the psychobiological framework of temperament and character and extensions to the anthropological paradigm known as cultural materialism.[4–6] Unlike many models, biosocial dynamics is broad in scope and can be formed into clinical, individual, and community level frameworks.

In addition to violence, biosocial dynamics is applicable to a wide array of traditional social problems. This chapter will outline the major components of the biosocial dynamic perspective from an individual-level focus to a socio-cultural evolutionary focus. An integrated model of liability to violence informed from the biosocial dynamic perspective will be delineated. Future research directions will be highlighted and discussed.

■ Biosocial Dynamics

Biosocial Dynamics: The Individual

Theories of violence that focus strictly on social factors must confront the inescapable role of the individual actor. As such, the necessity for understanding the psychobiological complex that comprises the individual in relation to behavior is paramount. This is particularly acute given long-standing, robust findings on career criminality. These findings have demonstrated that a small percentage of individuals—approximately 5 to 10% of the population—account for a majority of crimes against persons.[7–9] In total, findings from these and many other studies have demonstrated the asymmetrical nature of violence, meaning that violence is not evenly distributed. In other words, some people are persistently more violent than others.

Cloninger's Work on Temperament and Character

There have been multiple attempts at developing models of human personality that structure the various dimensions of personality along an optimal number of universal factors. These structural models of personality typically describe and organize personality among three to seven factors. Robert Cloninger, professor of psychiatry, psychology, and genetics at Washington University in St. Louis, has spent much of his professional career developing, refining, and testing personality models. His current approach involves a model comprised of four temperament dimensions and three character dimensions.[10–12]

Temperament can be defined as an individual's emotion-based tendency to respond to sensory stimuli in certain ways. Temperament is moderately heritable, meaning that there is a substantial biological basis to its formation. With respect to Cloninger's model, temperament is approximately 50% heritable, and each of the temperament factors is influenced by multiple genes. In addition, temperament is also moderately stable throughout life. Character, on the other hand, is less heritable, involves agency, and is influenced by socially mediated learning. Character involves higher-order thought or cognitive processes and plays a substantial role in mental self-governance. Character development is a function of underlying temperament and environmental variables.

Temperament is comprised of four factors: Harm avoidance, novelty seeking, reward dependence, and persistence. Three domains are necessary to describe character. These character factors are self-directedness, cooperativeness, and self-transcendence (see **Table 5.1**). Both temperament and character are measured by an inventory of questions (Temperament and Character Inventory or TCI) that "tap" these factors. Temperament and character relate broadly to the triune brain[13,14]—an evolutionary depiction of brain development consisting of a ba-

Table 5.1	**Descriptors of Temperament and Character Factors**	
	High Score	**Low Score**
Temperament Factor		
Harm avoidance	Fearful	Daring
	Shy	Outgoing
Novelty seeking	Exploratory	Reserved
	Impulsive	Deliberate
Reward dependence	Sentimental	Detached
	Warm	Cold
Persistence	Industrious	Lazy
	Enthusiastic	Underachiever
Character Factor		
Self-directedness	Responsible	Blaming
	Purposeful	Aimless
	Disciplined	Undisciplined
Cooperativeness	Helpful	Hostile
	Compassionate	Revengeful
	Principled	Opportunistic
Self-transcendence	Spontaneous	Contrived
	Acquiescent	Controlling
	Spiritual	Materialistic

Adapted from Cloninger[10] and Svrakic et al.[12]

sic reptilian (basal ganglia) brain, a mammalian (limbic system) brain, and a neo-mammalian (neocortex) brain. In simple terms, temperament is related to the mammalian brain, while character emerges from the neocortex or neomammalian brain. Because there can be multiple temperament and character configurations based on individual differences, there are no mechanical, one-way, linear relationships. Thus, according to Cloninger and his colleagues, the relations are non-linear, meaning that more than one configuration can give rise to several character combinations and vice versa. In fact, research has demonstrated that personality development follows the non-linear form of a complex adaptive system.[15]

Although not the sole or dominant structural model of personality, Cloninger's model nonetheless possesses several advantages. First, the temperament and character model has been based on external etiological criteria derived from basic biological and psychological research. As such, it is more conceptually and empirically rooted in basic psychobiological research, as opposed to models developed primarily from inductively driven empirical surveys of individuals. Second, the model has been developed to cope with non-linearity and be consistent with principles from complex adaptive systems (more about this later in the chapter). This is potentially important because science is increasingly discovering that non-linear dynamics are necessary to understand a broad range of phenomena.

Relationship to Existing Theories of Violence

Most research using the TCI has been executed toward distinguishing subtypes of personality psychopathology based on temperament configurations. For example, antisocial personality disorder—the psychiatric category most associated with violence, predatory behavior, criminality, and substance abuse—is associated with low scores on harm avoidance and reward dependence and high scores on novelty seeking. Cloninger's temperament and character model has much to offer the study of violent behavior among individuals.

Interestingly, two individual-level constructs that have received much research attention by criminologists and psychologists are low self-control and psychopathy. Self-control theory in criminology began with Michael Gottfredson and Travis Hirschi's *A General Theory of Crime* in 1990.[16] Since its publication the low self-control construct has garnered much research attention and empirical support.[17–19] From a TCI perspective, persons with low self-control can be described as low in harm avoidance, persistence, and self-directedness and high on novelty seeking. Meanwhile, psychopathy is a very old construct that has been a valuable tool in the prediction of violence among adults and juveniles.[20–23] From a TCI perspective, psychopaths are low in facets of harm avoidance, reward dependence, cooperativeness, and self-directedness and high in novelty seeking. Not surprisingly, the overall mapping of antisocial personality disorder, low self-control, and psychopathy theoretically indicates significant convergence between these constructs in that they all appear in similar locations on similar dimensions. However, there is recognized heterogeneity in antisocial personality disorder and psychopathy with primary (deficient emotional experience) and secondary types (high in anxiety).[24-26] This heterogeneity can potentially be better understood from a multidimensional personality system such as the TCI, with primary psychopathy being low in harm avoidance and secondary psychopathy high in harm avoidance and anxiety features. Predation behavior is more closely associated with the instrumental aggression related to primary versions of these constructs, which often involve revenge (low levels of cooperativeness) and deliberation and blaming (low levels of self-directedness). From a psychiatric diagnostic point of view, primary antisocial personality disorder is characterized by its convergence with narcissism, while secondary antisocial personality converges with borderline personality disorder. Future empirical research using the TCI can potentially refine the convergent and divergent validity further. Future studies will also need to study temperament and character in terms of the interrelated forms of violence, instrumental and reactive.

What is particularly useful about conceptualizing violence psychopathology by employing the TCI is that it brings basic research on the psychobiological roots of personality to bear. There is the additional advantage of being able to use the same system to understand health personality functioning as well as common mental health disorders such as anxiety and depression. Miller and colleagues, using the five factor model of personality to study psychopathy, have found that psychopathic features represent extreme variants of normal personality. The major limitation of the temperament and character model, as well as other individual-level approaches, is that successive levels of context that surround the habitats of violence are not delineated.[27]

Biosocial Dynamics: The Sociocultural System

In order to address successive levels of socio-cultural influences that surround the psychobiological complex of the individual person, the strategy of cultural materialism represents a synergistic fit. Cultural materialism is applicable to research activity and theory development throughout the social sciences and has been largely developed, refined, and popularized by its most notable proponent, anthropologist Marvin Harris. Beginning with *The Rise of Anthropological Theory* in 1968, Harris has continued to refine the paradigm and test it against a wide variety of cultural phenomena. Although traditionally centered in anthropology, cultural materialism is relevant to any scientific field concerned with the similarities and differences in human social life. According to cultural materialists, societies can be broken down into a tripartite conception involving infrastructural, structural, and symbolic-ideational sectors. *Infrastructure* represents the domains of production, such as subsistence and related technologies, and reproduction, such as demographic patterns and child-rearing practices. *Structure* denotes the organization of domestic and political economy as expressed in their attending institutions. The *symbolic-ideational sector* refers to a society's religious, philosophical, and ideological features. Cultural materialism posits that all three sectors are causally linked and interdependent. However, because infrastructure attends most directly to satisfying the drives and propensities of human nature within a specific habitat, this sector receives causal priority. It is this interaction of sectors and the factors comprising them that bear upon the ordinary means in which humans survive and reproduce that provides the "materialism" to the overall strategy.[28–32]

Although not a leading paradigm in the social sciences, cultural materialist scholarship has nonetheless been significant. The body of work includes theories and research findings from various topics, such as general evolution, world systems perspectives, warfare, social stratification and ethnic relations, and demographic issues, migration and settlement.[33–38] To my knowledge, there has been no attempt to integrate the cultural materialist approach with individual theories of personality and temperament or in utilizing the approach in violence scholarship.

The Universal Pattern and Societal Evolution

As previously mentioned, the universal structure of socio-cultural systems is comprised of infrastructure, structure, and a symbolic ideational sector. Further, this pattern and its relative power rests upon the premise that certain behavioral and mental processes are more directly essential to the survival, vigor, and well being of humans than others. Examples include sex drive, hunger, thirst, sleep, language, requirements for affective nurturance, nutritional and metabolic processes, vulnerability to mental and physical disease, and susceptibility to stress by darkness, cold, heat, altitude, moisture, lack of oxygen, and other ecological endangerments. These basic requirements are thought to represent the biopsychological constants of human nature. Cultural materialists argue that the infrastructure is the main causal center of socio-cultural systems. It is believed that this sector directly facilitates the expression of the aforementioned constants. Thus, infrastructure constitutes the primary point of interaction between biology and culture and therefore represents an ideal point of contact with the well-developed psychobiological complex delineated by Cloninger's personality theory. The mode of production consists of the technology and the practices employed by human beings for expanding or limiting basic subsistence production, especially the production of food and other forms of energy, given the constraints and opportunities provided by a specific technology interacting with a specific habitat. The mode of reproduction consists of the technology and practices employed by human beings for expanding, limiting, and maintaining population size.

The arrangement of cultural materialist priorities from infrastructural variables onto structural and finally the symbolic-ideational (superstructure) sphere reflect the remoteness of variables to the connection between nature and culture (**Table 5.2**). The second of three major subsystems of socio-cultural systems is the structure. Structure, consisting of domestic and political economy, is seen as secondary to infrastructure in terms of causal importance. Domestic economy pertains to the organization of reproduction and basic production, exchange, consumption within

Table 5.2	Examples of Infrastructure, Structure, and Symbolic-Ideational Variables

Infrastructure Variables: Mode of Production

Technological advancements	Road transportation
Food manufacturing	Trail transportation
Textile manufacturing	Water transportation
Chemical manufacturing	Air transportation
Metals manufacturing	Rail transportation
Machinery manufacturing	Fossil fuel reserves
Lumber manufacturing	Crude petroleum
Electrical manufacturing	Coal
Crop production	Natural gas
Farmlands	Animal waste
Livestock production	Geothermal heat
Mineral resources	Hydroelectric power
Territorial size	Climate
Soils and vegetation	Supply and utilization of water
Pollution and deforestation	

Infrastructure Variables: Mode of Reproduction

Morbidity rates	Population characteristics (age, sex, ethnicity)
Immigration	Fertility
Population density	Disease
Urban/Rural	Nurturance of infants
Suicide	Mating patterns
Mortality rates	Migration
Medical control of demographic pattern (conception, abortion, infanticide)	

Table 5.2	**Continued**	

Structural Variables

Family composition	Government structure	Interest rates
Family wealth	(leadership,	Inflation
Family debt	compensation processes)	Gross domestic product
Personal wealth	National division of labor	Gross national product
Personal debt	Taxation	Foreign aid
Domestic hierarchies	Income stratification	Banking
Domestic division of labor	War	Government regulations of
Family socialization	Police	business
Social sanctions	Criminal justice	Budgets
Age and sex roles	Law/crime rates (political/	Employment rates and
Expenditures	corporate crime)	processes
Rates of consumption	Tribute	(unemployment)
Political organizations,	Corporate structure	Voting patterns
clubs, associations,	(leadership,	
parties	compensation,	
	hierarchies)	

Symbolic-Ideational Variables

Art forms (aesthetics)	Print media	Educational values and
Music	Literature	ideologies
Sports	Marketing and advertising	Taboos
Recreational activities	Religious practice and	Magic
Folklore	ideologies	Superstitions
Myths	Political ideologies	Racial and ethnic
Rituals	Ethical ideologies	ideologies
Electronic media	Class ideologies	

primary groups. Political economy entails the organization of reproduction, production, exchange, and consumption within and between secondary institutions and governing bodies. The third major subsystem of socio-cultural system denotes the essential realm of ideas and symbolic entities.

Relationship to Existing Theories of Violence

In general, violence researchers and criminologists have not taken advantage of cultural materialism as a guiding paradigm in understanding contextual influences and aggregate patterns. Dominant theoretical perspectives are variants on social ecological theory—namely collective efficacy, social capital, institutional anomie, and social disorganization. Although these are useful theories, from a biosocial dynamic point of view, these theories are situated in the middle between the psychobiological knowledge of person-based theories and societal evolutionary perspectives. As such, these constructs are dependent variables in need of explanation and mediator/moderator variables in need of modeling. Changes in infrastructure-level processes such as technologies of subsistence can explain the formation of these phenomena. These types of sociological theories suffer from their disconnection to bio-psychological findings on the one hand and evolutionary principles such as selection processes (natural or cultural) on the other. The theories employ only a restricted range of transdisciplinary research, and as a result there is limited cross-pollination of new innovations that occur in various knowledge fields. Cultural materialism provides a series of contextual levels consistent with Cloninger's temperament and character paradigm in which each successive level is the context in which the lower level adapts and changes. Further, both are rooted in how humans and their cultures evolved across time from simple hunter-gatherer societies to contemporary information-age societies.

Complex Adaptive Systems

Because temperament and character interact within a psychobiological complex and the tripartite conception favored by cultural materialists depicts a system, both positive and negative feedback are essential aspects of its operation. *Negative feedback* refers to any system-maintaining innovation that modifies a divergence that preserves the fundamental characteristics of the system. *Positive feedback* denotes system-changing innovations. In the case of cultural materialism, changes initiated in the modes of production and reproduction are more likely to produce amplifications that reverberate throughout the domestic, political, and ideological sectors than vice versa. Innovations or changes initiated in the structural sectors are less likely to produce system-changing or positive feedback, and innovation or changes in the superstructure are still less likely to change the entire system. Again, this is due to their remote relationship with crucial infrastructural components. Contingency and emergence are two fundamental processes that influence the understanding of complex phenomena.

■ Applications

An Integrative Biosocial Dynamic Liability Model

The integrated model (**Figure 5.1**) incorporates biosocial variables in the underlying etiology that influences the temperament and character factors in relation to violence and predation. This undertaking is important because it begins the process

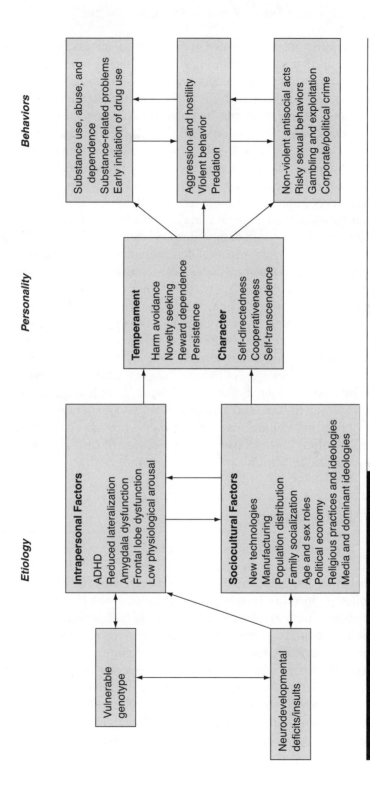

Figure 5.1 An Integrated Biosocial Dynamic Model for Liability to Violence and Predation.

of examining the relationships between causal factors for violence and predation syndromes that have their multifactor origins in both individual level biological factors and socio-cultural factors, which constrain behaviors and add levels of context. In addition, this exercise is important for directing future prevention and intervention efforts. It should be noted that this depiction is a heuristic tool and thus is not a direct reflection of all the complexity that may exist.

The manifestations of violence and predatory behavior usually appear early. Children and adolescents who are persistently violent and prey on others will have an earlier age of onset of offending and illicit substance use, display greater criminal versatility, and exhibit verbal and physical aggression. It is proposed that the network of temperament and character traits is modulated by environmental factors, displaying both dampening and catalytic effects. However, trait stability resists complete environmental determination. This is partly attributable to the heritability of personality, which studies consistently show accounts for 40 to 50% of the variance in personality traits.[39] Although similar in vein to Gottfredson and Hirschi's latent-trait approach,[16] this particular theoretical perspective is more dynamic, less reductive, and is open to a broader array of research-based factors. Thus, serious and persistent antisocial behavior is viewed as a phenotypic expression of different underlying genotype and person-environmental interactions. Sturdy bio-psychological etiological factors include attention deficit-hyperactivity disorder, frontal lobe dysfunction, low autonomic arousal, birth complications such as brain trauma, and genetic factors. As apparent under the rubric of socio-cultural factors, cultural materialist variables provide a context consistent with patterns involved in societal evolution. Because of this, aggregate-level theories of violence and predation can also be explored.

■ Conclusion

The necessity for transdisciplinary solutions to violence is critical. The range of findings on different aspects of violent behavior needs organization and greater conceptual direction. To this end, a biosocial dynamic transdisciplinary approach is offered. Specifically, this perspective combines the person-level strengths of Cloninger's temperament and character paradigm with the macro-evolutionary power of cultural materialism. As both are universal, consistent with selection principles, biologically-rooted, and capable of coping with non-linearity, the fit between the two paradigms is harmonious. Specific biosocial theories and research questions can be derived from the conceptual model. A sample of research questions include: To what extent has the range of targets of predatory behavior altered based on the shift to information-age technologies? What are the additional constraints or opportunities for control? What are the latent profiles of violent offenders, and what are their character configurations?

Beyond its considerable research capacity, biosocial dynamics can also be fashioned into an applied framework that can function at both the individual and community levels. With respect to temperament and character, this is facilitated by the ability of the TCI to measure and track changes across dimensions. For cultural materialism, material, structural, and ideational sectors can provide clinical community direction. Checklists based on this strategy can be formed that include questions such as the following: Has the project considered technologies related to subsistence and manufacturing? Has the project considered population characteristics (e.g., age, sex, ethnicity, birth rates), disease patterns and their potential pressures on project goals? Has the project considered family socialization patterns, age and sex roles and related social sanctions? Are project goals in alignment with pre-existing religious and secular ideologies?

Despite the dominance of discipline-specific socialization and the tendency to view the world from a "sociological" or "biological" point of view, there is a growing realization that these perspectives are stagnant and limited. As proponents of these perspectives continue to dig their heels in and hang on to their most cherished assumptions, the momentum of transdisciplinary syntheses will likely continue unabated. One such synthesis, *biosocial dynamics*, can potentially be quite useful in researching and organizing findings associated with violent behavior including providing guidance toward effective treatment and prevention.

References

1. Harris, M. (1974). *Cows, Pigs, Wars and Witches: The Riddles of Culture*. New York: Random House.
2. Caspi, A., Moffitt, T. E. (2006). Gene-environment interactions in psychiatry: Joining forces with neuroscience. *Nat Rev Neurosci* 7:583–590.
3. Laub, J. H. (2006). Edwin H. Sutherland and the Michael Adler report: Searching for the soul of criminology seventy years later. *Criminology* 44:235–258.
4. Cloninger, C. R. (2004). *Feeling Good: The Science of Well-Being*. New York: Oxford University Press.
5. Harris, M. (1994). Cultural materialism is alive and well and won't go away until something better comes along. In Robert Borofsky (Ed.), *Assessing Cultural Anthropology*. New York: McGraw Hill.
6. Harris, M. (1999). *Theories of Culture in Postmodern Times*. Walnut Creek, CA: AltaMira Press.

References

7. DeLisi, M. (2005). *Career Criminals in Society*. Thousand Oaks, CA: Sage.
8. Wolfgang, M. E., Figlio, R. M., Sellin, T. (1972). *Delinquency in a Birth Cohort*. Chicago: University of Chicago Press.
9. Tracy, P. E., Wolfgang, M. E., Figlio, R. M. (1990). *Delinquency Careers in Two Birth Cohorts*. New York: Plenum.
10. Cloninger, C. R. (1999). A new conceptual paradigm from genetics and psychobiology for the science of mental health. *Austral NZ J Psychiatr* 33: 174–186.
11. Cloninger, C. R., Svrakic, D. M., Pryzbeck, T. R. (1993). A psychobiological model of temperament and character. *Arch Gen Psychiatr* 50:975–989.
12. Svrakic, N. M., Svrakic, D. M., Cloninger, C. R. (1996). A general quantitative theory of personality development: Fundamentals of a self-organizing psychobiological complex. *Dev Psychopathol* 8:247–272.
13. Massey, D. S. (2002). A brief history of human society: The origin and role of emotion in social life. *Am Sociol Rev* 67:1–29.
14. MacLean, P. D. (1990). *The Triune Brain in Evolution: Role in Paleocerebral Functions*. New York: Plenum Press.
15. Cloninger, C. R., Svrakic, D. M., Svrakic, N. M. (1997). Role of personality self-organization in development of mental order and disorder. *Dev Psychopathol* 9:881–906.
16. Gottfredson, M. R., Hirschi, T. (1990). *A General Theory of Crime*. Stanford, CA: Stanford University Press.
17. Cauffman, E., Steinberg, L., Piquero, A. R. (2005). Psychological, neuropsychological, and physiological correlates of serious antisocial behavior in adolescence: The role of self-control. *Criminology* 43:133–176.
18. DeLisi, M., Vaughn, M. G. (2007). The Gottfredson-Hirschi critiques revisited: Reconciling self-control theory, criminal careers, and career criminals. (Unpublished manuscript in review).
19. Pratt, T. C., Cullen, F. T. (2000). The empirical status of Gottfredson and Hirschi's general theory of crime: A meta-analysis. *Criminology* 38:931–964.
20. Blair, J., Mitchell, D., Blair, K. (2005). *The Psychopath: Emotion and the Brain*. Oxford, UK: Blackwell.
21. Cleckley, H. (1976). *The Mask of Sanity*, 5th edition. St. Louis, MO: Mosby.
22. Hare, R. D. (1996). Psychopathy: A clinical construct whose time has come. *Crim Justice Behav* 23:25–54.
23. Vaughn, M. G., Howard, M. O. (2005). The construct of psychopathy and its role in contributing to the study of serious, violent, and chronic youth offending. *Youth Violence Juvenile Justice* 3:235–252.
24. Newman, J. P., MacCoon, D. G., Vaughn, L. J., Sadeh, N. (2005). Validating a distinction between primary and secondary psychopathy with measures of Gray's BIS and BAS constructs. *J Abnorm Psychol* 114:319–323.

25. Ross, S. R., Lutz, C. J., Bailley, S. E. (2004). Psychopathy and the five factor model in a non-institutionalized sample: A domain and facet level analysis. *J Psychopathol Behav Assess* 26:213–223.

26. Skeem, J. L., Poythress, N., Edens, J. F., et al. (2003). Psychopathic personality or personalities? Exploring potential variants of psychopathy and their implications for risk assessment. *Aggress Violent Behav* 8:513–546.

27. Miller, J. D, Lynam, D. R., Widiger, T. A., Leukefeld, C. (2001). Personality disorders as extreme variants of common personality dimensions: Can the five-factor model adequately represent psychopathy? *J Personality* 69:253–276.

28. Harris, M. (1968). *The Rise of Anthropological Theory: A History of Theories of Culture*. New York: Thomas Crowell.

29. Harris, M. (1977). *Cannibals and Kings: The Origins of Cultures*. New York: Random House.

30. Harris, M. (1979). *Cultural Materialism: The Struggle for a Science of Culture*. New York: Random House.

31. Harris, M. (1984). Animal capture and Yanomano warfare: Retrospective and new evidence. *J Anthropol Res* 40:183–201.

32. Harris, M., Ross, E. (1987). *Death, Sex, Fertility: Population Regulation in Pre-Industrial and Developing Societies*. New York: Columbia University Press.

33. Chase-Dunn, C., Hall, T. D. (1997). *Rise and Demise: Comparing World-Systems*. Boulder, CO: Westview Press.

34. Depres, L. (1975). *Ethnicity and Resource Competition in Plural Societies*. The Hague: Mouton.

35. Ferguson, B. (1989). Game wars? Ecology and conflict in Amazonia. *J Anthropol Res* 45:149–206.

36. Gross, D. (1974). Protein capture and cultural development in Amazonia. *Am Anthropol* 77:526–549.

37. Leavitt, G. (1986). Ideology and the materialist model of general evolution. *Social Forces* 65:525–553.

38. Sanderson, S. (1990). *Social Evolutionism: A Critical History*. Oxford, UK: Basil Blackwell.

39. Bouchard, T. J. (2004). Genetic influence on human psychological traits: A survey. *Curr Dir Psychologic Sci* 13:148–151.

References

Early Risk Factors for Young Homicide Offenders and Victims

6

David P. Farrington
University of Cambridge

Rolf Loeber
University of Pittsburgh

Rebecca Stallings
University of Pittsburgh

D. Lynn Homish
State University of New York at Buffalo

Homicide is the second leading cause of death for persons aged 15 to 24 in the United States after accidents and before suicide.[1] On the basis of 1997 data, 1 in 40 African American males is murdered compared with 1 in 280 Caucasian males. The peak ages at which males died were between ages 18 and 25; more than 100 per 100,000 African American males and more than 10 per 100,000 Caucasian males.[2] The rates of homicide offenders and victims in ages 13–17 and 18–24 increased from 1985 to a peak in 1993, then declined. For ages 18–24, the rates at the peak in 1993 were almost double the rates in 1985; for ages 13–17, the rates at the peak in 1993 were almost triple the rates in 1985. For ages 18–24, the peak homicide offending rate in 1993 was 280 per 100,000 for African Americans and 30 per 100,000 for Caucasians; the peak homicide victimization rate in 1993 was 190 per 100,000 for African Americans and 20 per 100,000 for Caucasians.[3]

In general, the ages of offenders and victims are positively correlated, with the peak risk for 19- and 20-year-olds killing other 19- and 20-year-olds. Most Caucasian victims (84%) are killed by Caucasian offenders, and similarly most African American victims (91%) are killed by African American offenders. Most homicide offenders aged 18–24 killed with a gun; in the peak year of 1993, there were three times as many gun homicides as homicides by other means by this age group.[4,5]

There has been a great deal of research on the characteristics of young homicide offenders. Retrospective case-control studies show that they tend to come from broken homes and violent families, have experienced parental alcoholism and child abuse, have low school achievement, and have run away from home, truanted, and been suspended from school. Not surprisingly, they also tend to have prior arrest histories. Much less is known about the backgrounds of young homicide victims. However, it is known that assault victims disproportionately tend to have committed offenses themselves.[6,7]

Kathleen Heide pointed out that "the available literature on juvenile homicide offenders is retrospective in nature. To say something definitive about etiological factors associated with youth murder requires longitudinal studies of children."[8] Only two previous such studies of youth homicide have been performed, both in the Pittsburgh Youth Study. Loeber and his colleagues studied the characteristics of 11 boys killed and 29 wounded by guns.[9,10] Compared with control groups, these boys tended to have low academic achievement, depressed mood, poor parental supervision, poor parent-boy communication, behavior problems of the father, the family on welfare, and low socioeconomic status. They also investigated factors that predicted violent offenders out of all boys and factors that predicted homicide offenders out of all violent boys. The factors that predicted homicide offenders were a high risk score, a positive attitude to substance use, conduct disorder, carrying a weapon, gang fighting, persistent drug use, selling hard drugs, peer delinquency, peer substance use, and being held back in school.[9,10]

■ Current Focus

The key questions addressed in this research are:

1. Which risk factors, measured at the beginning of a prospective longitudinal survey, predict homicide offenders and homicide victims out of a community sample 4–15 years later? This question has never been addressed before.

2. How accurately can homicide offenders and victims be predicted at ages 7–13?

3. To what extent are risk factors similar for homicide offenders and victims?

4. Do early risk factors predict homicide offenders more accurately than homicide victims? This would be expected if homicide offenders were more antisocial and deviant than homicide victims.

5. Do behavioral and attitudinal risk factors predict more accurately than explanatory risk factors? This would be expected to the extent that behavioral and attitudinal factors reflected the same underlying construct (e.g., an antisocial personality) as homicide offenders. By definition, explanatory factors measure a different underlying construct. However, it is less clear that behavioral and attitudinal factors would predict homicide victims more accurately, because it is less clear that being a homicide victim reflects an underlying antisocial personality or any other key hypothetical construct (e.g., low self-control, criminal propensity, deviance, etc.).

6. Are racial differences in the prevalence of homicide offenders and victims attributable to racial differences in early risk factors?

■ Methodology

Samples

The Pittsburgh Youth Study is a prospective longitudinal survey of the development of offending and antisocial behavior in three samples of about 500 Pittsburgh boys, totalling 1,517 boys. At the time they were first contacted in 1987–1988, random samples of first, fourth, and seventh grade boys enrolled in Pittsburgh public schools were selected.[11,12] At that time, 72% of all children residing in Pittsburgh attended public schools. The city of Pittsburgh covers the inner city population of about 370,000 (in 1990) out of the Pittsburgh-Beaver Valley Metropolitan Statistical Area of about 2,243,000.

Out of about 1,000 boys in each grade selected at random for a screening assessment, about 850 boys (85%) were actually assessed. The boys completed a self-report questionnaire about antisocial behavior while their primary caretakers completed an extended Child Behavior Checklist, and their teachers completed an extended Teacher Report Form.[13–15] We will refer to the primary caretaker as the mother because this was true in 94% of cases. Participants did not differ significantly from the comparable male student population in their scores on the California Achievement Test (CAT) or in their racial composition (African American or Caucasian).

From the screening assessment, a risk score was calculated for each boy indicating how many of 21 antisocial acts he had ever committed. Information from the boy, mother, and teacher was combined. The risk score was used to select the sample for follow-up, consisting of approximately the 250 most antisocial boys in each grade and about 250 boys randomly selected from the remaining 600. Hence, the screening sample of about 850 per grade was reduced to a follow-up sample of about 500 per grade. In the first follow-up assessment 6 months after the screening assessment, the three samples of boys were aged (on average) 7, 10, and 13, respectively. This paper compares child risk factors measured in the screening and first follow-up assessments (in 1987–1988) with later information about homicide offenders and victims.

Risk Factors

Risk factors were classified as explanatory or behavioral/attitudinal. Explanatory variables were those that clearly did not measure antisocial behavior, while behavioral/attitudinal variables could have reflected the boy's antisocial behavior. For example, a young mother and poor parental supervision were classified as explanatory variables, while being truant or suspended from school were classified as behavioral variables.

The most contentious variable was peer delinquency. We classified this as a behavioral variable because three-quarters of the delinquent acts committed by the boys were committed with their peers. Therefore, boys who had committed delinquent acts usually had delinquent peers. Also, Farrington and colleagues found that peer delinquency was the strongest correlate of a boy's delinquency in between-individual correlations (both measured at the same time) but did not predict a boy's later delinquency within individuals. They concluded that peer delinquency was not a cause of a boy's delinquency but measured the same underlying construct as delinquency. In contrast, poor parental supervision was correlated with delinquency between individuals and predicted delinquency within individuals.[16]

The 21 explanatory risk factors measured in 1987–1988 and used in the present study were as follows:

Child: Low guilt, HIA (hyperactivity-impulsivity-attention deficit), old for the grade (has been held back), low achievement (both according to the California Achievement Test and according to mother–teacher ratings), depressed mood, callous-unemotional.[17]

Parental: Young mother (a teenager when the boy was born), father seeking help for behavior problems (rated by the mother, so available for all fathers whether present or absent), parental substance use.

Child-rearing: Poor parental supervision, physical punishment by the mother, poor parent–boy communication.

Socioeconomic: Low socioeconomic status (the Hollingshead measure, based on parental education and occupational prestige), family on welfare, broken family (missing biological parent), large family, small house, unemployed mother, bad neighborhood (both according to 1990 census data and according to mother ratings).

These factors were derived from the 40 distinct explanatory factors, excluding those not known for all three samples, those with a large amount of missing data (e.g., variables referring to the operative father or to the mother–father relationship), and those not strongly related to delinquency in 1987–1988 (odds ratio > 2.0). Some variables were added because they were related to violence (odds ratio > 2.0).[18] Most variables were based on interviews with mothers, and in a few cases supplemented by data from boys.

The 19 behavioral/attitudinal risk factors measured in 1987–1988 and used in the present paper were as follows:

Child behavior: Serious delinquency, covert behavior (concealing, manipulative, untrustworthy), physical aggression, nonphysical aggression, cruel to people, runs away, disruptive behavior disorder according to the Revised Diagnostic Interview Schedule for Children,[19] high risk score.

Child attitude: Favorable attitude to delinquency, favorable attitude to substance use.

Parental: Bad relation with parents, counter control (the bad behavior of the boy inhibits parental attempts at socialization).

Peer: Peer delinquency, delinquent or poorly socialized friends, bad relation with peers.

School: Suspended, truant, negative attitude to school, low school motivation.

For the present analyses, the explanatory and behavioral risk factors were dichotomized within each sample into, as far as possible, the "worst" quarter (e.g., the quarter with the lowest attainment or poorest supervision) versus the remainder. This dichotomization fostered a "risk factor" approach and made it easy to study the cumulative effects of several risk factors. It also made all variables directly comparable by equating sensitivity of measurement and permitted the use of the odds ratio as a measure of strength of relationship, which has many advantages.[20] In the Pittsburgh Youth Study, conclusions about the most important explanatory variables for delinquency were not greatly affected by using dichotomous as opposed to continuous variables, or by different dichotomization splits.[21]

Dichotomizing the variables within each sample made all the samples comparable and made it possible to combine them. Arguably, the quarter of the youngest sample with the poorest parental supervision (for example) were comparable to the quarter of the oldest sample with the poorest parental supervision, even though the absolute levels of parental supervision were different in all three samples.

Homicide Offenders and Victims

Information about homicide offenders and victims was obtained from searches of local, state, and federal criminal records, interviews with the participants, searches of local newspapers, and the local coroner's office. Based on information collected up to February 2006, 33 of the study participants had been convicted of homicide. Eight were from the youngest sample, 13 from the middle sample, and 12 from the oldest sample. The first homicide attributable to a study participant was committed in 1992; the offenders committed their homicides between ages 15 and 26 (median age 19). Their victims' ages ranged between 1 and 61 years (median age 22). The weapon used was a gun in 24 cases; in other cases, the weapons used were hands (2 cases), knives (2), a brick (1), a metal rod (1), an automobile (1), a cord (1), and matches (in a case of homicide by arson). The motives were retaliation (12), robbery (7), a drug deal gone wrong (5), gang-related (3), domestic (1), arson (1), and mental problems (1); in 3 cases the motives were not known by the police.

Until February 2006, 30 of the study participants had died because of homicide (and 12 had died from other causes). Two were from the youngest sample, 12 from the middle sample, and 16 from the oldest sample. The first homicide victim was killed in 1993, and all victims died between ages 16 and 27 (median age 21). The weapon used was a gun in 27 cases. One participant killed someone and then was killed himself. He was counted as an offender, leaving 33 homicide offenders and 29 homicide victims.

In addition to 33 participants convicted of homicide, 30 have been arrested for homicide but not convicted (up to February 2006). Some of these may be convicted in the future, but many were not convicted either because they terrorized potential witnesses and/or because the evidence was too weak. Some, of course, may have been innocent. These 30 individuals were excluded from the analyses. A further 4 individuals who died between ages 13 and 14 for reasons other than homicide were also excluded, on the grounds that they were not at risk of becoming homicide offenders or victims. Excluding these 34 cases left 33 homicide offenders, 29 homicide victims, and 1,421 controls.

■ Results

Race Differences in Homicide

In light of national statistics, it is not surprising that we found that African American males were more likely than Caucasian males to be homicide offenders and victims: 28 of the 33 offenders (85%) were African American, as were 27 of the 29 victims (93%), both figures disproportionate to the overall composition of the population (African Americans comprised 780 of the 1,421 controls, or 55%). Prospectively, 3.4% of African American males were convicted of homicide, compared with 0.8% of Caucasian males, and 3.2% of African American males were killed, compared with 0.3% of Caucasian males. Weighting back to the population of Pittsburgh public schools, 2.7% of African American males were convicted of homicide, compared with 0.5% of Caucasian males; and 2.6% of African American males were killed, compared with 0.3% of Caucasian males. Unweighted data are used in this chapter, because the main interest is in studying predictions for individuals rather than making population estimates.

For ease of exposition, this chapter presents retrospective rather than prospective percentages (**Table 6.1**). The odds ratio (OR) for race versus homicide offenders was 4.6, while the OR for race versus homicide victims was 11.1. The confidence intervals are large because of the small numbers of homicide offenders and victims.

Later Features

Table 6.1 also shows the relationship between classic homicide features (guns, gangs, and drugs) and homicide offenders and victims. These features were measured in multiple data waves before any male was a homicide offender or victim. They are not studied as early risk factors in this paper.

				Odds Ratio	
Table 6.1	**Features of Homicide Offenders and Victims**				
Feature	% of Controls (1421)	% of Offenders (33)	% of Victims (29)	C-O	C-V
African American	55	85	93	4.6*	11.1*
Carried gun	6	20	33	4.0*	8.0*
Used weapon	8	25	29	3.8 *	4.5*
Gang member	14	30	19	2.6*	1.4
Persistent drug user	19	39	25	2.8*	1.5
Sold marijuana	8	28	21	4.2*	2.9*
Sold hard drugs	8	31	30	5.5*	5.1*

Abbreviations: C-O, contrasting controls and offenders; C-V, contrasting controls and victims. Offenders and victims were not contrasted because of small numbers.
*$P < .05$

Homicide offenders were not always more antisocial than homicide victims. In particular, homicide victims were more likely to carry guns (33%) than homicide offenders (20%). The OR for victims (8.0) was twice as great as the OR for offenders (4.0). Also, homicide victims were about as likely as homicide offenders to have used a weapon (e.g., when attacking someone or in a gang fight or robbery) or to have sold hard drugs. However, homicide offenders were more likely to be gang members, persistent drug users, and to have sold marijuana.

Explanatory Predictors

Eight of the 21 explanatory factors significantly predicted homicide offenders: broken family, bad neighborhood (according to the census), old for the grade (held back), family on welfare, low guilt, a young mother, an unemployed mother, and low socioeconomic status (**Table 6.2**). The strongest predictor was coming from a broken family: 88% of homicide offenders had a missing biological parent (usually the father) by the first year of the study compared with 62% of controls (OR = 4.4).

Nine of the 21 explanatory factors significantly predicted homicide victims: a broken family, low achievement (according to the California Achievement Test), low guilt, old for the grade, behavior problems of the father, HIA, family on welfare, callous-unemotional, and large family size (Table 6.2). Again, the strongest predictor was a broken family; 90% of homicide victims had a missing biological parent compared with 62% of controls (OR = 5.2).

Based on explanatory risk factors, homicide offenders were not more extreme than homicide victims; if anything, the odds ratios for predicting victims were greater than for predicting offenders. However, it was noticeable that most of the significant predictors of homicide offenders were socioeconomic/demographic factors: a broken family, a bad neighborhood, the family on welfare, a young mother, an unemployed mother, and low socioeconomic status. In contrast, most of the significant predictors of homicide victims were individual factors: low achievement, low guilt, old for the grade (held back), HIA, and callous-unemotional.

Explanatory Risk Scores

A logistic regression analysis was carried out to investigate which of the 8 significant predictors of homicide offenders were independent predictors. Three variables were significant or nearly significant in a stepwise analysis: A bad neighborhood (Likelihood Ratio Chi-squared or LRCS = 13.22, P = .0003), old for the grade (LRCS = 9.21, P = .002), and a young mother (LRCS = 2.85, P = .091). In the final model, the partial odds ratios were 3.2 for a bad neighborhood, 3.1 for old for the grade, and 2.0 for a young mother.

Table 6.2	Explanatory Predictors of Homicide Offenders and Victims		
Predicting Offenders	**% of Controls (1421)**	**% of Offenders (33)**	**Odds Ratio**
Broken family	62	88	4.4*
Bad neighborhood (C)	32	67	4.2*
Old for grade	25	55	3.6*
Family on welfare	43	71	3.3*
Low guilt	25	48	2.9*
Young mother	21	41	2.6*
Unemployed mother	25	45	2.5*
Low socioeconomic status	26	45	2.4*
Predicting Victims	**% of Controls (1421)**	**% of Victims (29)**	**Odds Ratio**
Broken family	62	90	5.2*
Low achievement (CAT)	24	60	4.8*
Low guilt	25	59	4.3*
Old for grade	25	52	3.2*
Father behavior problems	17	38	3.0*
Hyperactivity	17	38	2.9*
Family on welfare	43	67	2.7*
Callous-unemotional	24	44	2.5*
Large family size	22	38	2.2*

Abbreviations: C, census measure; CAT, California Achievement Test measure.
*$P < .05$

An explanatory risk score was calculated for each boy based on the number of these three risk factors that he possessed. **Table 6.3** shows how much this risk score predicted homicide offenders; for example, 0.6% of boys with none of these three risk factors were homicide offenders, compared with 9.2% of boys with all three risk factors. Hence, there was significant predictability but also a high false positive rate. Retrospectively, 19 of the 33 homicide offenders (58%) were among the one-fifth of the boys with two or three of these risk factors. Comparing boys with 0–1 risk factors with boys with 2–3 risk factors, OR = 5.8; comparing boys

Table 6.3	Explanatory Risk Scores			
Predicting Offenders	No. of Controls	No. of Offenders	Row %	Column %
Score				
0	655	4	0.6	12.1
1	491	10	2.0	30.3
2	207	13	5.9	39.4
3	59	6	9.2	18.2
Predicting Victims	No. of Controls	No. of Victims	Row %	Column %
Score				
0	333	1	0.3	3.9
1	527	5	0.9	17.2
2	336	6	1.8	20.7
3–4	220	17	7.2	58.6

Predicting offenders: OR = 5.8 (01 vs. 23); OR = 5.1 (012 vs. 3); AUC = .771
Predicting victims: OR = 5.9 (01 vs. 234); OR = 7.7 (012 vs. 34); AUC = .796
Abbreviations: OR, odds ratio; AUC, area under the ROC curve.

with 0–2 risk factors with boys with 3 risk factors, OR = 5.1. The area under the ROC Curve (AUC) = .771.

A logistic regression analysis was also carried out to investigate which of the 9 significant predictors of homicide victims were independent predictors. Four variables were significant or nearly significant in a stepwise analysis: low guilt (LRCS = 17.59, $P < .0001$), low achievement (LRCS = 9.56, $P = .002$), broken family (LRCS = 6.47, $P = .011$), and large family size (LRCS = 3.76, $P = .053$). In the final model, the partial odds ratios were 4.5 for broken family, 3.3 for low achievement, 3.8 for low guilt, and 2.3 for large family size.

An explanatory risk score was then calculated for each boy based on the number of these four risk factors that he possessed. Table 6.3 shows how much this risk score predicted homicide victims; for example, 0.3% of boys with none of these four risk factors became homicide victims, compared with 7.2% of boys with three or four of these risk factors. Retrospectively, 17 of the 29 homicide victims (59%) were among the one-sixth of the boys with three or four of these risk factors. Comparing boys with 0–1 risk factors with those with 2–4 risk factors, OR = 5.9; comparing boys with 0–2 risk factors with those with 3–4 risk factors, OR = 7.7. The AUC = .796. Hence, the prediction of homicide victims was at least as accurate as the prediction of homicide offenders.

■ Why Does Race Predict Homicide Offenders and Victims?

It is plausible to suggest that race predicts homicide offenders and victims because African American and Caucasian boys differ on predictive risk factors. According to this hypothesis, race should not predict homicide offenders and victims after controlling for predictive risk factors. Indeed, after entering the 8 significant explanatory risk factors in a logistic regression analysis, race did not significantly predict homicide offenders. After entering the 9 significant explanatory risk factors in a logistic regression analysis, race was still a significant predictor of homicide victims (LRCS = 4.61, P = .032). However, the predictive power of race was considerably reduced after controlling for other risk factors. It might be concluded that race predicts homicide offenders and victims primarily because of racial differences in predictive risk factors. The most important risk factors that were significantly associated with race and that predicted homicide offenders and/or victims were a bad neighborhood, a broken family, the family on welfare, and a young mother.

Behavioral/Attitudinal Predictors

Ten of the 19 behavioral/attitudinal factors significantly predicted homicide offenders: a high risk score, suspended from school, disruptive behavior disorder, a favorable attitude to delinquency, serious delinquency, a favorable attitude to substance use, peer delinquency, truancy, covert behavior (concealing, manipulative, untrustworthy), and cruelty to people (**Table 6.4**). The strongest predictor was a high risk score in the screening assessment, based on antisocial behavior: 85% of homicide offenders had a high risk score, compared with 49% of controls (OR = 5.8).

Fourteen of the 19 behavioral/attitudinal factors significantly predicted homicide victims: serious delinquency, suspended from school, a high risk score, truancy, non-physical aggression, covert behavior, a bad relation with peers, a bad relation with parents, physical aggression, low school motivation, peer delinquency, cruelty to people, bad friends, and disruptive behavior disorder

Table 6.4	Behavioral Predictors of Homicide Offenders and Victims		
Predicting Offenders	**% of Controls (1421)**	**% of Offenders (33)**	**Odds Ratio**
High risk score	49	85	5.8*
Suspended	43	79	5.0*
Disruptive behavior disorder	23	55	4.0*
Favorable attitude to delinquency	23	55	4.0*
Serious delinquency	29	61	3.8*
Favorable attitude to substance use	24	52	3.4*
Peer delinquency	24	52	3.4*
Truant	38	61	2.6*
Covert behavior	24	42	2.3*
Cruel to people	25	42	2.3*
Predicting Victims	**% of Controls (1421)**	**% of Victims (29)**	**Odds Ratio**
Serious delinquency	29	72	6.5*
Suspended	43	75	4.0*
High risk score	49	79	3.9*
Truant	38	69	3.7*
Nonphysical aggression	25	55	3.7*
Covert behavior	24	54	3.6*
Bad relation with peers	26	55	3.5*
Bad relation with parent	24	52	3.3*
Physical aggression	27	52	3.0*
Low school motivation	37	63	2.9*
Peer delinquency	24	45	2.6*
Cruel to people	25	45	2.5*
Bad friends	25	45	2.4*
Disruptive behavior disorder	23	39	2.1*

*$P < .05$

(Table 6.4). The strongest predictor was serious delinquency: 72% of homicide victims were serious delinquents compared with 29% of controls (OR = 6.5). Based on behavioral risk factors, homicide offenders were not more extreme than homicide victims; in fact, there were more significant results in predicting victims than in predicting offenders.

Behavioral Risk Scores

A logistic regression analysis was carried out to investigate which of the 10 significant predictors of homicide offenders were independent predictors. Five variables were significant or nearly significant in a stepwise analysis: a favorable attitude to delinquency (LRCS = 14.77, $P < .0001$), disruptive behavior disorder (LRCS = 12.01, $P = .0005$), suspended from school (LRCS = 9.49, $P = .002$), a high risk score (LRCS = 4.89, $P = .027$), and a favorable attitude to substance use (LRCS = 3.07, $P = .080$). In the final model, the partial odds ratios were 3.0 for high risk score, 2.8 for suspended from school, 2.2 for disruptive behavior disorder, 2.1 for a favorable attitude to delinquency, and 2.1 for a favorable attitude to substance use.

A behavioral risk score was then calculated for each boy based on the number of these five risk factors that he possessed. **Table 6.5** shows how much this risk score predicted homicide offenders; for example, 0.6% of boys with 0–1 of these five risk factors were homicide offenders, compared with 11.1% of boys with 4–5 risk factors. Again, there was significant predictability but also a high false positive rate. Retrospectively, 22 of the 33 homicide offenders (67%) were among the quarter of the boys with three or more of these risk factors. Comparing boys with 0–2 risk factors with those with 3–5 risk factors, OR = 5.9; comparing boys with 0–3 risk factors with those with 4–5 risk factors, OR = 9.5. The AUC = .797.

A logistic regression analysis was also carried out to investigate which of the 14 significant predictors of homicide victims were independent predictors. Three variables were significant in a stepwise analysis: serious delinquency (LRCS = 23.01, $P < .0001$), a bad relation with parents (LRCS = 5.14, $P = .023$), and truancy (LRCS = 4.21, $P = .040$). In the final model, the partial odds ratios were 4.4 for serious delinquency, 2.4 for a bad relation with parents, and 2.3 for truancy.

A behavioral risk score was then calculated for each boy based on the number of the three risk factors that he possessed. Table 6.5 shows how much this risk score predicted homicide victims; the example, 0.5% of boys with none of these three risk factors became homicide victims, compared with 9.9% of boys with all three of these risk factors. Retrospectively, 21 of the 29 homicide victims (72%) were among the quarter of the boys with two or more of these risk factors. Comparing boys with 0–1 risk factors with those with 2–3 risk factors, OR = 7.4; comparing boys with 0–2 risk factors with those with all 3 risk factors, OR = 7.3. The AUC = .788. The behavioral prediction of homicide victims was not significantly less accurate than the behavioral prediction of homicide offenders.

Comparing Predictors of Homicide Offenders and Victims

In comparing ORs, natural logarithms of ORs (LORs) were used, in order to convert this ratio variable into a linear scale. The LORs for explanatory predictors

Table 6.5	Behavioral Risk Scores			
Predicting Offenders	**No. of Controls**	**No. of Offenders**	**Row %**	**Column %**
Score				
0–1	703	4	0.6	12.1
2	355	7	1.9	21.2
3	230	6	2.5	18.2
4–5	128	16	11.1	48.5
Predicting Victims	**No. of Controls**	**No. of Victims**	**Row %**	**Column %**
Score				
0	589	33	0.5	10.3
1	458	55	1.1	17.2
2	290	1212	4.0	41.3
3	82	99	9.9	31.0

Predicting offenders: OR = 5.9 (012 vs. 345); OR = 9.5 (0123 vs. 45); AUC = .797
Predicting victims: OR = 7.4 (01 vs. 23); OR = 7.3 (012 vs. 3); AUC = .788
Abbreviations: OR, odds ratio; AUC, area under the ROC curve; SD, standard deviation of AUC.

of homicide offenders and victims were significantly correlated ($r = .45, P = .041$). There were 8 significant explanatory predictors of homicide offenders and 9 significant explanatory predictors of homicide victims. Four factors significantly predicted both: old for the grade, low guilt, the family on welfare, and a broken family.

The LORs for behavioral predictors of homicide offenders and victims were almost significantly correlated ($r = .40, P = .089$). There were 10 significant behavioral predictors of homicide offenders and 14 significant behavioral predictors of homicide victims. Eight factors significantly predicted both: a high risk score, truancy, serious delinquency, covert behavior, suspended from school, cruel to people, peer delinquency, and disruptive behavior disorder. Over all 40 predictors (explanatory and behavioral), the LORs for homicide offenders and victims were significantly correlated ($r = .44, P = .004$). Therefore, the strongest predictors of homicide offenders tended also to be the strongest predictors of homicide victims.

It was expected that homicide offenders would be more antisocial and deviant than homicide victims, and hence that homicide offenders would be predicted more accurately than homicide victims. However, this was not the case. For explanatory predictors, the geometric mean OR was 2.1 for predicting victims and 1.9 for predicting offenders. For behavioral predictors, the geometric mean OR was 2.7 for predicting victims and 2.3 for predicting offenders. These ORs were not significantly different, but they show that homicide victims were predicted at least as well as homicide offenders. Not surprisingly, behavioral predictors were somewhat more accurate than explanatory predictors.

Of the 21 explanatory predictors, 9 predicted homicide offenders more strongly and 12 predicted homicide victims more strongly. Of the 19 behavioral risk factors, 6 predicted homicide offenders more strongly and 13 predicted homicide victims more strongly. Hence, young homicide offenders were not more extreme than young homicide victims in their possession of either explanatory or behavioral risk factors.

■ Conclusion

This is the first prospective longitudinal study of characteristics of homicide offenders and victims. However, it has a number of limitations. In particular, the numbers of homicide offenders and victims are small (making it difficult to compare them directly), and results obtained in the city of Pittsburgh may not be generalizable to the United States. Also, the results are to some extent provisional, since the numbers of homicide offenders and victims (especially from the youngest sample) will continue to increase over time. The results apply to young homicide offenders and victims.

Nevertheless, this paper shows that explanatory and behavioral risk factors measured in the first year of the study significantly predicted homicide offenders and victims between 4 and 15 years later. Importantly, young homicide victims were at least as deviant as young homicide offenders, and victims were generally predicted as accurately as offenders. For example, 61% of homicide offenders and 72% of homicide victims had already committed serious delinquency (burglary, vehicle theft, robbery, assault, or rape), compared with 29% of controls.

The strongest predictors of homicide offenders tended also to be the strongest predictors of homicide victims. However, among the significant explanatory predictors, homicide offenders tended to be predicted by sociodemographic factors and homicide victims tended to be predicted by individual factors. Thus, victims tended to be individually deviant while offenders tended to be socially deprived. African American boys disproportionately tended to be homicide offenders and victims. However, the race differences were much reduced after controlling for risk factors associated with race, notably a bad neighborhood, a broken family, the family on welfare, and a young mother.

Risk scores showed how much homicide offenders and homicide victims could be predicted in the first year of the study. Typically, fewer than 1% of the least at-risk boys, compared to about 10% of the most at-risk boys, became homicide offenders (and similar results were obtained in predicting homicide victims). These risk scores overestimate the degree of prospective predictive accuracy in a new sample, because they retrospectively choose the best predictors in this particular sample. However, the predictability of homicide offenders and homicide victims would be increased by including later features such as guns, gangs, and drugs.

One possible interpretation of these results is that multiple early risk factors (including socioeconomic deprivation and low school attainment) cause an antisocial lifestyle involving guns, gangs, and drugs, that increases the risk of being involved in a homicide either as an offender or as a victim. Further research is needed to test this theory and to investigate why sociodemographic factors are more important for homicide offenders while individual factors are more important for homicide victims.

■ Acknowledgments

Work on this paper was supported by Grants 96-MU-FX-0012 and 2005-JK-FX-0001 from the Office of Juvenile Justice and Delinquency Prevention, Grant 50078 from the National Institute of Mental Health, and Grant 411018 from the National Institute on Drug Abuse. Points of view or opinions in this paper are those of the authors and do not necessarily represent the official position or policies of the U.S. Department of Justice, the National Institute of Mental Health, or the National Institute on Drug Abuse.

1. Hoyert, D. L., Arias, E., Smith, B. L., et al. (2001). *Deaths: Final Data for 1999*. Hyattsville, MD: National Center for Health Statistics.
2. Federal Bureau of Investigation (2003). *Crime in the United States, 2001*. Washington, DC: U.S. Department of Justice.
3. Cook, P. J., Laub, J. H. (1998). The unprecedented epidemic in youth violence. Pp. 27–64 in M. Tonry, M. H. Moore (Eds.), *Youth Violence*. Chicago: University of Chicago Press.
4. Snyder, H. N., Sickmund, M. (1999). *Juvenile Offenders and Victims: 1999 National Report*. Washington, DC: Office of Juvenile Justice and Delinquency Prevention.
5. Fox, J. A., Zawitz, M. W. (1999). *Homicide Trends in the United States*. Washington, DC: Bureau of Justice Statistics.
6. Lauritsen, J. L., Laub, J. H., Sampson, R. J. (1992). Conventional and delinquent activities: Implications for the prevention of violent victimization among adolescents. *Violence Vict* 7:91–108.
7. Rivara, F. P., Shepherd, J. P., Farrington, D. P., et al. (1995). Victim as offender in youth violence. *Ann Emergency Med* 26:609–614.
8. Heide, K. M. (2003). Youth homicide: A review of the literature and a blueprint for action. *Int J Offender Therap Compar Criminol* 47:6–36, p. 25.
9. Loeber, R., DeLamatre, M., Tita, G., et al. (1999). Gun injury and mortality: The delinquent backgrounds of juvenile victims. *Violence Vict 14*, 339–352.
10. Loeber, R., Pardini, D., Homish, D. L., et al. (2005). The prediction of violence and homicide in young men. *J Consult Clin Psychol* 73:1074–1088.
11. Loeber, R., Farrington, D. P., Stouthamer-Loeber, M., van Kammen, W. B. (1998). *Antisocial Behavior and Mental Health Problems: Explanatory Factors in Childhood and Adolescence*. Mahwah, NJ: Lawrence Erlbaum.
12. Loeber, R., Farrington, D. P., Stouthamer-Loeber, M., White, H. R. (in press). *Violence and Serious Theft: Development and Prediction from Childhood to Adulthood*. New York: Routledge.
13. Loeber, R., Stouthamer-Loeber, M., van Kammen, W. B., Farrington, D. P. (1989). Development of a new measure of self-reported antisocial behavior for young children: Prevalence and reliability. Pp. 203–225 in M. W. Klein (Ed.), *Cross-National Research in Self-Reported Crime and Delinquency*. Dordrecht, Netherlands: Kluwer.
14. Achenbach, T. M., Edelbrock, C. S. (1983). *Manual of the Child Behavior Checklist and Revised Child Behavior Profile*. Burlington, VT: University of Vermont Department of Psychiatry.
15. Edelbrock, C. S., Achenbach, T. M. (1984). The teacher version of the Child Behavior Profile: Boys aged 6 though 11. *J Consult Clin Psychol* 52:207–217.
16. Farrington, D. P., Loeber, R., Yin, Y., Anderson, S. J. (2002). Are within-individual causes of delinquency the same as between-individual causes? *Crimin Behav Mental Health* 12:53–68.

References

17. Frick, P. J., O'Brien, B. S., Wootton, J. M., McBurnett, K. (1994). Psychopathy and conduct problems in children. *J Abnorm Psychol* 103:700–707.

18. Farrington, D. P., Loeber, R., Stouthamer-Loeber, M. (2003). How can the relationship between race and violence be explained? Pp. 213–237 in D. F. Hawkins (Ed.), *Violent Crime: Assessing Race and Ethnic Differences*. Cambridge: Cambridge University Press.

19. Costello, A., Edelbrock, C. S., Kalas, R., et al. (1982). *The Diagnostic Interview Schedule for Children, Parent Version (revised)*. Worcester, MA: University of Massachusetts Medical Center.

20. Fleiss, J. L. (1981). *Statistical Methods for Rates and Proportions*, 2nd edition. New York: Wiley.

21. Farrington, D. P., Loeber, R. (2000). Some benefits of dichotomization in psychiatric and criminological research. *Crim Behav Mental Health* 10:100–122.

Generality of Deviance and Predation: Crime-Switching and Specialization Patterns in Persistent Sexual Offenders

7

Patrick Lussier
Simon Fraser University

Benoit Leclerc
University of Montreal
Philippe-Pinel Institute of Montreal

Jay Healey
Simon Fraser University

Jean Proulx
University of Montreal
Philippe Pinel Institute of Montreal

Contrary to public perception, empirical studies have constantly shown that persistent sex offenders constitute a small sub-group of the sex offender population. Indeed, only a small sub-group of sex offenders tends to persist over time, as recidivism rates tend to be approximately 10 to 15% over a period of about five years after release.[1] This small sub-group has attracted a lot of attention from the criminal justice system. Such attention led to the development of various risk assessment tools designed to help practitioners screening persistent offenders. Many characteristics have been identified, and theoretical models have been proposed.[2,3] In the meantime, however, the behavior of persistent sexual offenders has been overlooked to a great extent. One could reasonably question what those risk assessment tools are really predicting, as the criterion used to develop those instruments is "sexual recidivism," which includes much heterogeneity in its manifestations. Of interest is the fact that many predictors of sexual recidivism are related to offending characteristics, such as having offended against an extrafamilial, male, prepubescent victim. The purpose of this study is to build on previous studies to further understand the sexual criminal activity of persistent sexual offenders.[4] Emphasis here is on the tendency for that sub-group of offenders to switch from one sex crime category to another. Building on the criminological literature, we investigated the sexual criminal versatility of persistent sex offenders and the associated risk factors.

■ Sexual Polymorphism and Crime-Switching Patterns in Sex Offenders

Sexual polymorphism refers to crime-switching patterns along several dimensions such as victim's age, gender, relationship to the offender, and nature of acts committed by the offender. Few studies have examined the level of sexual polymorphism and crime-switching patterns in the sexual criminal activity of sex offenders. Based on the current state of knowledge, there are three broad conclusions that can be drawn in regard to the offending patterns of persistent sexual offenders. First, Soothill and colleagues came to the conclusion that while sex offenders are generalists in their criminal offending, they tend to specialize in their sexual offending, confining themselves to one victim type.[5] Similarly, Radzinowicz also found specialization in victim choice, in that only 7% of his large sample of sex offenders had convictions for crimes against both male and female victims, a finding consistent with those of Gebhard and colleagues.[6,7] More recently, Cann, Friendship, and Gonza found that only about 25% of their sample of incarcerated sex offenders was versatile when considering victim's age and gender as well as the offender-victim relationship.[8] On the other hand, crime-switching patterns may vary as a function of the dimension of the sexual polymorphism considered. For instance, while they also found much stability as to the victim's gender, Guay et al. reported considerable versatility for those targeting adolescents.[4] Although offenders targeting children and those targeting adults remained in the same category, those offending against adolescents were likely to switch either to adults or to children. Guay and colleagues hypothesized that adolescents may be a sex surrogate choice when the preferred partner was not available.

Second, empirical studies conducted in clinical settings have shown a divergent picture of the sex offenders' crime switching pattern. Weinrott and Saylor argued that official data hide an enormous amount of sex crimes.[9] Using official data only, Weinrott and Saylor found that only 15% of their sample of offenders was versatile considering only three categories: adult females, extrafamilial children, and intrafamilial children. Using a self-reported computerized questionnaire, however, that number rose to 53%.[9] Similarly, Heil and his colleagues reported that incarcerated offenders in treatment are not versatile as to victim's age (7%) and gender (8%) when assessed with official data, but are when interviewed using a polygraph (70% and 36%, respectively). Less dramatic numbers, however, were reported for parolees, which might be explained by sampling differences (i.e., incarcerated offenders were more serious offenders) and the fact that admitting a crime was a prerequisite to enter treatment.[10] Abel and Rouleau's well-publicized study, conducted under strict conditions of confidentiality, showed that 42% of their sample targeted victims in more than one age group, 20% targeted victims of both gender, and 26% committed both hands-on and hands-off crimes, such as exhibitionism.[11] The study and findings, however, have been criticized on methodological grounds.[12] On the other hand, similar results have been reported elsewhere in a sample of sex offenders assessed in a forensic psychiatric institution. For example, 30% of rapists admitted to acts of heterosexual pedophilia.[13]

The overlapping nature of different forms of sexually deviant acts found in the clinical studies is counterintuitive to current typological models of sex offenders based on the characteristics of the offense. The victim's gender, the victim's age, the offender-victim relationship, the level of sexual intrusiveness, and the level of force used during the commission of the crime are some examples of criteria that have been used over the years to classify sex offenders.[14,15] The limited evidence does not allow one to make firm conclusions as to whether or not those results invalidate current typological models. In fact, it remains unclear whether clinical studies found a general pattern of sexual polymorphism among most sex offenders or whether a sub-group of generally deviant sex offenders were found. In any case, this raises the possibility of a common cause to different forms of deviant sexual acts. One possible candidate that has been raised in recent years is the construct of sexualization or hyper-sexuality.[16,17] High sexualization refers to a disinhibited sexuality characterized by sexual preoccupation (e.g., excessive time spent thinking about sexual matters), sexual compulsivity (e.g., overwhelmed by sexual fantasies) and impersonal sex (e.g., preference for partner variety). Individuals characterized by a high sexualization might experience more difficulties in controlling their sexual urges. It is thus reasonable to propose that those sex offenders characterized by a disinhibited sexuality might have different means of sexual expression to fulfill their sexual needs. Therefore, an individual with high sexualization might be more likely to seek out for sexual gratifications in different contexts and different places. A high sexualization has been shown to be related to frequency of sexual offending in a sample of incarcerated sex offenders.[18]

Third, Smallbone and Wortley came to the conclusion that diversity in paraphilic activities may be a function of general deviance. Indeed, looking at different activity paraphilia (e.g., voyeurism, frotteurism, sexual sadism, etc.) in a sample of child molesters, they found that a scale measuring the versatility of sexual deviance correlated significantly and positively with nonsexual offending. In other words, as the frequency of offending increases, so does the versatility in paraphilic interests and behaviors.[19] Similarly, Lussier, LeBlanc, and Proulx found in a sample of recidivists, all of which having committed a sex crime, that versatility in sex offending was strongly related to versatility in non-sexual non-violent offending, as well as versatility in non-sexual violent crime. Furthermore, using structural equation modeling, they found that such pattern of general versatility was related to an early-onset and persistent antisocial behavior. In other words, sex offenders characterized by a life-course persistent antisocial tendency were more likely to show much versatility in their sexual offending.[20] In that regard, Guay et al. hypothesized that crime-switching in sexual offending might be partly explained by low self-control.[4] Gottfredson and Hirschi have described individuals with low self-control as impulsive, characterized by a tendency to pursue easy, risky, and immediate gratifications requiring no special abilities in spite of more long-term negative consequences.[21] A few emerging studies have shown that low self-control increases the risk of committing a sex crime. It is reasonable to propose that the sexual behavior of sex offenders lacking control over their behavior might take different expressions given the opportunity to do so.[22]

■ Current Focus

The current studies conducted to date provide two different pictures of the persistent sexual offenders, one being specialized in one sex crime category and another being characterized by much versatility. The current study will try to address such contradictory findings by looking at the sexual offending patterns of persistent sexual offenders. While earlier studies have looked mainly at victim's characteristics to assess crime specialization/versatility, we somewhat expand the scope by also looking at the nature of the sexual acts committed. In that regard, using kappa coefficients of agreement, Sjöstedt et al. found that the stability of the acts committed (e.g., violence, penetration, physical contact) was fair at best (i.e., kappa < .40) across offenses.[23] The analytic strategy chosen here is in keeping with the long tradition of empirical studies in criminology having looked at the specialization in general offending.[24] Furthermore, we found very few studies that had looked at individual differences related to crime-switching patterns in sexual offending. In fact, to our knowledge, only one empirical study has looked at the individual differences related to sexual polymorphism. Cann et al.[8] found that versatile sex offenders showed elevated scores on the Static-99, a risk assessment procedure designed to assess the risk of sexual recidivism specifically for sex offenders. Although interesting, these results are problematic considering that most of the items included in the Static-99 are related to the victims' (e.g., a male victim) and offenses' characteristics (e.g., sexual crime without contact). In other words, those results are not surprising, as more versatile sexual offending patterns are more likely to tap different indicators on the risk assessment scale. Furthermore, those results do not provide avenues of explanation for sexual polymorphism. Based on our current review of the literature two competing hypotheses will be empirically tested:

$H_{(1)}$: Sex offenders with high sexualization are more versatile in their sexual offending.

$H_{(2)}$: Sex offenders with low self-control are more versatile in their sexual offending.

■ Methodology

Subjects

The initial sample consisted of 553 adult males who had been convicted for a sexual offense. A total of 216 adult males convicted of a sexual offense against a minimum of two victims and having received a prison sentence of at least two years were included in this study. All of these individuals were incarcerated at the Regional Reception Centre of Ste-Anne-des-Plaines (in the province of Quebec, Canada) at the time of the study. They were consecutive admissions between April 1994 and June 2000 at the Regional Reception Centre, a maximum-security federal institution run by the Correctional Service of Canada. This facility admits all individuals sentenced to a minimum of two years for the purpose of risk and treatment-needs assessment. The average stay in this institution is about 6 weeks, permitting completion of correctional assessment procedures prior to the individual's transfer to an institution suited to his risk level and treatment needs. Their criminal history revealed that, on average, they were first convicted at age 35.2 (sd = 15.2; range = 18.1–73.9).

Procedures

Data used to create scales measuring behavioral antecedents were collected in a semi-structured interview with each subject. Each subject was interviewed only once by a member of the research team unaware of the research questions and hypotheses. Participation in this study was strictly voluntary. Subjects included in this study signed a consent form indicating that the information gathered would be used for research purposes only. Interviewers were all graduate students in criminology and psychology trained by a licensed forensic psychologist to conduct semi-structured interviews using a computerized questionnaire. Quality of data collected was controlled by completing interrater agreement. Interrater agreement was measured on the basis of 16 interviews conducted jointly by two raters (the principal research assistant and the second author). Ratings were done independently following these interviews, which were conducted by one interviewer in the presence of the other. The mean kappa was .87, which represents very strong agreement. Note that interrater agreement analysis was not conducted for the developmental behavioral indicators (i.e., self-control, and sexualization). Moreover, as participants granted access to their correctional files, official sources of information (e.g., police reports, victim statements, psychological assessments, etc.) were also used to validate information, when possible, obtained in interview. When disagreements were found between information gathered during the semi-structured interview and those collected from official files, official data were used.

Independent Variables

Age

The offender's age has been shown to be empirically related to sexual recidivism in that younger offenders are more likely to sexually re-offend, but this effect varies greatly across studies.[25] More recently, it has been argued that this relationship might be more complex than it appears. Thornton suggested that this trend might be due to the presence of differential recidivism rates between those offenders in their early twenties versus those in their sixties.[26] Similarly, Doren raised the possibility tha this effect might not hold true for all ages, as recidivism rates appear not to vary much between age 40 and 60.[27] In the present study, age is defined as the age of the offender at the start of the current incarceration. On average, sex offenders included in this sample were 43.1 years old (sd = 12.6; range = 20–75).

Marital Status

A meta-analysis has shown that being single (i.e., never married) is significantly related to sexual recidivism. In the present study, 41% of our sample had never been married, 35% were in a relationship (e.g., common law, married), 24% were either divorced or separated or widowed. The variable was coded as follows: (0) has been/being in a relationship; (1) being single/never married.

Ethnic Origin

Although ethnic origin has been extensively studied in the field of criminology, it has been somewhat overlooked in the field of sexual aggression. In total, 88% were Caucasian, 6% were African American, 4% were Native American while nearly 2% were Hispanic. This variable was dichotomized (0 = Non-Caucasian; 1 = Caucasian).

Educational Achievement

Educational achievement refers to the highest level of schooling completed. In our sample, 26% had some elementary level education, 61% had some high-school education while 12% had either some college or university level education. For the purpose of this study, this variable was dichotomized (0 = More than elementary level education; 1 = Elementary level education or higher).

Number of Convictions

To examine an association between a diversity index of activity paraphilia and frequency of general offending, we included in the analysis the total number of convictions. Our sample had on average 3.9 convictions (sd = 4.0; range = 1–20). In total, only 28.4% of our sample had a prior record for a sex crime.

Low Self-Control

The construct of low self-control was operationalized using four behavioral indicators of general deviance. The scale of authority-conflict (alpha = .70) includes four items related to being defiant at home and at school including: being disruptive in class, running away from home, being rebellious against an authority figure, being short tempered. The scale of reckless and imprudent behavior (alpha = .63) includes three items related to alcohol abuse, substance abuse, and dangerous behaviors. The scale of covert behavior (alpha = .61) is composed of five items that relate to being dishonest, deceitful, and committing concealing acts: repetitive and frequent lying, theft, selling drugs, fraud, and other property crime. Finally, the scale of overt behavior (alpha = .61) includes five items related to vandalism and acts of non-sexual aggression: major violence, serious violence, assault, cruelty against animals, and vandalism. These four scales included items related to childhood (0 to 12) and adolescence (ages 13 to 17) measured using a 3-point scale: (0) did not commit the behavior; (1) committed the behavior either in childhood or adolescence, and; (2) committed the behavior in both childhood and adolescence). The score of the four scales were standardized and summed. Therefore, a higher score on the scale reflects lower self-control.

Sexualization

Following our previous studies, the construct of sexualization was operationalized using three behavioral indicators. First, the scale of impersonal sex (alpha = .64) include four items: age at first sexual contact, age at first sexual intercourse, number of sexual partners (divided by age) and, having used the service of prostitutes (0 = no; 1 = yes). The scale of sexual compulsivity (alpha = .68) is based on the following seven items: (a) age at first masturbation; (b) compulsive masturbation; (c) the average frequency of masturbation per week prior to incarceration, of which we isolated the 25th percentile with the highest frequency, (d) being overwhelmed by deviant sexual fantasies, lifetime; (e) being overwhelmed by non-deviant sexual fantasies, lifetime; (f) having deviant sexual fantasies one year prior to the sex crime for which they were incarcerated; and (g) the presence of a paraphilia (e.g., bestiality, fetishism, etc.) using the DSM-IV criteria developed by the American Psychiatric Association. Finally, the scale of sexual preoccupation (alpha = .63) includes three items relating to the use of pornographic magazines, movies, as well as frequenting strip clubs. The scores on the three scales were standardized and summed. A high score on this scale indicated a high sexualization.

Dependent Variables

Police records were consulted to determine the criminal activity in adulthood. The number of victims refers to the total number of victims for the index offenses. On average, sexual aggressors included in this sample have been charged for 3.4 victims (sd = 4.5; range = 2–65).

Crime Categories

There is no general consensus as to how sex crime should be categorized. Earlier work has focused mostly on distinguishing the age and the gender of the victim as well as the nature of the offender-victim relationship. Two main dimensions of the sexual criminal activity were considered in the present study, that is, the victim's characteristics, and the characteristics of the sexual act. First, the victim's characteristics included the following three key dimensions: (a) victim's gender (1 = male; 2 = female); (b) victim's age (1 = between 0 and 12; 2 = between 13 and 17; 3 = 18 or more); (c) relationship between the offender and the victim (1 = stranger; 2 = intrafamilial; 3 = known and familiar; 4 = known but unfamiliar). We also took into consideration, three dimensions related to the characteristics of the sexual acts: (a) the presence or absence of sexual contact

(1 = hands-off; 2 = hands-on); (b) level of sexual intrusiveness (1 = fondling, rubbing, and masturbation; 2 = oral sex; 3 = anal, vaginal penetration), and; (c) level of physical force (1 = no force used; 2 = minimal force to gain compliance of the victim; 3 = excessive force used). Considering their importance as distinct dimension related to persistence in sexual re-offending, we investigated their relevance in regard to specialization and crime-switching. Transition matrices were performed for each of the six dimensions described here.

Transition Matrices

Crime-switching patterns across sex crimes were investigated in order to examine the tendency for sex offenders to specialize in a particular crime-type. We analyzed the sex crime transition for the first five victims. We focused here on the first five victims because of the dropping out of offenders and the small sample size as more victims were considered in the analysis. Due to missing data, it was possible to chronologically order the victims for 210 individuals. Because 210 offenders had two victims, but only 36 had at least five victims, we therefore only considered the first four crime transitions. Hence, 210 offenders had one crime transition (from crime #1 to crime #2), 100 had a second transition (from crime #2 to crime #3), 64 had a third transition (from crime #3 to crime #4), and 36 had four transitions (from crime #4 to crime #5).

Diversity Index

Following the work of Agresti and Agresti, diversity indexes were computed for different dimensions of the sexual offending activity.[28] The application of the diversity index in criminology is well-known.[29,30] The diversity index refers to the probability that any two offenses randomly selected from an individual's criminal history are in different categories. In order to compute the diversity index (D), one has to determine the number of crimes categories (k), where p_i equals the proportion of crimes for each of the $i = 1, 2, \ldots k$ categories identified. Then, D can be computed as follows:

(Eq. 7.1)
$$D = 1 - \sum_{i=1}^{k} p_i^2$$

The D index can be characterized by the following set of properties. First, D does not consider the chronological order of the offenses. Therefore, this allows measuring the level of specialization taking all offenses into consideration simultaneously. Second, the minimum score of D is 0, indicating perfect or complete specialization (e.g., all offenses fall into one category). Third, D is "a function of both the number of categories of both the number of categories and the dispersion of the population among the categories."[28] Therefore, a D indicating complete versatility will vary according to the number of offense categories considered—i.e., $D_{max} = (k - 1)/k$. Hence, if 4 offense categories are considered, D will vary from .00 (complete specialization) to .75 (complete versatility).

■ Results

Crime-Switching Patterns

Transition Matrices

In **Table 7.1**, crime-transitions were analyzed using three victims' characteristics. First, looking at the gender of the victim, we found much evidence for stability and specialization in both offenders against female victims and offenders against male victims. For offenders against female the probability of repeating against the same victim remained constantly over .90 across the four transitions while it remained constantly over .80 for offenders against male victims. Second, looking at the age of the victim, we found more evidence of crime-switching patterns. Those offending against children tend to limit themselves to children as the probability coefficient remained higher than .80 across offenses. If switching did occur, child molesters were more likely to revert to adolescents (range = .09–15) than to adults (range = .00–.05). Offenders against adolescents showed relatively lower rate of specialization, as the probabilities of re-offending against the same age-category varied between .47 and .71 across offenses. On the other hand, when switching did occur, it was mainly for a child victim (range = .28–.53).

Finally, as for those having offended against adults, probabilities of specialization varied between .54 and .90 across offenses. When switching did occur, offenders against adult victims were more likely to revert to adolescents (range = .10–.36) rather than child victims (range = .00–.11). Third, the nature of the relationship between the offender and the victim was considered for each crime transition. Individuals having offended against strangers (range = .80–1.00) and those having offended known-unfamiliar (range = .73–.93) showed relatively higher level of crime specialization across offenses. On the other hand, those having offended against a family member (range = .61–88) or a known-familiar (range = .64–1.00) victim showed relatively lower levels of specialization. For intrafamilial offenders, when switching did occur, it rarely involved stranger victims, but mostly known-familiar and unfamiliar victims. Similarly, when crime switching did occur for known-familiar victims, it almost never involved stranger victims, but mostly intrafamilial and known-unfamiliar victims.

In **Table 7.2**, crime-transitions were also investigated using offense variables, that is, the nature of offense, the level of sexual behavior intrusiveness achieved in the offense, and the level of physical force adopted during the offense. It shows that offenders tended to remain stable in the nature of the offense from

Table 7.1 Crime-Transitions Based on Victim's Characteristics

Victim's Gender[a]	Female (T_{+1})	Male (T_{+1})
Female	T_1=.92 (131) T_2=.90 (55) T_3=.94 (32) T_4=.95 (18)	T_1=.08 (12) T_2=.10 (6) T_3=.06 (2) T_4=.05 (1)
Male	T_1=.20 (13) T_2=.10 (4) T_3=.10 (3) T_4=.19 (3)	T_1=**.80 (53)** T_2=**.90 (35)** T_3=**.90 (26)** T_4=**.81 (13)**

Victim's Age[b]	Child (T_{+1})	Adolescent (T_{+1})	Adult (T_{+1})
Child	T_1=**.82 (116)** T_2=**.81 (51)** T_3=**.86 (31)** T_4=**.91 (20)**	T_1=.15 (21) T_2=.14 (9) T_3=.11 (4) T_4=.09 (2)	T_1=.03 (4) T_2=.05 (3) T_3=.03 (1) T_4=.00 (0)
Adolescent	T_1=.28 (11) T_2=.30 (7) T_3=.53 (9) T_4=.29 (2)	T_1=**.53 (21)** T_2=**.65 (15)** T_3=**.47 (8)** T_4=**.71 (5)**	T_1=.20 (8) T_2=.04 (1) T_3=.00 (0) T_4=.00 (0)
Adult	T_1=.11 (3) T_2=.07 (1) T_3=.00 (1) T_4=.00 (0)	T_1=.36 (10) T_2=.29 (4) T_3=.10 (1) T_4=.33 (2)	T_1=**.54 (15)** T_2=**.64 (9)** T_3=**.90 (9)** T_4=**.67 (4)**

Offender-Victim Relationship[c]	Stranger (T_{+1})	Intrafamilial (T_{+1})	Known-familiar (T_{+1})	Known-unfamiliar (T_{+1})
Stranger	T_1=**1.00 (21)** T_2=**1.00 (11)** T_3=**.88 (7)** T_4=**.80 (4)**	T_1=.00 (0) T_2=.00 (0) T_3=.00 (0) T_4=.00 (0)	T_1=.00 (0) T_2=.00 (0) T_3=.00 (0) T_4=.00 (0)	T_1=.00 (0) T_2=.00 (0) T_3=.13 (1) T_4=.20 (1)
Intrafamilial	T_1=.03 (2) T_2=.00 (0) T_3=.06 (1) T_4=.00 (0)	T_1=**.73 (55)** T_2=**.88 (21)** T_3=**.61 (11)** T_4=**.75 (6)**	T_1=.11 (8) T_2=.04 (1) T_3=.11 (2) T_4=.13 (1)	T_1=.13 (10) T_2=.08 (2) T_3=.22 (4) T_4=.13 (1)
Known-familiar	T_1=.00 (0) T_2=.04 (1) T_3=.00 (0) T_4=.00 (0)	T_1=.13 (8) T_2=.18 (5) T_3=.06 (1) T_4=.00 (0)	T_1=**.71 (45)** T_2=**.64 (18)** T_3=**.75 (12)** T_4=**1.00 (8)**	T_1=.16 (10) T_2=.14 (4) T_3=.19 (3) T_4=.00 (0)
Known-unfamiliar	T_1=.06 (3) T_2=.03 (1) T_3=.09 (2) T_4=.00 (0)	T_1=.02 (1) T_2=.11 (4) T_3=.09 (2) T_4=.07 (1)	T_1=.10 (5) T_2=.14 (5) T_3=.00 (0) T_4=.00 (0)	T_1=**.82 (42)** T_2=**.73 (27)** T_3=**.82 (18)** T_4=**.93 (14)**

Note: Probabilities are shown, with sample size in brackets.

a. T_1 = Transition 1 (n = 209), T_2 = Transition 2 (n = 100), T_3 = Transition 3 (n = 63), T_4 = Transition 4 (n = 35).
b. T_1 = Transition 1 (n = 209), T_2 = Transition 2 (n = 100), T_3 = Transition 3 (n = 64), T_4 = Transition 4 (n = 35).
c. T_1 = Transition 1 (n = 210), T_2 = Transition 2 (n = 100), T_3 = Transition 3 (n = 64), T_4 = Transition 4 (n = 36).

Table 7.2 Crime-Transitions Based on Offense Characteristics

Presence of Physical Contact Between Offender and Victim[a]

	Hands-off (T_{+1})	Hands-on (T_{+1})
Hands-off	T_1 = .50 (6) T_2 = .71 (5) T_3 = .71 (5) T_4 = .75 (3)	T_1 = .50 (6) T_2 = .29 (2) T_3 = .29 (2) T_4 = .25 (1)
Hands-on	T_1 = .05 (10) T_2 = .02 (2) T_3 = .04 (2) T_4 = .12 (4)	**T_1 = .95 (188) T_2 = .98 (90)** **T_3 = .96 (53) T_4 = .88 (29)**

Level of Intrusiveness Achieved[b]

	Fondling, rubbing, masturbation (T_{+1})	Oral sex (T_{+1})	Penetration (T_{+1})
Fondling, rubbing, masturbation	**T_1 = .48 (21) T_2 = .76 (19)** **T_3 = .65 (13) T_4 = .83 (10)**	T_1 = .18 (8) T_2 = .04 (1) T_3 = .10 (2) T_4 = .08 (1)	T_1 = .34 (15) T_2 = .20 (5) T_3 = .25 (5) T_4 = .08 (1)
Oral sex	T_1 = .21 (7) T_2 = .15 (4) T_3 = .33 (4) T_4 = .17 (1)	**T_1 = .64 (21) T_2 = .50 (13)** **T_3 = .50 (6) T_4 = .68 (4)**	T_1 = .15 (5) T_2 = .35 (9) T_3 = .17 (2) T_4 = .17 (1)
Penetration	T_1 = .23 (25) T_2 = .28 (11) T_3 = .10 (2) T_4 = .27 (3)	T_1 = .15 (17) T_2 = .05 (2) T_3 = .24 (5) T_4 = .27 (3)	**T_1 = .62 (69) T_2 = .67 (26)** **T_3 = .67 (14) T_4 = .46 (5)**

Physical Force Adopted to Commit the Offense[c]

	No force (T_{+1})	Only force necessary (T_{+1})	Excessive force (T_{+1})
No force	**T_1 = .90 (101) T_2 = .95 (56)** **T_3 = .95 (38) T_4 = .86 (18)**	T_1 = .05 (5) T_2 = .05 (3) T_3 = .03 (1) T_4 = .14 (3)	T_1 = .05 (6) T_2 = .00 (0) T_3 = .03 (1) T_4 = .00 (0)
Only force necessary	T_1 = .06 (4) T_2 = .04 (1) T_3 = .00 (0) T_4 = .17 (2)	**T_1 = .88 (56) T_2 = .88 (22)** **T_3 = .92 (12) T_4 = .75 (9)**	T_1 = .06 (4) T_2 = .08 (2) T_3 = .08 (1) T_4 = .08 (1)
Excessive force	T_1 = .03 (1) T_2 = .07 (1) T_3 = .00 (0) T_4 = .00 (0)	T_1 = .24 (8) T_2 = .07 (1) T_3 = .10 (1) T_4 = .00 (0)	**T_1 = .74 (25) T_2 = .86 (12)** **T_3 = .90 (9) T_4 = 1.00 (3)**

Note: Probabilities are shown, with sample size in brackets.

[a] T_1 = Transition 1 (n = 210), T_2 = Transition 2 (n = 99), T_3 = Transition 3 (n = 62), T_4 = Transition 4 (n = 37).

[b] T_1 = Transition 1 (n = 188), T_2 = Transition 2 (n = 90), T_3 = Transition 3 (n = 53), T_4 = Transition 4 (n = 29).

Cases that included hands-off offenses were excluded from this analysis.

[c] T_1 = Transition 1 (n = 210), T_2 = Transition 2 (n = 98), T_3 = Transition 3 (n = 63), T_4 = Transition 4 (n = 36).

one transition to another especially for hands-on offenses. For offenders who committed hands-on offense, the probability of repeating the same pattern across crimes remained higher than .88. Although the number of offenders who committed hands-off offense is very small, 50% of them committed hands-on offense at their second crime, suggesting a low rate of specialization among those offenders. Thereafter, these offenders remained more stable from one crime to the next (range = .71–.75). At the opposite of the offense nature, the level of intrusiveness achieved in the offense varied considerably over the sequence of crimes, suggesting more evidence of crime-switching patterns. Only 48% of offenders who fondled, rubbed, and/or masturbated their victim for their first crime did so in their second. Thereafter, the probability of subsequently achieving these sexual behaviors are 76%, 65%, and 83% in the second, third, and fourth transitions, respectively, showing a low rate of specialization. If switching did occur, those offenders were more likely to perform penetration (range = .08–.34) rather than oral-genital sex (range = .04–.18), thus not following a gradual escalation in the intrusiveness of sexual behaviors achieved. However, offenders who performed more intrusive sexual behaviors, that is, oral-genital sex (range = .50–.68) and penetration (range = .46–.67) showed a higher rate of specialization and thus more stability across crimes than those who first adopted less intrusive sexual behaviors. It should be noted that for offenders who performed more intrusive sexual behaviors, percentages across transitions are quite low, suggesting that offenders are not necessarily achieving more intrusive sexual behaviors from one crime to the next. Much like the nature of offense, evidence for stability and specialization were found for the level of physical force adopted during the offense. Offenders who did not adopt physical force during their first crime repeated this pattern over the sequence of crimes (range = .86–.95). A quite similar pattern is observed for both offenders who adopted only the force necessary to commit the offense (range = .75–.92) and those who used excessive force (range = .74–1.00). In the latter case, however, when switching did occur, offenders who used excessive force were more likely to only adopt the physical force necessary to commit the offense (range = .00–.24) rather than using no force (range = .00–.07). Overall, results suggest that offenders are quite stable regarding the level of physical force adopted during the offense.

The Diversity Index

Bivariate Analyses

Table 7.3 presents the means and standard deviations (bottom row) of the five diversity indexes computed as well the bivariate relationships between those indexes and the characteristics of the offenders. Overall, the diversity indexes did not seem to vary according to the socio-demographic characteristics of the

Table 7.3	Bivariate Associations Between Diversity Indexes and Individual Characteristics				
	Diversity Indexes for Victim's Characteristics[c]			Diversity Indexes for Offense Characteristics[c]	
	Gender	Age	Relationship	Intrusiveness	Force
Age[a]	.01	−.12[†]	.11	.04	−.16*
Ethnicity (Caucasian)[b]	−.92	−.82	−.65	−.74	−.36
Marital Status (Single)[b]	−.56	−.66	−1.12	−.47	−.17
Education (Elementary)[b]	−1.48	−1.86[†]	−.94	−.78	−1.48
Number of Convictions[a]	.01	−.01	−.10	−.02	.10
Number of Victims[a]	.04	.10	.17*	.15*	−.03
Level of Sexualization[a]	−.04	.06	−.09	.19**	.05
Low Self-control[a]	.01	.14*	−.08	.05	.15*
N	214	213	214	216	216
Mean	.07	.17	.17	.26	.09
Standard deviation	.16	.23	.23	.25	.18
Range	.00–.50	.00–.67	.00–.67	.00–.75	.00–.63

[a]Continuous variables tested with Pearson's r.
[b]Categorical variables tested with Mann-Whitney U. Z scores are presented.
[c]Logarithmic transformations were used on each of the diversity indexes for bivariate analyses.
[†]$P < .10$; *$P < .05$; **$P < .01$

offenders. Younger offenders appeared to be more versatile in terms of the level of physical force used to commit the offense, suggesting that older offenders might be more specialized in that regard. There was also a tendency for younger offenders to be more versatile as to the age of the victims selected, but the effect was only marginally significant. Moreover, less educated offenders tended to be more versatile in terms of the nature of relationship with their victims, but the effect was small and marginally significant. Interestingly, the number of convictions was not significantly related to any of the diversity indexes. In other words, the tendency to be more versatile in sexual offending was relatively independent of the tendency to re-offend for any type of crime. On the other hand, versatility as to the nature of the relationship with the victim and sexual intrusiveness were both significantly related to the number of victims. In other words, as the frequency of sexual offending increases, offenders appeared to be more versatile in terms of the victim they select (e.g., stranger, intrafamilial, etc.) and the nature of the sexual acts being committed (i.e., hands-off, fondling, etc.). Level of sexualization was also significantly related to the diversity index of sexual intrusiveness suggesting that offenders showing a higher level of sexualization are more likely to have a wider repertoire of sexual acts being committed across offenses. Sexualization was not significantly related to any other diversity index. Finally, low self-control was significantly related to both the diversity index of age and level of force used. Hence, offenders with lower level of self-control were more likely to offend against more than one age category as well as using a wider range of level of physical force to commit their crime.

Multivariate Analyses

Multivariate analyses were conducted in order to find whether self-control and sexualization increased versatility in sexual offending independently of socio-demographic and offending characteristics. Considering that the skewed distribution of the five diversity index violated the assumption of normal distribution in OLS regression, we used probit regression models. **Table 7.4** presents results of the probit regression models for each of the five diversity indices. Probit coefficients and the associated standard errors are reported for each independent variable entered in the regression model. For each regression model, we controlled for the other diversity indices in order to avoid spurious relationships. Looking at the results from the probit regression models, different sets of predictors emerged for the five diversity indices. For the diversity index of gender, only one factor emerged as statistically significant, that is, the diversity index of sexual intrusiveness. For the age of the victim, six of the twelve factors entered in the model were statistically related to a higher score on the diversity index. Being Caucasian with a lower school achievement, a lower number of convictions, and a higher number of victims, with higher scores on both the scale of low self-control and the diversity index of violence were statistically associated with a tendency to offend against more than one age category. Only one factor was significantly related to the offender-victim relationship diversity index. Those offenders with more victims were more likely to offend against more than one category of victim. Four of the twelve factors entered in the probit regression model were related to the diversity index of sexual intrusiveness. A higher number of victims, a higher level of sexualization as well as higher scores on the diversity index of gender and force used to commit the sex crime were all related to more versatility as to the nature of sexual acts committed to the victim across offenses. Finally, only one of the twelve factors emerged as a significant predictor of the diversity index of force used to commit the sex crime. Indeed, higher scores on the diversity index of sexual intrusiveness were associated with higher scores on the diversity of violence.

Table 7.4 Prediction of Diversity Indices Using Probit Regression Models

	Diversity Indexes for Victim's Characteristics[c]			Diversity Indexes for Offense Characteristics[c]	
	Gender	Age	Relationship	Intrusiveness	Force
Age	−.01 (.14)	−.01 (.01)	.00 (.04)	.00 (.01)	−.01 (.01)
Ethnicity (Caucasian)	.56 (.43)	.83 (.37)*	.29 (.34)	−.17 (.34)	.19 (.41)
Marital Status (Single)	−.11 (.24)	.04 (.21)	−.05 (.21)	.12 (.21)	−.16 (.24)
Education (Elementary)	.32 (.26)	.47 (.23)*	.28 (.22)	.40 (.23)+	−.32 (.28)
Number of Convictions	−.05 (.14)	−.32 (.12)**	.09 (.12)	−.10 (.12)	.07 (.14)
Number of Victims	.13 (.10)	.26 (.09)**	.22 (.09)*	.21 (.09)*	.01 (.10)
High Sexualization	−.06 (.06)	−.02 (.05)	−.04 (.05)	.19 (.05)***	−.05 (.06)
Low Self-control	.05 (.09)	.15 (.07)*	−.05 (.08)	.02 (.07)	.04 (.08)
Gender Diversity Index (log)	–	−.57 (.74)	.09 (.68)	1.96 (.72)**	−.65 (.82)
Age Diversity Index (log)	−.46 (.62)	–	−.11 (.52)	−.14 (.53)	−.02 (.01)+
Relationship Diversity Index (log)	−.11 (.58)	−.18 (.51)	–	.66 (.50)	.63 (.57)
Intrusiveness Diversity Index (log)	1.50 (.58)*	−.32 (.50)	.77 (.49)	–	1.24 (.57)*
Force Diversity Index (log)	−.96 (.82)	1.26 (.64)*	.66 (.63)	1.44 (.67)*	–
N	209	209	209	209	209
Goodness-of-fit	215.61	204.22	209.32	205.14	207.94
(df)	(196)	(196)	(196)	(196)	(196)

+P < .10, *P < .05, **P < .01, ***P < .001

■ Discussion

Following the footsteps of criminal career researchers, the analytical strategy used here help us in identifying six main conclusions about crime-switching patterns and specialization in sexual offending. First, crime-switching in sex offending is rather multidimensional. Clearly, diversity index were relatively independent from one another and associated with different individual characteristics. Therefore, contrary to Abel and Rouleau's observations,[11] we found little evidence supporting their conclusion that sex offenders offend against different types of victims in different contexts. Second, the level of crime-switching varies from one crime-type to another. On one hand of the continuum, victim's gender and level of physical force are relatively stable across crime-transitions, while on the opposite end of the continuum, the victim's age and sexual intrusiveness involves more crime-switching. Interestingly, it is those two dimensions, for which more evidence of crime-switching was found, that were more strongly related with individual characteristics of the offenders. Third, the notion of preference is relevant and of importance in the understanding of persistence in sexual offending. We thus concur with Soothill and his colleagues to a certain extent in that the level of stability and specialization found for certain aspects of offending (e.g., targeting children) suggest that it is far from being purely random upon certain situational contingencies.[5] Although the notion of preference might first appear to be in contradiction with the impulsive nature of those crimes, the notion of self-control remains of importance, since one must recognize an opportunity as such before acting upon it. Fourth, the concept of sex surrogate might also play a part in stimulating crime-switching. This appears to be especially true for those having offended against adolescent victims, who might represent the second best option in the absence of the preferred victim-type (i.e., children or adults). This situation appears to be true for both child molesters and rapists. Of importance, and in keeping with the sex surrogate hypothesis, is that very few child molesters also offended against adults and vice-versa. Fifth, there is some commonality between crime switching patterns as some diversity indexes tend to co-vary together. It thus raises the possibility that the same factors (not tested here) might be linked to different crime-switching patterns, such as force and intrusiveness. Sixth, versatility appears to be increasing as a function of repetition of the sexually deviant behavior, especially for victim's age, offender-victim relationship and sexual intrusiveness. The more they offend against different victims, the more their sexual criminal repertoire tends to diversify. This might partly explain discrepancies reported in earlier studies as clinical samples including more serious and persistent offenders should report more evidence of crime-switching. In order to interpret those findings we offer some hypotheses drawn from the rational-choice theory model of offending.

Crime Switching and Rational Choice

Rational choice approach theorists propose different offending models, each implying a different decision process influenced by a different set of factors. One of those is the continuing involvement model which refers to the continuation stage of the offender's criminal career. Clarke and Cornish stipulate that as a result of generally positive reinforcement, the frequency of offending increases until it reaches some optimum level.[31] Thus, the rewards of crime (e.g., money, dominance over others, sexual gratification) are of special importance in continuance. Apart from situational variables such as opportunities, and inducements that trigger the decision to commit a crime, Clarke and Cornish also summarize three categories of variables of importance at this stage of the criminal career: 1) increase in professionalism or offending experience, 2) changes in lifestyles and values (e.g., enjoyment of this "delinquent" life, development of justifications for criminal behavior), and 3) changes in peer group (networks of delinquent peers).[31] Following this perspective, a key result emerging from our study is that each polymorphism indicator seems to involve a different continuation process as predicted by a different set of variables. Indicators that showed much variability across offenses are the age of the victim and the level of sexual behavior intrusiveness achieved in the offense. More specifically, the tendency to offend against more than one age category across sexual offenses could be viewed as a "general deviance" type of continuation while the tendency to achieve a different level of sexual intrusiveness from one crime to the next may be considered as a "predation" type of continuation in crime.

The tendency to offend against more than one age category is driven principally by factors such as a high level of low self-control, and the tendency to be versatile across offenses in terms of the level of force adopted to commit the crime. Offenders who sexually abuse victims regardless of their age (children, adolescents, women) may be versatile offenders overall—that is, offenders who commit a wide range of criminal acts with no strong inclination to specialize in a specific type of crime or pattern of criminal acts. As they are characterized by low self-control, they may not be able to resist crime opportunities in order to satisfy their immediate and various needs (e.g., money, sexual gratification, dominance over others), but rather exploit every target or victim regardless of their characteristics. In that matter, the decision to sexually abuse regardless of the age of the victim might simply be spontaneous and the consequence of crime opportunities low self-control offenders encounter in the course of their "career." However, this interpretation is somewhat simplistic. One should note that these offenders are versatile in the level of force they employed to commit their crime, suggesting that skills are at least required in some offenses. More importantly, one should note that offenders who abused an adult or a child initially tend to switch to adolescent victims as a sex surrogate, suggesting that the phenomenon of crime-switching regarding the age is not totally random. Offenders may decide to look first at whether they can satisfy their needs with a victim that most closely resembles their initial victims in terms of physical attractiveness. Thus, offenders are versatile enough to switch to adolescent victims, but not totally as they still follow a certain path of stability. In other words, low self-control would not by itself account for the tendency to offend against more than one age category, but rather contributes to this type of continuance. Nonetheless, this type of involvement in sexual offending could be referred to as a "general deviance" type of continuation.

Offenders who achieve a different level of sexual intrusiveness across offenses are principally characterized by high sexualization, the tendency to abuse victims of both gender, and to adopt a different level of physical force across offenses. It could be argued that these offenders are also versatile, but low self-control is not predictive of the intrusiveness diversity. Recall that high sexualization refers to a disinhibited sexuality characterized by sexual preoccupation, sexual compulsivity, and impersonal sex. Having a higher level of sexualization, these offenders instead represent a group more oriented toward committing sex offenses which is supported by the association found between high sexualization and the frequency of sexual offending within the same sample of offenders. Thus, it is expected that those individuals experience more difficulties in controlling their sexual urges and exploit different opportunities to satisfy these urges, which might also explain why they tend to abuse victims of both gender. Furthermore, given the predictive nature of the level of physical force diversity (i.e., no force, minimum force, excessive force), one could also expect that those offenders acquired different and effective means to commit their crime and satisfy their sexual needs. Recent evidence suggests that modus operandi strategies are purposeful, that is the more strategic offenders are the most efficient in increasing victim participation and sexual intrusiveness during sexual episodes.[32] The capacity to adopt efficient strategies for the purpose of achieving sexual gratification emerges as of special significance in that continuance process. In fact, across offenses, successive trials may lead offenders toward more intrusive sexual behaviors such as penetration. This may in turn reinforce sexual offending as a mean to satisfy sexual needs especially for those characterized by a high sexualization. In this continuance process, we might be somewhat in the presence of an interdependence cycle of offending between high sexualization (the propensity), force diversity (the means), and sexual intrusiveness diversity (the outcome). Disinhibited sexuality combined to force diversity would favor the commission of a wider variety of sexual behaviors in terms of intrusiveness which in consequence would contribute to increase further disinhibition and so on. Although we cannot adequately verify this hypothesis in this study, the continuance phenomenon resulting from positive reinforcement highlighted by Clarke and Cornish is clearly of importance here.[31] This type of pursuing sexual offending in the course of a criminal career could be referred as a "predation" type of continuation in crime. Finally, it should be noted that evidence of sexual intrusiveness versatility raises doubts concerning the possibility that sexual offenders may limit themselves to a specific type of sexual behavior across offenses. Hence, recall that gender diversity predicts the intrusiveness diversity index. If one assumes that offenses are purposive and that positive reinforcement might occur, this possibility is rather unlikely.

Like any study, the present investigation is not without methodological limitations. This is an exploratory study and the findings should be interpreted as such. It is based on a small sample of Canadian federal inmates, which may not be representative of all sex offenders. Furthermore, it is possible that the retrospective and self-reported nature of the data used might have favored some biases in the reporting of sex crimes. The use of official data as well, however, might have reduced the impact of those biases. Also, this study is based on offending data that is censored since the criminal activity of the offenders included in the study is still active. Since some of the offenders will eventually re-offend, it is important to consider that our study only looks at a snapshot of the sexual criminal activity of adult sex offenders.

References

1. Lussier, P. (2005). The criminal activity of sexual offenders in adulthood: Revisiting the specialization debate. *Sexual Abuse: J Res Treatm* 17:269–292.
2. Hanson, R. K., Morton-Bourgon, K. E. (2005). The characteristics of persistent sexual offenders: A meta-analysis of recidivism studies. *J Consult Clin Psychol* 73:1154–1163.
3. Beech, A. R., Ward, T. (2004). The integration of etiology and risk in sexual offenders: A theoretical framework. *Aggress Violent Behav* 10:31–63.
4. Guay, J. P., Proulx, J., Cusson, M., Ouimet, M. (2001). Victim-choice polymorphia among serious sex offenders. *Arch Sexual Behav* 30:521–533.
5. Soothill, K., Francis, B., Sanderson, B., Ackerley, E. (2000). Sex offenders: Specialists, generalists or both? *Br J Criminol* 40:56–67.
6. Radzinowicz, L. (1957). *Sexual Offences: A Report of the Cambridge Department of Criminal Justice*. London: MacMillan.
7. Gebhard, P. H., Gagnon, J. H., Pomeroy, W. B., Christensen, C. V. (1964). *Sex Offenders: An Analysis of Types*. New York: Harper & Row.
8. Cann, J. Friendship, C., Gonza, L. (2007). Assessing crossover in a sample of sexual offenders with multiple victims. *Legal Criminol Psychol* 12:149–163.
9. Weinrott, M. R., Saylor, M. (1991). Self-report of crimes committed by sex offenders. *J Interpers Viol* 6:286–300.

10. Heil, P., Ahlmeyer, S., Simons, D. (2003). Crossover sexual offenses. *Sexual Abuse: J Res Treat* 15:221–236.

11. Abel, G. G., Rouleau, J. L. (1990). The nature and extent of sexual assault. Pp. 9–22 in W. L. Marshall, D. R. Laws, H. E. Barbaree (Eds.), *Handbook of Sexual Assault: Issues, Theories and Treatment of the Offender*. New York: Plenum Press.

12. Marshall, W. L. (2007). Diagnostic issues, multiple paraphilias, and co-morbid disorders in sexual offenders: Their incidence and treatment. *Aggress Viol Behav* 12:16–35.

13. Bradford, J. M., Boulet, J., Pawlak, A. (1992). The paraphilias: A multiplicity of deviant behaviors. *Can J Psychiatr* 37:104–108.

14. Groth, A. N., Birnbaum H. J. (1979). *Men Who Rape*. New York: Plenum Press.

15. Knight, R. A., Prentky, R. A. (1990). Classifying sexual offenders: The development and corroboration of taxonomic models. Pp. 23–54 in W. L. Marshall, D. R. Laws, H. E. Barbaree (Eds.), *Handbook of Sexual Assault: Issues, Theories and Treatment of the Offender*. New York: Plenum Press.

16. Kafka, M. P. (1997). Hypersexual desire in males: An operational definition and clinical implications for males with paraphilias and paraphilia-related disorders. *Arch Sexual Behav* 26:505–526.

17. Knight, R. A., Sims-Knight, J. E. (2003). Developmental antecedents of sexual coercion against women: Testing of alternative hypotheses with structural equation modeling. Pp. 72–85 in R. A. Prentky, E. S. Janus, M. Seto (Eds.), *Sexual Coercive Behavior: Understanding and Management*. New York: New York Academy of Sciences.

18. Lussier, P., Leclerc, B., Cale, J., Proulx, J. (2007). Developmental pathways of deviance in adult sex offenders. *Crim Justice Behav* (in press).

19. Smallbone, S. W., Wortley, R. K. (2004). Criminal diversity and paraphilic interests among adult males convicted of sexual offenses against children. *Int J Offender Therap Compar Criminol* 48:175–188.

20. Lussier, P., LeBlanc, M., Proulx, J. (2005). The generality of criminal behavior: A confirmatory factor analysis of the criminal activity of sex offenders in adulthood. *J Crim Justice* 33:177–189.

21. Gottfredson, M., Hirschi, T. (1990). *A General Theory of Crime*. Stanford, CA: Stanford University Press.

22. Lussier, P., Proulx, J., LeBlanc, M. (2005). Criminal propensity, deviant sexual interests and criminal activity of sexual aggressors against women: A comparison of explanatory models. *Criminology* 43:249–281.

23. Sjöstedt, G., Långström, N., Sturidsson, K., Grann, M. (2004). Stability of modus operandi in sexual offending. *Crim Justice Behav* 31:609–623.

24. Farrington, D. P., Snyder, H. N., Finnegan, T. A. (1988). Specialization in juvenile court careers. *Criminology* 26:461–488.

References

References

25. Hanson, R. K., Bussiere, M. T. (1998). Predicting relapse: A meta-analysis of sexual offender recidivism studies. *J Consult Clin Psychol* 61:646–652.
26. Thornton, D. (2006). Age and sexual recidivism: A variable connection. *Sexual Abuse: J Res Treat* 18:123–135.
27. Doren, D. (2006). What do we know about the effect of aging on recidivism risk for sexual offenders? *Sexual Abuse: J Res Treat* 18:137–157.
28. Agresti, A., Agresti, B. F. (1978). Statistical analysis of qualitative variation. *Sociol Methodol* 9:204–237.
29. Piquero, A., Paternoster, R., Mazerolle, P., et al. (1999). Onset age and offense specialization. *J Res Crime Delinq* 36:275–299.
30. Sullivan, C. J., McGloin, J. M., Pratt, T., Piquero, A. (2006). Rethinking the "norm" of offender generality: Investigating specialization in the short-term. *Criminology* 44:199–233.
31. Clarke, R. V., Cornish, D. B. (1985). Modeling offenders' decisions: A framework for research and policy. Pp. 147–185 in M. Tonry, N. Morris (Eds.), *Crime and Justice: An Annual Review of Research*. Vol. 6. Chicago: University of Chicago Press.
32. Leclerc, B., Tremblay, P. (2007). Strategic behavior in adolescent sexual offenses against children: Linking modus operandi to sexual behaviors. *Sexual Abuse: J Res Treat* 19:23–41.

Comparing Women and Men Who Kill

8

Jennifer Schwartz
Washington State University

Homicide is a rare occurrence, especially among women. But how rare? Are some women more likely to kill than other women? Have women increased their involvement in homicide as they've increased their involvement in paid work and other previously male domains? When women kill, do they go about it differently than men? How does being a woman, or being a man, shape the *ways* in which people commit homicide? What accounts for the large difference in male and female homicide offending? Do women and men kill for the same reasons or do sources of homicide differ by gender? This chapter will review the literature on homicide offending and present data from the *Supplementary Homicide Reports* to address these questions about similarities and differences in female and male homicide offending.

Less than 1% of all crimes committed last year were homicide offenses. This crime nonetheless is the focus of much attention from the media and from criminologists who systematically study crime, in part because of the severity of the offense. Criminologists also study homicide because it is the most accurately measured offense and the offense for which we have the most statistical information at the national level. Moreover, the characteristics of homicide events are very similar to those for aggravated assault and other forms of violence. Therefore, in studying homicide offending, we also learn about the causes and contexts of violence more generally. In exploring female and male homicide patterns, we get a more holistic picture of violent offending as well as a sense of how similar or different the behaviors of the two sexes are. It should be noted, however, that gender differences are *more* apparent for offenses that are more serious in nature; gender similarities are greatest for minor sorts of violence, such as simple assault.

The *Supplementary Homicide Reports* (SHR) are official, police-recorded statistics on almost all murders and non-negligent manslaughter incidents in the United States. Police record information on a voluntary basis on over 90% of the homicides of which they are aware. The FBI has accurately and consistently compiled these reports since the late 1970s. The reports include demographic characteristics of the victims and offenders, their relationship to one another, and the situational features of the homicide incident, such as weapon used, motives, or circumstances. Because the SHR data include information on homicides still under investigation, information is incomplete for about 25% of the cases. Therefore, the involvement of young males is probably understated because they are more typically the perpetrators in the more difficult-to-solve stranger homicide cases. By using advanced statistical procedures to gain precision, we can "guess" the characteristics of offenders based on their victims, minimizing the missing data problem.[1] Therefore, the SHR data present a fairly detailed nationwide portrait of homicide incidents, offenders, and victims. These data also allow researchers to describe changes in homicide offending over time. The SHR data are used to detail the extent of female and male homicide offending. Then, in tandem with more detailed case analyses, we generate a portrait of the female and male homicide offenders.

■ Extent of Female and Male Homicide Offending

Of the 16,097 homicide victims identified in 2004, the most recent year for which FBI data are available, 3541 (22%) were women. Male and female victimization rates per 100,000 were 8.7 and 2.4, respectively. As demonstrated by these statistics, homicide is a rare phenomenon. In comparison, deaths resulting from heart disease, accidents, and pneumonia are all far more common than deaths resulting from homicide, but in all of these scenarios—including homicide—the death rate for men far exceeds the death rate for women. This gender disparity is even larger for homicide offending. In 2004, police were able to identify 18,196 homicide offenders, 16,458 of whom were men and 1,738 of whom were women. Homicide offending rates for 2004 were 11.5 per 100,000 men and 1.2 per 100,000 women. Females make up only 10% of homicide offenders. Thus, the large majority of perpetrators and victims of homicide are men.

Among both female and male homicide offenders, young adults (ages 18–24) have the highest rates of offending. Classified by gender and race, black males have higher homicide rates than white males, and black females have higher homicide rates than white females. Taken together, the offending rates of adolescent white girls (14–17) are exceptionally low—fewer than 1 girl in 100,000 is arrested for homicide. Black males aged 18–24 have the highest homicide offending rates (185 per 100,000). In between the two extremes are homicide rates of white males followed by black females. Within race groups, women make up a similar proportion of all homicide offenders—11% of white and 8% of black homicide offenders are women.

Homicide offending peaked in the early 1990s and has since declined so that current rates are lower than those in the early 1980s.[2] Rates of offending by black males dropped sharply in the mid-1990s and continue to decline, albeit at a slower pace. The trends of white males mirrored those of black males, but the declines were not as steep and seem to have leveled off by the early 2000s. The homicide rates of black and white females match one another and are characterized by steady declines since the 1980s. Driving the downward trend is a large drop in women's rates of intimate-partner homicide (we discuss trends in various sorts of homicide in more detail later in this chapter). The homicide rates of 14–17-year-olds are slightly elevated in the early 1990s; adolescent rates are less driven by intimate-partner homicide, in part because of lower exposure to intimate partners and lesser access to guns than other subgroups.

Generally female trends in homicide mirror male trends in homicide, though women's involvement has been and remains very low in comparison to men. In fact, female representation among homicide offenders is somewhat lower today than it was almost 25 years ago (about 13% in 1980 compared to about 11% today). This consistency holds across age groups. Female representation dropped most sharply in the early 1990s when male rates were rapidly increasing, but the continued lower representation of females indicates female rates moved in tandem with male rates. The gender gap for 14–17-year-olds temporarily narrowed in the late 1990s and early 2000 because female declines were not as dramatic as male declines in that age group. The main conclusion, though, is that the gender gap in homicide has *widened* somewhat since the 1980s for all age- and race-groups.

The gender gap was declining even when effects of the women's movement might have been strongest in the 1980s and when women's arrest rates for assault were rising in the early 1990s. This stability in the gender gap is at odds with the widely held perception that women are becoming more violent, as suggested by the narrowing gender gap in arrests for assault offenses.[3] Some have interpreted increases in women's assault arrests as the ill effects of changing gender roles that have made female behaviors more masculine. Overall trends in homicide suggest otherwise.

In this chapter, however, we further explore the idea that changing gender roles have altered the context of women's offending. If this is the case, we would expect women to increasingly kill strangers in felony-related homicides—in the past, a distinctly male scenario. Or, perhaps female–female violence would be more likely as women start to interact with one another more like men do, including using violence to solve problems. On the other hand, if gender roles have *not* changed, or have not changed in a way that affects homicide and violent crime, we'd expect stability in the context of women's and men's offending. We generate and examine statistics that indicate if the extent and type of homicide committed by women and men have changed from 1980 to the present. Aside from addressing the theoretical debate regarding the effects of social change on women's homicide offending patterns, there are other good reasons to study female homicide, despite its statistical rarity.

■ Why Study Female Homicide?

Some might question why we need to study female homicide. There are a number of reasons why such study is necessary. First, despite its low incidence, women's homicide offending may have wider-reaching consequences for future crime trends than male offending because women are the primary caregivers for children in our society. Incarcerated female homicide offenders are more likely to leave children behind compared to other types of female offenders and compared to male offenders of all types. Though obviously it is not desirable for children to have homicidal mothers, female offenders tend to direct their aggression against abusive partners rather than their children, and most do not have any prior arrests.

Second, no other violent crime is measured as accurately and precisely as homicide offending, making homicide a good barometer for violent offending generally, despite homicide's comparatively low frequency. Indeed, many criminologists consider homicide to be an overly successful assault. Therefore, similar distributional patterns in victim–offender relationship, motive, and so forth, likely hold for assault offending. Note, however, that the gender gap systematically narrows as less serious violence is considered so that women are far more involved in simple assault (~25% of arrests), which includes minor harm such as scratching or shoving, versus aggravated assault (~20%) or homicide (~10%).

Third, studying female homicide offending, and comparative research more generally, can help clarify our current understanding of causes of violent offending. If women's homicide patterns do not fit with dominant theories of crime, these discrepancies should challenge criminologists to refine their explanations of criminal offending. Moreover, studying female homicide offending is useful in and of itself for further understanding and demonstrating the pervasive influence of gender on behavior, even in extreme actions like taking the life of another. Men and women kill in ways that reflect their gender roles. We now explore patterns of female and male homicide to demonstrate this point.

■ Women's and Men's Offending Patterns: A Statistical Comparison

Criminologists can characterize female and male homicide offending as either very similar or very different from one another depending on the lens one uses to view homicide offending. There are many ways to study gender differences in homicide offending, ranging from interviews with convicted offenders, to in-depth analyses of legal documents generated in the criminal justice system, to secondary data analysis of police records. Each methodology produces a slightly different picture of gender and homicide, making it important to look at multiple sources of evidence. Regardless of methodology, findings must be interpreted, and one's theoretical orientation to gender differences—whether one views women and men as fundamentally alike or essentially different—likely colors this interpretation. The truth is probably somewhere in the middle—there are both gender similarities and differences in homicide offending. Consider the following prototypical examples of a male homicide versus a female homicide:

> *The offender, Stephen, and the victim, Mark, have each spent the evening drinking in bars with friends before happening to go to the same nightclub. By this time, about 1 a.m., both men were drunk. Stephen and Mark had seen each other around before, but didn't really know each other. For reasons that are not obvious, Mark, with his friends watching nearby, makes repeated derogatory comments to Stephen. Mark had a reputation for getting into fights. Stephen, with his friends looking on, tells Mark to "fuck off" and, on a subsequent occasion, warns him he'll hit him if Mark provokes him again. Stephen has been arrested before, but has not served time for a violent offense. Mark makes a verbal threat, Stephen lands one solid blow to Mark's face, and Mark falls to the floor unconscious. Mark dies of a brain hemorrhage.[4]*

> *During five years of marriage, both the offender and her husband drank heavily. Things were OK until the last year of marriage, when he would drink and become violent. He would beat her, sometimes to the point of where she had to go to the emergency room of a local hospital. . . . One night, after he had been drinking to excess, he heard her talking on the telephone. He thought it was another man and became enraged. He began to strangle her with the telephone cord. She freed herself and ran into the kitchen. He started to strangle her with his hands. She reached into the sink where she found a knife that she used to stab him to death.[5]*

Based on these two cases, how alike or different are these two homicide cases? The two events are similar in that neither homicide was planned but rather resulted from an argument, spurred in part by the use of alcohol, which escalated into physical violence. Both incidents took place late at night, probably on a weekend. Both victims were male and, to some extent, provoked their attack. The circumstances surrounding these two deaths, however, might also be characterized as very different. The male's victim is a casual acquaintance or stranger, whereas the female offender was married to her victim. Though the female offender could claim self-defense and had no prior record, the male offender was not protecting himself, and both he and the victim had previous involvements with the law. Finally, the location of the two events differed—the female offender killed at home, and the male offender in public at a bar. We more systematically explore these differences in delineating a portrait of male and female homicide offenders, by drawing on the *Supplementary Homicide Reports*.

Table 8.1 displays female and male rates (columns 1–6), which are standardized measures of the extent of various types of homicide, the gender gap (columns 7–9), a standardized measure of female representation in homicide offending relative to males, and offender profile percentages (columns 10–15), which reveal the distribution of homicide characteristics among women or men. Examining changes in the gender gap within each category of homicide is instructive because it gives an indication of women's relative involvement compared to men in each sort of homicide and whether there have been gender-specific changes in the nature of homicide offending over time. We also discuss the rates underlying these trends and, in this way, succinctly summarize changes in homicide offending over time. The offender profiles are useful for understanding if the composition of female homicide offenders has changed over time—such as toward more female-on-female violence or toward greater victimization of strangers. Following the presentation of statistical portraits of female and male offenders, we utilize case studies and qualitative analyses to gain a more in-depth picture of typical female and male homicide offenders. Throughout, we point out gender differences and similarities.

Victim-Offender Relationship

Perhaps the most crucial gender difference in homicide offending is in who women and men kill. Overwhelmingly, females kill family members. In fact, almost 60% of female homicide offenders kill an intimate partner, child, or other family member. Men, in comparison, kill a family member about 20% of the time. In almost one-third of female homicides, her victim is a boyfriend, husband, or former partner. Children are the next most common targets of women's homicide (19%). In comparison, about 13% of men's homicides are against intimates and 3% are against children. Consequently, the large majority of women's victims,

Table 8.1 Male and Female Homicide Rates per 100,000, Female Percentages, and Offender Profile Percentages: 1980, 1990, 2003

Homicide Type	Male Rates[a]			Female Rates[a]			Female Percentage[b]			Profile Percentage, Males[c]			Profile Percentage, Females[c]		
	(1) 1980	(2) 1990	(3) 2003	(4) 1980	(5) 1990	(6) 2003	(7) 1980	(8) 1990	(9) 2003	(10) 1980	(11) 1990	(12) 2003	(13) 1980	(14) 1990	(15) 2003
Victim-Offender Relationship															
Stranger	10.7	12.3	5.1	0.53	0.40	0.31	5	3	6	25	27	29	7	7	10
Acquaintance	22.6	24.8	8.5	2.2	2.0	1.0	9	7	11	53	55	49	29	33	33
Family Total[d]	5.7	5.1	3.9	3.0	2.2	1.2	35	30	24	22	19	22	64	61	57
Intimate Partners	5.1	4.6	2.2	3.8	2.4	0.87	43	34	28	12	10	13	49	40	29
Children	1.0	1.0	0.59	0.71	0.84	0.58	42	45	50	2	2	3	9	14	19
Other Family	3.4	2.8	1.1	0.45	0.43	0.26	12	13	19	8	6	6	6	7	9
Child Homicide															
Infant (Under 1)	0.33	0.47	0.28	0.29	0.44	0.24	47	49	47	22	27	22	37	47	37
Toddler (ages 1–5)	0.80	0.79	0.66	0.38	0.41	0.32	33	34	33	52	46	52	49	44	49
Kids (ages 6–12)	0.41	0.47	0.34	0.11	0.09	0.09	21	16	21	27	27	27	14	9	14
Motives/Circumstances															
Argument	11.7	12.7	6.2	0.82	0.82	0.49	7	6	7	56	50	47	66	61	45
Felony-Related	1.2	3.5	2.1	0.02	0.05	0.04	2	2	2	25	27	26	10	14	17
Gang-Related	26.2	23.2	11.3	5.2	3.5	1.3	17	13	10	17	15	19	24	25	37
Other	8.4	6.9	4.6	2.0	1.4	1.1	19	17	19	3	8	9	0.3	1	2
Weapon															
Gun	32.7	34.7	20.0	4.8	2.8	1.2	13	8	6	66	68	70	60	48	41
Knife	13.0	11.8	6.3	2.6	2.4	1.3	17	17	17	26	23	22	33	41	42
Force	3.6	3.9	2.1	0.48	0.51	0.37	12	12	15	7	8	7	6	9	12
Poison/Drugs	0.07	0.07	0.12	0.03	0.05	0.09	32	41	43	0.1	0.1	0.4	0.4	1	3
Other	0.36	0.33	0.15	0.08	0.10	0.06	19	23	28	1	1	1	1	2	2

[a]Rates represent three-year averages: 1980 (1979, 1980, 1981); 1990 (1989, 1990, 1991); 2003 (2001, 2002, 2003); Rates are adjusted for the sex composition of the country and for changes in SHR coverage over time. The population base includes ages 12–64.
[b]Female Percentage = Female Rate / (Female Rate + Male Rate)*100 percent
[c]Profile Percentage = (Offense Count/Total Count of All Offenses)*100 percent. **Note:** May not sum to 100 percent due to rounding.
[d]"Family Total" includes intimate partners (spouses, ex-spouses, common law partners, and boy/girlfriend), children, and other family members (e.g., parent, sibling, cousin).

roughly 75%, are men. Likewise, 75% of males' victims are men, but male of-fenders' targets are mostly acquaintances—about half the time. Men kill strangers (29%) more often than they kill family members (22%). In contrast, women rarely kill strangers (10%) and only sometimes kill acquaintances (33%).

Importantly there is *no marked shift among women in the relational aspects* of their homicide offending profile. If gender roles were shifting in ways that af-fected homicide offending patterns, we'd expect to see a shift toward stranger or, perhaps, acquaintance homicide. There is no such shift. The distribution of women's victims has remained essentially the same over the past 25 or so years—about 60% family, 30% acquaintances, and 10% strangers. One notable change, however, is the decrease in the percent of victims who are intimate partners (from 49% of women's victims to 29%).

Women's rates of intimate partner homicide have dropped precipitously since 1980; by comparison, women's intimate partner rates in 1980 were four times higher than current rates. Men's rates of intimate partner violence have dropped as well, but not as much as women's rates (men's rates in 1980 were about twice as high as present rates). In fact, women's rates of homicide are down since 1980 for every victim-offender relationship category and family sub-category, though by far the greatest decline is in intimate partner homicide. De-clines in male acquaintance and stranger homicides are also notable. Rates of each dropped by more than half since 1990; 1990 rates were marginally higher than rates in 1980. Since 1990, declines in male rates of stranger and acquaintance homicide outpaced female declines.

The gender gap in homicide offending is greatest for stranger homicides; fe-males have consistently made up about 5–7% of those identified as a perpetra-tor of a stranger homicide. Women's representation in homicides against acquaintances is also low and unchanged; between 1980 and the present, about 7–10% of these offenders were women. The gender gap is narrowest for homi-cides against family members (including intimates). Over 25% of homicides against family are committed by female offenders. This represents quite a drop from 40% of offenders in 1980, and women are still underrepresented as offenders given they make up half the population.

Women are not underrepresented as homicide offenders when we examine those who victimized young children (ages 0–12). Women constituted almost half of offenders arrested for child homicide. Female involvement in child homi-cide declines with victim age so that the gender gap is 50% for infanticides, 33% for toddlers, and 21% for kids. These gender gap percentages are nearly identi-cal to those for 1980 and 1990. In terms of victim selection, women more often offend against infants (37% of child victims), while males offend against kids (27% of child victims). But toddlers are most vulnerable, making up about half of both women's and men's non-adult victims.

Motives and Circumstances

The immediate motivation for the majority of both women's and men's homicides are arguments and fights. Nearly half of all homicides, committed by men or women, occur because of some sort of argument or fight, such as a conflict over money or property, anger over one partner cheating on another, severe punishment of a child or abuse of a partner, retaliation for an earlier dispute, or a drunken fight over an insult or other affront. It is important to note that qualitative analyses, discussed in more depth below, show that many female homicides that result from an argument are often directed against the violence or abuse of a partner and may be viewed as "extra-legal" self-help, or even self-defense, though also categorized as arguments in these data are incidents of severe child abuse. Less common are arguments with friends, neighbors, or acquaintances that end in homicide.[6]

The second most common male homicide circumstance is felony-related.[7] About 25% of men's homicides compared to about 15% of women's homicides occur within the context of committing another felony. Almost half the time these sorts of homicides are related to a robbery. Other felony-related homicides are related to drug dealing (1 in 5 felony homicides for men; 1 in 8 for women) or, less commonly, burglary, arson, sex offenses, or theft. Of note, female felony homicide offenders often co-offend with male partners.[8]

In the SHR data, some 70% of female felony homicide offenders had a partner compared to 50% of male felony homicide offenders. In contrast, roughly 25% of offenders of either sex had a co-offender when the homicide resulted from a fight or argument. Felony-related homicides are more likely to be committed with a partner, particularly among women. Qualitative accounts suggest that the crime partners of women are often boyfriends and that the women play a more secondary role. It is more likely that the male planned the offense—to the extent that planning occurred—and that he brought the weapon, especially if it was a gun. That women's homicide is often related to men's violence—either as a co-offender or in response to abuse—is consistent with past studies of women's assault and use of other forms of violence.[9] Women's homicides, if not related to a fight, are next most often categorized as "other." Since the 1990s, women's homicides increasingly are categorized as other so that now over 1/3 of women's homicides are of unknown origin. This trend is also present for men (increasing from 15 to 19% of homicides), but "other" homicides are less common among men compared to felony-related homicides.

The smallest proportion of homicides for both men and women are those that are gang-related. Only about 1–2% of women's homicides are gang-related and this low level of involvement has not changed over time. Less than 50 women in the entire United States were identified as being a participant in a gang-related homicide between 2001 and 2003. For men, the percentage of gang-related homicides increased from 3% to 9% over the past 20 years, with most of the increase taking place in the late 1980s. The proportion of male homicides motivated by gang involvement has increased, in part, because all other types of homicides declined more precipitously than did gang-related homicides. In sum, both sexes most often kill in the context of an argument or fight, but men's homicide more often is felony-related whereas women are next most often involved in "other" sorts of homicides.

The gender gap in homicide offending is narrowest for uncategorized "other" sorts of homicide offenses and homicides stemming from an argument. The gender gap is largest for gang- and felony-related offenses. This pattern holds across each decade we examine, indicating that any changes in women's homicide motivation generally have mirrored changes in men's motivations. Since at least 1980, female involvement in gang-related homicides has remained at 2%, felony-related homicides at 7%, and "other" homicides at 17–18%. Rates of involvement in these three types of homicide declined evenly for women and men. Felony-related and "other" homicide rates are currently about half what they were in the 1980s. Rates of gang-related violence increased in the 1990s for both women and men; though declining, rates in 2003 remain somewhat higher than 1980s rates. All other offense types are at lower levels now than in 1980.

The greatest declines, though, have occurred in homicides motivated by arguments and these declines have been more substantial among women than men. Women's relative involvement in homicides stemming from an argument dropped sharply, by nearly half since 1980 (17% in 1980 versus 10% in 2004). Women's rates are only one-fifth what they were in 1980; men's rates have been cut by more than half. The sustained decline in female partner violence rates mainly is responsible for the widening of the gender gap in argument-related homicides.

To summarize, women's and men's homicides are most likely to be sparked by arguments or fights, but gender differences are more notable in the extent of involvement in felony- and gang-related homicides. Though the SHR data lack detail in terms of offender motivations, case studies and qualitative accounts show important gender differences in the content of arguments, with women more often engaging in self-defensive violence. There has been little, if any, shift in the immediate circumstances surrounding women's homicide; women and men most often kill in the context of a heated argument. Changes in the circumstances surrounding female homicide generally follow a similar pattern as those of men. Notably, though, women's involvement in the most common type of homicide—argument-motivated—has declined more substantially than males' involvement owing to declining rates of female partner violence.

Offense Characteristics

Some offense characteristics, such as the time and day of the incident, are similar for females and males. Homicides occur more often on weekends and late at night. Female homicide offending usually takes place in her and/or the victim's home; male homicides are more likely to occur in public places, such as bars or other public locations. This gender difference occurs primarily because the settings in which women kill intimate partners and children differ from the settings where men kill acquaintances and strangers.

In terms of weapon used, men are far more likely than women to use guns. Females were involved in only 6% of the homicides perpetrated with a gun. Female representation has declined since 1980 when 13% of gun offenders were women. In fact, a woman today is as likely to use a knife as a gun to commit her homicide whereas in the past 60% of female homicides were committed with a gun. Note that this shift is mainly due to the steeper declines in women's rates of gun violence compared to declines in homicides committed with knives. Gun homicide rates of males have also declined, but only since 1990. Men's homicides still tend to be committed primarily with guns (65–70% over 1980–2003).

Interestingly women are equally represented with men in homicides in which the victim is poisoned or drugged. Otto Pollak asserted that a large portion of the gender gap in offending might be due to women's more surreptitious style of committing crimes, citing poisoning as a means of women secretly engaging in homicide. This style of offending, he explained, was required by women's smaller physique but facilitated by women's domestic social role as caregiver (e.g., via opportunities presented when preparing food).[10] Criminologists today would likely concur that female crime is more hidden than male crime, but would attribute this to the typically less serious nature of women's offending compared to men's. Criminologists also agree that homicide is the most accurately measured offense and women's overall involvement compared to men is very low. Whether or not Pollak's assertion was true at the time, today fewer than 100 women each year are *detected* killing a victim with poison or drugs. Only a fraction of female homicides were by poisoning or drugs (e.g., ranging from less than 1% to 3%). With around 20,000 "unintentional" poisonings a year, there is always the potential that untold numbers of women are getting away with murder.

Offender Background

Like many offenders, female and male homicide offenders come from economically and educationally disadvantaged backgrounds and communities. Female offenders have low educational attainment, on average the 11th grade level. Both sexes of homicide offenders, if employed, tend to work in a menial occupation, though for women it is in the service sector and for men it is more likely in a blue collar occupation. Women's rates of homicide tend to be high where male rates are also high, such as urban areas.[11]

In comparison to male homicide offenders, fewer women had a prior record or felony offense. It is estimated that upwards of 75% of male homicide offenders had previously been arrested, many repeatedly and for felony offenses. Previous research suggests that most (70%) female homicide offenders do not have a prior felony record, though many (about 60%) have prior arrests for misdemeanors. Many of these arrests are likely to be for assault, possibly related to domestic abuse, status violations as a juvenile (such as running away from abuse in the home), or minor property crimes, such as shoplifting, credit card fraud, or check forgery. Very few women had ever been previously incarcerated, compared to one-fifth of the men arrested for homicide.[6] It is clear that female homicide offenders are not immersed in criminal subcultures to the same extent as male homicide offenders.[12]

Compared to other types of female offenders, female homicide offenders were more likely to be from a solid family background, to have children, and to a have stable living arrangement prior to the offense. Female murderers appear to have somewhat higher levels of problem drinking, but lower levels of drug use compared to other female offenders. These patterns again indicate that female homicide offenders are not often part of the criminal subculture. These differences also reflect the influence of domestic violence on women's offending patterns. In sum, the background characteristics of female and male offenders are similar: they tend to be characterized by poverty, low educational attainment, and no or low-quality employment. Yet female homicide offenders are less likely to have a prior record, especially for more serious offenses and less likely to be involved in a drug or criminal subculture. Gender differences in previous criminal involvements and opportunities for offending clearly shape the context, or type, of offending for women and men.

■ Women's and Men's Offending Patterns: A Qualitative Comparison

Previous case studies shed additional light on the family and gendered dynamics of women's and men's homicide. In this section, we draw on previous case studies and other in-depth modes of analysis to elucidate key gender differences (and similarities) in the ways in which men and women engage in homicide offending. We begin by considering the more unusual forms of female and male homicide offending, neonaticide for women and familicide for men; then, we describe the more common (though still rare) forms of female and male homicide, child and partner homicide for women and acquaintance and stranger homicide for men.

Child Homicide

A predominantly female form of homicide is neonaticide, when a mother kills her newborn child. These offenders are often young, unmarried women who may conceal pregnancy, give birth alone, and commit homicide using more "delicate" methods such as exposure, suffocation, or strangulation. These women may kill their newborn in fear of stigmatization should their pregnancy be detected, due to feeling unable to care for the child, or because of extreme stress or mental illness. Until an infant is a week old, its most immediate threat is its mother.[13]

Almost uniquely male are murder-suicides and family massacres (familicides), where a man kills his children, his partner, and possibly himself for reasons such as possessive jealousy, anger or vindictiveness towards a partner, loss of children through separation, or sometimes the inability to financially support his family any longer. The victims are usually biological children, older than most child victims, and killed with a gun. Like the women who commit neonaticide, these men may express feelings of powerlessness, of matters having gone beyond their control; they also express feelings of pain and/or anger.[14,15]

Both sorts of homicide sometimes demonstrate planning or forethought. Yet some offenses seemed to occur with little forethought, with the offenders showing signs of irrationality or imbalance, at least at the time of the incident if not previously. The more common situation of child homicide, for both women and men, arises not out of the intent to kill the child; rather it is the end result of harsh punishment (or discipline, from the parent's perspective). Consider the following two examples—the first a female description, the second a male description:

> *I was packing up my stuff [to move] and my son was acting up and I didn't know what to do, 'cause I don't understand nothing about disciplining a child, 'cause how I was raised by my own family, how they abused me and I didn't know what to do, so I took it out on my son and sent him to his room and I made him go to bed and he went to bed. I went near and he wasn't breathing, he stopped breathing, wouldn't breathe. I know he was sleeping and he didn't wake up. I hit him, I only hit him twice in the head with my hand. I don't know, with my shoe, my flat shoe in the head twice and that was it, and I sent him to his room 'cause I didn't want to hit him no more . . . It was very hard for me 'cause I didn't know what to do. The only thing I knew was to take him to the doctor when he needed to go to the doctor and feed him and keep him clean, that was it. I didn't know how to love him, 'cause I didn't have, didn't love myself, I didn't know how to love him.*[16] *—female offender*

Austin was sitting on the floor eating a packet of chips and he started crying. I picked him up and whacked him on the bum three or four times with an open hand. I put him down and he was still crying. I picked him up and shook him (to) shut him up . . . I didn't lose my cool, I was just annoyed . . . I was just annoyed because I couldn't hear the video. He was getting on my nerves.[14] —*male offender*

The homicides of these and other preschool children tend to be more brutal than those of infants killed by their mothers. These child victims likely had suffered from abuse by their mother or, especially, their father for much of their young lives. Female offenders were usually the primary caretaker. Many of the women report having felt socially isolated, trapped by their responsibilities at a young age. The male child homicide offenders shared more in caretaking responsibilities than most men. The males were often stepfathers or other men living with the family.

The mother, though often married or partnered, tends to commit the crime alone, in the bathroom or bedroom, using manual force (hitting, kicking, choking, drowning). It is unlikely she was under the influence of drugs or alcohol at the time. Women filicide offenders often claim innocence or that it was an accident, though more than 6 in 10 children (ages 2–5) had multiple wounds. Half the women arrested for child homicide had recorded child abuse histories, particularly those who killed a preschooler (ages 2–5). A large minority of the women were abused themselves as children. Conviction charges typically are lower than the initial murder charge in 80% of cases, suggesting lesser culpability or some mitigating circumstances upon weighing the evidence.[17]

Men initially attempt to deny or cover up their role in the homicide, sometimes persuading their partners to support their story. Case files show male offenders saying "I was just playing;" that the child was "accident-prone;" or that the child "fell downstairs." The child's death was not likely premeditated, but the physical evidence often showed signs of prior abuse and that extreme aggressive acts precipitated the child's death.

Although these acts are inexcusable, in general, these families were enmeshed in stressful circumstances—money troubles and unemployment, frequent fights with their partner, high poverty communities. About 70% of murdered children resided in severe urban poverty. Higher rates of child homicide (and child maltreatment) occur in socially disorganized communities—communities characterized by poverty and social isolation, single-parent family structures, and conflicting behavioral norms regarding the use of violence as a means of problem solving. This suggests that child homicide is, in part, rooted in the social organization of society. Intimate partner rates, too, tend to be higher in communities characterized by high poverty, social isolation, and such.

Partner Homicide

Exploring homicide directed against intimate partners paints a very different portrait of female and male homicide offenders. Remember that women's homicidal behavior and violence is most often directed against a partner rather than a child. In fact, a woman's decision to kill her partner may be motivated be a desire to protect her children (or herself). Angela Browne's landmark study of women who killed their abusive husbands compared to women who escaped abuse showed few differences among the two groups of women. Their victims, however, differed: Men who more frequently and severely assaulted or raped their partners, made more death threats, frequently used alcohol or drugs, and abused the children were more likely to be killed. Patterns of violence escalated more among the women who killed their husbands, prompting Browne to conclude "women's behavior seemed to be primarily in reaction to the level of threat and violence coming in." What appears to trigger the homicide, despite the long history of abuse, is the feeling that her death or, importantly, the safety of her children is at stake based on an event out of proportion with past "normal" violent events (e.g., physical abuse of a child or discovery of sexual abuse of a daughter).[18] As many as 60% of women were being abused at the time they killed their partner and women who kill their partners were unlikely to be the first to use force in the event precipitating the homicide.[19]

Qualitative analyses suggest that women's homicide, and their violence more generally, often revolves around relational concerns. Female motives for violence often involve self-defensive acts against abusive male partners, risk taking to protect emotional commitments and valued relationships, or co-offending with male partners, the latter of which will be described shortly. Moreover, a myriad of studies show that female violence mainly occurs only under extreme stress or repeated provocation, such as in the case of aggression against small children or in response to male instigated violence including domestic abuse and assault.[20,21] Indeed, some have characterized women's violence as a form of "extra-legal" self help because women typically only kill in situations they perceive as life-threatening. Males, on the other hand, are more likely than women to kill as a result of jealousy or rage, trivial arguments, or in the course of committing another felony.

Male homicide offenses against partners are dominated by motives of possessiveness, jealousy, abuse and control, and arguments. Men's violence in these cases is aimed at preventing the woman from leaving, retaliating for her departure, or forcing her to return. Some studies indicate that women who are separated from their partners are at an elevated risk of violent victimization, including homicide. When men kill partners, it often represents the culmination of a prolonged history of abuse. Another motive related to possessiveness is sexual jealousy, such as over a suspected or known infidelity (e.g., love triangles). Motives relating to perceived infidelity or termination of the relationship, center on themes of male domination and control whereas females are the majority of offenders when the motive is self-defense. A portrait of female homicide offenders as women acting in self-defense out of desperation would be one-dimensional, however, as there have always been some women who are motivated by material wealth and financial gain, revenge, involvement in a criminal subculture or gang, or the wish to continue an illicit affair.[22]

Acquaintance and Stranger Homicide

Female-on-female violence most frequently is directed against neighbors, their intimates' other sex partner, or friends and acquaintances; it should be noted, however, that as many as a third of female-on-female homicide victims are daughters of the offender. Offenders who kill another (unrelated) woman tend to be younger in age than the average female offender. Women kill other women in fights over men, to prevent a romance from occurring, to preserve their sexual or social reputation, and as a result of an ongoing feud. For example, two neighbors had an ongoing feud over neighborhood matters. On this occasion, the two women were struggling in the kitchen and, as a result, the offender's 3-year-old child was inadvertently injured. The offender responded by stabbing the other woman in the chest one time, killing her. Though extreme, this incident also reflects female offenders' greater willingness to aggress to protect a loved one. Other female–female violence may result from fights related to gossip or jealousy, disrespect (e.g., negatively evaluating another girl's appearance), and interactions with another woman's boyfriend—all of which may be regarded generally as reputational challenges.[23] Importantly, the extent of female–female homicides has not risen over the past 25 years, as some might expect if women truly have become more violent. Female-on-female homicides continue to make up less than 2% of total homicides; roughly 25% of women's victims were other women in 1980, 1990, and presently.

Though it is rare that a woman will kill a stranger, when this occurs the victim is likely to be a man and, about half the time, it is in the context of committing another felony offense, namely robbery. In these situations, women often co-offend with men, though women typically play an ancillary role. Many of the women charged with a robbery-related homicide are ultimately considered accessories to the homicide rather than major actors, and men usually have brought the weapon (80% of the time) and initiated the violence. Women who co-offend are probably romantically involved with their crime partners (~75%); men, by comparison, mainly co-offend with other men and therefore are far less likely to be romantically involved (14%). Thus, even when women aren't offending *against* their intimates, women's violence is intimately tied with men because they are offending *with* their intimates. Female felony-related stranger homicides are next most often perpetrated in the context of prostitution; to some extent these homicides may be self-defensive because prostitutes may be severely victimized by their clients (e.g., beaten, robbed, raped). Prostitutes are also known to sometimes rob their clients, perhaps with the help of "their man," so "prostitution-related" homicides may also reflect robberies "gone bad." About one-third of stranger homicides by women result from a fight or argument, usually with a man, but 30% of the time with a woman.

By far the most common homicide situation is male-on-male violence. Indeed, men are the most likely victims of homicide (and violent crime generally) as well as the more common perpetrators. As with female offenders, most male homicide is often the result of an argument. The nature of male disputes with other males, however, differs markedly in character from the types of domestic arguments that spur women to violence. Male–male homicide events often result from what appears to be a minor or trivial provocation, such as a shove, insult, or the "wrong look" among friends and acquaintances, or, less often, strangers. These events typically occur in a place of leisure, such as bars, parties, barbecues, parks, or on the streets, where groups of young men may congregate. Insults or threats appear to escalate and develop "spontaneously" into violence, though amplification is often facilitated by the use of alcohol and the presence of young male peers and a social audience. At some point, both parties must interpret the exchange as requiring retaliation and mutually agree to aggression.[24]

Why would such seemingly trivial slights with so little consequence cause a person to risk death? What seems absurdly trivial to some provides males, throughout the social strata, the opportunity to demonstrate masculinity through these "honor contests." Lower class males may develop a stronger allegiance to street norms and aggressive means of demonstrating masculinity than middle- and upper-class males, who more strongly prescribe to mainstream society's norms relating to problem solving. Whereas middle- and upper-class males may have myriad opportunities to "do masculinity," lower class males living in concentrated urban poverty may, over time and as an adaptation to persistent economic strain, place stronger collective emphasis on more achievable goals than financial success, such as respect and prestige conferred to those with a street reputation. Violations of the "code of the street"—sustained eye contact or a disrespectful demeanor, for example—can be lethal.[25,26]

Male homicide offenders are more likely to be immersed in street culture. Compared to female homicide offenders who are unlikely to have a prior felony record, male offenders (and sometimes victims) tend to have lengthy arrest and, for some, imprisonment histories. Moreover, many male offenders often have long histories of unemployment. Though male–male status contests are the predominant form of male homicide, two other distinctly male patterns are felony-related homicide and gang-related killings. These types of homicide also stem from male involvement in criminal subcultures. Upwards of 95% of gang homicides are perpetrated by males against males, both of whom are likely to be in (rival) gangs. Motives for gang homicide often are similar to those for non-gang homicide—retaliation in order to save face and to establish social position, though gang interactions tend to be more conflict-oriented than other groups of youth. Felony-related homicide is also viewed by some as a means of displaying masculinity via demonstrating willingness to engage in risky behavior with the potential for violence.[27]

■ Conclusion

Though the motivational and situational contexts of homicide offending may differ markedly by gender, males and females appear to be subject to the same social and cultural influences on homicide offending. That is, when it comes to forces outside the individual, men and women are more alike than different in the factors that increase the likelihood of homicide and other violent offending. For example, places with high levels of male homicide tend to have correspondingly high levels of female homicide, though male homicide rates greatly exceed female rates in all places. A number of studies have also shown that women's homicide trends tend to mirror men's trends in homicide offending. Both of these facts provide indirect evidence that women and men experience similar pushes toward violence. The considerably smaller set of studies that has directly compared causes of women's and men's homicide has concluded that similar social forces are at work in producing men's and women's violence—namely, concentrated poverty, inequality, and single-parent family structures weaken allegiance to mainstream norms regulating the use of violence as well as inhibit the capability of residents to exert informal social control. Of note, these conditions are associated with all sorts of homicide offending, including partner homicide, child homicide, gang killings, and so on. These "milieu effects" are felt by females and males alike, though males more readily respond to these conditions with violence than do females, explaining *some* gender differences in offending levels.[28–32]

The stronger influence on men of one's immediate surroundings only partially explains why females are so much less likely than men to kill, why women need a higher level of provocation before turning to serious violence, and why women so infrequently kill a rival female, use a gun, or engage in felony offenses or gang violence. These differences in the extent and context of female and male homicide offending might be attributed to differences in *the organization of gender*. Gender norms and stereotypes surrounding femininity and masculinity are less or more compatible with violence (and involvement in the criminal underworld). Violence by females is more stigmatizing whereas violence by males is more status enhancing. Women's violence tends to be restrained by an "ethic of care," where women are expected to maintain and establish social relationships and be more responsive to the needs of others. Men are conditioned more towards status seeking, competition, and distributive justice. Gender socialization works to limit female motivations for violence, but it heightens male motivations. Further, males have greater opportunity to commit violence as they tend to be less supervised than females, allowing greater and more frequent contact with male peers and engagement in violence-likely social situations (e.g., parties, "hanging out," involvement in criminal enterprises). Females, on the other hand, are more closely watched, limiting exposure to violence-likely situations.[33] There also is a good deal of evidence that sexism in male peer groups and in the underworld limits the extent and nature of female involvement in crime groups, regardless of a woman's ability or desire to engage in criminal violence.[34]

Homicide is rare, particularly for women who make up about 10% of homicide offenders. Relative to men, female involvement has not changed much over time. Whether change in women's propensity for violence is measured using overall rates of homicide or "masculine" homicide classifications such as stranger homicide or intra-sex homicide, there is little evidence that women have become more violent over the past 25 years. This meshes with other studies on girls' and women's assault patterns, which show that females today are not more likely to commit assault (though they do appear more prone to *arrest* for assault). Importantly, there has been no marked shift among women in their homicide offending profile over time.

Women's homicide patterns are marked by victims who are closest to them—partners and children. Only rarely do women kill strangers. When a woman kills, it is likely she was under extreme pressure and/or provoked by fear for her life or for the sake of someone close to her (e.g., children), though sometimes her motives are less altruistic (e.g., committing another felony, often with her romantic partner, or fighting with another woman). Men's relational patterns of homicide are more heavily weighted by friends, acquaintances and strangers and the event typically takes place in a public place, perhaps where alcohol and an audience are present. Men often kill over matters that appear to be trivial—minor insults or minimal physical contact—yet these challenges are viewed by participants as requiring a response in order to defend one's masculinity, particularly if the offenders are involved in street culture. When a man kills his partner it is rarely out of mortal fear but usually in response to jealousy or other control motive.

Men and women kill in ways that uniquely reflect their gender roles and related social positions. As such, the context of homicide differs substantially by gender. Contexts of offending, such as the target of aggression, specific motivation, and commission of the crime, are profoundly shaped by gender roles and opportunities, which differ markedly based on gender. Thus, women's aggression tends to be directed at intimate partners who may precipitate their own death and children with whom these women spend much of their time. Men's homicide occurs more often in the context of the criminal underworld and in public spaces. The backgrounds and the social structural conditions underpinning homicide, however, are quite similar for women and men. Communities marked by social disorganization cause both women and men to be more susceptible to dealing with problems via the use of violence (even if the targets of aggression differ). Thus, temporal and spatial patterns of female and male homicide tend to be the same. Because female homicide is so intertwined with male homicide, solutions that address the structural conditions associated with violence should apply equally well to females and males. Yet, there is also a need to take into account the gendered ways in which people offend if we hope to prevent future homicides from occurring.

References

1. Fox, J. A. (2004). Missing data problems in the Supplementary Homicide Reports: Imputing offender and relationship characteristics. *Homicide Stud* 8:214–254.
2. Fox, J. A., Zawitz, M. W. (2003). *Homicide Trends in the United States*. Washington, DC: U.S. Department of Justice, Bureau of Justice Statistics.
3. Steffensmeier, D., Schwartz, J., Zhong, H., Ackerman, J. (2005). An assessment of recent trends in girls' violence using diverse longitudinal sources: Is the gender gap closing? *Criminology* 43:355–406.
4. Brookman, F. (2005). *Understanding Homicide*. London: Sage, p. 128.
5. Brownstein, H. H., Spunt, B. J., Crimmins, S., et al. (1994). Changing patterns of lethal violence by women. *Women Crim Justice* 5:99–118.
6. Jurik, N., Winn, R. (1990). Gender and homicide: A comparison of men and women who kill. *Viol Victims* 5:227–242.
7. Wilbanks, W. (1983). The female homicide offenders in the U.S. *Int J Women's Stud* 6:302–310.
8. Schwartz, J., Steffensmeier, D. (2007). The nature of female offending: Patterns and explanation. Forthcoming in R. Zaplin (Ed.), *Female Offenders: Critical Perspective and Effective Interventions*. Sudbury, MA: Jone & Bartlett.
9. Miller, J. (1998). Up it up: Gender and the accomplishment of street robbery. *Criminology* 36:37–66.
10. Pollak, O. (1950). *The Criminality of Women*. Philadelphia: University of Pennsylvania Press.

11. Scott, L., Davies, K. (2002). Beyond the statistics: An examination of killing by women in three Georgia counties. *Homicide Stud* 6:297–324.

12. Suval, E. M., Brisson, R. C. (1974). Neither beauty nor beast: Female criminal homicide offenders. *Int J Criminol, Penol* 2:23–34.

13. Gartner, R., McCarthy, B. (2006). Killing one's children: Maternal infanticide and the dark figure of homicide. Pp. 91–114 in K. Heimer and C. Kruttschnitt (Eds.), *Gender and Crime: Patterns in Victimization and Offending*. New York: New York University Press.

14. Alder, C., Polk, K. (1996). Masculinity and child homicide. *Br J Criminol* 36:396–411.

15. Daly, M., Wilson, M. (1988). *Homicide*. Hawthorne, NY: Aldine de Gruyter.

16. Crimmins, S., Langley, S., Brownstein, H. H., Spunt, B. J. (1997). Convicted women who have killed children. *J Interpers Viol* 12:49–69.

17. Mann, C. R. (1996). *When Women Kill*. Albany, NY: SUNY.

18. Browne, A. (1987). *When Battered Women Kill*. New York: The Free Press.

19. Johnson, H., Hotton, T. (2003). Losing control: Homicide risk in estranged and intact intimate relationships. *Homicide Stud* 7:58–84.

20. Bailey, W., Peterson, R. D. (1995). Gender inequality and violence against women: The case of murder. Pp. 174–205 in J. Hagan, R. D. Peterson (Eds.), *Crime and Inequality*. Stanford, CA: Stanford University Press.

21. Dobash, R., Dobash, R. E., Wilson, M., Daly, M. (1992). The myth of sexual symmetry in marital violence. *Social Prob* 39:71–91.

22. Weisheit, R. (1993). Structural correlates of female homicide patterns. Pp. 191–206 in A. W. Wilson (Ed.), *Homicide: The Victim-Offender Connection*. Cincinnati: Anderson Publishing Co.

23. Miller, J., Mullins, C. W. (2006). Stuck up, telling lies, and talking too much: The gendered context of young women's violence. In K. Heimer, C. Kruttschnitt (Eds.), *Gender and Crime: Patterns of Victimization and Offending*. New York: New York University Press.

24. Polk, K. (1998). Males and honour contest violence. *J Homicide Stud* 3:6–29.

25. Anderson, E. (1999). *Code of the Street*. New York: W. W. Norton.

26. Messerschmidt, J. (2004). *Flesh and Blood: Adolescent Gender Diversity and Violence*. Totowa, NJ: Rowman, Littlefield Publishers.

27. Short, J. F., Strodtbeck, F. L. (1965). *Group Process and Gang Delinquency*. Chicago: University of Chicago Press.

28. Kubrin, C. (2003). Structural covariates of homicide rates: Does type of homicide matter? *J Res Crime Delinq* 40:139–170.

29. Schwartz, J. (2006). Effects of diverse forms of family structure on women's and men's homicide. *J Marriage Family* 68:1292–1313.

30. Schwartz, J. (2006). Family structure as a source of female and male homicide in the United States. *Homicide Stud* 10:253–278.

References

References

31. Steffensmeier, D. J., Haynie, D. (2000). The structural sources of urban female violence in the United States. *Homicide Stud* 4:107–134.
32. Steffensmeier, D. J., Haynie, D. (2000). Gender, structural disadvantage, and urban crime: Do macrosocial variables also explain female offending rates? *Criminology* 38:403–438.
33. Bottcher, J. (1995). Gender as social control. *Justice Q* 12:33–57.
34. Steffensmeier, D., Terry, R. (1986). Institutional sexism in the underworld: A view from the inside. *Sociol Inq* 56:304–323.

Gang Involvement and Predatory Crime

9

Jean Marie McGloin
University of Maryland

Recent decades have witnessed a large growth in street gang presence and activity. By 2004, the National Youth Gang Center estimated that there are approximately 760,000 street gang members and 26,000 street gangs across nearly 3,000 jurisdictions in the United States. This proliferation has not been limited to urban centers, rural and suburban areas across the nation have also seen a dramatic increase in street gangs. At the same time, gangs have shown an expansion of members' age and ethnicity, as well as an increase in female membership.[1-5] Membership in street gangs is not simply reserved for young, minority males. These apparent quantitative and qualitative shifts in the character of street gangs and gang membership are interesting, but they do not compel the attention of criminologists in isolation. If gangs are simply self-formed groups of individuals who adopt a common name, have some sense of longevity, and have a basic organization, then they would arguably not be in the purview of criminological focus. After all, we rarely find ourselves in the business of studying sports teams or fraternities.

Instead, it is the *criminal* element that invites our attention. Research has long suggested that predatory crime is somehow part, if not a product, of gang life. Indeed, as the prevalence of street gangs increased nationally, Chicago saw a 500% growth in gang-motivated homicides in Chicago from 1987–1994, while the increase in homicides from 1999–2001 in California was fully attributable to an upswing in gang homicides in Los Angeles County.[6,7] For such reasons, scholars and practitioners alike invest resources in understanding the relationship between gang involvement and offending behavior. This chapter reviews these linkages, paying particular attention to the theoretical mechanism that underlies it, as well as considers what may be uniquely criminogenic about gang membership. It also discusses the implications of this linkage, focusing on policy and intervention considerations.

■ Gang Involvement and the Increased Risk of Offending

A number of studies have found that gang members tend to be more serious offenders than their non-gang counterparts and that they are responsible for a disproportionate amount of crime. For example, data from the Rochester Youth Development Study reveal that gang members are significantly more likely to report involvement in violence than non-gang members.[8] At the same time, 30% of youth in this sample self-reported gang membership, but they were responsible for 65% of the reported delinquent acts over a four-year period.[9,10] This disproportionate involvement emerged across levels of crime seriousness as well as for violent and property crime. Similarly, approximately 14% of the subjects in the Denver Youth Study over a four-year period reported being gang members but were responsible for 79% of the reported serious violence and 71% of the reported serious property crime.[11] Gang members in this sample self-reported approximately two to three times more delinquency than non-gang members. Sara Battin and her colleagues investigated this pattern within the Seattle Social Development Project. They found that gang members comprised 15% of the sample, but were responsible for approximately 58% of the general delinquent acts reported over a four-year period. As with the other studies, results from the Seattle data revealed that this disproportionate involvement spanned across an array of crime types, including assault, robbery, and theft.[12,13]

It is important to highlight three points about these findings. First, despite the varying geographic locations and the range of gang membership prevalence, gang members consistently were more serious delinquents and were responsible for the lion's share of crime. Second, these findings were based on self-reports. Thus, it is not the case that this relationship simply reflects a systematic bias of official records being more likely to capture the behavior of gang members than that of non-gang members. Finally, this trend cuts across types of predatory crime. It was not exclusive to a specialized type of crime, such as robbery, which suggests a general connection between gang membership and offending behavior.

Interestingly this "risk" of gang involvement for offending appears to exist on a continuum. David Curry, Scott Decker and Arlen Egley acknowledge that most gangs are loosely organized and that the process of affiliation or disaffiliation is rarely rapid or spontaneous.[14] Full-fledged gang membership is often a gradual process and, accordingly, there are distinctions in the extent to which individuals are affiliated or associated with street gangs; some individuals may not be distinctly gang members or non-gang members, but their associations and linkages rather place them somewhere in the middle. Relying on a survey of middle school students in St. Louis, Curry and his colleagues found that 15% reported being a past or current gang member and nearly 49% reported at least some association with gangs (e.g., had gang members as friends, wore gang colors, flashed gang signs, or hung out with gang members) though they did not identify themselves as gang members. Both self-reported and official recorded delinquency showed a rank-order relationship with the level of gang involvement. Gang members reported the most delinquency and were most likely to have court referral records, followed by youth associated with gangs and non-gang youth, respectively. In short, the increased risk of delinquency is not specific to gang membership, but also extends to individuals who associate with street gangs.[14]

Just as the division between gang and non-gang members is not always clear-cut, but rather exists on a spectrum, not all gang members are the same. Research has long shown that gang members vary in the extent to which they are committed to or embedded in street gangs. Most often, scholars distinguish between core members, who are involved in many gang activities and have more stable memberships, and peripheral members, who are relatively less involved and have more transient stays in the gang. Some research has moved past this relatively simple dichotomy, however. For example, Jean McGloin found that gang members in Newark occupied a range of social positions and roles in street gang networks. For our purposes, it is important to note that the more involved and embedded members tend to be more criminally active when compared to peripheral, less embedded members.[15] Indeed, research has revealed that being a central member of a delinquent group serves to amplify one's incidence of criminal behavior.[16] This, along with the previous findings, underscores the robustness of the linkage between gang involvement and predatory crime. Even so, however, these results do not necessarily reveal what this linkage *means*.

Some people may presume that this relationship suggests that gang involvement causes delinquent behavior, but this is not the only possible interpretation. Individuals who gravitate towards gang involvement may be different somehow than individuals who do not. If so, this linkage reflects enduring individual-level differences in criminal propensity, not some detrimental impact of gang involvement. It therefore would seem prudent for theorists, researchers, practitioners and policy-makers to study this relationship with more depth.

■ Why Is There a Relationship Between Gang Involvement and Crime?

Scholars have long debated the theoretical "meaning" of gang membership in much the same way as they have debated the relationship between having deviant peers and an increased likelihood of offending. Traditionally, this linkage serves as a place of intersection between learning and control theories of crime, which adopt decidedly different viewpoints. Other perspectives, such as opportunity theories, certainly have the ability to comment on the importance of deviant peers with regard to offending, but learning and control theories nonetheless have largely defined and structured this debate.

The *socialization or facilitation model* views gang involvement/membership as causally meaningful. Based primarily on propositions from differential association and social learning theories, it assumes that the normative processes of the gang/delinquent peer group create and sustain delinquents.[17,18] As a consequence of gang involvement, individuals learn to commit crime because this primary social environment provides access to definitions favorable towards committing crime, to sources of reinforcement for delinquent/criminal behavior, and to a number of delinquent models for observational learning. Simply, without this social–psychological context, the individual might not engage in delinquency, thus the gang is criminogenically important and deserves our attention (see **Figure 9.1**).

In contrast, the *selection model* asserts that gang membership does not hold any causal significance with regard to delinquency. Instead, this model argues that the relationship is spurious; a common factor explains both gang membership and delinquency, as Figure 9.1 demonstrates. Drawing on findings by control theorists, it proposes that an individual will offend when social controls or self-control are weak.[19-21] Under the premise of "birds flock together," more serious delinquents self-select into gangs. Therefore, the gang simply reflects the already established tendencies of its members; it does not cause delinquency. As part of their general theory of crime, Michael Gottfredson and Travis Hirschi state "adventuresome and reckless children who have difficulty making and keeping friends tend to end up in the company of one another, creating groups made up of individuals who tend to lack self-control. The individuals in such groups will therefore tend to be delinquent, as will the group itself."[20] Thus, Gottfredson and Hirschi assert that since low self-control underlies both involvement with street gangs and delinquency.

Some researchers have recognized that couching this discussion in a single, unidirectional pathway is not the most productive enterprise. Rather, it might be more accurate to consider the possibility that controls, learning environments and delinquency influence each other in a reciprocal manner. Accordingly, Ter-

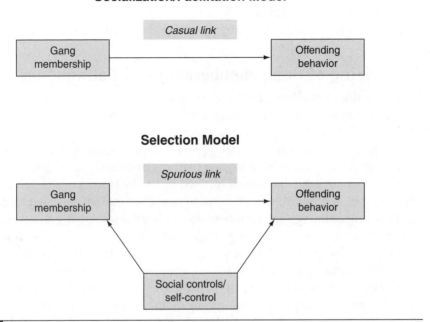

Figure 9.1 Models of Gang Delinquency

ence Thornberry suggested an interactional perspective that accounts for bidi-rectional relationships among social controls, delinquent peers, and delinquency. The *enhancement model* is influenced by this perspective and proposes that peo-ple who are part of gangs may be different than their non-gang counterparts even before membership, but the group processes nonetheless encourage and amplify delinquent behavior.[22,23] In short, it represents a middle-ground or compromise between the control and learning sides of this theoretical debate.

These perspectives all have conceptual merit and can potentially explain the linkage between gang involvement and a heightened risk of offending. In order to truly shed insight on which theoretical perspective has the most merit, re-searchers have turned to longitudinal data. Doing so allows a finer investigation of connection between the *timing* of gang membership and criminal behavior, about which the selection and socialization models offer divergent predictions. According to the selection model, when comparing gang members and non-gang members over time, the former should always be more delinquent and there should be no systematic change in this behavior during the time of gang mem-bership. Since gang membership is simply a reflection of a person already being more delinquent due to other causal factors, such as self-control, being an active member of the gang should have no facilitating effect. In contrast, the socialization model argues that these two groups would look very similar before and after gang membership, but that during the time of membership, gang members would be more active in delinquency due to the criminogenic social context.

The Timing of Gang Membership and Delinquency

Finn Esbensen and David Huizinga investigated the temporal relationship between gang membership and delinquent behavior in order to shed insight on this theoretical debate.[24] First, they confirmed the cross-sectional relationship between gang membership and delinquency, that is, gang members were more criminally active than their non-gang delinquent counterparts. Then, turning to four years of available data, they focused in on the timing of the subjects' gang membership, if applicable, and delinquency. The findings revealed that offending prevalence among gang members was higher than non-gang subjects even before membership began, which provides initial support for the selection model. The results also provided some support for the socialization model, however, since the offending prevalence among gang members declined subsequent to leaving the gang. When looking at individual-level patterns of offending, they discovered that offending rates among gang members were particularly pronounced during the time of membership—though they engaged in more crime than their non-gang counterparts before joining the gang. This divergence became more pronounced during the time of active membership. This investigation provided the most support for the enhancement model. Although youth who are already more delinquent may gravitate towards gangs, there is also something criminogenic about the gang that amplifies their behavior.[24]

Thornberry and his colleagues also investigated this premise with male youth from the Rochester Youth Development Study.[8] Their investigation largely provides support for the socialization model. Since gang members only had higher rates of crimes against persons than non-gang members when actively part of the gang.[8] More recently, Gordon and colleagues relied on ten years of data from the Pittsburgh Youth Study for their inquiry. They discovered that boys who joined gangs were more delinquent than their non-gang counterparts before they were active members, which provided some support for the selection model. They also found that criminal behavior increased significantly among gang members when they were actively part of the gang and diminished after leaving the gang, thus providing the strongest support for the enhancement model. Interestingly, this pattern emerged across an array of dependent variables, including self-reports, parent reports and teacher reports of delinquent behavior.[25]

On the whole, studies vary in the extent to which they provide support for each model, although the enhancement explanation tends to have the strongest standing. It also appears generally clear that gangs do provide some facilitating effect with regard to delinquency, even if gang members were more criminally active prior to membership. The natural question that follows, therefore, is why gang membership acts as a facilitator. Given that researchers and theorists often group findings on gang membership with those on deviant peers, it is not unreasonable to ask whether the same mechanism is at work. Is it that gang members are simply exposed to a greater number of more serious delinquent peers? If so, then there is nothing uniquely criminogenic about the gang or gang membership, per se, but rather gangs are simply another form of a delinquent peer group.

In an empirical investigation of this question, Gordon and colleagues found that exposure to delinquent peers was one socializing mechanism at work for gang members, though it did not completely explain the relationship between gang membership and heightened delinquency.[25] Relying on a different dataset, Battin et al. also investigated whether delinquent peer associations were able to explain the effect gang membership has on criminal involvement, measured both via self-reports and official records. They found that being a gang member exerted an effect on delinquency above and beyond having delinquent friends. These two investigations therefore suggest that there is something uniquely criminogenic about gang membership.[12]

■ What Might Be Unique About Gang Membership?

In considering what it is about gang membership that might cause and support increased criminal behavior, a number of possibilities emerge. This section elaborates on one primary possibility, namely the interactive social processes that are part of gang life. Although a street gang is arguably a type of delinquent peer group, it is a particularly powerful social network that often embraces predatory and violent behavior. Street gangs have the power to constrain the behavior of their members so that individuals behave in a manner consistent with the values, norms, and symbolic nature of the group.[26]

Individuals who gravitate towards gang involvement are often marginalized from acquiring status in general society via legitimate means.[27,28] To be sure, threats to one's status often shed insight on the origin of gangs and gang membership; still, it is important to recognize that vying for status within the gang is also an important process. James Short and his colleagues have argued that studying the social process of negotiating social status within the gang often provides more insight into understanding the behavior of gang members than does considering one's status in reference to society at large.[29,30] This is somewhat similar to Elijah Anderson's discussion of the disadvantaged underclass, who adapt to their socio-economic context, which includes the perceived continual threat of violence, by adopting a "code of the street." Part of this code entails the notion that failing to address transgressions or actions of disrespect will only serve to invite them more often in the future. Like this subculture, the nature of gang life can structure certain expectations and support social processes that facilitate the offending behavior of gang-involved youth.[31]

Hughes and Short studied gang members in Chicago and noted that: ". . . several gang members lost status within the gang after becoming 'too committed' to school or family . . . the gang context was conducive to violence, and for gang youth, willingness to fight was often critical to status management."[30] Moreover, Scott Decker reviewed interview data from 99 gang members in St. Louis and argued that gang violence was an expressive result of interactive social processes. In particular, he suggested that violent behavior among gang members emerged out of collective behavior, whereby real or perceived "threats" set an escalating, dynamic interaction in motion, which culminated in violence through retaliation. Empirical data has found support for this argument.[32,33] For example, Pizarro and McGloin reviewed over five years worth of homicide data in Newark, New Jersey and discovered that escalating dispute embedded within group contexts predicted gang related-homicides.[34]

In short, offending behavior often becomes an intimate part of acquiring and maintaining social status within the gang, which might help us to understand the mechanism whereby gangs facilitate predatory behavior. Gang membership comes with particular expectations about behavior and interactions—expectations that shape and influence individuals who are involved in street gangs. The initiation for some gang members is an inherently violent process, consisting of being "beat in," which sends a resonating message about the meaning and expected interactional processes of gang life.[35] It is not surprising that gang membership has been established as a correlate and a predictor of gun ownership, gun possession, and gun use.[36–39] Indeed, Terence Thornberry et al. found that gang members in the Rochester Youth Development Study were approximately *ten times* more likely to carry a firearm than non-gang members.[26] Consistent with the previous discussion, the often-cited reasons for such activities include protection/self-defense from other gangs, intimidation, and status. Unfortunately, these violent expectations often have dire consequences. In a rather grim commentary, Scott Decker and Janet Lauritsen followed up 99 gang members five years after interviewing them. Of the 51 subjects found, 19 were dead, 2 were in prison and 4 were in wheelchairs.[40]

This label of "gang member" or "gang-involved" may also spark assumptions of an individual's behavior from those outside the gang. For instance, Finn Esbensen and his colleagues found that gang members and non-gang members look quite similar across an array of psycho-social variables, though individuals in the former group were more likely to perceive having been labeled as bad or disturbed by their teachers. Accordingly, individuals involved in gangs may not only perceive expectations from within the gang about social interactions and behavior that are tied to status and respect, but they might also perceive expectations from those in larger society to act or behave in a violent fashion.[41] Under the premise of labeling theory, this may set a self-fulfilling prophecy in motion. Taken together, external labels and internal expectations can interact and cumulatively push an individual towards predatory crime as he or she becomes involved in street gangs.[42] This discussion is only one example of what might make gang involvement uniquely risky, but it provides some points for consideration.

■ Policy Implications

That gang members are responsible for a disproportionate amount of crime clearly warrants intervention strategies and resources. In addition, that something unique about gang involvement amplifies individual-level offending behavior further underscores this focus. A vast array of gang prevention and intervention programs exist, though our sense of "what works" is fairly limited. It would seem relatively straightforward to determine which strategies are best suited to combat gangs and prevent gang membership, but programs rarely define their problem of interest with clarity (e.g., intimidation of the public by gang members, an increased homicide rate attributed to gangs, an increasingly violent drug market related to an influx of gangs, an increase in commercial robberies attributed to a small group of gang members), let alone complete a process or outcome evaluation.[43] Even so, the purpose of this chapter is not to review the sea of intervention strategies, but rather to elaborate on implications for anti-gang programs in light of the previous discussion about the linkage between gang involvement and predatory crime.

The first implication is that prevention strategies are clearly warranted. Prevention programs are directed at the general population, which is in contrast to intervention strategies that are directed at at-risk populations or groups. This chapter has illustrated that there is a facilitating effect to gang membership, one that extends to individuals who associate with gangs, as well. Therefore, only directing policies or programs at individuals who are already gang members or gang associates would miss the opportunity to prevent these linkages and reduce the risk of increased offending.

One prevention program that is relatively well-known is Gang Resistance and Education Training, or G.R.E.A.T., which is a school-based curriculum in which law enforcement officers act as instructors. The middle-school portion of the curriculum is a thirteen-week course in which lessons center around preventing gang involvement and delinquency, while promoting life skills and pro-social ties within families and the community. Results from an early cross-sectional evaluation indicated some moderate success, but a longitudinal evaluation was less promising.[44] Although the efficacy of G.R.E.A.T. is not clear, it is important to note that programs that attempt to prevent the development of linkages to gangs do and *should* exist.

Not all individuals who are linked to the gang are equal in their connections. Some people are merely associates, and within the category of "gang member" there is variation in the extent to which people are involved and embedded in the gang. With this in mind, as well as the positive relationship evidenced between the extent of gang involvement and offending behavior, it would be unwise to subject all gang-involved youth to the same intervention strategy. For example, peripheral members might be persuaded to terminate their gang involvement more easily, perhaps through a social service-based strategy, when compared to core/central gang members who may require more law enforcement resources. With regard to the former group, social service providers could intervene and potentially prevent an individual from becoming further enmeshed in the gang, thereby reducing the heightened risk of becoming more serious offenders. At the same time, levels of involvement in the gang may reflect gradations in the "dangerousness" posed to public safety, further suggesting a benefit to differentiating among the types and extent of linkages to street gangs.

Mark Fleisher has argued that "gangs are social networks composed of individual gang members, and that gang member behavior is determined in part by a gang member's location in the structure of the social network. That location in the social network structure determines opportunities and constraints that expand or limit a gang member's choices."[45] Not surprisingly, therefore, recent work has argued that intervention and suppression techniques should be cognizant of social positions within the gang and not treat all individuals in the same manner. Programs would be well-served by seeing gangs as social networks in which positions and the extent of "gang involvement" varies.

One manner in which to do this is to appeal to a particular method during the problem analysis phase–network analysis. The primary purpose of network analysis is to reveal the presence of any regular patterns in social relationships: rather than focusing on attributes of individuals, it focuses on the associations or linkages among people.[46,47] McGloin recently described a network analysis of gang members in Newark, New Jersey.[15] The data included information on various social connections among gang members, including who was related to whom, who was incarcerated in the same correctional facility and who hung out and committed crime together. As part of this analysis, it became clear that individuals exist on a spectrum of involvement with the gang, across a range of linkages. This kind of problem analysis could directly inform policy and prevention decisions about how to allocate resources. For example, a core member who is central to the street gang and heavily involved in serious crime warrants law enforcement attention. This can be further underscored if this core person is the primary linkage to the gang for a number of peripheral members. Under such hypothetical circumstances, focusing on this person would address an individual who is responsible for a disproportionate amount of crime and it would coincidentally cleave of other persons' linkage to gang involvement, potentially ending the facilitating context for delinquency.[15]

It is also important to be cautious that intervention programs do not have the unintended consequence of strengthening an individual's linkage to the gang. Law enforcement attention on gangs, through arrest, patrol, surveillance, and other suppressive tactics, can serve as a powerful external source of cohesion. It provides the group with a common point of conflict and solidified identity, setting a self-fulfilling prophecy in motion.[48] Such a risk is not limited to suppressive tactics. For example, the Los Angeles Group Guidance Project offered tutoring, counseling, and recreational activities to the local gangs in an attempt to integrate street gang members into the pro-social community. Unfortunately, this program provided the gang members with more opportunities to socialize and become more linked to each other, producing a more cohesive gang that was involved in more crime. In short, it is terribly important for policy-makers and those part of an intervention to consider the level of gang involvement when planning a strategy and to continually assess whether that involvement is changing as a consequence of the tactics (either for the better or the worse).

■ Conclusion

This chapter discussed the positive correlation between gang involvement and predatory crime. Although scholars have long known that such a link exists, both in terms of an individual's increased likelihood of offending and gang members being responsible for a disproportionate amount of crime, they have contested meaning of this relationship. Whereas the socialization/facilitation model argues that gang membership plays a causal role in offending behavior, the selection model maintains that this relationship merely reflects more serious offenders self-selecting into gang membership. Evidence presented in this chapter suggests that gangs do have a facilitating effect on delinquency, above and beyond simply being exposed to delinquent peers. The unique criminogenic nature of gang involvement compels us to carefully consider intervention strategies that are cognizant of the gradations that exist regarding gang involvement. In doing so, such interventions may disproportionately affect the crime rates, as well as evidence greater success through the intelligent allocation of resources.

References

1. Crane, J., Boccara, N., Higdon, K. (2000). The dynamics of street gang growth and policy response. *J Policy Mod* 22:1–25.
2. Curry, G. D., Decker, S. H. (2003). *Confronting Gangs: Crime and the Community*, 2nd edition. Los Angeles: Roxbury.
3. Howell, J. C. (1998). *Youth Gangs: An Overview*. Washington, DC: Office of Juvenile Justice and Delinquency Prevention.
4. Howell, J. C., Moore, J. P., Egley, A. (2002). The changing boundaries of youth gangs. Pp. 3–18 in C. R. Huff (Ed.), *Gangs In America, III*. Thousand Oaks, CA: Sage.
5. Miller, W. B. (2001). *The Growth of Youth Gang Problems in the United States: 1970–1998*. Washington, DC: Office of Juvenile Justice and Delinquency Prevention.
6. Block, C. R., Christakos, A., Jacob, A., Przybylski, R. (1996). *Street Gangs and Crime: Patterns and Trends in Chicago*. Chicago: Illinois Criminal Justice Information Authority.
7. Tita, G., Abrahamse, A. (2004). *Gang Homicide in L.A., 1981–2001. Perspectives on Violence Prevention, Number 3*. Sacramento, CA: California Attorney General's Office.
8. Thornberry, T. P., Krohn, M. D., Lizotte, A. J., Chard-Wierschem, D. (1993). The role of juvenile gangs in facilitating delinquent behavior. *J Res Crime Delinq* 30:55–87.
9. Thornberry, T. P., Burch, J. H. (1997). *Gang Members and Delinquent Behavior*. Washington, DC: Office of Juvenile Justice and Delinquency Prevention.
10. Thornberry, T. P. (1998). Membership in youth gangs and involvement in serious and violent offending. Pp. 147–166 in R. Loeber, D. P. Farrington (Eds.), *Serious and Violent Juvenile Offenders: Risk Factors and Successful Interventions*. Thousand Oaks, CA: Sage.
11. Huizinga, D. H. (1997). *Gangs and the Volume of Crime*. Paper presented at the annual meeting of the Western Society of Criminology, February 14–16, Honolulu, HI.
12. Battin, S. R., Hill, K. G., Abbott, R. D., Catalano, R. C., Hawkins, J. D. (1998). The contribution of gang membership to delinquency beyond delinquent friends. *Criminology* 36:93–115.
13. Hill, K. G., Lui, C., Hawkins, J. D. (2001). *Early Precursors of Gang Membership: A Study of Seattle Youth*. Washington, DC: Office of Juvenile Justice and Delinquency Prevention.
14. Curry, G. D., Decker, S. H., Egley, A. (2002). Gang involvement and delinquency in a middle school population. *Justice Q* 19:275–292.
15. McGloin, J. M. (2005). Policy and intervention considerations of a network analysis of street gangs. *Criminol Public Policy* 4:607–636.
16. Haynie, D. L. (2001). Delinquent peers revisited: Does network structure matter? *Am J Sociol* 106:1013–1057.

17. Akers, R. L. (1998). *Social Learning and Social Structure: A General Theory of Crime and Deviance*. Boston: Northeastern University Press.

18. Sutherland, E. H. (1947). *The Principles of Criminology*, 4th edition. Philadelphia: Lippincott.

19. Glueck, S., Glueck, E. (1950). *Unraveling Juvenile Delinquency*. Cambridge, MA: Harvard University Press.

20. Gottfredson, M. R., Hirschi, T. (1990). *A General Theory of Crime*. Stanford, CA: Stanford University Press.

21. Hirschi, T. (1969). *Causes of Delinquency*. Berkeley: University of California Press.

22. Thornberry, T. P. (1987). Toward an interactional theory of delinquency. *Criminology* 25:863–891.

23. Elliott, D. S., Menard, S. (1996). "Delinquent friends and delinquent behavior: Temporal and developmental patterns." Pp. 28–67 in J. D. Hawkins (Ed.), *Delinquency and Crime: Current Theories*. New York: Cambridge University Press.

24. Esbensen, F., Huizinga, D. (1993). Gangs, drugs, and delinquency in a survey of urban youth. *Criminology* 31:565–587.

25. Gordon, R. A., Lahey, B. B., Kawai, E., et al. (2004). Antisocial behavior and gang membership: Selection and socialization. *Criminology* 42:55–87.

26. Thornberry, T. P., Krohn, M. D., Lizotte, A. J., et al. (2003). *Gangs and Delinquency in Developmental Perspective*. New York: Cambridge University Press.

27. Thrasher, F. (1927). *The Gang: A Study of 1,313 Gangs in Chicago*. Chicago: University of Chicago Press.

28. Cloward, R. A., Ohlin, L. E. (1960). *Delinquency and Opportunity: A Theory of Delinquent Gangs*. New York: Free Press.

29. Short, J. F., Strotdbeck, F. L. (1965). *Group Process and Gang Delinquency*. Chicago: The University of Chicago Press.

30. Hughes, L. A., Short, J. F. (2005). Disputes involving youth street gang members: Micro-social contexts. *Criminology* 43:43–76.

31. Anderson, E. (1999). *Code of the Streets*. New York: W.W. Norton.

32. Decker, S. H. (1996). Collective and normative features of gang violence. *Justice Q* 13:243–264.

33. Decker, S. H., Van Winkle, B. (1996). *Life in the Gang: Family, Friends, and Violence*. New York: Cambridge University Press.

34. Pizarro, J., McGloin, J. M. (2006). Gang homicides in Newark: Collective behavior or social disorganization? *J Crim Justice* 34:195–207.

35. Vigil, J. D. (1996). Street baptism: Chicano gang initiation. *Human Organiz* 5:149–153.

36. Bjerregaard, B., Lizotte, A. J. (1995). Gun ownership and gang membership. *J Crim Law Criminol* 86:37–58.

References

References

37. Lizotte, A., Howard, G. J., Krohn, M. D., Thornberry, T. P. (1997). Patterns of illegal gun carrying among young urban males. *Valparaiso Law Rev* 31:375–394.
38. Lizotte, A. J., Krohn, M. D., Howell, J. C., et al. (2000). Factors influencing gun carrying among young urban males over the adolescent-young adult life course. *Criminology* 38:811–834.
39. Luster, T., Oh, S. M. (2001). Correlates of male adolescents carrying handguns among their peers. *J Marriage Family* 63:714–726.
40. Decker, S. H., Lauritsen, J. (2006). Leaving the gang. Pp. 21–40 in A. Egley, C. L. Maxson, J. Miller, M. W. Klein (Eds.), *The Gang Reader*, 3rd edition. Los Angeles: Roxbury.
41. Esbensen, F. A., Huizinga, D., Weiher, A. W. (1993). Gang and non-gang youth: Differences in explanatory factors. *J Contemp Crim Justice* 9:94–116.
42. Lemert, E. M. (1951). *Social pathology: Systematic Approaches to the Study of Sociopathic Behavior*. New York: McGraw-Hill.
43. McGloin, J. M. (2005). *Street Gangs and Interventions: Innovative Problem Solving with Network Analysis*. Washington, DC: Office of Community Oriented Policing Services.
44. Esbensen, F. A., Osgood, D. W., Taylor, T. J., et al. (2001). How great is G.R.E.A.T.? Results from a longitudinal, quasi-experimental design. *Criminol Public Policy* 1:87–118.
45. Fleisher, M. S. (2002). Doing field research on diverse gangs: Interpreting youth gangs as social networks. Pg. 200 in C. R. Huff (Ed.), *Gangs in America, III*. Thousand Oaks, CA: Sage.
46. Knoke, D., Kuklinski, J. H. (1982). *Network Analysis*. Thousand Oaks, CA: Sage.
47. Wasserman, S., Faust, K. (1994). *Social Network Analysis: Methods and Applications*. New York: Cambridge University Press.
48. Klein, M. W., Crawford, L. Y. (1968). Groups, gangs, and cohesiveness. Pp. 63–75. F. Short (Ed.), *Gang Delinquency and Delinquent Subcultures*. New York: Harper & Row.

Still Psychopathic After All These Years

Matt DeLisi
Iowa State University

Michael G. Vaughn
University of Pittsburgh

"His mouth is full of curses and lies and threats; trouble and evil are under his tongue. He lies in wait near the villages; from ambush he murders the innocent, watching in secret for his victims. He lies in wait like a lion in cover; he lies in wait to catch the helpless; he catches the helpless and drags them off in his net. His victims are crushed, they collapse; they fall under his strength."

—*Psalms 10:7–9 (cited in Meloy and Gacono, 1998[1])*

"Humans have long been concerned by or fascinated with the concept of evil and the people thought to personify evil. Say the word psychopath and most people can easily conjure up an image of someone they believe to embody the word."

—*James Blair, Derek Mitchell, and Karina Blair[2]*

With a clinical and criminological history that spans more than two centuries, psychopathy is among the most popular, controversial, and empirically evaluated constructs in the behavioral sciences. Robert Hare, arguably the most accomplished psychopathy researcher noted that even those opposed to the very idea of psychopathy cannot ignore its potent explanatory and predictive power—if not as a formal construct, then as a static risk factor.[3] Indeed, some researchers have found evidence indicating that psychopaths constitute a taxon or natural, discrete class of persons among the criminal population.[4,5] In this chapter, we argue that psychopathy is the purest, most parsimonious, and, frankly, best explanation of serious antisocial and violent behavior. More than any other theory of crime, the construct of psychopathy brilliantly forges the connection between the individual-level traits of the actor and his antisocial behavior.

Psychopathy is a clinical construct usually referred to as a personality disorder defined by a constellation of interpersonal, affective, lifestyle, and behavioral characteristics that manifest in wide-ranging antisocial behaviors. The characteristics of psychopathy read like a blueprint for violence. Psychopaths are impulsive, grandiose, emotionally cold, manipulative, callous, arrogant, dominant, irresponsible, short-tempered persons who tend to violate social norms and victimize others without guilt or anxiety. In short, they are human predators without conscience. At the heart of psychopathy is the complete unfeeling for other people, evidenced by callous-unemotional traits, remorselessness, and the absence of empathy. They do not experience the feelings that naturally inhibit the acting out of violent impulses and their emotional deficiency is closely related to general under-arousal and the need for sensation-seeking.[6] Because of this vacancy in the moral connection to other people, psychopaths are qualitatively distinct from other offender groups. But psychopaths are more than qualitatively distinct from other offenders: they are *quantitatively* worse. A study by David Simourd and Robert Hoge speaks to the virulence of the personality disorder even among a sample of dangerous criminals. Simourd and Hoge examined the case histories of 321 felons incarcerated for violent crimes. Of the sample, 36 inmates were psychopaths and 285 were not. Compared to non-psychopaths, psychopaths had more previous, total, violent, noncompliant, and different types of criminal convictions; more arrests; greater criminal sentiments and pride in antisocial behavior; and almost without exception, greater needs in terms of supervision.[7]

What is the prevalence of psychopathy in the general population? It is difficult to know since population-based studies have not been carried out; however, studies in correctional facilities have shown that approximately 25% of persons with antisocial personality disorder, a psychiatric disorder closely associated with psychopathy, meet criteria for psychopathy.[8] And since psychiatric epidemiological studies of antisocial personality disorder indicate that approximately 4% of the adult population possesses this disorder, we can infer an estimate of roughly 1% for psychopathy.[9]

If one is interested in understanding criminal violence, psychopathy is a good place to start. This chapter briefly highlights empirical issues pertaining to criminological theory, career criminality and recidivism, murder and sexual offending, and institutional violence as they relate to psychopathy. While these concepts are informed by many academic disciplines and constituted by an array of topical areas, psychopathy is central to each.

■ Criminological Theory

One of the most popular and widely-studied theories of crime is the general theory of crime advanced by Michael Gottfredson and Travis Hirschi, which asserts that low self-control is the chief variable that predicts crime and analogous behaviors.[10] The profile of persons with low self-control is well known; however, consider the following description of criminal offenders:

> *". . . over-evaluation of immediate goals as opposed to remote or deferred ones; unconcern over the rights and privileges of others when recognizing them would interfere with personal satisfaction in any way; impulsive behavior, or apparent incongruity between the strength of the stimulus and the magnitude of the behavioral response; inability to form deep or persistent attachment to other persons . . . poor judgment and planning in attaining defined goals . . . almost complete lack of dependability of and willingness to assume responsibility; and, finally, emotional poverty."[11]*

While this reads like a description of an offender with low self-control, it is actually a profile of psychopathic offenders published in 1948. Indeed, the core characteristics in Gottfredson and Hirschi's general theory of crime (e.g., hot tempered, impulsive, action-oriented, unempathetic, inability to delay gratification) could be construed as a softened abbreviation of psychopathy. In this way, the most talked-about, controversial, and cited theory in mainstream criminology borrows much of its empirical heft from the construct of psychopathy.[12]

Psychopathy has proven useful in the integration of previously disparate literatures. For instance, Donald Lynam has shown that a small cadre of children with hyperactivity, impulsivity, attention problems (e.g., ADHD), and conduct disorder are afflicted with a virulent strain of psychopathology best described as "fledgling psychopathy." Lynam's work has strengthened developmental psychology, psychopathology, and criminology by illustrating the worst of the worst in terms of violent and antisocial behavior and how it unfolds over the lifespan.[13,14] For instance, in one of the earliest studies of adolescent psychopathy, Adelle Forth and her colleagues found that psychopathic youths had criminal histories with more previous violent offending and institutional violence.[15] Even as adolescents, psychopathic offenders are more likely than non-psychopathic youths to receive a swift juvenile court referral, commit a violent offense upon release, and engage in both instrumental, or "cold-blooded" and reactive or "hot blooded" forms of aggression.[16–18]

Others, such as Michael Vaughn and David Farrington, suggest that psychopathy could be the useful construct to organize the study of serious, violent antisocial behavior among children and adolescents.[19,20] For instance, three notable longitudinal studies, the Denver Youth Survey, Pittsburgh Youth Study, and Rochester Youth Development Study have shown that between 14 and 17% of the youths in these samples are habitual offenders who account for 75 to 82% of the incidence of criminal violence. These adolescents in Denver, Pittsburgh, and Rochester tended to be "multiple problem youth" who experienced an assortment of antisocial risk factors, such as mental health problems, alcoholism and substance abuse histories, and sustained criminal involvement. Within this violent group, a small minority of youths were the most frequent, severe, aggressive, and temporally stable delinquent offenders. These youths, all of them males, were reared in broken homes by parents who themselves had numerous mental health and parenting problems. These boys were also noticeable by their impulsivity, emotional and moral insouciance, and total lack of guilt with which they committed crime. In other words, these studies indicate that the most violent young offenders in the United States display many of the characteristics of psychopathy.[21]

Even those who are critical of the notion of using psychopathy as a general theory of crime recognize how parsimoniously and accurately it describes crime and violence.[22] For the more extreme forms of crime, psychopathy is an intuitive heuristic for understanding behavior; however, it seems too severe when attempting to explain mundane forms of crime. For instance, it might seem foolish to suggest that behaviors such as shoplifting, forgery, and drunk driving are the expression of psychopathy since they are more common and often committed by seemingly "normal" persons. However, the very nature of minor crimes like stealing and drunk driving tells something about the offender, namely those who are willing to take from others, satisfy their desires at the possible expense of others, and flagrantly violate law and morality. To borrow from Gottfredson and Hirschi, all crimes are acts of force and fraud against others in the pursuit of self-interest. This is not unlike psychopathy.

■ Career Criminality and Recidivism

It is well-established that a minority of criminals perpetrate the majority of crimes in a population. Career criminals begin their antisocial careers early, commit greater and more varied crimes, and are the most violent.[23] Various scholars have empirically explored the links between psychopathy and assorted dimensions of career criminality, especially recidivism and noncompliance with criminal justice sanctions. Grant Harris and his colleagues examined the recidivism rates of 169 male offenders released from a psychiatric facility and followed-up one year later.[24] Nearly 80% of psychopathic offenders committed a new violent offense. Moreover, psychopathy was the strongest predictor of recidivism. In fact, its effects were *stronger than the combined effects of sixteen background, demographic, and criminal history variables.*[24] In the Pittsburgh Youth Study, boys who presented with psychopathic traits were between 480 and 630% more likely to be multiple problem offenders. They were the most frequent, severe, aggressive, and stable delinquents who were prone to externalizing disorders but seemingly immune from internalizing disorders, such as anxiety.[21]

Recently, David Farrington explored etiological predictors of psychopathy using data from the Cambridge Study in Delinquent Development, a 40-year prospective longitudinal survey of the criminal careers and social histories of 411 London males.[25] Using the PCL-R: SV (Screening Version), Farrington compared the offending careers of the top 11% of the sample who scored 10 or above on the PCL-R: SV (deemed the most psychopathic) to the remaining members of the panel. The most psychopathic group totaled significantly more convictions, greater involvement in the criminal justice system, and presented with more criteria for antisocial personality disorder diagnosis. Nearly half of these men were chronic offenders. An assortment of background factors was predictive of psychopathy at age 48. The strongest predictors (with corresponding odds ratios) were uninvolved father (6.5), physical neglect (5.9), convicted father (5.1), low family income (4.6), and convicted mother (4.5).[25]

Due to this study's empirical strength, it has been suggested that with respect to persistence, frequency, and severity, male psychopaths constitute the most violent population of human aggressors known.[26] Mary Ann Campbell and her colleagues studied 226 incarcerated adolescent offenders and found that about 9% exhibited high levels of psychopathic traits; however, this small selection of youths had the most violent and versatile criminal histories.[27] Richard Rogers and his colleagues' analysis of 448 prisoners found that, as children, psychopathic inmates forced others into sexual activity, were physically cruel to others, used weapons in fights, deliberately destroyed property, committed arson, and were cruel to animals, among other crimes.[28] In the Cambridge Study in Delinquent Development, children with psychopathic personalities were significantly likely to be chronic offenders and these traits exerted predictive power of criminal behavior decades later.[29] Importantly, high scores on psychopathy measures have also been correlated with early-onset for violent offending.[30] Finally, Michael Vaughn and Matt DeLisi explored the relationship between psychopathic personality traits and career criminality among a large sample of more than 700 incarcerated adolescents. Youths who presented with psychopathic characteristics were approximately 300 to 400% more likely than offenders without psychopathic traits to be classified as career criminals. Subsequently, they found that psychopathy measures were moderately able to correctly classify career criminal membership between 70 and 73%. When higher threshold specifications were used, the classification accuracy improved to an impressive 88%, much of it relating to impulsivity, callousness, fearlessness, and narcissism.[31] Interestingly enough, some of the interest in psychopathy centers on the notion that their behavior is in some way innate. A recent analysis of 626 twin pairs indicated that nearly 50% of variation in fearless dominance (resiliency to internalizing disorders) and impulsive antisociality (liability to externalizing deviance) was attributable to genes.[32] Put another way, the constellation of negative personality traits imbued in psychopathy have been there since the beginning of the psychopath's life.

What feature of psychopathy among adolescents is particularly worrisome? Recent research suggests that callous-unemotional traits may be the pathway that leads to severe and persistent aggression in youth. For instance, in a sample of 169 adolescents, Dustin Pardini found that low empathy was mediated by a non-concern for the consequences of punishment. If social learning and behavior conditioning principles have little impact on restraining behaviors then these youth are relatively "free" to do as they please.[33] Similarly, in a sample of 376 boys and 344 girls, Darrick Jolliffe and David Farrington found that these same low empathy traits were associated with increased frequency of bullying behavior overall, and violent bullying among the boys. It appears that the hallmark feature of primary psychopathy—lack of conscience—may be recognizable among children and adolescents.[34]

Several meta-analyses have indicated that psychopathy is the indispensable predictor of violent recidivism among children, adolescents, and especially adults.[35-37] For instance, among a sample of incarcerated American adolescents, psychopathic youths recorded higher levels of instrumental violence, violence where the victim required medical attention, assaults with deadly weapons, and both self-reports and criminal records of violence.[38] Among Canadian detained adolescents, psychopathic youths were more likely to offend after release from custody, committed more nonviolent and violent crimes, and recidivated more quickly than others.[39] As recidivists, psychopaths are quicker, more productive, and more severe once released back to the community.

■ Murder and Sexual Offending

The violence perpetrated by psychopaths is more instrumental, dispassionate, and predatory than other offenders as such psychopathy is an important risk factor for homicide and sexual offending. Much of this pertains to the ease with which psychopaths can inflict violence. A recent study published in *Nature* found that psychopathic murderers have diminished negative reactions to violence compared to non-psychopaths and other violent offenders as if violence was a facile, unexceptional event.[40] For serial murder and single sexual homicides, psychopathy is a basic personality characteristic of the offender.[41,42] For instance, Theodore Millon and Roger Davis suggest that many murderers could be characterized as malevolent psychopaths, which is a particularly negative subtype of offender characterized as belligerent, mordant, rancorous, vicious, brutal, callous, and vengeful.[43] What does psychopathic malevolence look like? Park Dietz and his colleagues conducted a descriptive study of 30 sexually sadistic criminals. All of these men intentionally tortured their victims for sexual arousal. Their crimes often involved careful planning, the selection of strangers as victims, approaching the victim under a pretext, participation of a partner, beating victims, restraining victims and holding them captive, sexual bondage, anal rape, forced fellatio, vaginal rape, foreign object penetration, telling victims to speak particular words in a degrading manner, murder or serial killings (most often by strangulation), concealing victims' corpses, recording offenses, and keeping personal items belonging to victims.[44] These are some call signs of psychopathy, albeit coupled with sexual sadism.

A study of 125 murderers found that more than 93% of homicides committed by psychopaths were "cold-blooded," in that they were instrumental, completely premeditated, and were not preceded by an explosive emotional interaction, such as an argument. Stephen Porter and his colleagues compared sexual homicides committed by psychopathic and non-psychopathic offenders in Canadian prisons. They found that nearly 85% of psychopathic murderers engaged in some degree of sadistic behavior during the course of their murder. Moreover, homicides committed by psychopaths contained significantly greater levels of gratuitous and sadistic violence.[45] Citing a study conducted by the Federal Bureau of Investigation, Robert Hare noted that more than half of the law enforcement officers killed on duty were murdered by offenders that matched the personality profile of the psychopath.[46]

Paul Mullen reviewed data suggesting that mass killers were isolated individuals who had rarely established themselves in effective adult roles. Persons who committed massacres were usually men roughly 40 years old, who had been bullied or isolated as children, demonstrated an affinity or preoccupation with weaponry and violence, and showed psychopathic-like personalities marked by rigid/obsessive beliefs, delusional suspiciousness, narcissism, and grandiose ideas that they had been persecuted.[47] Wade Myers examined the psychiatric history, criminal history, and family background of 16 juvenile sexual homicide offenders and discovered a laundry list of severe risk factors, many of them related to psychopathy. The most prevalent of these traits were an impaired capacity to feel guilt, neuropsychiatric vulnerabilities, serious school problems, child abuse victimization and family dysfunction, history of interpersonal violence, prior arrests, sadistic fantasy, psychopathic personality, and personality disorder diagnosis. Nearly 90% had elevated psychopathy scores.[48] Matt DeLisi interviewed 500 adult offenders with a minimum of 30 prior arrests. The sample included 42 murderers, 80 rapists, and 38 kidnappers. All of these offender groups showed versatility evidenced by multiple arrests for assorted violent and property crimes, recurrent imprisonments, and criminal careers that averaged roughly 25 years.[49] During interviews, the most violent offenders, especially the rapists, demonstrated prototypical psychopathic traits, such as pathological lying, irresponsibility, malevolent egocentricity, pronounced anger, and little regard for their victims.

Psychopathy figures prominently in the personality profile of sexually offending groups. Roy Hazelwood, the renowned FBI profiler, and Janet Warren developed profiles of serial sexual offenders based on actual cases. They described impulsive serial sexual offenders as persons motivated by a sense of entitlement and the perception that anything (or anyone) is there for the taking—in other words, classic psychopathic symptoms.[50] Based on data from 329 Canadian prisoners, Stephen Porter and his colleagues found that a substantial number of various sex offenders are psychopaths. Specifically, 64% of inmates with convictions for rape and child molestation, 36% of rapists, 11% of intra-familial child molesters, and 6% of extra-familial child molesters were psychopaths.[51] Psychopathy also escalates risk among adolescent sex offenders. Heather Gretton and her colleagues studied 220 adolescent males in an outpatient sex offender treatment program to assess linkages between psychopathy and recidivism. Youths with high psychopathy scores on the Psychopathy Checklist Revised Youth Version (PCL:YV) posed multiple threats to public safety. They were more likely than other offenders to escape from custody, violate probation, and commit violent and non-violent crimes after release. Moreover, some highly psychopathic youths exhibited deviant sexual arousal as measured by phallometric tests.[52]

Although the relationship between psychopathy and sexual offending is multifaceted, it is undeniable that psychopathy figures prominently. Raymond Knight and Jean-Pierre Guay summarized 50 years of research on the topic and arrived at three general conclusions. First, psychopaths are significantly more likely than non-psychopathic criminals to rape and are over-represented in clinical samples of sexual offenders. Additionally, psychopathic traits predict rapacious behavior among non-criminal samples. Second, psychopaths constitute a small subgroup of rapists that are extraordinarily violent and recidivistic. Third, the underlying processes that contribute to psychopathy are similar to those of sexually coercive behavior.[53] In other words, psychopathy is inextricably linked to the most heinous forms of violent criminal behavior.

■ Institutional Violence

Psychopathy is a strong predictor of whether an inmate will continue to misbehave while incarcerated especially for the most physically aggressive types of offenses.[54] In fact, psychopathic inmates tend to be the most aggressive and difficult-to-manage inmates.[55] Glenn Walters conducted a meta-analysis of 41 studies and found a moderate correlation between psychopathy and institutional adjustment ($r = .27$). The studies encompassed adults and juveniles, offenders from four countries, various follow-up periods, and inmates from prisons, forensic hospitals, and psychiatric facilities. Upon release, psychopaths were significantly likely to commit general, violent, and sexual recidivism.[56] Robert Hare and his colleagues found that psychopathic inmates accumulated more incident reports for violating prison rules, were more likely to assault staff, and were more likely to assault other inmates. Nearly one in two psychopaths (with scores greater than 30 on the PCL-R) had assaulted another inmates.[57] Similarly, Sarah Spain and her colleagues found that psychopathic adolescents accumulated more total, violent, verbal, and administrative violations while in custody and also had significantly worse treatment outcomes. In other words, psychopathic youths took much longer to complete or achieve minimal success in treatment.[58] Among a sample of adjudicated adolescents, Daniel Murrie and his colleagues found that the risk of prison violence increased 10% for each point above the mean PCL-R score. And Mairead Dolan and Charlotte Rennie found that youth psychopathy scores were predictive of assault on others in a secure facility.[59]

The link between psychopathy and institutional violence has also been found among mentally disordered offenders. Kirk Heilbrun and his colleagues administered the PCL to 218 clients following admission to an inpatient forensic hospital. Significant correlations between the PCL total scores and both nonphysical and physical aggression during the first two months of hospitalization were observed. The PCL total scores were also significantly correlated with post-discharge arrests for violent offenses. Psychopathic inpatients totaled significantly more aggressive incidents during the first two months of hospitalization. Moreover, psychopathy was significantly related to frequency of seclusion or restraint, suggesting that for mentally disordered offenders, psychopathy may serve as a risk factor for institutional aggression.[60]

That psychopathic offenders have poorer adjustment to correctional supervision likely justifies the most punitive forms of criminal sanction. For example, in a sample of 450 sexually violent offenders in Florida, Jill Levenson and John Morin found that for each point above the mean score on the PCL-R, offenders were 49% more likely to be civilly committed or selected for involuntary confinement after serving a prison sentence. Inmates who met the standard cut score of 30 were 490% more likely to be selected for civil commitment. In conjunction with diagnosed paraphilias, psychopathy correctly predicted commitment recommendations in 90% of cases.[61]

In the public mind, psychopaths are deserving of the death penalty perhaps because of the label psychopath. John Edens and his colleagues presented vignettes of a 16-year-old murderer, described as having classic psychopathic symptoms, to research respondents. These respondents were 130% more likely to recommend that youths should be sentenced to death if they have psychopathic traits. Moreover, respondents indicated that youths should not receive treatment in prison.[62]

■ Conclusion

Criminal offenders are a heterogeneous group diverse by gender, race, ethnicity, social class, criminality, criminal history, offense type, risk and protective factors, and personality. Anyone who has worked with criminal offenders in a correctional setting can rather quickly identify recurrent characteristics of serious offenders, however. When considering the most violent types of offenders, for instance—those with convictions for murder, rape, kidnapping, armed robbery, etc.—several thoughts come to mind. First, virtually all of the most violent offenders are male; predatory violent behavior is simply less prevalent among women. The majority of incarcerated violent offenders had an adverse, often abusive childhood, and most were raised in poverty. These demographic and social correlates are not the only commonalities among violent criminals. Interpersonally, one is immediately struck by their global irresponsibility and basic refusal to handle the important obligations of adult social roles, such as maintaining relationships, maintaining employment, and maintaining sobriety. Incarcerated violent offenders tend to be mean-spirited and insensitive, exceedingly manipulative, and utterly narcissistic. On their rap sheets are found multiple arrests for various crimes committed at high rates across their lifespans. There is a synergy between the violent criminals' personality traits, lifestyle, and observed behavior that dovetails so exquisitely that it is as if their criminality is wrapped up in a box. That box is psychopathy.

Psychopathy is an efficient and protean way to understand and explain crime because the traits that constitute psychopathy correspond to the elemental characteristics of crime itself: a self-serving, uncaring violation of another person. Recent advances in criminological theory, such as self-control construct in the general theory of crime, are essentially shorthand for psychopathy. For the extremes of criminal behavior, psychopathy is the *sine qua non* criminological explanation, one with a long and recurrent history. While other explanatory constructs are also important, it is clear that psychopathic traits are important to understand not only murder, but also serial murder, sadistic murder, and sexually violent murder. In this way, we believe that the construct and theory of psychopathy is inescapable. It is clear, concise, internally consistent, and perhaps most importantly, plausible. It efficiently conveys how criminal atrocities can flow from people who because of their lack of empathy, selfish desires, and deficient conscience impose a heavy toll on society.

1. Meloy, J. R., Gacono, C. B. (1998). The internal world of the psychopath. Pp. 95–109 in T. Millon, E. Simonsen, M. Birket-Smith, R. D. David (Eds.), *Psychopathy: Antisocial, Criminal, and Violent Behavior*. New York: The Guilford Press.

2. Blair, J., Mitchell, D., Blair, K. (2005). *The Psychopath: Emotion and the Brain*. Malden, MA: Blackwell, p. 1.

3. Hare, R. D. (1998). Psychopaths and their nature: Implications for the mental health and criminal justice systems. Pp. 188–212 in T. Millon, E. Simonsen, M. Birket-Smith, R. D. David (Eds.), *Psychopathy: Antisocial, Criminal, and Violent Behavior*. New York: The Guilford Press.

4. Harris, G. T., Rice, M. E., Quinsey, V. L. (1994). Psychopathy as a taxon. *J Consult Clin Psychol* 62:387–397.

5. Skilling, T. A., Quinsey, V. L., Craig, W. M. (2001). Evidence of a taxon underlying serious antisocial behavior in boys. *Crim Justice Behav* 28:450–470.

6. Herpertz, S. C., Sass, H. (2000). Emotional deficiency and psychopathy. *Behav Sci Law* 18:567–580.

7. Simourd, D. J., Hoge, R. D. (2000). Criminal psychopathy: A risk-and-need perspective. *Crim Justice Behav* 27:256–272.

8. Hart, S. D., Hare, R. D. (1996). Psychopathy and antisocial personality disorder. *Curr Opin Psychiatr* 9:129–132.

9. Hare, R. D. (1996). Psychopathy: A clinical construct whose time has come. *Crim Justice Behav* 23:25–54.

10. Gottfredson, M. R., Hirschi, T. (1990). *A General Theory of Crime*. Stanford, CA: Stanford University Press.

11. Gough, H. G. (1948). A sociological theory of psychopathy. *Am J Sociol* 53:359–366, p. 362.

12. Wiebe, R. P. (2003). Reconciling psychopathy and low self-control. *Justice Q* 20:297–336.

13. Lynam, D. R. (1996). Early identification of chronic offenders: Who is the fledgling psychopath? *Psychol Bull* 120:209–234.

14. Lynam, D. R., Gudonis, L. (2005). The development of psychopathy. *Ann Rev Clin Psychol* 1:381–407.

15. Forth, A. E., Hart, S. D., Hare, R. D. (1990). Assessment of psychopathy in male young offenders. *Psychol Assess*. 2:342–344.

16. Brandt, J. R., Kennedy, W. A., Patrick, C. J., Curtin, J. (1997). Assessment of psychopathy in a population of incarcerated adolescent offenders. *Psychol Assess* 9:429–435.

17. Stafford, E., Cornell, D. G. (2003). Psychopathy scores predict adolescent inpatient aggression. *Assessment* 10:102–112.

18. Loper, A., Hoffschmidt, S., Ash, E. (2001). Personality features and characteristics of violent events committed by juvenile offenders. *Behav Sci Law* 19:81–96.

References

References

19. Vaughn, M. G., Howard, M. O. (2005). The construct of psychopathy and its potential contribution to the study of serious, violent, and chronic youth offending. *Youth Viol Juv Justice* 3:235–252.
20. Farrington, D. P. (2005). The importance of child and adolescent psychopathy. *J Abnorm Child Psychol* 33:489–497.
21. Loeber, R., Farrington, D. P., Stouthamer-Loeber, M., et al. (2002). Male mental health problems, psychopathy, and personality traits: Key findings from the first 14 years of the Pittsburgh Youth Study. *Clin Child Family Psychol Rev* 4:273–297.
22. Walters, G. D. (2004). The trouble with psychopathy as a general theory of crime. *Int J Offender Therap Compar Criminol* 48:1–16.
23. DeLisi, M. (2005). *Career Criminals in Society*. Thousand Oaks, CA: Sage.
24. Harris, G. T., Rice, M. E., Cormier, C. A. (1991). Psychopathy and violent recidivism. *Law Human Behav* 15:625–637.
25. Farrington, D. P. (2006). Family background and psychopathy. Pp. 229–250 in C. J. Patrick (Ed.), *Handbook of Psychopathy*. New York: The Guilford Press.
26. Harris, G. T., Rice, M. E., Lalumiere, M. (2001). Criminal violence: The roles of psychopathy, neurodevelopmental insults, and antisocial parenting. *Crim Justice Behav* 28:402–426, p. 406.
27. Campbell, M. A., Porter, S., Santor, D. (2004). Psychopathic traits in adolescent offenders: An evaluation of criminal history, clinical, and psychosocial correlates. *Behav Sci Law* 22:23–47.
28. Rogers, R., Salekin, R. T., Sewell, K. W., Cruise, K. R. (2000). Prototypical analysis of antisocial personality disorder: A study of inmate samples. *Crim Justice Behav* 27:234–255.
29. Farrington, D. P. (2000). Psychosocial predictors of adult antisocial personality and adult convictions. *Behav Sci Law* 18:605–622.
30. Forth, A. E. (1995). *Psychopathy and Young Offenders: Prevalence, Family Background, and Violence*. Program Branch Users Report. Ontario, Canada: Minister of the Solicitor General of Canada.
31. Vaughn, M. G., DeLisi, M. (2007). Were Wolfgang's chronic offenders psychopaths? *Journal of Criminal Justice*, in press.
32. Bloningen, D. M., Hicks, B. M., Krueger, R. F., et al. (2005). Psychopathic personality traits: Heritability and genetic overlap with internalizing and externalizing psychopathology. *Psychol Med* 35:637–648.
33. Pardini, D. A. (2006). The callousness pathway to severe violent delinquency. *Aggress Behav* 32:590–598.
34. Jolliffe, D., Farrington, D. P. (2006). Examining the relationship between low empathy and bullying. *Aggress Behav* 32:540–550.
35. Dolan, M., Doyle, M. (2000). Violence risk prediction: Clinical and actuarial measures and the role of the psychopathy checklist. *Br J Psychiatr* 177:303–311.

36. Edens, J. F., Skeem, J. L., Cruise, K. R., Cauffman, E. (2001). Assessment of 'juvenile psychopathy' and its association with violence: A critical review. *Behav Sci Law* 19:53–80.

37. Howard, M. O., Williams, J. H., Vaughn, M. G., Edmond, T. (2004). Promises and perils of a psychopathology of crime: The troubling case of juvenile psychopathy. *J Law, Policy* 14:441–483.

38. Murrie, D. C., Cornell, D. G., Kaplan, S., et al. (2004). Psychopathy scores and violence among juvenile offenders: A multi-measure study. *Behav Sci Law* 22:49–67.

39. Corrado, R. R., Vincent, G. M., Hart, S. D., Cohen, I. M. (2004). Predictive validity of the psychopathy checklist: Youth version for general and violent recidivism. *Behav Sci Law* 22:5–22.

40. Gray, N. S., MacCulloch, M. J., Smith, J., et al. (2003). Forensic psychology: Violence viewed by psychopathic murderers. *Nature* 423:497–498.

41. Geberth, V., Turco, R. (1997). Antisocial personality disorder, sexual sadism, malignant narcissism, and serial murder. *J Forens Sci* 42:49–60.

42. Myers, W. C., Monaco, L. (2000). Anger experience, styles of anger expression, sadistic personality disorder, and psychopathy in juvenile sexual homicide offenders. *J Forens Sci* 45:698–701.

43. Millon, T., Davis, R. D. (1998). Ten subtypes of psychopathy. Pp. 161–170 in T. Millon, E. Simonsen, M. Birket-Smith, R. D. David (Eds.), *Psychopathy: Antisocial, Criminal, and Violent Behavior*. New York: The Guilford Press.

44. Dietz, P. E., Hazelwood, R. R., Warren, J. (1990). The sexually sadistic criminal and his offenses. *Bull Am Acad Psychiatr Law* 18:163–178.

45. Porter, S., Woodworth, M., Earle, J., et al. (2003). Characteristics of sexual homicides committed by psychopathic and non-psychopathic offenders. *Law Human Behav* 27:459–470.

46. Hare, R. D. (1999). Psychopathy as a risk factor for violence. *Psychiatric Q* 70:181–197.

47. Mullen, P. E. (2004). The autogenic (self-generated) massacre. *Behav Sci Law* 22:311–323.

48. Myers, W. C. (2004). Serial murder by children and adolescents. *Behav Sci Law* 22:357–374.

49. DeLisi, M. (2001). Extreme career criminals. *Am J Crim Justice* 25: 239–252.

50. Hazelwood, R. R., Warren, J. I. (2000). The sexually violent offender: Impulsive or ritualistic? *Aggress Viol Behav* 5:267–279.

51. Porter, S., Fairweather, D., Drugge, J., et al. (2000). Profiles of psychopathy in incarcerated sexual offenders. *Crim Justice Behav* 27:216–233.

52. Gretton, H. M., McBride, M., Hare, R. D., et al. (2001). Psychopathy and recidivism in adolescent sex offenders. *Crim Justice Behav* 28:427–449.

References

53. Knight, R. A., Guay, J. (2006). The role of psychopathy in sexual coercion against women. Pp. 512–532 in C. J. Patrick (Ed.), *Handbook of Psychopathy*. New York: The Guilford Press.

54. Edens, J. F., Buffington-Vollum, J. K., Colwell, K. W., Johnson, D. W., Johnson, J. K. (2002). Psychopathy and institutional misbehavior among incarcerated sex offenders. *Int J Forens Mental Health* 1:49–58.

55. Dolan, M., Blackburn, R. (2006). Interpersonal factors as predictors of disciplinary infractions in incarcerated personality disordered offenders. *Personality Indiv Diff* 40:897–907.

56. Walters, G. D. (2003). Predicting criminal justice outcomes with the psychopathy checklist and lifestyle criminality screening form: A meta-analytic comparison. *Behav Sci Law* 21:89–102.

57. Hare, R. D., Clark, D., Grann, M., Thornton, D. (2000). Psychopathy and the predictive validity of the PCL-R: An international perspective. *Behav Sci Law* 18:623–645.

58. Spain, S. E., Douglas, K. S., Poythress, N. G., Epstein, M. (2004). The relationship between psychopathic features, violence, and treatment outcome: The comparison of three youth measures of psychopathic features. *Behav Sci Law* 22:85–102.

59. Dolan, M., Rennie, C. (2006). Psychopathy checklist: Youth version and youth psychopathic trait inventory: A comparison study. *Personality Indiv Diff* 41:779–789.

60. Heilbrun, K., Hart, S. D., Hare, R. D., Gustafson, D., Nunez, C., White, A. (1998). Inpatient and post-discharge aggression in mentally disordered offenders: The role of psychopathy. *J Interpersonal Viol* 13:514–527.

61. Levenson, J. S., Morin, J. W. (2006). Factors predicting selection of sexually violent predators for civil commitment. *Int J Offender Therap Compar Criminol* 50:609–629.

62. Edens, J. F., Guy, L. S., Fernandez, K. (2003). Psychopathic traits predict attitudes toward a juvenile capital murderer. *Behav Sci Law* 21:807–828.

The Heterogeneity of Predatory Behaviors in Sexual Homicide

11

Eric Beauregard

University of South Florida

The first obstacle to characterizing sexual homicide is the absence of any legal definition. When investigators attempt to solve a murder and decide whether it is sexual in nature, they rely on two types of information: testimony—from either the murderer or someone else—and physical evidence, of which the crime scene is the key source. According to Robert Ressler and his colleagues, a murder can be considered sexual if at least one of the following is true: 1) the victim is found totally or partially naked; 2) the genitals are exposed; 3) the body is found in a sexually explicit position; 4) an object has been inserted into a body cavity (anus, vagina, mouth); 5) there is evidence of sexual contact; 6) there is evidence of substitutive sexual activity (e.g., masturbation and ejaculation at the crime scene) or of sadistic sexual fantasies (e.g., genital mutilation). The main obstacle to the exploitation of this type of evidence is that some police officers do not recognize its sexual character.[1]

Another problem related to the definition of sexual homicide has been the failure of some researchers to take into account differences in the sex and age of the victims. In several cases, in fact, murders of women, men, and children have been considered to belong to a single category, despite the lack of evidence that these types of sexual homicide are part of a homogenous phenomenon. On the contrary, the absence of such evidence makes it essential that definitions of sexual homicide consider the age and sex of the victims.

This chapter addresses different issues related to the heterogeneity of sexual murderers and sexual homicides. The first section deals with the different types of sexual murderers of women and the existing classifications based on their criminal behaviors. The second section addresses the sexual murder and murderers of men. After looking at some of their differences and similarities with sexual murderers of women, this section ends by suggesting a classification specific to sexual murderers of men. Finally, the third section investigates sexual murderers of children and their crimes, especially the differences and similarities they share with sexual murderers of women.

■ Sexual Murderers of Women

To our knowledge, ten typological studies of sexual murderers have been conducted.[1–10] These typological studies reveal four types of sexual murderers, with each study describing between two and four types. Two types of sexual murderer are consistently reported in the various studies: angry and sadistic. In addition, we also find the sexual murderer who kills to eliminate witnesses. Finally, some studies include a residual category which includes types such as the "power-assertive," "power-reassurance," "mixed," and the "neuropsychological dysfunction."

Despite terminological variations from study to study, sadistic and angry murderers present a number of consistent characteristics. To illustrate this point, we have grouped in **Tables 11.1 and 11.2** the primary characteristics of sadistic and angry sexual murderers.

Sexual murderers who kill the victim to eliminate any witnesses have as their primary intent the sexual assault of their victim; the murder is merely instrumental. This type of murderer is often described as less likely to have had long-term emotional relationships and his phallometric (sexual interests measured by penile plethysmography) profile is deviant. His victims are unknown to him and often younger than 30, and his sexual assault is characterized by coitus and some sadistic elements. The murder may or may not be premeditated, and may be panicky or cold-blooded, depending on his criminal experience. Usually, the victim's wounds are restricted to a single site on the body, and the victim is found lying on her back. Often, the crime is committed, and the victim's corpse found, at the site at which first contact between the murderer and the victim occurred.

The typological studies of sexual homicide conducted to date suffer from several limitations. Firstly, most of the studies comprise a wide spectrum of sexual murderers (serial and non-serial murderers, sexual murderers of women, men, children), completely ignoring the specific characteristics of each group. It should also be noted that some studies have limited themselves to a single source of data, such as clinical observations, self-reported information, or data from official

Table 11.1	Summary of the Characteristics of the Sadistic Sexual Murderer

Characteristics of the Murderer	Pre-Crime Phase
<ul><li>mobility</li><li>high intelligence</li><li>post-secondary education</li><li>preference for work placing him in contact with authority or death</li><li>cruelty towards animals</li><li>enuresis during childhood</li><li>fire-setting</li><li>tendency to be isolated</li><li>antisocial, narcissistic, schizoid, and obsessive-compulsive personality disorders</li><li>severe psychopathy</li><li>lack of empathy</li><li>history of breaking and entering</li><li>history of sexual crimes</li><li>fascination for objects related to police work</li><li>possession of violent pornography and detective magazines</li><li>paraphilias: cannibalism, vampirism, necrophilia, fetishism, masochism, transvestitism, voyeurism, exhibitionism, obscene telephone calls</li><li>sexual sadism</li><li>serial sexual crimes</li></ul>	<ul><li>impressive amounts of unexpressed aggression</li><li>very elaborate sadistic fantasies</li><li>fantasy world more important to him than reality</li><li>situational stress</li><li>often murders after a blow to his self-esteem</li><li>"hunts" his prey</li><li>selection of a specific victim following surveillance</li><li>premeditation of crime</li><li>consumption of alcohol prior to the crime</li></ul>

Modus operandi	Post-Crime Phase
<ul><li>ruse and manipulation to approach the victim</li><li>victim unknown to him</li><li>isolated crime scene, chosen in advance, far from his residence</li><li>vehicle used in commission of crime</li></ul>	<ul><li>moving of the corpse</li><li>hiding of the corpse</li><li>modus operandi reflects control</li><li>absence of weapons or evidence at the crime scene</li><li>interest in media coverage of the crime</li></ul>

Table 11.1	Continued

Modus operandi	Post-Crime Phase
• presence of instruments of torture or of a rape kit	• possible change of job or city after the crime
• modus operandi reflects sadistic fantasies	• may volunteer to help during the investigation
• victim held captive for several hours, with recording of aggression	• relatively normal behavior between crimes
• consumption of alcohol during the crime	• absence of remorse for his acts
• submission of victim demanded	• pleasure in describing the horror of his acts
• victim tied up and gagged	• low profile during incarceration
• fellatio by victim	
• anal or vaginal penetration of victim	
• possible sexual dysfunction	
• insertion of objects in various body cavities	
• prolonged and ritualized torture	
• mutilation of genital organs	
• non-random pattern of wounds on the victim's body	
• pre-mortem mutilation	
• death by strangulation	
• sexual arousal elicited by violent acts committed on the victim, culminating in the murder	
• dismembering	
• retention of souvenirs belonging to the victim or taken from her	

sources, which precludes the possibility of using multiple sources of data to draw up a complete and detailed profile of the sexual murderer and his crimes. Additionally, while some studies have proposed models in which the murderer's motivation and personality have been inferred, none propose a standardized method that permits adequate evaluation of these elements. Furthermore, most of the studies—regardless of whether their approaches are rooted in clinical psychology or law enforcement—pay little attention to pre-crime-phase variables, including situational factors that may have precipitated the sexual homicide. Finally, several authors have constructed their typology on the basis of clinical judgment, which precludes any verification of the validity of their analyses.

Table 11.2	Summary of the Characteristics of the Angry Sexual Murderer

Characteristics of the Murderer	Pre-Crime Phase
• mid-20s • residence and workplace near crime scene • average intelligence • married or in a stable relationship • little work experience • socially incompetent • not socially isolated • difficulties with authority • impulsivity • anger • selfish • various non-specific personality disorders • low to moderate psychopathy • presence of severe mental disorders such as mood disorders • history of violence towards women • history of substance abuse • no consumption of pornography • sexual dysfunctions • absence of sadistic sexual fantasies	• depressive mood • suicidal ideation • feelings of anger • reduced alcohol consumption prior to the crime • victim selected from murderer's daily activities • victim selected from a familiar setting • victim stance • rage displaced towards victim • desire to kill • absence of premeditation

Modus operandi	Post-Crime Phase
• access to crime scene on foot • victim is known to murderer • victim older than murderer • crime scene outdoors • crime scene known to murderer • use of a weapon found at the crime scene • minimal use of physical restraints • reduced consumption of alcohol during the crime • anxiety during crime • explosive and violent attack • vengeance is displaced to a specific victim	• feelings of relief • corpse of victim left at the crime scene • corpse left in view • body found on its back • crime scene reflects lack of organization • no interest for media coverage of the crime

Table 11.2	Continued	
Modus operandi		**Post-Crime Phase**

- blows specifically directed towards victim's face
- wounds on several areas of the bodies
- humiliation and extreme violence
- possible sexual assault of the victim
- insertion of objects into various body cavities of the victim
- absence of sperm at the crime scene
- murder provoked by the victim's words or actions
- murder by strangulation
- post-mortem sexual acts and mutilation
- overkill

In light of the limitations just described, Beauregard and Proulx developed a typology of sexual murderers of adult women based on objective crime-scene criteria and multivariate analyses.[2] This analysis yielded two sub-groups of sexual murderers, namely sadistic and angry.

Sadistic Sexual Murderer

Sadistic murderers premeditate their crime and select a victim previously unknown to them. During the crime, these murderers humiliate their victims, in many cases physically restrain them, and mutilate them. The crime lasts more than 30 minutes, which increases the risk of being caught by police. This type of murderer tends to move or hide the victim's corpse in order to avoid its detection. Moreover, sadistic sexual murderers sometimes dismember and hide their victim's corpse, select victims with specific characteristics, oblige their victims to commit sexual acts, and torture their victims. On the other hand, sadistic murderers are less likely to leave their victims on their backs than angry murderers. Sadistic murderers present a positive affect prior to the crime, such as sexual arousal, calmness, or feelings of well-being, and they report having deviant sexual fantasies prior to their crime. This positive affect may be related to deviant sexual fantasies and may be the expression of strong feelings associated with the thrill associated with the hunt and capture of the victim. Further, it may be hypothesized that premeditation and deviant sexual fantasies favor the execution of certain acts (e.g., torture, mutilation, dismemberment) that instantiate the imagined crime scenario.

Angry Sexual Murderer

Angry murderers do not premeditate their crimes, and their victims are circumstantial. They do not usually humiliate, physically restrain, or mutilate their victims. The crime lasts less than 30 minutes, which decreases the risk of being caught by the police. The victim's corpse is often left at the crime scene. Furthermore, angry murderers present an anger affect prior to crime and report having experienced problems of loneliness and idleness prior to crime. We suggest that the differences in the relational problems of the two types of sexual murderers reflect differences in personality disorders. Our results demonstrate that angry murderers had a borderline personality disorder, indicative of a desire for contact with other people concomitant with an inability to obtain and maintain intimacy.[11] On the other hand, sadistic murderers exhibit schizoid and avoidant personality disorders, suggesting that they have renounced contact with other people in favor of fantasy worlds. This being so, it is understandable that no sadistic murderer reported problems of loneliness prior to committing his murder.

As can be seen, there exists different types of sexual murderers of women which is illustrated by their different offending patterns.[12] Most studies on the classification of sexual homicide have identified types congruent with the sadistic and the angry pathways. However, as it has been mentioned previously, these studies have mixed together sexual murderers of women, men, and children. But are they really all the same? When looking at studies on sexual murderers, the sexual homicide of women was the most frequently investigated; consequently, little research has been completed on other types of sexual murderers, especially on sexual murderers of men.

■ Sexual Murderers of Men

Sexual murderers of men correspond to the same definition of sexual homicide given by Ressler et al.[1] However, Drake identified other elements typical in cases of homosexual homicide: death does not occur on the offender's territory, no signs of forced entry, body found in the bedroom, signs of overkill and arson are evident, robbery occurred, and the victim lived alone.[13]

Homosexual Homicide Typology

To our knowledge, only one typology of sexual homicide of men has been developed. Based on his investigative experience, Geberth suggested a six-type classification of homosexual homicide. The "interpersonal violence-oriented disputes and assaults" are the most common type of sexual homicide of men. These are mostly the result of disputes between partners, ex-partners, or love triangles. This type of homosexual homicide may include instances where "ground rules" are not respected by one of the parties involved in the sexual activity (e.g., an older male attempting to carry the sexual activities beyond what has been negotiated). Often, these homicides are committed in a context of prostitution, where the prostitute or hustler denies being a homosexual and responds with extreme violence to this threat to his masculinity.

The second type of homosexual homicide identified by Geberth describes "murders involving forced anal rape and/or sodomy." These murderers are usually sexually motivated, but there is no sexual gratification associated with the killing. Death occurs mainly from the amount of force used to overcome the victim's resistance or in order to prevent identification.

The third type identified is the "lust murder." These homicides often present evidence of sadism and mutilation to the victim's genitals. The crime is meticulously premeditated according to the deviant sexual fantasies of the offender. According to Geberth, the offender will exhibit several characteristics of Hare's description of a psychopath, such as deception, superficial charm, and callousness.

"Homosexual serial murders" correspond to the fourth type identified by Geberth. They hunt for vulnerable victims that are easy to control, such as children and prostitutes. These homicides involve lust murders, thrill killings, and child killings as well as robbery homicides that are homosexually oriented. They can be characterized by acts of mutilation and dismemberment of the victim's body, performed in order to shock those who will find it, to facilitate its transportation, or simply to prevent the victim's identification.

In the "robbery/homicide of homosexuals," offenders hunt for potential victims engaging in high-risk behaviors (e.g., cruising) in locations known to be frequented by some homosexuals (e.g., gay bars, saunas). Others, either alone or in a group, will use homosexual prostitution as a vehicle to assault or rob a gay customer who is willing to pay to have sex. Finally, "homophobic assaults and gay bashing" incidents are performed by individuals showing an intense hatred for homosexuals.[14]

The typology by Geberth is interesting, particularly from an investigative viewpoint, because the main characteristics concern the crime scene. However, the pre-crime phase and the characteristics of the offenders are neglected by this perspective. In order to better understand sexual murderers of men, Beauregard and Proulx described a group of men who have killed another man in a sexual context as well as a new classification on this particular type of sexual murderer.[15]

Characteristics of Sexual Murderers of Men

Victimology

In cases of sexual homicide of men, the victims are generally older than their offenders. The murderers in the sample of Beauregard and Proulx are on average 27.8 years old at the time of the crime, compared to 33 years old for the victims.[15] These results are in agreement with studies on homosexual violence, which report that victims of homosexual homicides are usually older than the offender.[16,17]

Two thirds of the sexual murderers in Beauregard and Proulx's sample killed a victim who was of homosexual orientation.[15] Even if this particular result is not reported in other studies on sexual homicide, it suggests that the routine activities of some victims may put them more at risk for such crimes. A single homosexual man may look for sexual contact with unknown partners in gay bars, therefore increasing his risk of being victimized by a predator. Moreover, in half of the cases in the sample, victims were living alone. According to Marcus Felson, the absence of a "capable guardian" is a factor which increases the probability of a crime being committed by a motivated offender. Knowing that the victim lives alone assures the offender that there will be no witnesses and no one to interfere during the crime.[18]

Finally, in almost half of the cases the victims had used drugs or alcohol prior to the crime. This consumption of drugs or alcohol, combined with a desire to have sexual contact with another man, may have reduced the victims' ability to assess the potential dangers of bringing home a stranger. Furthermore, it is possible that victims under the influence of drugs or alcohol may be more vulnerable because they are less able to defend themselves during an attack.

Pre-Crime Factors

The majority of sexual murderers of male victims used alcohol and/or drugs before the crime. It can be hypothesized that the consumption of drugs or alcohol served as a disinhibitor, resulting in anger and violence for some sexual murderers of men. However, it is interesting to note that this consumption of drugs or alcohol is similar to the behavior demonstrated by some sexual murderers of adult female victims from Beauregard and Proulx's study.[15] Others reported that substance abuse in individuals who committed homicide and sexual assault is more serious than in the general population and could contribute to the crime by disinhibiting rage as well as stimulating sexual desire.[19,20]

Interestingly, Beauregard and Proulx's study showed that in almost half of the cases, financial problems prior to the crime were reported by sexual murderers of men.[15] This result, which is particular to this study, may be related to a motivation apart from sexual or vindictive motives for these sexual murderers. For some sexual murderers in the sample, sex was used to attract a victim for an intended theft crime, but because of unplanned situational elements (e.g., inability to control the victim), the planned theft degenerated into murder. Burglary has been linked to sexual homicide by other authors.[21]

Finally, only a minority of sexual murderers in the sample admitted to deviant sexual fantasies prior to the crime. This result corresponds with observations of sexual murderers of female victims in that only a minority of them is sexually motivated. For instance, Langevin and his colleagues found that 31% of sexual murderers reported sexual gratification as a motivation,[19] whereas 69% identified a fusion of anger and sexuality. In Beauregard and Proulx's study, 33% of sexual murderers of female victims reported deviant sexual fantasies before committing the crime.[2]

Crime Characteristics

Concerning crime characteristics, it is noteworthy that almost all crimes committed by sexual murderers of male victims were premeditated. For instance, Robert Ressler and his colleagues found that 86% of organized sexual murderers premeditated their offense compared to 44% for disorganized offenders.[1] In Grubin's study, a third of his sample planned the offense, whereas in Beauregard and Proulx's study, only 5% of sexual murderers who used the anger pathway premeditated the crime compared to 81% of sexual murderers who used the sadistic pathway.[2,22]

The use of a weapon is a crime characteristic that distinguishes sexual murderers of male victims from sexual murderers of female victims. The majority of offenders used a weapon to commit their crime in our research. Similarly, in the 37 cases of homosexual serial homicides reported by Geberth, 35 victims were killed either by a firearm or a knife.[14] According to Miller and Humphreys, a knife was used in 54% of cases of homosexual homicides, and in 19% of cases a firearm was used, often after being stabbed and assaulted. In sexual murderers of women, the preferred method used to kill the victim is strangulation.[23] Two possible explanations could account for such a difference. First, male victims possess greater physical strength than female victims, and offenders may want to prevent opposition or resistance. Second, it is possible that the use of a weapon is directly related to the premeditation of the crime, the weapon being used primarily to threaten and/or to control the victim during the burglary or sexual assault.

Mutilations rarely occur, a result that contrasts drastically with the literature on homicide of men, where mutilations, and especially overkill, are typical characteristics. Moreover, a study by Bell and Vila revealed that overkill was greater among homosexual victims of homicide compared to heterosexual victims. One possible explanation is that mutilation and/or overkill has not been well documented in the available data.[24]

Cases of sexual homicide usually present a certain degree of organization. Along with the premeditation of the crime and the use of a weapon, 60% of sexual murderers reported having moved or hidden the body after the crime. Hiding or moving the victim's body after the crime is usually an attempt to delay body discovery and conceal evidence. Moreover, it may provide more time for the offender to flee the crime scene, come up with a good alibi, or even to move to another city or another state. In cases of sexual homicides of men, it is possible that high organization is related to the crime location such as the offender's or the victim's residence. In those cases, it is crucial to move the victim's body in order not to be associated with the crime.

■ Towards a Typology of Sexual Murderers Against Men

Descriptions of sexual murderers of adult male victims provide some understanding of this particular type of sexual homicide and also of the main features. However, such descriptive analysis of each variable separately does not offer a clear picture of the context in which the crimes are committed. This is why a classification of sexual murderers who killed men is proposed that takes into account the entire criminal event of the sexual homicide, including the study of the offender, the victim, and the context of the crime.[25]

The Avenger

Individuals corresponding to this type of sexual murderer are usually involved in prostitution activities and can be of homosexual, heterosexual, or of bisexual orientation. The consumption of drugs and alcohol is an important feature of these murders. Most have been convicted of property and violent crimes before the murder. Most also have experienced psychological, physical, and sexual abuse during childhood. Moreover, the type of sexual activity requested by the client in a prostitution context, or a triggering event occurring during or after the sexual exchange, may elicit memories from the abuse, unleash the rage of the offender, and lead to the homicide. The offender is avenging himself directly on his current partner for all the grievances (present or past) of which he feels he has been a victim. The homicide is preceded by anger; it is usually committed by strangulation or by using a weapon of opportunity (kitchen knife, a pillow, phone cord). Because of the rage of this offender, evidence of expressive violence can be found on the victim, who is usually older than the offender.

The Sexual Predator

The second type of sexual murderer of male victims identified is the sexual predator. This offender is mainly motivated by deviant sexual fantasies. Homosexual in sexual orientation, he presents criminal antecedents of sexual crimes, especially against male children or adolescents. For these sexual murderers, the sexual assault and the homicide are premeditated. Most often, the targeted victim is an adolescent or a young man, unknown to the offender, and not necessarily of homosexual orientation. The offending process starts with the abduction/confinement of the victim, and sadistic acts (mutilations, sodomy, and humiliation) are performed during the crime. Evidence of expressive violence is found on the victim's body. The crime usually lasts more than 30 minutes, but it can go as long as 24 hours in some cases.

The Nonsexual Predator

The nonsexual predator is not motivated by anger or by deviant sexual fantasies. The homicide is not planned, but is more accidental or instrumental. The principal motivation for the crime is to rob the victim, and sex is used solely as a means of entrapment. In most of the cases, this type of sexual homicide can be described as a robbery that degenerated into the death of the victim because of his resistance. Predation is related to the choice of victim: often, this offender uses the visibility and the homosexual orientation of the victim to seduce him and to bring him to an isolated area (usually the victim's residence) where he will be able to commit his crime without interference. His hunting field is established according to the availability of targets and potential victims. Thus, gay bars, "cruising" bars, and places reputed to be frequented by homosexuals are attractive to this offender. The victim is chosen for his vulnerability (lives alone, reluctant to report a robbery to the police, feels guilty after being manipulated, etc.), his easy access (lives or goes often to the gay district), and his visibility (gay bars and gay district are usually frequented by homosexuals; some are very open about their sexual orientation).

The murderer may be heterosexual or homosexual; he may act alone or with the help of an accomplice. The crime may be committed with a weapon found on the crime scene or brought by the offender. Violence is instrumental in the sense that it serves to commit the burglary or to overcome the victim's resistance. Usually, the victim is not sexually assaulted, but sexual contact may occur between the offender and the victim in order to manipulate the victim. The sexual contact would serve to trap the victim. The crime phase is generally of short duration, with the offender leaving the crime scene right after the homicide. Sexual murderers of this type may use alcohol or drugs prior to the crime. Often, they have a diversified criminal career with an emphasis on crimes against property.

Beauregard and Proulx suggested that homosexual men are victimized mainly because of their situational vulnerability. Life habits or routine activities of these men may have increased their risk of becoming a victim of sexual homicide.[15] Routine activities theory demonstrates that the probability that a crime will occur depends on three factors: an attractive target, the absence of a capable guardian, and the presence of a motivated offender. As can be seen from these results as well as in other studies, male victims of sexual homicide generally live alone, they have used alcohol or drugs before the crime, they are reputed to not report certain crimes to the police, and some of them go to gay bars in order to get acquainted with a stranger or to "cruise." Thus, certain types of criminals choose these hunting fields in order to select an attractive and vulnerable target.

Sexual murderers of male victims exhibit a variety of motivating factors. Some are motivated by revenge, others by profit or sadistic fantasies. Interestingly, revenge and profit are motivations that have not been found in the sexual homicide of women. Moreover, these motivations are directly related to specific contexts (e.g., financial difficulties, prostitution), which once again highlight the importance of looking at the entire criminal event in sexual homicide.

Sexual murderers of men share some similarities with those who kill women. However, some of their offending patterns and motivations vary and are specific to this type of murderer, once again pointing to the heterogeneity of sexual murderers and sexual homicides. Individuals who kill children in a sexual context seem also to exhibit a specific offending pattern mainly influenced by different routine activities and a sadistic motivation.

■ Sexual Murderers of Children

Mainly because of the apparent low frequency of occurrence, empirical researches on sexual homicide and sexual murderers of children have been limited. As we previously mentioned, most of the research conducted on sexual homicide and sexual murderers has focused on those individuals who killed an adult woman. Because of the difficulties related to collecting information on these offenders, very few empirical studies have looked specifically at sexual homicide and sexual murderers of children.

Sexual Homicide of Children

The selection of a child victim could be related to the fact that they represent easy, weak, vulnerable, or available targets. In some instances, it may also be that some individuals present a deviant sexual preference and are sexually aroused and gratified by the suffering and the killing of a child victim.[26] This type of pedophile molests children with the express desire to physically harm the victims. Typically, the victim is a stranger and may be stalked and/or abducted from places where children tend to gather (e.g., playgrounds, schools, shopping centers). The crime is often premeditated, ritualized, and the victim's body may be mutilated. Moreover, these offenders report few contacts with children outside of their offense, rank low on social competences, and are more likely to be classified as sadists.[27,28]

Comparative Studies of Sexual Murderers of Children

To our knowledge, only three comparative studies involving sexual murderers of children have been conducted. Results from these studies revealed that sexual murderers were rated significantly higher on the Psychopathy Checklist-Revised (PCL-R), had a greater incidence of psychosis, personality disorders (antisocial), paraphilias (sadism), and addictions, and showed more deviant phallometric responses to depictions of sexual assaults of children and adults. Results suggested also that sexual murderers significantly more often victimized strangers and had been charged or convicted in the past of violent nonsexual and sexual offenses as compared to a non-homicidal group of sex offenders.[29,30]

According to Firestone et al., "there is a limited amount of psychological research available on men who commit sexual murders, and no distinction has been made between those who have victimized adults and those who victimized children."[31] Thus, in order to better understand sexual murderers of children, Beauregard and colleagues conducted comparisons with a group of sexual murderers of women on developmental, pre-crime, crime, and post-crime factors.[32]

Developmental Factors

Beauregard and his colleagues observed that sexual murderers of women report significantly more daydreaming and enuresis (during childhood) as compared to sexual murderers of children. As to the life and sexual history variables, a higher proportion of sexual murderers of women present frequent alcohol/drug abuse problems as compared to sexual murderers of children. Sexual murderers of children are, however, significantly more inclined to report experience of sexual abuse in childhood and deviant sexual fantasies than sexual murderers of women. These last two results are congruent with the attachment model of the development of sexual deviance.[33] According to this model, attachment reflects the bond between child and parent that provides the necessary security and confidence for the child to explore his world. The presence of negative childhood experiences—such as sexual abuse—may prevent the development of a secure attachment.[34] The failure to develop a secure attachment can lead to psychosocial deficits such as low self-esteem and lack of skills necessary to establish adequate relationship with peers.[35] The difficulty relating to peers can lead to seeking alternative means of fulfilling emotional and sexual needs in ways that do not challenge these deficits. It may be argued, therefore, that sexual scripts such as child molestation or even sexual homicide may be appealing to these offenders because it makes no demands on self-confidence and social skills that they lack and may be interpreted as an action that can provide the illusion of intimacy without fear of being rejected.[36] These scripts may be obtained through a social learning process by being exposed to or being a victim of sexual abuse.[37] Furthermore, these scripts may be used during masturbatory activities, thus pairing deviant sexual fantasies with orgasm and creating a conditioning process.[38] Negative childhood experiences, especially sexual abuse, may thus be seen as developmental risk factors leading to the offender's sexual preference for a child.[39] It is noteworthy that experience of sexual abuse during childhood and deviant sexual fantasies are also characteristics of sadistic offenders.[40]

The higher prevalence of deviant sexual fantasies in sexual murderers of children may be related to the motivations underlying sexual homicide. It may be hypothesized that sexual murderers of children are mainly sadistic, accounting for the importance of deviant sexual fantasies.[41] Sadists retreat from relationships with adults, where they typically have not been successful, and flee into a world of sexually coercive fantasies. Due to the amount of time they dedicate to their fantasies, they become elaborate and form an outlet for their unexpressed emotional states: rage, humiliation and suffering.[42] However, the use of coercive sexual fantasies as a coping strategy may prove insufficient if the sadist experiences unusually intense stressful events. The nature of this stress could be a generalized conflict, low self-esteem, or a feeling of rejection, as in the case of sexual murderers of children in our sample. Actualizing his fantasies through a sadistic sexual offense constitutes another coping strategy, which the sadist resorts to in order to deal with his internal distress.

Regarding the criminal career, sexual murderers of children present significantly more prior convictions for sexual crimes without contacts (e.g., indecent exposure, voyeurism, obscene phone calls) as compared to sexual murderers of women. Interestingly, this last result is congruent with previous studies on recidivism. Those who commit sexual crimes against children present a higher risk for sexual recidivism.[43] Hence, Hanson showed that the recidivism rate of rapists dropped gradually with age in adulthood, whereas for child molesters, it remained steady until the late forties.[44] According to Lussier, "it is not surprising then, that their criminal repertoire tends to include a more important proportion of sexual crimes."[45]

Pre-Crime Factors

Pre-crime factors include both predisposing and precipitating factors. Precipitating factors (48 hours prior to crime) are disinhibitors that are conceived as factors that favor sexual crimes. Predisposing factors (1 year prior to crime) represent an obstacle repetitively met by the individual in his life or a zone of vulnerability that has triggered the development of one or many ineffective coping strategies, such as avoidance, denial of emotions, or sexual deviance. Sexual murderers of children reported more perception of rejection and a generalized conflict, such as opposition or avoidance conducts toward a real or symbolic group of individuals in the year prior to the homicide as opposed to the sexual murderers of women. This is congruent with Lanning's explanation of sexual homicide of children; he states that in many cases, the use of lethal violence may be due to poor social and interpersonal skills of the offender. Because of this difficulty of interacting with others, especially with adults, those offenders may possibly target children because they are weak, vulnerable, and available (emotional congruence). This result also concurs with the finding that sexual murderers of children reported more generalized conflict as opposed to sexual murderers of women. According to Ward and Beech, perceived rejection and generalized conflict "can be viewed in terms of attachment insecurity leading to problems establishing intimate relationships with adults." Some sexual offenders with a *disorganized* attachment style "are likely to use sexual offending as one of several possible strategies of externally based control in response to the intense negative emotional states which are the sequelae of such an attachment style."[46]

In the 48 hours prior to the crime though, sexual murderers of women are significantly more prone to use alcohol and target a victim who is under the influence of drugs and/or alcohol. Almost all sexual murderers of children (90%) report prior contacts with the victim as compared to 56% of the sexual murderers of women. Further, a significantly larger proportion of sexual murderers of children uses pornography and is unemployed prior to committing the crime as compared to sexual murderers of women.

Crime Factors

The study by Beauregard et al. tested crime factors including crime phase variables and crime scene characteristics. Results showed that adult women are more often killed at night as compared to children. However, premeditation of the crime is significantly more frequent for sexual murderers of children as opposed to sexual murderers of women. Regarding crime scene characteristics, sexual murderers of children use strangulation to kill their victim, and they dismember and conceal the victim's body more often as compared to sexual murderers of women. These modus operandi characteristics, in addition to deviant sexual fantasies, are largely congruent with results from Dietz, Hazelwood, and Warren, which is probably the most complete study on the issue of the crime phase of sadistic offenders.[47] Their results showed that crimes of sadists were planned (93%), and the victim was usually unknown (83%). The victim was tortured (100%), tied up and gagged (87%), and sexual acts were diverse, including sodomy (73%), fellatio (71%) and vaginal intercourse (57%). When the victim was killed, it was often by asphyxia (58%) and the victim's corpse was concealed (65%). Furthermore, hiding the victim's body is an associated feature of sadism.

Finally, some of the significant differences between sexual murderers of children and sexual murderers of women can be better understood by a routine activity approach. For predatory crime, which usually depends on direct physical contact between the offender and the crime target, the routine activity approach emphasizes the importance of the daily activities of offenders and targets. As illustrated by our results, sexual murderers of women are more likely than sexual murderers of children to (1) be characterized by drug and/or alcohol abuse and dependence, (2) be characterized by frequent consumption of alcohol prior to the crime, (3) target a victim under the influence of drugs and/or alcohol, and (4) commit the crime at night. Thus, as part of their routine activities, these offenders are more likely to encounter potential victims in places where consumption of drugs or alcohol is involved. Hence, it is possible that these offenders will meet the victim in a bar, a club, or at a party where a potential victim has been consuming alcohol or drugs too, increasing her risk and vulnerability. Sexual murderers of children present a different pattern. Pedophile murderers were more likely to be unemployed prior to the crime, to have had prior contact with the victim, and to have used pornography prior to the crime as compared to sexual murderers of women. It may be hypothesized that sexual murderers of children spend some of their leisure time at home watching pornography and then go to places where potential victims gather (e.g., playgrounds, schools, and convenience stores) in order to establish prior contacts with victims (e.g., grooming). They wait for an opportunity, such as the absence of parents or guardians, and then attract the child victim to an isolated location where they will commit the assault and homicide. A recent study demonstrated that the type of victim (e.g., child versus adult women) would influence the hunting field of offenders (i.e., the type of area where offenders hunt for victims), which in turn is influenced by the victim's routine activities.[48]

Interestingly sexual murderers of children do not seem to present several offending patterns among them. Most present the core characteristics and predatory behaviors of the sadistic sex offender. However, situational factors leading to the commission of the crime are specific to this particular type of victims, which clearly suggest that sexual murderers of children are different from those individuals who kill a woman or a man in a sexual context.

■ Conclusion

Sexual homicide is a crime of a relatively rare occurrence, but it is the sexual crime that attracts the most attention from the media and the community, mainly due to apparent random victim selection. Moreover, this particular form of crime is difficult to understand because sex, normally associated with pleasure and creation, is linked to the painful, destructive act of killing. In order to make sense of these horrible crimes, it is important to investigate the offending processes of these murderers and the *entire* criminal event, which includes the offender, the victim, and the context of the crime. The results presented in this chapter clearly demonstrate that depending on the type of victims (women, men, and children), sexual murderers seem to be driven by different criminal motivations and will exhibit different predatory behaviors linked to specific routine activities.

A better understanding of the different types of sexual murderers is beneficial for at least two important actors of the criminal justice system: corrections and police. First, the knowledge on the different offending process of sexual murderers may help clinicians involved in treatment and in risk evaluation to better identify their offense cycle and factors that may be associated to high-risk situation. Second, the police may use this information in the criminal profiling process. The different offending pathways identified and their related characteristics may serve to better understand what happened on the crime scene and suggest a potential portrait of the offender.[49]

References

1. Ressler, R. K., Burgess, A. W., Douglas, J. E. (1988). *Sexual Homicide: Patterns and Motives*. New York: Lexington Books.
2. Beauregard, E., Proulx, J. (2002). Profiles in the offending process of non-serial sexual murderers. *Int J Offender Therap Compar Criminol* 46:386–399.
3. Beech, A. D., Fisher, D., Ward, T. (2005). Sexual murderers' implicit theories. *J Interpers Viol* 20:1366–1389.
4. Beech, A. D., Robertson, D., Clarke, J. (2001). *Towards a Sexual Murder Typology*. Paper presented October 31–November 3, 2001 at the Association for the Treatment of Sexual Abusers, San Antonio, TX.
5. Clarke, J., Carter, A. (1999). *Sexual Murderers: Their Assessment and Treatment*. Paper presented October 29–November 1, 1999 at the meeting of the Association for Treatment of Sexual Abusers, Orlando, FL.
6. Folino, J. O. (2000). Sexual homicides and their classification according to motivation: A report from Argentina. *Int J Offender Therap Compar Criminol* 44:740–750.
7. Keppel, R. D., Walter, R. (1999). Profiling killers: A revised classification model for understanding sexual murder. *Int J Offender Therap Compar Criminol* 43:417–437.
8. Kocsis, R. N. (1999). Criminal profiling of crime scene behaviors in Australian sexual murders. *Austral Police J* 53:113–116.
9. Meloy, R. J. (2000). The nature and dynamics of sexual homicide: An integrative review. *Aggress Viol Behav* 5:1–22.

10. Revitch, E., Schlesinger, L. B. (1981). *Psychopathology of Homicide*. Spring-field, IL: Charles C Thomas, Publisher.
11. Beck, A. T., Freeman, A. (1990). *Cognitive Therapy of Personality Disorders*. New York: The Guilford Press, p. 396.
12. Beauregard, E., Proulx, J., Brien, T., St-Yves, M. (2005). Colérique et sadique, deux profils de meurtriers sexuels [Anger and sadistic, two profiles of sexual murderers]. Pp. 203–232 in J. Proulx, M. Cusson, E. Beauregard, A. Nicole (Eds.), *Les Meurtriers Sexuels: Analyse Comparative et Nouvelles Perspectives*. Montréal, Québec: Les Presses de l'Université de Montréal.
13. Drake, D. S. (1999). Recognizing gay homicide. *Minnesota Gay Homicide Study*. http://www.chronline.org/PDFs/Research_Brief_Recognizing_Gay_Homicide2004.pdf. Accessed June 21, 2007.
14. Geberth, V. (1996). *Practical Homicide Investigation: Tactics, Procedures, and Forensic Techniques*, 3rd edition. Boca Raton, FL: CRC Press.
15. Beauregard, E., Proulx, J. (2007). A classification of sexual homicide against men. *Int J Offender Therap Compar Criminol*, 5:420–432.
16. Sagarin, E., Macnamara, D. E. (1975). The homosexual as a crime victim. *Int J Criminol Penol* 3:13–25.
17. Tremblay, P., Boucher, E., Ouimet, M., Biron, L. (1998). Rhetoric of over-victimization: The gay village as a case study. *Can J Criminol*. January:1–20.
18. Felson, M. (2002). *Crime and Everyday Life*, 3rd edition. Thousand Oaks, CA: Sage.
19. Langevin, R., Ben-Aron, M. H., Wright, P., et al. (1988). The sex killer. *Ann Sex Res* 1:263–301.
20. Yates, E., Barbaree, H. E., Marshall, W. L. (1984). Anger and deviant sexual arousal. *Behav Therap* 15:287–294.
21. Schlesinger, L. B., Revitch, E. (1999). Sexual burglaries and sexual homicide: Clinical, forensic, and investigative considerations. *J Am Acad Psychiatr Law* 27:227–238.
22. Grubin, D. (1994). Sexual murder. *Br J Psychiatr* 165:624–629.
23. Miller, B., Humphreys, L. (1980). Lifestyles and violence: Homosexual victims of assault and murder. *Qual Sociol* 3:169–185.
24. Bell, M. D., Vila, R. I. (1996). Homicide in homosexual victims: A study of 67 cases from the Broward County, Florida, medical examiner's office (1982–1992), with special emphasis on overkill. *Am J Forens Med Pathol* 17:65–69.
25. Meier, R. F., Kennedy, L. W., Sacco, V. F. (2001). Crime and the criminal event perspective. Pp. 1–27 in R. F. Meier, L. W. Kennedy, V. F. Sacco (Eds.), *The Process and Structure of Crime: Criminal Events and Crime Analysis*. New Brunswick: Transaction Publishers.
26. Lanning, K. V. (1994). Sexual homicide of children. *APSAC Advisor* 7:40–44.
27. Holmes, R. M. (1991). *Sex crimes*. Newbury Park, CA: Sage.

References

References

28. Holmes, S. T., Holmes, R. M. (2002). *Sex crimes: Patterns and behavior*, 2nd edition. Newbury Park, CA: Sage.
29. Firestone, P., Bradford, J. M., Greenberg, D. M., Larose, M. R. (1998). Homicidal sex offenders: Psychological, phallometric, and diagnostic features. *J Am Acad Psychiatr Law* 26:537–552.
30. Firestone, P., Bradford, J. M., Greenberg, D. M., Nunes, K. L. (2000). Differentiation of homicidal child molesters, nonhomicidal child molesters, and nonoffenders by phallometry. *Am J Psychiatr* 157:1847–1850.
31. Firestone, P., Bradford, J. M., Greenberg, D. M., et al. (1998). Homicidal and non-homicidal child molesters: Psychological, phallometric, and criminal features. *Sexual Abuse: J Res Treatment* 10:305–323, p. 306.
32. Beauregard, E., Proulx, J., Stone, M., Michaud, P. (2007). Sexual murderers of children: Developmental, pre-crime, crime, and post-crime factors. *Int J Offender Therap Compar Criminol*, in press.
33. Ward, T., Hudson, S. M., Marshall, W. L., Siegert, R. (1995). Attachment style and intimacy deficits in sexual offenders: A theoretical framework. *Sexual Abuse: J Res Treatment* 7:317–335.
34. Cicchetti, D., Lynch, M. (1995). Failures in the expectable environment and their impact on individual development: The case of child maltreatment. Pp. 32–71 in D. Cicchetti, D. J. Cohen (Eds.), *Developmental Psychopathology, Vol. 2: Risk, Disorder, and Adaptation*. New York: John Wiley.
35. Marshall, W. L., Hudson, S. M., Hodkinson, S. (1993). The importance of attachment bonds in the development of juvenile sex offending. Pp. 164–181 in H. E. Barbaree, W. L. Marshall, S. M. Hudson (Eds.), *The Juvenile Sex Offenders*. New York: The Guilford Press.
36. Marshall, W. L., Eccles, A. (1993). Pavlovian conditioning processes in adolescent sex offenders. Pp. 118–142 in H. E. Barbaree, W. L. Marshall, S. M. Hudson (Eds.), *The Juvenile Sex Offenders*. New York: The Guilford Press.
37. Laws, D. R., Marshall, W. L. (1990). A conditioning theory of the etiology and maintenance of deviant sexual preference and behavior. Pp. 209–229 in W. L. Marshall, D. R. Laws, H. E. Barbaree (Eds.), *Handbook of Sexual Assault: Issues, Theories, and Treatment*. New York: Plenum.
38. Abel, G. G., Blanchard, E. B. (1974). The role of fantasy in the treatment of sexual deviation. *Arch Gen Psychiatr* 30:467–475.
39. Lussier, P., Beauregard, E., Proulx, J., Nicole, A. (2005). Developmental factors related to deviant sexual preferences in child molesters. *J Interpers Viol* 20:999–1017.
40. Gratzer, T., Bradford, M. W. (1995). Offender and offense characteristics of sexual sadists: A comparative study. *J Forens Sci* 40:450–455.
41. Proulx, J., Blais, E., Beauregard, E. (2006). Sadistic sexual aggressors. Pp. 61–77 in W. L. Marshall, Y. M. Fernandez, L. E. Marshall, G. A. Serran

(Eds.), *Sexual Offender Treatment: Controversial Issues*. Winchester, UK: Wiley.

42. Proulx, J., McKibben, A., Lusignan, R. (1996). Relationship between affective components and sexual behaviors in sexual aggressors. *Sexual Abuse: J Res Treatment* 8:279–289.

43. Hanson, R. K., Steffy, R. A., Gauthier, R. (1993). Long-term recidivism of child molesters. *J Consult Clin Psychol* 61:646–652.

44. Hanson, R. K. (2002). Recidivism and age: Follow-up data from 4673 sexual offenders. *J Interpers Viol* 17:1046–1062.

45. Lussier, P. (2005). The criminal activity of sexual offenders in adulthood: Revisiting the specialization debate. *Sexual Abuse: J Res Treatment* 17:269–292, p. 283.

46. Ward, T., Beech, A. R. (2006). An integrated theory of sexual offending. *Aggress Viol Behav* 11:44–63, p. 55.

47. Dietz, P. E., Hazelwood, R. R., Warren, J. (1990). The sexually sadistic criminal and his offenses. *Bull Am Acad Psychiatr Law* 18:163–178.

48. Beauregard, E., Rossmo, D. K., Proulx, J. (2007). A descriptive model of the hunting process of serial sex offenders: A rational choice approach. *J Family Viol*, 22:449–463.

49. Beauregard, E. (2007). The role of profiling in the investigation of sexual homicide. Pp. 193–212 in J. Proulx, E. Beauregard, M. Cusson, A. Nicole (Eds.), *Sexual Murderers: A Comparative Analysis and New Perspectives*. Chichester, UK: Wiley.

Criminal Predatory Behavior in the Federal Bureau of Prisons

Glenn D. Walters

Federal Correctional Institution, Schuylkill, Pennsylvania

We have all heard the stories about inmates being raped or assaulted in prison; some of us may even have been deterred from committing a crime after hearing one of these stories. Rape and assault undoubtedly occur in American prisons and correctional facilities, but the vast majority of inmates are neither raped nor beaten senseless. Most, however, have been victims or perpetrators of predation in prison. The seeming paradox of high rates of predation coupled with low rates of sexual and nonsexual assault can be explained by the fact that predation comes in many forms, ranging from the overt and obvious to the covert and discreet. Predation assumes planning, yet the level of planning varies from inmate to inmate and from one predatory act to the next. Given the heterogeneous nature of the federal prison population, variety is the rule when it comes to predation. The goal of this chapter is to offer a model of inmate predation in the Federal Bureau of Prisons (BOP) that calls attention to two related but distinct strains of criminal predatory behavior: proactive and reactive.

■ The Scope of the Problem

Back in 1984 when I began working in the BOP, there were 32,000 inmates, 12,000 staff, and 44 different institutions in the federal prison system. Ronald

Reagan was running for reelection, Los Angeles was hosting the summer Olympics, and TV shows like *Dynasty* and *Dallas* were at the top of the Nielsen ratings. Twenty-three year later, the BOP has grown to 190,000 inmates, 35,000 staff, and 113 institutions. Hence, between 1984 and 2007 there was a 494% increase in the inmate population of the BOP, but only a 192% increase in staffing and a 157% increase in institutions. The density of institutions and the inmate-to-staff ratio have more than doubled in the past 23 years, from 727 inmates per institution in 1984 to 1681 inmates per institution in 2007 and from 2.69 inmates per staff member in 1984 to 5.43 inmates per staff member in 2007. To put it succinctly, BOP staff is increasingly being asked to do more with less.

What might account for the dramatic increase in the BOP inmate population over the past 23 years? The Sentencing Reform Act of 1984, which established determinate sentencing, abolished parole, and reduced the amount of good time inmates could earn, and mandatory sentencing charters enacted in 1986, 1988, and 1990 both raised the number of inmates entering prison and reduced the number of inmates leaving prison. However, these were not the only factors responsible for the rapid growth of the federal prison population between 1984 and 2007. America has been engaged in a war on drugs since the early 1900s, but the war gained new momentum in the late 1980s and early 1990s with the advent of several presidential initiatives. The drug war not only increased the BOP inmate population but also changed the population's composition. In 1984, 29% of the BOP inmate population was serving time for drugs; by 2007 the percentage had risen to 55%.

Federal statutes on gun control, immigration, child pornography, and carjacking as well as the Revitalization Act of 1997 in which the BOP took custody of all District of Columbia (DC) code felony offenders, not only increased the overall prison population but also introduced a new class of violent offender to the BOP. In 1984, the only violent crime the United States Attorney's Office was prosecuting to any extent was bank robbery; by 2007, murderers, rapists, assaulters, burglars, and child molesters were entering the system in record numbers. Changes in both the size and composition of the federal prison population may have contributed to a rise in violence within the BOP as exemplified by a 155% increase in the rate of inmate assaults on staff and a 206% increase in the rate of inmate assaults on other inmates between 1984 and 2007. In trying to make sense of these changes, I came up with a two-dimensional theory of criminal predatory behavior.

■ A Two-Dimensional Model of Criminal Predatory Behavior

In an attempt to understand criminal predatory behavior in the BOP, I developed several working theoretical models of criminality. I published my initial findings in a book on the criminal lifestyle and created an 80-item self-report measure, the Psychological Inventory of Criminal Thinking Styles (PICTS), to assess the eight thinking styles that I believed supported this lifestyle.[1] A continuing program of research and clinical observation has shown that these eight thinking styles can be grouped into two primary factors. I termed one factor proactive criminal thinking and the other factor reactive criminal thinking and constructed PICTS composite scores to measure each factor. I also began to notice similarities between the eight thinking styles measured by the PICTS and such crime-related psychological constructs as psychopathy and antisocial personality disorder. These observations eventually led to the formation of a general theory of criminal predatory behavior comprised of two interrelated factors, proactive criminality and reactive criminality.

The terms *proactive* and *reactive* were popularized by Kenneth Dodge in his work on aggression in children. Dodge and his colleagues observed that childhood aggression assumes one of two forms: instrumental or proactive aggression, and hostile or reactive aggression.[2,3] Proactive aggression is a goal-oriented behavior designed to achieve a tangible reward or objective, such as intimidating another child into giving up a prized possession. Reactive aggression, by contrast, is committed in retaliation for a perceived injustice or provocation, such as pushing a child who has bumped into you under the assumption that the bump was intentional. In comparing these two forms of aggression, Dodge held that while proactive aggression is cold-blooded, goal-directed, and calculated, reactive aggression is hot-blooded, affective, and unplanned. Although only a handful of studies have addressed the issue of proactive and reactive aggression in adults, results from these studies suggest that Dodge's proactive–reactive model may apply to adults as well as to children.[4,5]

Two studies conducted on PICTS measures of proactive and reactive criminal thinking provide preliminary support for the construct validity of the proactive–reactive model in adults. Research on children, for instance, demonstrates that proactive aggression is associated with positive outcome expectancies for aggression,[6] whereas reactive aggression is associated with hostile attribution biases.[7] In a study of incarcerated male federal prisoners, Walters determined that the PICTS Entitlement scale, a strong correlate of proactive criminal thinking, predicted positive outcome expectancies for crime but not hostile attribution biases, while the PICTS Cutoff scale, a strong correlate of reactive criminal thinking, predicted hostile attribution biases but not positive outcome expectancies for crime.[8] In a second study, Walters, Frederick, and Schlauch discovered that the PICTS proactive composite scale postdicted prior arrests for instrumental crimes like robbery and burglary but not reactive crimes like assault and domestic violence; conversely, the PICTS reactive composite scale postdicted prior arrests for reactive crimes but not prior arrests for proactive crimes.[9]

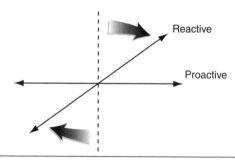

Figure 12.1   Proposed Relationship Between Proactive and Reactive Aggression in Children

Several important questions relating to proactive and reactive aggression in children appear to have been answered in recent years. First, there is growing consensus that proactive and reactive aggression are dimensions rather than categories.[10] Second, rather than falling at opposite ends of the same dimension, proactive and reactive aggression occupy different dimensions.[11] Third, although the proactive and reactive dimensions give rise to different sets of correlates, like the outcome expectancy–proactive and hostile attribution bias–reactive relationships described earlier, these two dimensions correlate .41 to .90 with one another,[12] thus giving rise to a correlated two-dimensional model (**Figure 12.1**). A two-dimensional model of criminal predatory behavior was consequently introduced using Dodge's work with childhood aggression as a theoretical guide. This was a developmentally informed theory that linked proactive and reactive aggression in children to proactive and reactive aggression and criminal thinking in adults.[13]

Criminal predation is a broad concept that encompasses proactive–reactive differences in behavior, affect, and cognition (**Table 12.1**). The purpose of this chapter is to determine whether adult proactive–reactive criminal predatory behavior parallels childhood proactive–reactive aggression, a purpose that will be addressed in three questions:

1. Does criminal predation, like childhood proactive–reactive aggression, form dimensions (quantitative distinctions) rather than categories (qualitative distinctions)?

2. If adult criminal predatory behavior, like childhood aggression, is dimensional in nature, then does it also partition into the proactive and reactive forms that have been observed in childhood aggression?

3. In the event proactive and reactive criminal predation are identified, is there evidence that these two strains of criminal behavior and thinking correlate with one another as do proactive and reactive childhood aggression?

Table 12.1	Behavioral, Affective, and Cognitive Features of Proactive and Reactive Criminal Predation	
Feature	Proactive	Reactive
Behavioral	Planned/Premeditated Scheming/Coldblooded Calculated/Manipulative	Spontaneous/Impulsive Emotional/Hotheaded Changeable/Capricious
Affective	Anticipation (of positive outcomes)	Anger (at perceived injustices)
Cognitive	Attitude of Privilege Rationalization	Loss of Focus Weak Personal Control

■ Dimensions or Categories?

An ongoing debate continues to rage over whether crime-related concepts like psychopathy, antisocial personality, and criminal lifestyle are best construed as dimensions or as categories. The dimensional view of criminal predatory behavior holds that offenders fall along one or more dimensions of predatory behavior and that individual differences between offenders are quantitative (differences in degree) rather than qualitative (differences in kind). The taxonomic view of predatory behavior maintains that offenders fall into discrete categories of individuals who do and do not engage in predatory behavior. Paul Meehl and his colleagues performed a valuable service to researchers interested in distinguishing between dimensional and taxonomic structure by creating the taxometric method. Taxometric procedures, such as mean above minus below a cut (MAMBAC), maximum covariance (MAXCOV), and maximum eigenvalue (MAXEIG), were constructed from statistical algorithms to assess the latent structure of psychopathological constructs like schizophrenia, depression, and anxiety and have been applied to crime-related constructs like psychopathy, antisocial personality, and criminal lifestyle.[14–19]

In the first study to investigate the latent structure of psychopathy with the taxometric method, Harris, Rice, and Quinsey collected Psychopathy Checklist-Revised (PCL-R) data on 653 mentally disordered offenders and observed taxonomic latent structure in items from Factor 2 of the PCL-R and in the eight individual items that correlated highest with the total PCL-R score.[20] Edens, Marcus, Lilienfeld, and Poythress have criticized Harris et al.'s choice of indicators (dichotomized), participants (mentally disordered forensic patients), and procedures (distributional analysis).[21] Conducting their own study on a group of 876 prison inmates and non-incarcerated court-ordered substance abuse patients, Edens and his colleagues found evidence of dimensional structure on the PCL-R, a finding that was replicated in several subsequent investigations.[21–24] Two self-report measures designed to assess psychopathy, the Psychopathic Personality Inventory (PPI) and the Levenson Self-Report Psychopathy scale (LSRP), also display dimensional structure when subjected to taxometric analysis.[25–27]

Ratings obtained from the DSM-IV diagnostic criteria for antisocial personality disorder showed signs of taxonicity when Skilling, Harris, Rice, and Quinsey studied a sample composed largely of participants from the earlier Harris et al. investigation.[28] Several more recently conducted studies, however, have produced results more consistent with a dimensional interpretation of the latent structure of antisocial personality. First, Marcus, Lilienfeld, Edens, and Poythress administered the Structured Interview for DSM-IV Axis II Personality Disorders (SCID-II) and Personality Diagnostic Questionnaire-4 (PDQ-4) to 1146 state inmates and non-incarcerated court-ordered substance abusers and found evidence of dimensional structure on both measures.[26] Second, Walters, Diamond, Magaletta, Geyer, and Duncan observed dimensional results when the three subscales of the Antisocial Features (ANT) scale of the Personality Assessment Inventory (PAI) were subjected to taxometric analysis, regardless of participant gender (male, female), race (white, black, Hispanic), or security level (low, medium, high).[29]

Taxometric research on two measures designed to assess features of a criminal lifestyle, a chart audit procedure known as the Lifestyle Criminality Screening Form (LCSF) and a self-report measure known as the Psychological Inventory of Criminal Thinking Styles (PICTS), showed consistent support for dimensional latent structure in a group of 771 male federal inmates.[30] A follow-up study determined that even when extreme scoring groups were employed, a situation conducive to the formation of pseudotaxa, the PICTS continued to exhibit dimensional structure.[31,32] Research conducted over the past several years on multiple measures of three crime-related constructs—psychopathy, antisocial personality, and criminal lifestyle—indicate that these constructs exist along one or more continua. The question that needs to be addressed next is whether these constructs form a single dimension or several different dimensions.

■ How Many Dimensions?

Now that it has been established with a reasonable degree of certainty that the latent structure of criminal predatory constructs like psychopathy, antisocial personality, and criminal lifestyle is dimensional, the next order of business is to calculate the number of individual dimensions that support criminal predation. The technique that researchers most often use to determine whether a set of variables falls along a single dimension or partitions into several different dimensions is factor analysis. In situations where a theory is available to guide our research efforts, confirmatory factor analysis is the recommended approach. The theory that will guide a structural equation modeling (SEM) confirmatory factor analysis of psychopathy, antisocial personality, and criminal lifestyle is that advanced by Walters, in which criminality is divided into two dimensions, proactive and reactive. It is accordingly reasoned that individual measures of psychopathy, antisocial personality, and criminal lifestyle should fit a two-dimensional model (proactive and reactive criminality) significantly better than alternate one-dimensional and three-dimensional models.

The one-dimensional model of criminal predation holds that psychopathy, antisocial personality, and criminal lifestyle converge on a single common trait or dimension, whereas the two-dimensional model of criminal predation maintains that psychopathy, antisocial personality, and criminal lifestyle form two overlapping dimensions, which in the current research context are referred to as proactive and reactive criminality. The three-dimensional model considered in the present set of analyses holds that psychopathy, antisocial personality, and criminal lifestyle form three separate dimensions, one for each construct or measure. The three-dimensional model can be viewed as a control model in the sense that it proposes greater commonality between different constructs from the same measure than between related constructs from different measures. This model will also be referred to as the *measures model* because it predicts that each measure constitutes a separate dimension.

In selecting measures for a confirmatory factor analysis of psychopathy, antisocial personality, and criminal lifestyle, it is imperative that we avoid comparing measures derived from different methods (self-report versus rating scale) because how a construct is measured (method) can have a profound effect on its pattern of correlation with other measures.[33] Thus, if we were to combine a behavioral measure of psychopathy (e.g., passive avoidance errors), with an interview-based measure of antisocial personality (e.g., SCID-II), and a self-report measure of criminal lifestyle (e.g., PICTS), this would skew the data in favor of the three-dimensional or measures model because of common method variance. In other words, measures of different constructs utilizing the same method are more likely to correlate than measures of the same construct utilizing different methods. Consequently, self-report measures of psychopathy (LSRP), antisocial personality (ANT), and criminal lifestyle (PICTS) that had previously yielded dimensional results were used to test the one-, two-, and three-dimensional models in the analyses described next.

In investigating the number of dimensions that support criminal predatory behavior, the one-dimensional model regressed the 13 LSRP, ANT, and PICTS scales onto a single latent factor (**Table 12.2**). The two-dimensional model, by comparison, regressed the LSRP Primary Psychopathy scale, the ANT Egocen-

Table 12.2	Descriptions and Factor Assignments for the Thirteen Indicators				
Measure	**Indicator**	**Description**	**1D**	**2D**	**3D**
LSRP	Primary Psychopathy	selfish, callous, manipulative, impulsive,	1	1	1
	Secondary Psychopathy	irresponsible, poor self-control	1	2	1
ANT	Antisocial Behaviors	history of behavior and conduct problems	1	2	2
PICTS	Egocentricity	self-centered, callous, remorseless	1	1	2
	Stimulus seeking	low tolerance of boredom	1	2	2
	Mollification	blaming, justifying, rationalizing	1	1	3
	Cutoff	rapid elimination of deterrents to crime	1	2	3
	Entitlement	ownership, privileged status	1	1	3
	Power orientation	exerting power and control over others	1	1	3
	Sentimentality	performing good deeds to excuse crime	1	1	3
	Superoptimism	unrealistic appraisal of criminal success	1	1	3
	Cognitive indolence	short-cut thinking, lack of critical reasoning	1	2	3
	Discontinuity	poor follow-through, lack of consistency	1	2	3

Abbreviations: LSRP, Levenson Self-Report Psychopathy scale; ANT, Personality Assessment Inventory Antisocial Features scale; PICTS, Psychological Inventory of Criminal Thinking Styles; 1D, one-dimensional model; 2D, two-dimensional model; 3D, three-dimensional model. Numbers under each dimensional model represent the dimension to which indicator was assigned.

tricity subscale, and the five PICTS scales that, according to the results of a study by Egan, McMurran, Richardson, and Blair, comprise a "willful criminality" factor (Mollification, Entitlement, Power Orientation, Sentimentality, and Superoptimism) onto a proactive latent factor and the LSRP Secondary Psychopathy scale, the ANT Antisocial Behaviors and Stimulus Seeking subscales, and the three PICTS scales that comprise a "lack of thoughtfulness" factor (Cutoff, Cognitive Indolence, Discontinuity) onto a reactive latent factor.[34] The three-dimensional or control model regressed each of the individual scales onto their respective measures: the LSRP Primary and Secondary Psychopathy scales onto a LSRP latent factor, the three ANT subscales onto an ANT latent factor, and the eight PICTS thinking style scales onto a PICTS latent factor.

SEM analysis of the three models in a preliminary sample of 139 male, medium-security federal inmates generated support for the absolute fit of the two-dimensional model as measured by the comparative fit index (CFI) and root mean square error of approximation (RMSEA) criterion.[35] In addition, relative fit analyses revealed that the two-dimensional model furnished a significantly better fit for the data than either the one-dimensional or three-dimensional models. The results of these analyses are suggestive—but far from conclusive—given the fact that reliable results for a SEM analysis require a sample size twice that of the present investigation to allow for at least 20 participants per measured variable ($20 \times 13 = 260$). Assuming that these initial findings hold up in a larger sample, there is preliminary support for the argument that—like childhood aggression—adult criminal predatory behavior partitions into two dimensions, proactive and reactive. The next step will be to determine whether these two dimensions are correlated, as with proactive and reactive childhood aggression, or whether they are independent of one another.

▪ Are the Dimensions Correlated or Independent?

The third question posed in this chapter is whether the putative proactive and reactive dimensions of criminal predatory behavior are correlated or independent. The proactive and reactive dimensions of childhood aggression have been found to correlate .41 to .90 with one another. Likewise, research studies conducted on the PCL-R Factor 1 and Factor 2 scores, the LSRP Primary and Secondary Psychopathy scales, and the PICTS proactive and reactive criminal thinking composite scales denote that the two dimensions correlate .40 to .72 with one another.[36–38] Therefore, adult predatory behavior parallels childhood aggressive behavior in the sense that both appear to be subsumed by two correlated dimensions referred to in this chapter as proactive and reactive criminality/aggression. One might therefore ask, what are the implications of this two-dimensional model of adult criminal predatory behavior?

▪ Implications of the Two-Dimensional Model

One implication of the dimensional nature of the two-dimensional model is that criminal predatory behavior is not a categorically distinct form of behavior but is an extension of normal aggressive behavior in both adults and children. Consequently, labeling someone a proactive or reactive predatory criminal may be inappropriate in that people differ in degree rather than in kind on the proactive and reactive dimensions of predatory criminal behavior. It would be more appropriate to identify a person's current level of proactive and reactive predatory criminal behavior and the situational factors that moderate his or her expression of one or both of these forms of criminal predation. There are policy implications to the dimensional structure of criminal predatory behavior as well. Popular measures of criminality like the PCL-R and DSM-IV criteria for antisocial personality disorder are sometimes included in death penalty and parole evaluations. In light of the dimensional latent structure of criminal predatory behavior, it would seem advisable that instead of relying on a single cutoff score, the entire range of scores or perhaps several cutoff scores on measures like the PCL-R should be considered in making death penalty and parole determinations.

Preliminary analysis denotes that criminal predatory behavior is supported by two different dimensions, proactive and reactive. One implication of this research finding is that different intervention strategies may be required to address these two forms of criminal predatory behavior. Although reactive criminality is best managed with skill development techniques like anger and stress management, proactive criminality requires that outcome expectancies for crime and criminal goals be explored and reevaluated. Many correctional programs do a good job of addressing the skill deficits and overriding issues that support reactive criminality, but few programs are equipped to handle the manipulative features of proactive criminality. Furthermore, parole/release decision-making generally takes into account the more observable aspects of reactive criminality but often overlooks the more subtle aspects of proactive criminality. Hence, effort needs to be directed at designing correctional programs that address both reactive and proactive criminality as well as creating guidelines for parole/release decision-makers that consider both reactive and proactive issues.

The fact that the proactive and reactive dimensions of criminal predatory behavior are correlated also has important theoretical, practical, and policy implications. Given the moderately high correlation that exists between proactive and reactive criminal predatory behavior, it will be relatively rare to find someone who is extremely high on one dimension and extremely low on the other dimension (i.e., a "pure" proactive or reactive criminal). We are more apt to find someone who is high on both dimensions or low on both dimensions. Shifting from the individual criminal offender to the individual criminal act, there is evidence that most criminal acts involve both proactive and reactive aggression/criminality, although the degree of each tends to vary from one criminal event to the next. Therefore, rather than be concerned with whether a particular offender is a proactive or reactive criminal, or whether a specific criminal act is a proactive or reactive criminal event, a more productive approach would be to consider the degree of proactive and reactive criminality currently being displayed by an individual offender or contained in an ongoing criminal event.

■ Conclusion

The present chapter describes a two-dimensional model of criminal predatory behavior that links adult criminal behavior to childhood aggressive behavior. As I mentioned at the beginning of this chapter, this is how I view criminal predatory behavior in the BOP as well as in general. Using data analyzed with the taxometric method, it was shown that adult criminal predatory behavior is dimensional in nature; using factor analysis, it was discovered that adult criminal predatory behavior partitions into two dimensions, proactive and reactive; and using correlational analysis, it was determined that these two dimensions are correlated rather than independent. To the extent that the proactive and reactive dimensions apply to both criminal and non-criminal human behavior, and given the dimensional nature of these constructs, additional research is required to understand the transition from proactive and reactive non-criminal behavior to proactive and reactive criminal behavior.

References

1. Walters, G. D. (1990). *The Criminal Lifestyle: Patterns of Serious Criminal Conduct.* Thousand Oaks, CA: Sage.
2. Dodge, K. A. (1991). The structure and function of reactive and proactive aggression. Pp. 201–218 in D. Pepler, K. Rubin (Eds.), *The Development and Treatment of Childhood Aggression.* Hillsdale, NJ: Erlbaum.
3. Dodge, K. A., Coie, J. D. (1987). Social-information processing factors in reactive and proactive aggression in children's peer groups. *J Pers Social Psychol* 53:1146–1158.
4. Cornell, D. G., Warren, J., Hawk, G., et al. (1996). Psychopathy in instrumental and reactive violent offenders. *J Consult Clin Psychol* 64:783–790.
5. Kockler, T. R., Stanford, M. S., Nelson, C. S., et al. (2006). Characterizing aggressive behavior in a forensic population. *Am J Orthopsychiatr* 76:80–85.
6. Crick, N. R., Dodge, K. A. (1996). Social information-processing mechanisms in reactive and proactive aggression. *Child Dev* 67:993–1002.
7. Dodge, K. A., Newman, J. P. (1981). Biased decision-making processes in aggressive boys. *J Abnorm Psychol* 90:375–379.
8. Walters, G. D. (2007). Measuring proactive and reactive criminal thinking with the PICTS: Correlations with outcome expectancies and hostile attribution biases. *J Interpers Viol* 22:1–15.
9. Walters, G. D., Frederick, A. A., Schlauch, C. (2007). Postdicting arrests for proactive and reactive aggression with the PICTS Proactive and Reactive composite scales. *Journal of Interpers Viol*, in press.
10. Dodge, K. A., Lochman, J. E., Harnish, J. D., et al. (1997). Reactive and proactive aggression in school children and psychiatrically impaired chronically assaultive youth. *J Abnorm Psychol* 106:37–51.

References

11. Poulin, F., Boivin, M. (2000). Reactive and proactive aggression: Evidence of a two-factor model. *Psychol Assess* 12:115–122.
12. Price, J. M., Dodge, K. A. (1989). Reactive and proactive aggression in childhood: Relations to peer status and social context dimensions. *J Abnorm Child Psychol* 17:455–471.
13. Walters, G. D. (2005). Proactive and reactive aggression: A lifestyle view. Pp. 29–43 in J. P. Morgan (Ed.), *Psychology of Aggression*. Hauppauge, NY: Nova Science Publishers.
14. Meehl, P. E. (2004). What's in a taxon? *J Abnorm Psychol 113*, 39–43.
15. Meehl, P. E., Golden, R. (1982). Taxometric methods. Pp. 127–181 in P. Kendall, J. Butcher (Eds.), *Handbook of Research Methods in Clinical Psychology*. New York: Wiley.
16. Meehl, P. E., Yonce, L. J. (1994). Taxometric analysis: I. Detecting taxonicity with two quantitative indicators using means above and below a sliding cut (MAMBAC procedure). *Psychol Reports* 74:1059–1274.
17. Meehl, P. E., Yonce, L. J. (1996). Taxometric analysis: II. Detecting taxonicity using covariance of two quantitative indicators in successive intervals of a third indicator (MAXCOV procedure). *Psychol Reports* 78:1091–1227.
18. Waller, N. G., Meehl, P. E. (1998). *Multivariate Taxometric Procedures: Distinguishing Types from Continua*. Thousand Oaks, CA: Sage.
19. Ruscio, J., Haslam, N., Ruscio, A. M. (2006). *Introduction to the Taxometric Method: A Practical Guide*. Mahwah, NJ: Lawrence Erlbaum.
20. Harris, G. T., Rice, M. E., Quinsey, V. L. (1994). Psychopathy as a taxon: Evidence that psychopaths are a discrete class. *J Consult Clin Psychol* 62:387–397.
21. Edens, J. F., Marcus, D. K., Lilienfeld, S. O., Poythress, N. G. (2006). Psychopathic, not psychopath: Taxometric evidence for the dimensional structure of psychopathy. *J Abnorm Psychol* 115:131–144.
22. Guay, J. P., Ruscio, J., Knight, R. A., Hare, R. D. (2007). A taxometric analysis of the latent structure of psychopathy: Evidence for dimensionality. *J Abnorm Psychol*, in press.
23. Walters, G. D., Duncan, S. A., Mitchell-Perez, K. (2007). The latent structure of psychopathy: A taxometric investigation of the Psychopathy Checklist-Revised in a heterogeneous sample of male prison inmates. *Assessment*, in press.
24. Walters, G. D., Gray, N.S., Jackson, R. L., et al. (2006). *A Taxometric Analysis of the Latent Structure of the Psychopathy Checklist: Screening Version*. Unpublished manuscript.
25. Marcus, D. K., John, S. L., Edens, J. F. (2004). A taxometric analysis of psychopathic personality. *J Abnorm Psychol* 113:626–635.
26. Marcus, D. K., Lilienfeld, S. O., Edens, J. F., Poythress, N. G. (2006). Is antisocial personality disorder continuous or categorical? A taxometric analysis. *Psychol Med* 36:1571–1582.

27. Walters, G. D., Brinkley, C. A., Magaletta, P. R., Diamond, P. M. (2006). Taxometric analysis of the Levenson Self-Report Psychopathy scale. Unpublished manuscript.
28. Skilling, T. A., Harris, G. T., Rice, M. E., Quinsey, V. L. (2002). Identifying persistently antisocial offenders using the Hare Psychopathy Checklist and DSM antisocial personality disorder criteria. *Psychol Assess* 14:27–38.
29. Walters, G. D., Diamond, P. M., Magaletta, P. R., et al. (2006). *Taxometric analysis of the Antisocial Features scale of the Personality Assessment Inventory in Federal prison inmates.* Unpublished manuscript.
30. Walters, G. D. (2006). *The latent structure of the criminal lifestyle: A taxometric analysis of the Lifestyle Criminality Screening Form and Psychological Inventory of Criminal Thinking Styles.* Unpublished manuscript.
31. Beauchaine, T. P., Waters, E. (2003). Pseudotaxonicity in MAMBAC and MAXCOV analyses of rating scale data: Turning continua into classes by manipulating observers' expectations. *Psychol Meth* 8:3–15.
32. Walters, G. D., McCoy, K. (2007). Taxometric analysis of the Psychological Inventory of Criminal Thinking Styles in male and female incarcerated offenders and college students. *Crim Justice Behav* 34:781–793.
33. Podsakoff, P. M., MacKenzie, S. B., Lee, J.-Y., Podsakoff, N. P. (2003). Common method biases in behavioral research: A critical review of the literature and recommended remedies. *J Applied Psychol* 88:879–903.
34. Egan, V., McMurran, M., Richardson, C., Blair, M. (2000). Criminal cognitions and personality: What does the PICTS really measure? *Crim Behav Mental Health* 10:170–184.
35. Arbuckle, J. L. (1999). *AMOS User's Guide* (Version 4.0). Chicago: SmallWaters.
36. Hare, R. D. (2003). *The Hare Psychopathy Checklist—Revised Manual* (2nd ed.). Toronto, Ontario, Canada: Multi-Health Systems.
37. Levenson, M. R., Kiehl, K. A., Fitzpatrick, C. M. (1995). Assessing psychopathic attributes in a noninstitutionalized population. *J Pers Social Psychol* 68:151–158.
38. Walters, G. D., Mandell, W. (2007). Incremental validity of the Psychological Inventory of Criminal Thinking Styles and Psychopathy Checklist: Screening Version in predicting disciplinary outcome. *Law Human Behav* 31:141–157.

References

Civil Commitment Laws for Sexual Predators

13

Roxann M. Ryan
Iowa Department of Public Safety

The research focus on violence against women in the last two decades led to new insights into the impact of sex offending on both victims and offenders. Despite extensive empirical research indicating that the vast majority of sexual assaults are committed by persons who either know the victim or are related to the victim, the stereotype of a serial rapist, stranger-in-the-bushes remains strong. Perhaps it was that vivid stereotypical view that generated policy makers' interest in addressing the problem of sexually violent predators in the 1990s and the early 21st century. Or, it may have been the new research on innovative treatment methodologies for sex offenders. Or, it may have been the research indicating that sex offenders are no different from other offenders in that a small percentage of offenders are responsible for a disproportionate amount of the offending. For the politicians who enact the laws, the motivation may well have been the strong, tough-on-crime campaign theme that often wins over voters. In all likelihood, there were many motivations behind the grand experiment in enacting laws that permit the civil commitment of sexually violent predators. Make no mistake: it is an *experiment*, and an expensive one at that.

It is not the first time that such experiments have occurred. In the 1930s, many states enacted sexual psychopath laws to provide an alternative disposition for offenders who were thought to suffer from unique mental or emotional disorders that caused them to become sexual offenders.[1] Those laws fell out of favor when it appeared that the treatment methods were ineffectual in "curing" the mental illnesses. In the 1970s and 1980s, a great deal of research was devoted to sex offender causation and treatment. Many experts felt that this in-depth study of sex offender treatment could lead to a more refined and broad-based approach to sex offender treatment. In addition, the focus changed from elimination of recidivism to reduction of recidivism.

In the 1990s, the treatment response changed to focus on specialized treatment programs for violent sex offenders, designed to reduce the risk of re-offending using a variety of treatment modalities. Singling out sex offenders for special treatment was justified on several grounds. First, sex offenders are one of the few types of offenders who tend to specialize in their criminal activity. Although other offenders are as likely to commit a different type of offense as they are to commit the same offense a second time, sex offenders who commit another crime are more likely to commit another sex offense.[2] Second, sex offenders tend to escalate the seriousness of their offenses over the course of their criminal lifetimes. Many sex offenders commit increasingly violent sex offenses as they continue their criminal careers. The impact of sex offenses on victims is particularly profound and often is directed toward children.[3] Third, a variety of treatment programs have been developed to address behavioral patterns, cognitive thinking skills, biological bases, and social skills behavior in sex offenders. Finally, social scientists have refined their ability to make risk predictions with respect to sex offenders. Advances in research design and statistical capacity have improved, so that the actuarial prediction of re-offense risk outperforms clinical predictions.[1]

The result of these research and policy considerations was a movement in the 1990s to adopt a specialized civil commitment program designed specifically for sexually violent predators, that is, sex offenders who are most likely to commit further sex offenses against victims who are unrelated to them. Nineteen states developed some form of sexually violent predator civil commitment laws by 2007. Civil commitment laws are quite different from criminal laws. Although both civil commitment and criminal conviction can affect fundamental liberty interests, the differences are stark. The goals are different, the processes are quite different, and the constitutional rights at stake are very different.

■ Goals

The goals of criminal law are manifold: retribution/revenge, incapacitation, or rehabilitation. Public policymakers do not necessarily agree on which of the many goals is paramount, and a criminal law may serve more than one goal. Regardless of the goal, the result is that the criminal offender can be incarcerated upon conviction and incur the loss of liberty. Although civil commitment also results in a loss of liberty, the goals of civil commitment are more circumscribed.[4] The focus is on protecting mentally ill persons from themselves and others. The goal is treatment of the mental health condition that will provide protection of persons, and if the only means to obtain that protection is civil commitment, then a loss of liberty for that individual is justified, at least until the risk of danger has been resolved. The assumption in a civil commitment action is that the involuntary commitment will last for a short time, often a matter of days or weeks.

Thus, both criminal conviction and civil commitment can result in the loss of liberty for an individual, but the reasons for the loss of liberty may be very different. The constraints on the institutions housing the individuals also are quite different. In a civil commitment action, there is a presumption that the person will be committed for purposes of treatment. Although the treatment is usually not characterized as "rehabilitation," as it is in the criminal context, there are similarities to criminal rehabilitation programs. The assumption is that civil commitment is a temporary situation and that the committed person will be released as soon as the person no longer poses a danger to self or others. There is no set time limit for commitment, and the constraints on the person are based entirely on the committed individual's risk to self or others.

In the criminal incarceration, however, the requirements for treatment are quite different. Although corrections officials are constitutionally required to provide basic health care to inmates, the treatment requirements are far more limited. The standards for required care are set by the Eighth Amendment's cruel and unusual punishment standard. If failure to provide health care would be considered "cruel and unusual punishment," then correctional officials must provide that health care. This is a minimal standard in comparison to the standards used in civil commitment.

These differing goals translate into contrasting perspectives between civil commitment and criminal conviction. Correctional officials generally focus their attention on maintaining order in the institution. Individuals are viewed as part of the whole population, people who need to be controlled, and their treatment programs are a secondary concern. Mental health care facility administrators who oversee persons who are civilly committed are focused instead on the individual treatment plans for each person committed. Their concerns for maintaining order are important, too, but their primary focus is on individual treatment plans. From the individual's perspective, the contrast between a prison environment and a civil commitment environment can be stark. Although the motivations of policy makers who enacted sexually violent predator laws certainly have been questioned, the use of civil commitment laws in addition to or in place of criminal laws necessarily implicates these contrasting goals.

■ Processes

Legal processes are based largely on the underlying goal of the system, so it is not surprising that the process of criminal conviction also is starkly different from the process of civil commitment. The criminal process is more widely understood. First and foremost, it is an adversary process in which the accused criminal defendant faces formal action by the government. The action is entitled, "State v. [defendant's name]" or "Commonwealth v. [defendant's name]." The government determines whether to charge a person with a crime based on the government's investigation of facts. A trial is held in which fact-finders determine beyond a reasonable doubt whether the person is guilty of the offense charged. If the person is found guilty, then a judge imposes the sentence prescribed by statute. Throughout the criminal process, the criminal defendant has the panoply of constitutional rights to protect against overreaching by the government.

A traditional civil commitment action generally is less adversarial. That is not to say that there is no animosity between parties involved in a civil commitment action. As a legal process, there are no "adversaries" in a civil commitment action. The action is entitled "In re Commitment of [person's name or initials]." The focus is on the individual facing civil commitment and whether that individual suffers from a mental health condition that poses a danger to self or others. Proof required for traditional civil commitment is a "clear and convincing evidence" standard, which is less demanding than "beyond a reasonable doubt," but more demanding than the civil standard of a preponderance of the evidence.

Civil commitment of sexually violent predators is somewhat different from traditional civil commitment, but it is more like civil commitment than criminal prosecution and conviction. States that have adopted sexually violent predator variations of civil commitment use standards that parallel traditional civil commitment. The primary difference is that sexually violent predator laws do not require proof of a type of mental health disorder that would support a traditional civil commitment action. For example, the Iowa legislature adopted a policy similar to that of many states:

> The [Iowa] general assembly finds that a small but extremely dangerous group of sexually violent predators exists which is made up of persons who do not have a mental disease or defect that renders them appropriate for involuntary treatment pursuant to the treatment provisions for mentally ill persons under chapter 229, since that chapter is intended to provide short-term treatment to persons with serious mental disorders and then return them to the community. In contrast to persons appropriate for civil commitment under chapter 229, sexually violent predators generally have antisocial

personality features that are unamenable to existing mental illness treatment modalities and that render them likely to engage in sexually violent behavior. The general assembly finds that sexually violent predators' likelihood of engaging in repeat acts of predatory sexual violence is high and that the existing involuntary commitment procedure under chapter 229 is inadequate to address the risk these sexually violent predators pose to society. The general assembly further finds that the prognosis for rehabilitating sexually violent predators in a prison setting is poor, because the treatment needs of this population are very long-term, and the treatment modalities for this population are very different from the traditional treatment modalities available in a prison setting or for persons appropriate for commitment under chapter 229. Therefore, the general assembly finds that a civil commitment procedure for the long-term care and treatment of the sexually violent predator is necessary.[5]

The goal of sexually violent predator civil commitment is similar to that of traditional civil commitment: treatment of a mentally disordered person who poses a risk to public safety. The process for achieving the goal is quite different. Lawmakers set the standards for civil commitment of sexually violent predators. They usually begin by defining their terms. The person who is the subject of the civil commitment has been characterized in several ways: as a sexually violent predator, a sexually dangerous person, or a sexually violent person.

Who Qualifies?

The term "sexually violent predator" generally refers to a person who has been convicted of or charged with a sexually violent offense and who suffers from a mental abnormality that makes the person likely to engage in predatory acts constituting sexually violent offenses if not confined in a secure facility. Generally, states have established two broad categories of sex offenders who may be civilly committed as sexually violent predators. The first group is *persons who are guilty of sex offenses.* This may include persons who were found guilty by a judge or jury, pleaded guilty, were found incompetent to stand trial, or were acquitted by reason of insanity after being charged with designated sex offenses. This provision usually applies to offenders who are currently incarcerated at the time that the sexually violent predator civil commitment action is initiated. The second group is *persons who commit a "recent overt act" warranting commitment.* Some sexually violent predator statutes also may include offenders who are not currently incarcerated, but who commit a "recent overt act," that is, an act that has either caused harm of a sexually violent nature or creates a reasonable apprehension of such harm.

Most sexually violent predator statutes also require proof of a history of "predatory" offenses. These definitions usually include more than serial rapists who stalk their victims. The term "predatory" refers to acts directed toward a person with whom a relationship has been established or promoted for the primary purpose of victimization. This generally excludes incest offenses, unless the offender has established a relationship with a child's caretaker for the primary purpose of sexually molesting the stepchild.

Standard of Proof

The standard of proof often is higher for a sexually violent predator civil commitment action than for a traditional civil commitment action. Many predator statutes require proof beyond a reasonable doubt rather than proof by clear and convincing evidence.

Mental Abnormality

The predator statutes also require proof of a "mental abnormality," rather than a "mental disorder." Much like the legal term "insanity," which has no equivalent term in the mental health profession, a "mental abnormality" is a legal term rather than a mental health term. The term "mental disorder" is used by the American Psychiatric Association to describe conditions that are included in the *Diagnostic and Statistical Manual* (DSM). A "mental abnormality," on the other hand, is defined as an abnormality that either predisposes a person to commit sex offenses or makes it more likely than not that the person will commit a sexual offense. For example, the Iowa statute provides that a "mental abnormality" is "a congenital or acquired condition affecting the emotional or volitional capacity of a person and predisposing that person to commit sexually violent offenses to a degree which would constitute a menace to the health and safety of others."[6]

Who Decides?

States set up a variety of ways to prosecute the cases. Some states put sole authority in the state attorney general. Other states put sole authority in the local county prosecutor. Some states allow for dual jurisdiction. Generally, the prosecutor has very broad discretion in making decisions about civil commitment, just as the prosecutor has broad discretion to bring criminal charges. Many states set up an elaborate process of screening to help prosecutors decide which civil commitment cases to bring. Because the sexually violent predator statutes are designed to identify only the most dangerous repeat sex offenders, a screening process helps to winnow the large pool of eligible sex offenders to a much smaller number who may qualify for the "sexually violent predator" designation.

Most statutes allow for two different types of screening processes. First, a prosecutor may initiate a civil commitment if a previously convicted sex offender commits a recent overt act. The standards vary among jurisdictions, but generally provide a great deal of discretion to the prosecutor to decide which civil commitment actions to pursue. Second, an institutional review can result in the screening of potential commitment candidates. When an institutional review process is used, many states develop an initial screening process that applies specific baseline requirements for civil commitment, for example, a minimum number of predatory sex offenses and no treatment gain shown. This initial screening process may include more than one step. For instance, one screening may occur within a prison, and a second screening may be done by a multidisciplinary group. In addition, preliminary screening may include some type of assessment by mental health professionals, who use actuarial risk assessment procedures to assess whether the person qualifies as being more likely than not to re-offend if not placed in a secure facility. Some states also include a prosecutor review committee that makes the final recommendation for filing a civil commitment action.

Several tools are available to assess the risk that an individual offender will re-offend. The Rapid Risk Assessment for Sexual Offense Recidivism (RRASOR) is a four-item test that is designed to measure a paraphilic component. It was validated by examining re-offense by 2,900 sex offenders in the United States, Canada and England. The highest possible score is 6. A high risk of re-offense is shown with a score of 5. The Minnesota Sex Offenders Screening Tool (MnSOST) and the Minnesota Sex Offender Screening Tool Revised (MnSOST-R) were developed by Doug Epperson in conjunction with the Minnesota Department of Corrections. These instruments are designed to measure sex offense recidivism. The MnSOST was first validated by examining re-offense by more than 250 sex offenders in Minnesota and has been replicated in other studies. A high risk of re-offense is shown by a score of 47 or more on the MnSOST and by a score of 8 or more on the MnSOST-R. The Static Risk Assessment 1999 (Static 99 or SRA 99) is a combination of two other actuarial instruments that have been validated. The Static 99 instrument measures both sex offense recidivism and violence recidivism. A high risk of re-offense is shown by a score of 6 or more. These tests are one means by which the data needed for decision-making can be generated.

Preliminary Procedures

When the screening process is completed, the civil commitment action begins with the filing of a petition, which must allege that the person is a sexually violent predator and state sufficient facts to support the allegation.[7] Every legal action must begin with some formal filing. Generally, the petition can be filed if the institutional review process results in a recommendation to file a civil commitment action, or if a prosecutor determines that the person has committed a "recent overt act." The person who is being civilly committed is called the "respondent." Because the liberty interest is at stake, a civil commitment respondent is entitled to have an attorney and if the respondent is indigent an attorney can be appointed.[8] Within three days after the petition is filed, the district court makes a preliminary determination about whether there is probable cause to believe that the person named in the petition is a sexually violent predator.[9] The rules of evidence do not apply, and the state may rely solely on the petition, or add documentary evidence or live testimony. If probable cause is found, then the respondent remains incarcerated until the trial is over. Once probable cause is found, the respondent also is ordered to be evaluated by a qualified professional. In some states, the mental health expert appears as a witness for the court. In other states, the expert is a prosecution witness and the defense is permitted to hire a different expert witness to evaluate the respondent.

Evaluation of Respondent

In the full evaluation of the respondent, the court-appointed expert supplements a review of the records by conducting a personal interview with the respondent in the case. This personal interview is designed to assess the potential factors that would reduce the risk of re-offending. This includes the respondent's treatment gains, indicating that the respondent has gained insight into his sex offense pattern and recognizes potential risks for future offending; and the respondent's relapse prevention plans, including any official supervision or informal supervision or support systems available to the respondent. The respondent can retain experts or professionals to perform independent examinations, at state expense.[10]

The rules of civil procedure, including pretrial discovery rules, apply in sexually violent predator civil commitment actions. This means that prosecutors are able to discover a great deal of information about respondents, while respondents are able to discover all of the prosecution's evidence before the trial as well. Application of civil rules of discovery also means that prosecutors can depose respondents in advance of trial—a procedure that is never available in a criminal case because it would violate the criminal defendant's right against self-incrimination. Civil commitment respondents do not lose their Fifth Amendment rights, but some courts have ruled that the respondent may be required to answer questions about previous crimes that either have been prosecuted or are no longer eligible for prosecution (either because the statute of limitations has run or because the prosecutor has given the respondent immunity from criminal prosecution). Respondents can be required to testify about the cases in which they were convicted, because there is no longer a Fifth Amendment privilege against self-incrimination as to those cases.

Treatment Before Trial

There is no constitutional or statutory right to specified pretrial treatment. In Iowa, the Iowa Supreme Court has suggested that it will not recognize a right to specified treatment,[11] and courts in other jurisdictions have rejected claims of a right to specified treatment.[12,13] The United States Supreme Court has recognized only a substantive due process right to "minimally adequate treatment"[14] and has recognized that even when adequate treatment may not be available public safety may demand some action by the government.[15]

Trial

Many states establish a short time-frame for trials to occur after the probable cause hearing, usually 90–120 days. Iowa law, for example, allows the respondent or the State to request a continuance based on good cause by the court in the due administration of justice. Because of lengthy delays in getting cases to trial, the statute now provides that "[i]n determining what constitutes good cause, the court shall consider the length of the pretrial detention of the respondent."[16] Given the lengthy pretrial discovery permitted under the rules of civil procedure, it is not unusual to have the trial date moved far beyond the statutory time limit. The fact-finder may be either a judge or a jury. Most states allow a jury to decide the question of civil commitment, although some states have left the decision solely to the judge. Some states allow the prosecution, the respondent or the judge to ask for a jury trial.

At the trial on the merits, the fact-finder must determine whether the respondent is a sexually violent predator—that is, whether the respondent is more likely than not to commit another sexually violent offense if not confined in a secure facility. Many states use a beyond-a-reasonable-doubt standard, although a few states use a "clear and convincing evidence" standard. The United States Supreme Court ruled in the *Winship* case that a criminal conviction requires proof beyond a reasonable doubt,[17] but a civil commitment action is not a criminal case, so a lower standard of proof is permissible.

The "reasonable doubt" definition varies among jurisdictions. For example, the Eighth Circuit Court of Appeals defines reasonable doubt as:

> *A reasonable doubt is a doubt based upon reason and common sense, and not the mere possibility of innocence. A reasonable doubt is the kind of doubt that would make a reasonable person hesitate to act. Proof beyond a reasonable doubt, therefore, must be proof of such a convincing character that a reasonable person would not hesitate to rely and act upon it. However, proof beyond a reasonable doubt does not mean proof beyond all possible doubt.[18]*

The Iowa definition is similar:

> *A reasonable doubt is one that fairly and naturally arises from the evidence or lack of evidence produced by the State. If, after a full and fair consideration of all the evidence, you are firmly convinced of the defendant's guilt, then you have no reasonable doubt and you should find the defendant guilty. But if, after a full and fair consideration of all the evidence or lack of evidence produced by the State, you are not firmly convinced of the defendant's guilt, then you have a reasonable doubt and you should find the defendant not guilty.*[19]

The definition of "clear and convincing" evidence also varies among jurisdictions. In Iowa, the term "clear and convincing" is defined as "Evidence is clear, convincing and satisfactory if there is no serious or substantial uncertainty about the conclusion to be drawn from it." In most states, when a jury decides whether to civilly commit, the decision must be by unanimous verdict of the jury.[19] If the fact-finder (whether it is the judge or the jury) is *not* satisfied that the respondent is a sexually violent predator, the court must order the respondent to be released from custody.

When a respondent is found to be a sexually violent predator, then the respondent is admitted to a treatment program. Those treatment programs generally are separate from other types of mental health treatment programs, because sexually violent predators are different from most civil commitment patients. The finding that the respondent is a sexually violent predator necessarily requires proof that the person is sexually dangerous, so it is inappropriate to put sexually violent predators with other civil commitment patients. In addition, the purpose of sexually violent predator treatment programs is different from traditional civil commitment programs. The sexually violent predator may suffer from a "mental abnormality" that is not treated in the same way as the mental disorders that warrant traditional civil commitment. The focus of the sexually violent predator treatment program is sex offending, which is not the primary focus of most civil commitment treatment programs.

■ What Happens in Commitment Programs?

Most sexually violent predator programs have dual purposes of protection of society and treatment of the committed person. The United States Supreme Court has not specifically ruled that treatment programs are required for sexually violent predator programs. In *Kansas v. Hendricks*, the United States Supreme Court said, "we have never held that the Constitution prevents a State from civilly detaining those for whom no treatment is available, but who nevertheless pose a danger to others."[20] The Court noted that persons with untreatable, highly contagious diseases might be involuntarily confined, or that confinement of dangerously insane persons who are untreatable also may be permitted.

The pledge to treat sexually violent predator patients varies among states, and there is no universally accepted treatment program for all sex offenders. The content of treatment programming varies among jurisdictions. Some states have a stronger emphasis on the treatment programs than others, and some states have seen rapid growth in their sexually violent predator programs, which makes effective treatment programs far more difficult to implement. Treatment is far more expensive than incarceration without treatment.

A standard, comprehensive treatment program consists of a five-phase treatment program with several treatment modalities that can be adapted to the individual needs of each patient. The standard treatment program can be completed in three to five years if the patient is cooperative and motivated to change. Individual treatment and group classes involving the first patient and the treatment staff begin immediately. Patients are instructed regarding the requirements for advancement through the program. During the first phase, patients complete classes on cognitive skills, victim empathy, relapse prevention, relationship skills, human sexuality, anger management, personal victimization and other topics that are universally accepted as critical components of a comprehensive treatment program for sex offenders.

Most programs develop treatment goals for each patient based upon the many factors identified in the treatment literature that are believed to contribute to sexual offending. These may include:

1. Thoroughly disclose sexual history
2. Insight into risk factors
3. Resolve victimization issues
4. Develop victim empathy
5. Develop solitary and interactive social skills
6. Develop strong cognitive coping skills
7. Modify deviant arousal
8. Complete relapse prevention plan
9. Demonstrate relationship and intimacy skills
10. Modify negative self-concept
11. Develop problem-solving skills
12. Demonstrate motivation to change

In most programs, patients are evaluated periodically (often review is every 90 days). Three objective, physiological measures may be included in the assessment process to assess treatment progress and these results are included in the patient's quarterly reports. Polygraph exams may assess patient honesty about the numbers and types of victims as well as types of sexual behaviors performed. Penile plethysmographic exams may be performed to determine each patient's sexual arousal patterns. This is important because research has demonstrated that sexual arousal to children is the number one predictor of recidivism by sexual offenders. An Abel assessment provides a physiological measure of the patients' sexual interests as measured by Visual Reaction Time technology.

For the treatment program staff, a Therapeutic Interaction Model involving seven components to therapeutic interactions can help to set the stage for a therapeutic environment. Using the acronym MEDICAL, the seven components of the treatment staff model include:

Modeling appropriate behavior

Empathizing with the patients

Deescalating agitated patients

Instructing patients in alternative behaviors

Confronting patients with firmness and compassion

Accepting and Affirming patients as worthwhile individuals, and

Listening actively to understand patients

The primary advantage of an indefinite civil commitment program for sex offenders is that the sex offender patients must consistently demonstrate progress and insight into their own offending in order to be seriously considered for release. In a prison (or in a commitment of a defined time), the sex offender can simply bide time until the release date. In an indefinite commitment, the progress must be real and sustained for a lengthy time period before any form of release is possible. Treatment of psychopathic sex offenders is different, and some experts suggest that psychopathic offenders should be separated from non-psychopathic patients in treatment because the psychopathic offender may appear to be benefiting from the treatment, when in fact the psychopathic offender is learning better techniques to avoid detection or responsibility.

As a matter of constitutional law, civilly committed patients must be evaluated periodically. In most states, the review of sexually violent predator patients occurs at least annually, with the results provided to the court for a determination as to whether the commitment should continue. In some states, the patient can petition for discharge at other times, but the courts have discretion to summarily deny a patient's request for discharge.

If the annual review hearing indicates that the patient's mental abnormality has changed so that it may be safe for the person to be at large, then a final hearing is scheduled to determine whether the patient should be released. Unless the prosecution demonstrates that the patient's mental abnormality or personality disorder remains such that the person is not safe to be at large and if discharged is likely to engage in acts of sexual violence, then the patient may be released. Statutes vary regarding the conditions for release, but virtually all states make provision for a transitional release, and set out the consequences for violations of conditional release. The conditions usually include recommitment for serious violations.

■ Constitutional Issues

Critics of civil commitment for sexually violent predators question the constitutionality of the process. The Supreme Court and most state courts have upheld the basic elements of the programs, however. The Supreme Court has examined several due process issues and rejected the constitutional challenges. States have rejected those same due process challenges, as well as other variations of due process challenges, such as vagueness (a complaint that the law does not adequately describe the prohibited behavior), the use of less restrictive alternatives to incarceration. State courts also have rejected constitutional challenges based on various criminal rights—ex-post facto (passing a criminal law that took effect after the person had already committed the offense), double jeopardy (repeated criminal punishment for the same offense), cruel and unusual punishment, equal protection (different treatment for sex offenders), and jury trial rights (unanimous verdict, number of jurors), speedy trial, competency to stand trial, and self-incrimination. Sexually violent predators also have raised a broad variety of evidentiary issues and procedural issues in the various state courts. Most state statutes have withstood the various challenges with some modifications in each state. Aside from various legal challenges, the two primary complaints about sexually violent predator civil commitment laws are (1) a general sense of fairness and concern about the selection of persons committed; and (2) prohibitive costs.

Fairness

It is often argued that regardless of any legal determinations of fundamental fairness under the due process clause, it is unfair to simply lock up sex offenders because of society's moral panic about offenders.

Why are sex offenders selected for indefinite commitment when other offenders are not included? Recidivism rates for sex offenders do not appear to be very different from recidivism rates for other offenders. Supporters of civil commitment argue that research on recidivism rates of sex offenders is questionable, because sex offenses are severely underreported. In addition, most civil commitment laws require several convictions for sex offenses which indicate a pattern of recidivism that indicates continued dangerousness. These repeat offenders are among the small percentage of offenders who are the most dangerous offenders. Supporters of civil commitment also argue that the impact of sex offending on the victims is greater than for other types of offenses, which justifies a different response to sex offenders than to other types of offenders.

Why are sex offenders confined indefinitely for "treatment" when no successful treatment program has yet been established? It seems unfair to confine a person as part of an experiment, when there is no evidence to indicate that the person can be successfully treated. Supporters of civil commitment respond that the small group of high-risk repeat sex offenders includes the persons who are most likely to have more victims. Society has a strong interest in avoiding this further victimization. In addition, given the nature of sex offending, indefinite and long-term commitment to a treatment program is most likely to show success. Sex offender treatment requires lengthy treatment, and sex offenders who have an end date to their confinement can conform to requirements during the time of confinement, but then continue their offending when they are released. Intense, long-term treatment is most likely to change the offender's view of themselves and the world and thereby reduce the likelihood of re-offending. In addition, treatment programs can benefit the offender in addressing the serious emotional and psychological problems that led them to sex offending.

Why are some sex offenders civilly committed when others are not? The selection process for choosing the "most dangerous" sex offenders is not based on clear, empirically supported criteria. Human behavior is difficult to predict yet it is these flawed predictions that form the basis for long-term civil commitment. The supporters of civil commitment respond that although human behavior is difficult to predict, proof of a long-term pattern of offending, coupled with proof of a mental abnormality that predisposes the person to commit those types of offenses, is sufficient to warrant commitment for purposes of treatment.

Cost

The cost of sexually violent predator civil commitment programming is estimated to average four times more than the cost for incarceration in prison.[21] Critics question whether the additional cost for civil commitment programming is justified, given the lack of proof that sex offender treatment works. Some sex offenders choose not to participate in programming, and there is no way to force compliance, yet the costs of security and programming do not decrease. Given that so few patients have been released from the programs, the costs are likely to continue to increase. Because the program costs are so high, there is a risk that the quality of the programs may decline as a result of cost-cutting measures. Monitoring of programs is limited—most are self-monitored—and standards for programming are not established. There are informal associations among the directors in the various states, but these groups are not authorized to evaluate treatment or other programs at the facilities. Public support for official monitoring is not as strong as the public support for the idea of confining dangerous sex offenders, so it may be difficult to provide formal monitoring mechanisms.

■ Conclusion

Societal response to sex offending has ebbed and flowed for many decades. The recent return to civil commitment of sex offenders harkens back to the efforts in the early 20th century. The new sex offender treatment programs have survived most of the legal challenges brought by the patients in the programs, but policy questions remain. Although research on sex offending has grown, the existing treatment programs have not been shown to eliminate sex offending. This raises significant policy questions about involuntary commitment to a program that may not work. Yet treatment is only one of the goals of an involuntary civil commitment program for sexually violent predators. Public safety also is a legitimate societal concern. Victims of sexual assault often suffer long-term consequences. If programs are developed to address the needs of repeat sex offenders who suffer from abnormalities that predispose them to commit more sex offenses, then the costs of victimization may be reduced.

From a policy perspective, it is difficult to turn back once the decision is made to adopt a civil commitment program for sexually violent predators. Even if the treatment programs fail to work and a decision is made to disband them, public safety and political concerns make it difficult to release sex offenders who have been found to be dangerous. The sexually violent predator civil commitment statues are indeed a grand experiment with very high stakes.

References

1. Becker, J., Murphy, W. (1998). What we know and don't know about assessing and treating sex offenders. *Psychol Public Policy Law* 4:116–137.
2. Miethe, T., McCorkle, R. C. (1998). *Crime Profiles: The Anatomy of Dangerous Persons, Places and Situations*. Los Angeles: Roxbury.
3. Koss, M., Harvey, M. (1991). *The Rape Victim: Clinical and Community Interventions*, 2nd edition. Thousand Oaks, CA: Sage.
4. Appelbaum, P. S. (1992). Civil commitment from a systems perspective. *Law Human Behav* 16:61–74.
5. Iowa Code § 229A.1 (2007).
6. Iowa Code § 229A.2(3) (2007).
7. Iowa Code § 229A.4(1) (2007).
8. Iowa Code § 229A.6(1) (2007).
9. Iowa Code § 229A.5 (2007).
10. Iowa Code § 229A.6(1) (2007).
11. *In re C.S.*, 516 N.W.2d 851 (Iowa 1994).
12. *James v. Wallace*, 382 F. Supp. 1177 (N.D. Ala. 1974).
13. *Apodaca v. Ommen*, 807 P.2d 939 (Colo. 1991).
14. *Youngberg v. Romeo*, 457 U.S. 307, 102 S. Ct. 2452, 73 L. Ed. 2d 28 (1982).
15. *Powell v. Texas*, 392 U.S. 514, 88 S. Ct. 2145, 20 L. Ed. 2d 1254 (1968).
16. Iowa Code § 229A.6(2) (2007).
17. *In re Winship*, 397 U.S. 358 (1970).
18. Eighth Circuit Model Instruction No. 3.11 (1992).
19. Iowa Code § 229A.7(3) (2007).
20. *Kansas v. Hendricks*, 521 U.S. 346 (1996).
21. Davey, M., Goodnough, A. Doubts rise as states hold sex offenders after prison. New York Times, March 4–7, 2007, available online at http://www.nytimes.com/2007/03/04/us/04civil.html?ex=1174276800&en=309030f49f197ff6&ei=5070

Prosecuting Criminal Predators

14

Denise Timmins
Iowa Attorney General's Office

I am an attorney. It's a profession of which I am proud to be a part. I am even more proud that I am a prosecutor. I know that none of the jokes and stereotypes generally associated with lawyers really applies to me. The negative images people have about attorneys are of ambulance chasers and slick corporate lawyers who profit from the misery of others. A prosecutor has a higher calling. We help make society a safer place. Because of our work, criminals go to prison, and hopefully they stay there for as long as the law allows. We are defenders of truth and justice.

Strangely, though, when I tell someone for the first time that I am a prosecutor, I usually receive one of two responses, neither of which is positive. The inquirer may smile politely and move as quickly as possible to another subject that does not involve the "dirty" details of my job. Too often, however, people want to have a prolonged discussion involving the intimate details of any recent case in which I have been involved. To someone outside of the criminal justice system, it all sounds like a good episode of *Law and Order*. We as prosecutors know it is reality.

Crime evokes interesting responses in people. No one will deny its existence. No one can. The media, both in news and entertainment programming, always seems ready to exploit human suffering. With television shows dramatizing and glorifying violent acts, and with news programs broadcasting increasingly graphic images of real violence, even the most unwilling viewer has to recognize the prevalence of violence in our society. However, even as most people acknowledge its existence, they will do everything possible to distance themselves from it. They tell themselves things like, "that doesn't happen here," or that they would never allow themselves to be in a situation like that. This allows them to shelter themselves from the reality of violence, replacing it with a comforting belief that those horrors exist elsewhere.

A prosecutor can never enjoy that comfort. Every day, prosecutors deal with the reality that comes from the gruesome details of another person's pain and suffering. Every day, prosecutors work to bring criminals to justice, and hopefully provide closure and healing to their victims. And every day, prosecutors deal with the worst of the worst: predators.

■ Criminal Predators

"Predator" is a term that is often misused. In today's media, the term is applied to almost any heinous act committed by an individual. My experience as a prosecutor has proved that definition to be too broad. There are limitless reasons for criminal acts, and usually those reasons are known only to the criminals who commit them. We do know, however, that a true predator is part of a small but extremely dangerous group of criminals. The live-in boyfriend who abuses his girlfriend or molests her young children is a danger to that specific pool of victims, but he is not likely to go outside of the home in search of other victims. The bookkeeper who embezzles thousands of dollars from her employer is more likely a criminal due to her employment circumstances and the temptation of easy money. It is not likely that she researched the classified ads and applied for a job where she would have access and control over a business's bank accounts. Most criminals are like the boyfriend and the bookkeeper. The common denominator is opportunity and easy access.

This should not minimize the seriousness of these crimes or lessen the responsibility of their perpetrators, but it does differentiate them from the predator. Predators are not driven by easy opportunities. Just like a true hunter would derive no pride from shooting a tethered deer, predators do not find satisfaction in an easy mark. They seek out their victims. They research and study them to know as much as they can. Their lives revolve around finding the next victim, and they use any means necessary to give themselves the advantage over their prey. Unlike an ordinary criminal, a predator's crime is his life, his identity. Predators thrive on the thrill of the hunt, and their successes only encourage them to continue.

In my experience, the two most common predatory criminals are sexual predators and financial predators. These two types of predators are surprisingly similar. While comparing sexual and financial crimes may seem like comparing apples to oranges, closer inspection leads to an understanding of the parallel motivations for these two categories of predators.

The biggest difference between the two is the crime itself. Obviously, sexual and financial crimes are glaringly different, and society's attitudes toward sex and money make the differences even more extreme. It seems obscene to even suggest the two have anything in common. Yet the similarities in the methods of the predators, and the effects of their crimes on their victims, become quite clear to the prosecutors who deal with these cases. For these prosecutors, these similarities simply cannot be overlooked. An important element in the prosecution of both sexual and financial predators is understanding how the predatory mind works and the process the predator uses to stalk his victim and finally strike his mark. Even as the overall approach to dealing with financial crimes is different from dealing with sexual crimes, so is the approach to dealing with regular financial and sexual criminals different from dealing with their predatory counterparts.

The first similarity between sexual and financial predators is in how they select their victims. Like their counterparts in the animal kingdom, human predators prey on the weak. Unlike animals, human predators are not motivated by a hunger for the food necessary for physical survival. Animals only take what they need; human predators have no such limitations. Their victims are limited only by availability, and while the animal predator seeks to fulfill only its basic needs, the human predator hunts more for self-gratification, the sense of power that comes from overcoming and defeating another victim.

The prime targets for the predatory criminal are children, the elderly, and people outside the societal norm, such as prostitutes or illegal drug users, who do not have the same defenses as the majority of society. These victims have weaknesses due to their age, their mental capacity, or their status; these weaknesses make them more desirable to the predator because of the advantages he has over such a victim. A predator may choose a child who is too young to verbalize the abuse he has inflicted on her. A child can more easily be intimidated into silence with threats toward the child's own safety, or that of his family, friends, or pets. An elderly person who has grown to trust a financial predator may take a longer time to discover that her bank accounts and retirement funds have slowly been drained, or, if she suffers from Alzheimer's or some other form of dementia, she may never comprehend what happened to the financial security she had hoped to pass on to her children and grandchildren. The predator who sexually assaults a prostitute counts on the fact that very few, if any, will believe her if she reports the rape. He knows that if he attacks an addict whose children were taken away due to neglect, no one is likely to listen to her or care.

Victim selection is extremely important to predators, and they choose carefully before striking.

Despite the differences in their actual crimes, the thought processes of sexual and financial predators are strikingly similar. First and foremost, there is a frightening disconnection from reality that allows them to justify their actions, no matter how heinous they would seem to a regular person. In my experience with predatory criminals, they truly believe that they are not doing anything wrong or immoral. Even though they understand that their actions are illegal, they believe that the law that is supposed to protect their victims is misguided or oppressive. A regular person will often tell himself that he has done nothing wrong or find some sort of justification for his wrongful actions in order to live with the knowledge of what he has done. It is possible that predators do the same, but it seems just as likely that they truly believe in the righteousness of their behavior. At this stage in my career, I cannot say for certain which is true. I am not sure anyone can, including the predators themselves, since their perception of what constitutes normal human behavior is so distorted.

The predators' lack of remorse is staggering, almost unbelievable. Sexual predators will claim that molested children actually enjoy sexual contact, and that it is a natural human behavior that has been wrongly outlawed by a prudish and oppressive society. They will claim that they were helping their adult rape victims live out fantasies, and that they had full consent for everything they did. Financial predators will blame their investments in sham corporations on bad judgment, or that they were fully authorized by their victims to do everything they did. Rarely do they take responsibility for their actions or acknowledge that their behavior was illegal or wrong. Even more rarely do they acknowledge or take responsibility for the physical, emotional, or financial harm they inflict on their victims.

Coupled with the predator's lack of remorse is an inflated sense of entitlement. Predators are almost childlike in their perception of ownership. Their desire for anything justifies the means to obtain it. If a predator wants sex, he should be able to have it with whomever he wants. If something horrible has happened to the predator at some point in his life, then someone else should suffer the same level of violence and degradation. A predator who needs a new car or wants to take a trip to some exotic location finds a new victim in order to pay for their pleasure with someone else's money.

This sense of entitlement is most obvious in financial predators. They invest a great deal of time and effort in grooming their victims. They "take care" of them for so long before they strike that they feel completely justified in taking their victims' money. The financial predator believes that the victim owes him for everything that he has done. The stolen finances amount to a self-imposed service fee for befriending an elderly victim. It is a payment due for all of the time it took to learn enough about the victim to be able to empty her bank account or retirement fund. To financial predators, it is not theft or embezzlement, it is simply taking what they have coming to them, what should already be theirs because they deserve it.

Predators rarely accept blame for their actions. On those infrequent occasions when I have seen a predator that I am prosecuting take responsibility for his crime, it was because he believed doing so would work to his benefit. This usually happens at a sentencing hearing, when the predator is trying to convince the court to impose a light sentence. Otherwise, the actions of predators are the fault of other people or of outside influences that are beyond their control. Blaming the victim is commonplace. Sexual predators will often speak of "promiscuous children." They may also blame the victims' parents, claiming that "if the parents had taken better care of their children, I would never have had access to them." The typical excuse for financial predators is "it was just business." They also blame their victims for not paying better attention to the fine print or being gullible enough to believe that any investment could be a "sure thing."

Drugs, alcohol, and other addictions are also common excuses for either type of predator. They claim that they would not normally molest, rape, or assault somebody, or that they understand that stealing money is wrong, but they just could not control their behavior. If they had not been drinking, on drugs, or gambling, they never would have committed those crimes. Prosecutors quickly learn how to defeat these arguments because we hear them so often. Alcohol and drugs can never be allowed to be recognized as the cause of criminal activity. As prosecutors, we have to recognize these excuses as just another item in an endless list of ways the predator will try to present himself as the victim, rather than the criminal.

Many people outside of law enforcement would be surprised to learn that the crimes of sexual and financial predators cause similar effects on their respective victims. Some may even be offended by the idea of comparing a rapist and a white collar criminal in such a manner. While it is obvious that the victims of sexual assault endure a different sort of trauma than the victims of financial crimes, the core feelings and emotions endured by both sets of victims are surprisingly similar. Shame, anger, embarrassment, and fear are common reactions reported by both types of predatory victims. It is common knowledge that far too many rapes go unreported because the victim feels ashamed of what has happened. In the same way, many victims of financial predators choose not to report their crimes because they are embarrassed that they placed their trust in someone who, in retrospect, was obviously not trustworthy. They do not want anyone to think they were fools or suckers, and they absorb the financial loss rather than give anyone that opportunity.

Rape victims will feel anger that they were violated in such a personal way, that another person took something that most people consider intimate and private and forced it upon them. The financial victim has also had something personal and private taken from her, something that most people share only with a trusted few, and will feel the same kind of anger, despite the fact that she has been violated in a completely different manner. A rape victim will feel embarrassed about having to tell a police officer, a doctor, or a judge and jury all of the degrading details of the assault in order to convict the sexual predator. A financial victim is likewise reluctant to share the details leading up to her loss, perhaps because every detail is an opportunity for anyone who can hear to think she was foolish to trust the predator in the first place. An elderly person who is still clinging to independence may not want to report the crime because people might think she is no longer capable of handling her own finances, as well as other areas of her private life.

Finally, both sets of victims feel fear. Victims of sexual predators fear that, due to the nature of sexual crimes and society's attitude toward sex in general, they could be looked upon as promiscuous or immoral, despite the fact that they had no choice in what happened to them. Financial victims fear that their families might step in and take away their personal and financial freedom, that they could be placed in a nursing home, or have their checkbook and credit cards taken away. However, there are fears that are common to both victim pools. They fear that the predator will retaliate if they report the crime. They fear that family members and friends will treat them differently or act differently around them. They fear that they will be partially blamed for the crime. They fear that they will never feel safe and secure, that they will never trust anyone again.

■ Legal Procedures

Charging

A case always comes to a prosecutor after the fact. The crime has been committed and the damage has been done. We cannot change what happened to the victim. We can only help them by holding the offender accountable for his actions. The process begins with a file on the prosecutor's desk. This file contains most, if not all, of the relevant information necessary to prosecute the case. At this point, we decide who will be charged and with what crime. Interpreting the information in the file is like putting together a puzzle. Each fact is just one piece. Some of those pieces are more important than others, but each has a place in determining what shape the puzzle takes. How well all the pieces fit together helps determine the level of crime that will be charged. A missing piece could reduce a kidnapping case into a charge of simple assault. As prosecutors, we organize, compartmentalize, and dissect every piece of information in order to determine what charge we will be able to bring to court.

The charging stage is important when prosecuting a predator. Both financial and sexual predators come with the mindset that they have done nothing wrong. Most predators that actually get caught have prior experience in getting away with their crimes either because they were never caught before, or, for those who have been arrested or even convicted, because the consequences for their crimes were too light.

One reason for this is that too often prosecutors will take into consideration things that should have no effect on the level of the initial criminal charge. A prosecutor may worry that the young victim of a child molester might have trouble holding up under cross-examination, so he charges the predator with a lesser crime in hopes of pleading out the case before it reaches trial. In a financial case involving an elderly Alzheimer's patient, the prosecutor may decline to file the case because the victim is in poor health and unable to testify, despite the fact that there is a well-documented paper trail of evidence that led to the predator's arrest in the first place.

Obviously a prosecutor needs hard facts in order to charge a crime. With that said, second-guessing the proper criminal charge because of how a witness might act gives the predator an unnecessary and unfortunate advantage. In a case with a well-documented investigation, the need for a live witness is a myth. Certainly, having a good witness on the stand can help sway a jury's feelings about a case, but a good case is based on facts, not emotions. The prosecutor's responsibility is to charge the case as the facts support it, and then let the other concerns sort themselves out. Certainly there are cases that sometimes have to be dismissed due to concerns with witnesses or evidence, but a strong investigation almost always reveals facts that can be presented in some way.

There is only one person who benefits from a prosecutor's undercharging or declining to charge a case, and that person certainly is not the victim: It is the predator himself. This is a person who has already absolved himself of any blame or responsibility, and the failure to fully and properly charge him for his crime only confirms that belief. Once again, he will walk away from his crime with little or no consequence. Even worse, he is now even more convinced than ever that no one can or will do anything to prevent him from striking other victims. That belief will empower him to seek out more victims and to continue with his destructive behavior.

Discovery

The pieces to the prosecutor's puzzle start to fit together during the discovery process. This is when motions are filed, hearings are held, and depositions are conducted. The process allows both the prosecution and the defense to get a feel for the case and to begin formulating a strategy for the best way to present their cases to the jury. For the predator, this is where the games really begin. Predators are masters of manipulation. They have to be: whether it is a sexual predator luring a child into his home or a financial predator hoping to clean out an elderly person's pension fund, the predator must know the best ways to make another person believe and trust him, when in reality he knows that he is really acting only out of concern for his own self-interests.

This art of manipulation does not end when a predator enters the judicial system. If anything, it is intensified, because the stakes become so much higher. Until an arrest, the predator who is unable to manipulate his prey into doing what he wants can simply move on to a new mark. Once that predator has been charged with a crime, however, failing to convince the right people of his innocence means a loss of freedom, and with it, a loss of opportunities for more victims while he is incarcerated. For the predator, the courts are a new arena with new players against whom he must pit his manipulative skills.

These skills are most obvious with financial predators. The financial predator's lifeblood is his ability to charm and manipulate others. It is how he thrives in business. Since he has always presented himself to his victims and to society as an honest, hard-working, educated man in a business suit, he is quite comfortable in a room full of attorneys. When he enters into negotiations or even into the courtroom with a prosecutor, he is at the top of his game, because he truly believes that he is the smartest person in the room. He will attempt to establish from the beginning that he is the one who is in charge of the situation. Once he feels he has established control, he will bring out all of the reasons why he is not the one responsible for what happened to his victim, and he will appear quite charming while he attempts to minimize the effects of his crime or insists that he has been wrongly accused.

The financial predator's charm can make convincing the victim that the predator is actually a criminal the most difficult aspect of the discovery stage. Often, the victim does not want to believe that the predator is not the person he appears to be. While the victim of a sex crime understands immediately that a crime has occurred and that she was the target, financial crime victims often have to be convinced of that fact. Financial predators choose their prey wisely. Most often, their targets are elderly people. They take time to form relationships. They take their victims to church or to the grocery store. They visit them on a regular basis when no one else does. More than one victim has told me that although they would like to get their money back, they do not want anything done to the predator who took it. For these people, the predator is the only person who takes care of them or cares about them.

The relationship that the financial predator creates with his victim is parasitic, but to the victim it seems symbiotic. The predator creates a situation where the victim comes to rely on him for basic physical and emotional needs. This dependence makes it difficult for the victim to sit in the same room with the predator during a deposition. Many victims do not want to tell a prosecutor about what happened to them, because they understand that assisting the prosecution means that this person that they trusted and befriended really did something horrible to them. This betrayal of trust is simply more than many victims want to deal with.

Sexual predators are as skilled in the art of manipulation as their financial counterparts, but they tend to use different techniques. Since they are usually less educated and less charming than financial predators, for them the discovery process becomes a new opportunity to assault their victims. They expect their attorneys to embarrass and humiliate their victims by asking intimate, personal, and often irrelevant questions. While their attorneys grill their victims, they take the opportunity to apply what is often their best form of manipulation: intimidation. They cannot speak to the victims during the questioning, but they will attempt to stare their victims down, or some will continually tap a pencil or find some other way to constantly remind their victims that they are in the room, and that they are listening to every word of every answer the victim gives. They will use whatever body language they can to nonverbally let the victims know that providing evidence against them is a dangerous thing to do, that there will be retribution against the victim once these legal issues have been resolved.

Imagine sitting in a room with the very person who violently raped you, while his attorney questions everything you did before, during, and after the assault. Keeping self-control in this situation is a daunting task for anyone, especially since sexual predators are as savvy in their choices of victims as financial predators are. As stated before, many sexual assault victims are chosen because of their status in society. Children are easy prey for predators. They are easy to control because they can be easily threatened and intimidated. Out of fear for their own safety or for the safety of their loved ones, they do not always tell anyone what was done to them, and when they do tell, they unfortunately are not always believed.

The same is true for adult victims of sexual assault. Who would believe a stripper or a prostitute who claims she was raped? How reliable can an addict be when she tells police that she was held at knifepoint and assaulted? Sexual predators understand how society judges those outside of the mainstream, and therefore choose victims who are not accepted, not well-liked, or not likely to be believed, knowing that doing so increases their chances of walking away from their crimes without fear of consequences.

Because of the predator's inherent ability to manipulate the system and intimidate or charm his victims, the prosecutor must do everything possible to protect the victim during the discovery process. We have a duty to make the victim feel safe and involved while participating in the judicial process. We must help victims understand that, despite their fears, at the end of the process comes healing and the opportunity to move beyond what happened to them.

Many tools are available to help us do this. Whether the case involves a financial or sexual predator, the prosecutor should ask for and receive no-contact orders for the victims. Don't get me wrong: a no-contact order is not some magical device that protects a victim from any wrongdoing by the predator. It is a piece of paper. However, it is our first opportunity to give the victims a sense of safety and empowerment and to also assert further control over the predator. It also provides recourse to the prosecutor if the defendant decides to violate the order by contacting a victim. If the predator has been released pre-trial, that violation gives the prosecutor an easy opportunity to get the predator off the streets and into a jail cell where he belongs. Swift action following a violation also lets the victim know that law enforcement is going to do everything they can to protect them as the judicial process moves forward.

It is also important for the prosecutor to limit the line of questioning that is allowed during depositions of the victim prior to the deposition itself. This is especially true for victims of sexual predators. In almost all states, the victim's prior sexual history is not admissible during trial. Since this is the case, the defense attorney should not be allowed to ask about it during a deposition. For the defense, the only purpose of such questions is to embarrass and intimidate a witness in hopes of scaring them out of testifying during the trial. It is exactly what the sexual predator wants, and should be stopped before it is ever allowed to start.

Prosecutors should also refer victims to any services that might be available to them. Prosecutors are only a small part of the healing process, and it is important in every case that the prosecutor works with other agencies or community groups to provide a well-rounded support system for the victim. Financial victims can be referred to local agencies or nonprofits that are willing to help them get their finances back in order. Sexual assault victims should be referred to local shelters or to counseling services that can help them begin to deal with their trauma. These services cannot change what happened to the victims, but they do give them ways to cope. They help them live their lives normally again, which initially seems impossible for many victims.

Voir Dire

Trial is the part of my job that I love the most. Athletes spend countless hours conditioning their bodies and practicing their skills to prepare for competition. Musicians rehearse a piece of music over and over before performing it in front of an audience. The same is true for the prosecutor. We spend months preparing for a case. Long hours are spent with witnesses, preparing them for what they could be asked while on the stand. We work late into the night preparing questions for witnesses and preparing evidence to present to a judge and jury. And as much as we try to avoid it, we become emotionally vested in every case. Well before I go to trial, I know for a fact that the predator is guilty, and that he needs to be put in prison to protect his victims and the rest of society from the dangers he presents. As the trial begins, it is time for me to take what I already know and convince twelve other people to believe it as well.

Everything starts with jury selection. Out of a room full of strangers, the prosecutor is expected to find the twelve people who would be the most fair-minded for the trial. Jury selection is not an opportunity to directly present the case to the jurors—that comes later. It is the first chance the prosecutor has to prepare the jurors for what will be presented to them during the trial. Jury selection is my time to present the problems in my case and to see which potential jurors are willing to accept my line of thought. For example, in a financial case, many defense attorneys will base their strategy on the fact that the victim willingly gave her money to the defendant in full knowledge of his intended uses of it and the risks involved with the "investment opportunity" proposed by the predator. I can tailor my questions to potential jurors to address that defense before the defense attorney has the opportunity to present it in detail. The most common defense in sexual assault cases is that the victim consented to the sexual contact. Potential jurors must be questioned to discover what they think defines consent and how they may view whatever contact the victim may have had with the predator. The issue of consent is absolutely vital in selecting jurors for most sexual assault cases.

Much has been written about jury selection and the best strategies for choosing a favorable jury. My experience as a prosecutor says to go with your gut. A juror may appear to have everything going for him in terms of his background and how he answers your questions, but if there is something that simply does not feel right about him, strike him from the jury pool. Your gut is always right in jury selection.

Trial

After the jury has been selected, I get to tell my side of the story during opening arguments. Television courtroom dramas make it seem like cases are won and lost during closing arguments, but criminal attorneys on both sides of the aisle know the opposite to be true. A strong opening is vital. If I tell the story wrong, I may never get the jury back on my side. The opening statement is the prosecutor's opportunity to present the facts, to show the jury an overview of the evidence, and to make human the victims of the case. Of course, the defense will follow by tearing apart every detail of the prosecutor's opening argument, but if the story is told right, the jurors can see through rhetoric, or at least be able to have an open mind as the trial evolves.

When presenting the facts of the case through witnesses and evidence, the prosecutor must be well-organized and persuasive. Jurors are like anyone else: they need to have the evidence presented to them in a manner that allows them to process it as well as possible. Jurors also need to understand the story from the very beginning. The victim is the most important person in the prosecutor's story, and she needs to be on the witness stand at the beginning of the trial, regardless of where she fits into the actual timeline of events. Police officers who responded to the crime, doctors and nurses who treated the assault victim, and detectives and accountants who investigated financial records are all important to the case, but they cannot personalize the crime for the jury. Only the victim can put a face on it. Only the victim can let the jury know that the crime was committed against a real person. In the victim, jurors can see the actual effects of the crime on another human being, and as the victim's testimony unfolds, they can begin to identify with the victim, or see similarities between the victim and people they know from their own lives outside of the courtroom.

Unfortunately, the victim is not always available to testify due to death, age, illness, or some other reason. If that is the case, the prosecutor needs to begin with a witness who is close to the victim. Even without the victim present, it is vital to humanize that person for the jury. In the abstract, it is far too easy for the defense to present the victim as consenting, unreliable, or even the actual cause of the crime. That becomes much more difficult once the prosecution has made the victim real for the jury.

Cross examination of the predator can be the most challenging aspect of a trial. While a defendant always has the choice whether or not to take the witness stand, most predators choose to do so. Their sense of entitlement and confidence in their skills of manipulation lead them to believe that they can talk their way out of anything. They are practically compelled by their own arrogance to take the stand, thinking that once the jury hears their side of the story, it is impossible that they would end up with anything except for a verdict of not guilty.

Some of them are more skilled at testifying than others, but in the end, their stories simply cannot stand up against solid evidence. The sexual predator who claims that his victim consented to their sexual contact has a hard time explaining how that is possible when the knife he used to threaten her or pictures of the injuries he caused to her are entered into evidence. A financial predator's claim that his victim knowingly and voluntarily gave the predator control of his finances unravels quickly when the jury learns that the victim is ninety years old, suffers from Alzheimer's, and has nothing to live on after his bank account and pension fund were emptied.

Still, I am constantly amazed at the sincerity that predators are able to project from the witness stand. They are that good at lying. Fortunately, a trial is not a simple matter of two people having their say before the case goes to the jury. Through witness testimony and undisputable evidence such as DNA or a well-documented paper trail, a prosecutor can chip away at the predator's story piece by piece. A good story is helpful, but it ultimately fails when confronted with solid evidence.

During closing arguments, the prosecutor has to go back and reassemble the puzzle for the jury. Evidence comes into a trial piecemeal. There is so much information for the jury to process, and many important pieces of evidence will have been forgotten by the time the trial comes to a close. Other evidence gets presented, and jurors become confused about what its purpose is in relation to the overall case. That is why the prosecutor must use closing arguments to show the jury the big picture of the case, and how all those pieces of evidence fit into that big picture. I retell what really happened. I re-emphasize what evidence really matters. I remind them why they should find my evidence to be more believable and more reliable than the defense's. It is during closing where the prosecutor applies the facts of the case to the law. The law says that these particular acts are a crime. In the end, the jury must understand that these acts were committed by the defendant, how and why he did it, and that it is their responsibility to hold him accountable for his actions.

Verdict

After all the hours of preparation, all of the arguments, all of the time and money spent on bringing a predator to justice, everything rests on the final decision of twelve people. Everything comes down to one or two words as the verdict is read: Guilty or not guilty. A prosecutor has to prepare the victim and other interested parties for either outcome. I always let them know that regardless of the verdict, everyone has done the best they can do. Whether the predator is sent to prison or he walks out of the courtroom a free man, they need to feel proud of themselves for standing up to him, for doing what is right and speaking out against him and speaking the truth about what happened. And I always tell them that, no matter how well they testified, no matter how strong the evidence was, no matter how badly the predator incriminated himself on the stand, there is no such thing as a sure thing once the case is in the hands of the jury.

A guilty verdict always brings with it a sense of relief. At that point, I know that justice has been done, and I feel rewarded for all of the hard work and long hours I put into the case. For the victim, however, it does not make everything right. The guilty verdict is only a small part of the healing process, and while it does help bring closure to that part of the victim's life, it does not and cannot magically make the pain and suffering disappear. I hear from so many victims that they expected to feel happy or relieved when they heard the word "guilty," but in reality they felt the same anger or emptiness or whatever it was they felt before the verdict.

Victims endure unthinkable emotional pain, and a guilty verdict never takes that pain away, but it does allow them to move forward in the healing process.

With the verdict, they can put behind them the ordeal of maneuvering through the judicial process and instead move on to the all-important process of dealing with their emotions and putting their lives back together however they can. This process can take many forms, but it is always easier to proceed with once the trial has ended and the predator has been found guilty.

As a prosecutor, I also experience mixed emotions with every guilty verdict. I receive great satisfaction in knowing that the predator will spend time behind bars, and that it will hopefully be a very long time before he is able to harm another person. There is a lot of pride in knowing the part I played to make that possible.

With that, however, there is a sense of emptiness for me as well. After the dust has cleared and the excitement of the trial is over, so much of it seems to be such a pointless waste. All of those skills that the predator used to commit his crime and then try to avoid the consequences could have made him a highly productive member of society. Had he made different choices, he could have been successful in so many different areas of life. Instead, he chose a life where he benefited from the pains of others, and instead of contributing to society he will now waste his life and large amounts of taxpayer money in prison. The victim's life has been completely and irrevocably changed by the predator's actions, and there is no going back there either. As a result, the lives of those around the victim are changed as well. So many lives changed, ruined, or destroyed, all because of the malicious acts of one person.

No matter how many of these cases I prosecute, I doubt I will ever understand predators and why they commit the crimes they do. I have no desire to. My sympathies lie with the victims. As far as I am concerned, there is no justification strong enough to excuse these predators from responsibility for their actions. Besides the fact, to truly and fully understand a predator, means that you actually are one.

■ Conclusion

Winning and losing are both part of the job for a prosecutor. I hate to lose, but it is something that a good prosecutor learns to deal with. Dealing with losing is vital for any prosecutor, not only to keep her sanity, but also to keep trying cases. Difficult cases are easily lost, but they are still worth trying. There are prosecutors who will claim they have never lost a case. There is a reason for that: they never try the difficult ones, those cases that are high-risk in terms of getting a conviction, but necessary because the same predator who makes the case so difficult is the one who most needs to be put into prison.

Predators are a disease in our society and prosecutors are only able to treat the disease after it starts. Fortunately, there are people in other fields who study and research the root causes of the disease, working to find out what causes predators to do what they do, and searching for ways to prevent people from ever becoming predators. I can only hope they have success, but until that time, I know that I will always have a job.

Institutional Misconduct Among Capital Murderers

15

Mark D. Cunningham
Private-Practice Forensic Psychologist

An understanding of the prison behavior of capital offenders has accelerated rapidly in recent years as a result of large-scale digitized correctional databases becoming available for study. This has yielded an increasingly detailed and reliable illumination of the comparative rates and correlates of prison misconduct among prison inmates in general, and more specifically among convicted murderers and capital offenders. Still, the body of studies examining the prison misconduct of murderers and capital murderers remains limited. This is surprising, given the national and international interest in American capital jurisprudence and the implications that the prison misconduct of capital murderers have for attitudes regarding the death penalty, for juror determinations in capital sentencing cases, for life-without-parole sentencing, and for the confinement of death-sentenced inmates.

Studies providing inferential or direct data regarding the institutional misconduct of capital murderers have utilized six broad types of samples (see **Table 15.1**):

1. Convicted murderers in the general prison population.[1–3]
2. Inmates sentenced to life-without-parole.[4–6]
3. Capital offenders sentenced to life terms, i.e., never sentenced to death.[7,8]

Table 15.1 Assaultive Rule Violations of Murderers, Capital Murderers, and Comparison Inmates

Study	Sample	Follow-up Interval	Rate of Assaults		
			Capital	Comparison	
Sorensen & Cunningham[1]	51,527 system-wide, Florida	2003 (12 months)		0.034 annual	
	5,010 1st degree murderers			0.032 annual	
	3,256 2nd degree murderers			0.038 annual	
	1,320 lesser homicide			0.021 annual	
	837 any homicide	(2002 admission)		0.042 annual	
	13,251 no homicide	(2002 admission)		0.037 annual	
	450 any homicide	(2002 admt. close custody)		0.044 annual	
	3,663 no homicide	(2002 admt. close custody)		0.082 annual	
Sorensen & Cunningham[2]	1,659 murderers, Texas	2001–03 (initial)		0.045 cum. preval.	
		M = 20 months		0.070 cum. preval.	
	223 lesser homicide				
	1,108 murder				
	328 capital murder (life)		0.162 cum. preval.		
Sorensen & Pilgrim[3]	6,390 murderers, Texas	1990–99 (initial)		.024 annual	
		M = 4.5 years		.084 cum. preval.	
				(serious assault)	
Life-without-parole inmates					
Cunningham et al.[4]	149 MS-DS, Missouri	1991–2002 (M = 6.7 yrs)	0.076 annual		
	1,054 LWOP	(M = 4.3 yrs)			
	2,199 parole eligible	(M = 1.5 yrs)	0.425 annual	0.096 annual	
Cunningham & Sorensen[5]	9,044 long-term inmates in close custody, Florida	1998–2003 (initial)			
	1,897 LWOP	M = 3.4 years		0.074 cum. preval.	
	1,985 30+ year sentence	M = 3.4 years		0.061 cum. preval.	
	1,726 20–29 year sentence	M = 3.2 years		0.072 cum. preval.	

Sorensen & Wrinkle[6]	1,469 15–19 year sentence	M = 3.3 years		0.097 cum. preval.
	1,967 10–14 year sentence	M = 3.2 years		0.117 cum. preval.
	648 murderers, Missouri	1977–92		0.218 cum. preval.
	93 Death Row	M = 6.62 years	0.237 cum. preval.	
	323 LWOP	M = 6.66 years	0.176 cum. preval.	
	232 LWP (2nd degree)	M = 7.13 years		0.224 cum. preval.
Capital murderers sentenced to life terms				
Cunningham & Sorensen[2]	136 capital murderers, Texas	2001–2004 (initial)	0.094 annual	
		M = 2.37 years	0.14 cum. preval.	
Marquart et al.[8]	107 CLS murderers, Texas	1974–88 (M = 7.2 yrs)		0.026 annual
	38,246 system-wide, Texas	1986	0.12 annual	
	1,712 high security, Texas	1986	0.20 annual	
Sorensen & Wrinkle[6]	See above			
Former death-sentenced murderers				
Akman[9]	69 FDR, Canada	1964–65 (2 yrs)	0 cum. preval.	
	7,447 system-wide, Canada	1964–65 (2 yrs)		0.007 annual
Bedau[10]	55 FDR, New Jersey	1907–60 (53 yrs)	0 cum. preval. (serious assault)	
Edens et al.[11]	See below		(serious assault)	
Marquart et al.[8]			(serious assault)	
Marquart et al.[16]	156 LS, Texas (128 murderers/28 rapists)	1973–88 (M = 11 yrs)	(serious assault)	0.10 cum. preval. (serious assault)

Table 15.1 (Continued)

Study	Sample	Follow-up Interval	Capital	Comparison
Marquart & Sorensen[12]	533 FDR, nationwide (453 murderers, 80 rapists)	1973–1988		0.031 cum. preval.
Reidy et al.[13]	On DR (M = 6.7 years)	0.054 annual		
	Post-DR (M = 9.3 years)	0.028 annual		
		(serious assaults)		
Wagner[14]	100 FDR, Texas	1924–72 (M = 12 yrs)	0.20 cum. preval.	
Death row inmates				
Edens et al.[11]	155 DR, expert predicted, Texas			
	65 DR executed	M = 12 years	0.046 cum. preval.	
	42 DR	M = 8 years	0.071 cum. preval.	
	48 DR/FDR	M = 22 years	0.042 cum. preval.	
		(serious assaults)		
Marquart et al.[14]	421 DR, Texas	1974–1988	0.107 cum. preval.	
Reidy et al.[13]	See above			
Mainstreamed death-sentenced inmates				
Cunningham et al.[4]	See above			

Abbreviations: DR, Death Row; FDR, Former Death Row; DR/FDR, tenure on death row and post death row in general prison population; MS-DS, Mainstreamed Death Sentenced; LS, Life Sentence; CLS, Capital Life Sentence; LWOP, Life-without-Parole; LWP, Life with Parole; cum. preval., cumulative prevalence rate; annual, annual frequency rate.

4. Capital offenders initially sentenced to death at trial, but who subsequently gained relief by commutation, retrial, or other remedy.[9–14]

5. Death-sentenced inmates on death row.[13,15,16]

6. Death-sentenced offenders who are mainstreamed in the general prison population rather than being maintained on a segregated death row.[4]

The findings of correctional research regarding these categories of murderers and capital murderers will be illustrated in the sections that follow.[17,18] The implications of these findings for questions confronting correctional procedures or public policy will be highlighted to illustrate the practical applications of this research. Finally, emerging research on the correlates of prison violence among murderers and capital murderers will be considered.

■ Are Murderers More Likely than Other Offenders to Engage in Violence in Prison?

Three large-scale studies have examined misconduct among convicted murderers in the general prison population, with only one of these providing comparative data with non-murderers. Sorensen and Pilgrim retrospectively reviewed the disciplinary records of 6,390 murderers in Texas prisons who had been convicted between 1990 and 1998. During prison tenures averaging four and a half years, 8.4% of these offenders were disciplined for violent acts. The prevalence rates of specific misconduct varied by the severity of the assault: 0% homicide of staff, 0.1% homicide of inmate, 0.5% aggravated assault on staff, 4.4% assault on inmate with a weapon, 4.2% fight with a weapon, and 0.2% other violence. From these prevalence rates, Sorensen and Pilgrim extrapolated that a convicted murderer is projected to commit serious violence during a 40-year term in prison at probabilities of: 16.4% likelihood of serious assault, 1% likelihood of aggravated assault on staff, and 0.2% likelihood of a homicide of an inmate.[3]

In a subsequent study, Sorensen and Cunningham examined the prison behavior of 1,656 convicted murderers who had been admitted to the Texas prison system in 2001–2003. Averaging 22 months in prison at the time of this study, 8.5% of the convicted murderers had engaged in an assault and 2.17% in an assault with serious injury, with annual frequency rates of 71.7 and 12.5 per 1,000 inmates, respectively. Again, comparisons were not made with the misconduct rates of inmates who had been convicted of other offenses.[2] These two studies have impressive sample sizes and provide important base rate data illuminating the frequency and prevalence rates of prison violence during an initial phase of incarceration among convicted murderers. Neither, however, answers the question of whether convicted murderers are more likely to engage in violence in prison.

A large-scale study in the Florida Department of Corrections does address this issue, as well as illustrating how sample selection in a study can be varied to control for inherent flaws. Sorensen and Cunningham compared the prison misconduct of various overlapping cohorts of convicted murderers and other offenders in Florida prisons. Most broadly, the 2003 disciplinary records of all inmates serving the entire 2003 calendar year ($N = 51,527$) were compared in terms of the type of offense that had resulted in their conviction. This sample included 9,586 inmates who had been convicted of some form of homicide, of whom 5,010 had been convicted of first degree murder. The first degree murderers had better disciplinary records, and equivalent annual prevalence rates of assault, as compared to other offenders: assault 2.6%, assault with injury 0.6%, and assault with serious injury 0.2%. This analysis, while informing how conviction offense was related to prison violence in any given year, did not control for the murderers being deeper in their sentences and thus older. Both of these factors have been associated with lower rates of institutional violence and thus could confound comparisons of murderers with other offenders.

Another analysis examined the 2003 disciplinary records of a cohort of inmates who entered prison in 2002 ($N = 14,088$). Even this analysis, however, did not control for whether the respective inmates were held at the same level of custody. Accordingly, a third sample consisted of inmates who entered prison in 2002 and were assigned to close custody ($N = 4,113$). An analysis was also conducted to determine if murderers were disproportionately represented in various forms of assault. Regardless of the sample or analysis or severity of violence specified, convicted murderers were not more likely to be involved in institutional violence.

The emerging conclusions of these studies indicate that only a minority of convicted murderers are cited for violence in prison, with progressively lower prevalence rates for more serious prison violence. Convicted murderers are no more likely to be involved in assaultive misconduct in prison than offenders convicted of other crimes.

■ Are Offenders Convicted of More Severe Forms of Homicide More Likely to Be Violent in Prison than Offenders Convicted of Less Severe Forms of Homicide?

Whether offenders who have been convicted of more severe forms of homicide are more likely to be involved in prison violence than those convicted of less serious forms is unclear. Two studies referenced above examined the misconduct of homicide offenders by the severity of the homicide (e.g., capital, first degree, second degree, manslaughter), with contradictory results. A severity-related effect was strongly observed in research on Texas homicide offenders, with capital murderers exhibiting higher rates of assault and assault with serious injuries than offenders who had been convicted of lesser forms of homicide. Among convicted murderers in Florida prisons, however, first degree murderers and second degree murderers had equivalent rates of assaults, regardless of severity. In a third study in the Missouri Department of Corrections, detailed in a subsequent section, Sorensen and Wrinkle reported that life-sentenced capital offenders and second degree murderers had equivalent rates of prison assaults.[6]

Severity of homicide therefore has an inconsistent relationship to assaultive misconduct in prison, apparently varying by correctional department. This inconsistency potentially illustrates the role of "institutional" variables, as opposed to "personal" variables in the occurrence of prison violence.[19]

▪ Do Female Homicide Offenders Engage in Prison Violence at Different Rates than Male Murderers?

Data in respect to rates of misconduct among women were drawn from the general population of inmates and convicted homicide offenders in the general prison population. Whether female inmates, or more specifically female homicide offenders, exhibit different base rates of assaultive misconduct in prison is controversial. In a large scale study *not* restricted to homicide offenders, Harer and Langan reported that serious assaults by female inmates in the federal Bureau of Prisons occurred at one-twelfth the rate of such assaults among males.[20] Similarly, among convicted homicide offenders in the Texas Department of Criminal Justice (TDCJ) during an initial confinement period of 6 to 30 months, females exhibited equivalent rates of assault, but had no incidents of serious assaults. Somewhat inconsistent with both of the above studies, however, females in the Florida Department of Corrections demonstrated similar prevalence rates of assault at all levels of severity during their first year in confinement as compared to male inmates.[21] Institutional homicides by female inmates are apparently extraordinarily rare, with none occurring in the history of the Federal Bureau of Prisons.[20]

We conclude, therefore, that the data are mixed regarding whether female inmates or female homicide offenders are less frequently involved in prison violence. There are trends pointing to females being less likely to engage in serious assaults, particularly prison homicides.

■ Are Life-Without-Parole Inmates Unmanageable and Predatory Because They Have Nothing to Lose?

"I think that life sentences without parole do create a segment of the prison population who have no hope. They know that they are going to be there for life, and they have nothing to lose. And I think it does create a terrific security problem for prison officials and for the staffs that work in prisons."—Harris County [Houston] Assistant District Attorney Roe Wilson, in testimony before the Judicial Committee of the Texas Senate in opposition to Senate Bill 348 (2003 legislative session).[22]

Comparisons of life-without-parole and parole-eligible inmates have been undertaken in three studies, each comparing rates of prison misconduct among life-without-parole (LWOP) and parole-eligible inmates, to illuminate an assertion that life-without-parole inmates represent a particular prison security and management problem. In two of these studies, LWOP inmates had rates of prison misconduct that were equivalent to parole-eligible inmates. The largest involved a substantial sample of long-term inmates admitted to the Florida Department of Corrections 1998–2002, including 1,897 inmates sentenced to LWOP terms and 7,147 other close custody inmates serving 10–30+ years.[5] Retrospective review of the 1998–2003 disciplinary records of these inmates revealed that the likelihood and pattern of disciplinary infractions and potentially violent rule infractions among LWOP inmates were broadly similar to those of other long term inmates. Also notable, during their initial years in their LWOP sentences ($M = 3.3$ years) when they would be considered to be most at risk of violence, only 0.6% of the LWOP inmates were cited for an assault with serious injury.

Consistent with these findings, Sorensen and Wrinkle found that convicted murderers in the Missouri Department of Corrections exhibited similar rates of assaultive misconduct, regardless of whether they had been sentenced to LWOP or parole-eligible life sentences.[6] More specifically, this study compared the disciplinary records (1977–1992) of 323 LWOP inmates who had been convicted of capital murder and 232 inmates sentenced to life with parole for second degree murder. Approximately 20% of these inmates were sanctioned for an assault in prison during this period of time. Two-thirds of these assaults were minor and one-third were serious. During the 15-year study period, approximately 1.2% killed another inmate.

Interestingly, in another study LWOP inmates were markedly *less* frequently involved in assaultive misconduct in prison. Cunningham, Sorensen, and Reidy compared 960 LWOP inmates to 1,503 parole-eligible inmates in a high-security prison in the Missouri Department of Corrections (1991–2002).[4] The LWOP inmates were half as likely to have been cited for violent misconduct as the parole-eligible inmates with whom they were serving time in the same correctional facility. As often occurs in research design, the methodology of this study is double-edged. It provided for side-by-side comparisons within the same prison, but this restriction to a single facility limits generalization of the findings.

Thus, LWOP inmates are not a disproportionate source of violence in prison. This conclusion rests on data from an aggregate of over 12,000 inmates, drawn from two correctional jurisdictions, and encompassing over two decades of retrospective records review. Although a rationale of "nothing to lose" has intuitive appeal, it is not borne out when the comparative prison behavior of LWOP inmates is examined. The findings of these studies were presented to the Texas Legislature in 2005. Texas subsequently became the 38th state to provide a LWOP sentencing option at capital sentencing. Eleven states without the death penalty also have LWOP sentencing.

■ Are Capital Offenders Likely to Perpetrate Serious Violence in Prison?

> "He absolutely will, regardless of whether he's inside an institution-type setting or whether he's outside. No matter where he is, he will kill again. . . . He would be a danger in any type setting, and especially to guards or other inmates. No matter where he might be, he is a danger."—Sentencing phase testimony of James Grigson, M.D., in State of Texas v. Rodriquez, a death-penalty case.[23]

Only three studies have reported on the prison behavior of capital offenders who received life sentences rather than the death penalty at their capital trials, none of which were available during the era of Dr. Grigson's recurrent testimony in Texas capital cases (Dr. Grigson gave testimony quite similar to that quoted above in over 100 death penalty cases in Texas). In 1989, Marquart, Ekland-Olson, and Sorensen reported on 107 Texas capital defendants who had been convicted 1974–1988 and sentenced to capital life terms after their juries had rejected the Texas capital sentencing "special issue," i.e., "whether there is a probability that the defendant would commit criminal acts of violence that would constitute a continuing threat to society."[8,16,24] Averaging just over seven years in prison at the time of retrospective file review, 12% of these inmates had been sanctioned for violent misconduct. Interestingly, the annual frequency of violent misconduct among these 107 Texas capital life offenders (0.026) was substantially lower than that exhibited by inmates system-wide (0.117) or non-capital inmates at a similar high security level (0.195).

Sorensen and Wrinkle examined assaultive misconduct rates among 323 LWOP-sentenced capital murderers (1977–1992), finding a prevalence rate of assaults of approximately 20%.[6] This rate was similar to that exhibited by second degree murderers. A broader comparative analysis of assaults among all inmates in the Missouri Department of Corrections was not reported.

A third study by Cunningham and Sorensen described rates of assaultive prison misconduct among 136 Texas capital offenders during the initial phase (M = 2.37 years) of their life sentences.[7] As anticipated, prevalence rates decreased as the severity of the misconduct increased (i.e., any potentially violent act = 0.368; assaultive violations = 0.14; assaults with serious injury = 0.051; homicide = 0). Comparison data with an admission cohort of non-capital inmates was not available. The capital inmates did, however, exhibit higher rates of assaultive prison misconduct than an admission cohort of inmates who had been convicted of non-capital forms of homicide.

A handful of other studies have reported on the institutional conduct of inmates who had initially been sentenced to death, but whose sentences were subsequently revised to life terms by commutation, retrial and sentence to life, or capital case dismissal. These reports inform considerations of whether these offenders constitute a long-term threat to institutional safety, but only following the initial years of incarceration when violence is most likely to occur.

In 1972, the death penalty, as it was then being practiced, was declared unconstitutional by the U.S. Supreme Court in *Furman v. Georgia* (1972). Two of these studies examined capital offenders from the pre-*Furman* era.[10,14] Though not providing specific misconduct rates, Bedau reported that among 55 New Jersey capital offenders released from death row to the general prison population 1907–1960, none had institutional histories that adversely affected their parole determinations.[10] Wagner reported that among 100 Texas offenders who obtained relief from their death sentences 1924–1971, during general prison population tenures averaging 12 years, 80% were not sanctioned for serious institutional violence (i.e., murder, aggravated assault, sex by force, striking a guard, or escape) and none assaulted a correctional officer.

Four other studies have illuminated the post-relief institutional conduct of death-sentenced offenders who were removed from death row under *Furman* or during the post-*Furman* era. Among 533 capital offenders commuted nationwide under *Furman*, 31.5% were subsequently sanctioned for violent misconduct in the general prison population. Marquart, Ekland-Olson, and Sorensen reported on 92 Texas offenders who had been sentenced to death under the "special issue," i.e., "whether there is a probability that the defendant would commit criminal acts of violence that would constitute a continuing threat to society," but subsequently obtained relief.[25] During ensuing tenures averaging six years in the general prison population, their annual rate of serious violent rule infractions among these former condemned prisoners was 0.0161, well below that exhibited by other general population inmates. A smaller study of 39 former death-sentenced inmates in Indiana by Reidy, Cunningham, and Sorensen reported that 20.5% were involved in violent acts in the general prison population following their removal from death row, and only one-third of these acts resulted in serious injury.[13] Edens and his colleagues reported on the violent prison misconduct of 48 former death-sentenced inmates where a mental health expert had testified at their death penalty trials in Texas predicting that they would be a "future danger."[11] Examining violent misconduct both while on death row and following relief from their death sentences, 4% of these inmates were sanctioned for serious assaults.

Only a minority of capital offenders are disciplined for serious prison violence. Further, the trend is toward these offenders not being a disproportionate risk of prison violence as compared to other inmates. This finding appears consistent whether these convicted capital murderers are on death row pending a death sentence, or in the general prison population as a result of a life sentence at trial or relief from their death sentences. Even the capital murderers for whom there was an expectation by mental health experts or jurors of future violence were unlikely to be involved in prison violence.

◼ Do Death-Sentenced Inmates Require Segregated and Super-Maximum Confinement?

Studies of Inmates on Death Row

Four studies have reported on rates of institutional violence among death-row inmates.[25] In the largest of these, Marquart, Ekland-Olson, and Sorensen retrospectively reviewed the disciplinary records of offenders who had passed through the Texas death row 1974–1988 ($N = 421$).[8] They reported that 45 inmates (10.7 percent) assaulted correctional staff or other inmates during the 15 years encompassed by the retrospective review, equivalent to the prevalence rate of aggravated/weapons assaults demonstrated by convicted murderers and rapists in Texas prisons who were serving life sentences. Two death row inmates (0.47 percent) killed another inmate. Given the much higher rate of inmate homicide in the general prison population during this era, it is unclear whether the prevalence rate of prison homicide exhibited by the death row inmates was disproportionate. Obviously, the death row inmates were under higher security and did not have the same opportunities for violence as inmates in the general population. However, during this era, many Texas death-sentenced inmates worked in a death row garment factory with objects that could serve as weapons, and had routine meal and recreation contact interaction with staff and other inmates.

Sorensen and Wrinkle reported on 93 inmates who had passed through death row in Missouri 1977–1992.[6] Twenty-four percent were cited for assaultive misconduct during this tenure. In another retrospective review, Reidy, Cunningham, and Sorensen examined the disciplinary records of 39 Indiana capital offenders who had gained relief from their death sentences between 1972 and 1999. During their tenures on death row, which averaged 6.7 years, 25.6% were involved in violent misconduct.[13]

In a fourth study, Cunningham, Sorensen, and Reidy compared the rates of inmate and staff assaults among Arizona death row inmates ($N = 127$) to those exhibited by the general prison population of the Arizona Department of Corrections in fiscal year 2003 ($N = 30,000$).[15] The death row inmates had a one-year rate of assault of .78 per 100 inmates, compared to 3.26 per 100 among all inmates in that prison system. Because it was possible the death-sentenced inmates had "aged out" of serious prison misconduct by virtue of their averaging a longer time in prison on their current conviction than other inmates in Arizona DOC (119 months vs. 36.9 months), their rate of assault since admission to death row was analyzed. Neither their average annual rate of 3.96 per 100 inmates, nor the average annual rate of 3.42 per 100 inmates if a psychotic outlier inmate were excluded, were significantly different than that exhibited by non-death sentenced inmates. The prevalence rate of serious violent misconduct among Arizona condemned inmates was 17.3% during their entire tenure at risk on death row. Also informative, 52% of the death row inmates had three or fewer disciplinary infractions of any sort since admission to death row, and 16.5% had never had a disciplinary write-up. Cunningham et al. characterized this as "a rather remarkable adaptation by a significant proportion of these inmates—particularly given their time at risk."[4]

Studies of Mainstreamed Death-Sentenced Inmates

Rather than maintaining death-sentenced inmates on a segregated death row, since 1991 Missouri has maintained an innovative policy of making death-sentenced inmates eligible for *all* housing and programming assignments in a high security prison. In other words, they are intermingled in their cell and unit assignments, work roles, programming, recreation, and visitation with non-death inmates. As with any other inmate in this high security prison, assignments and activities were determined by inmate conduct and not sentence. Cunningham, Reidy, and Sorensen reported that the 149 death-sentenced inmates who had been mainstreamed in the risk period of this study (1991–2002) exhibited an annual rate of violent misconduct of 0.076.[4] This rate was equivalent to inmates serving life-without-parole (0.096) and substantially lower than that observed among parole-eligible inmates (0.425) within the same correctional facility. In fact, holding other factors constant, the death-sentenced and life-without-parole inmates were about half as likely to be sanctioned for violent misconduct. These reports by Cunningham and colleagues represented the first "apples to apples" comparison of the prison conduct of death-sentenced and non-death sentenced inmates under the same conditions of confinement. This research also represented a quantitative validation of Missouri's groundbreaking policy in mainstreaming rather than segregating death-sentenced inmates. Administrators in the Missouri Department of Corrections have attributed the success of this policy to staff initiative and a "web of incentives" developed to influence inmate behavior.[26]

The security-driven rationale that death-sentenced inmates require segregated, super-maximum conditions of confinement to deter assaults against inmates and staff is not supported by available research. If, as research appears to demonstrate, such conditions do not serve a legitimate penal interest, they are arguably in violation of the Eighth Amendment, which bars cruel and unusual punishment.[27,28]

■ What Factors Are Correlated with Prison Violence Among Capital Offenders?

Validation studies of risk assessment instruments and actuarial models comprise a rapidly expanding literature that is examining factors correlated with violence in prison and among capital offenders. This complex arena of inquiry could easily be a chapter in its own right. Much of this research has focused on broad samples of prison inmates, with inferential application to capital offenders. My colleagues and I have examined correlates of prison misconduct among admission cohorts of inmates, prisoners in higher security classifications, and homicide offenders.[29]

As the "counterintuitive" findings reviewed in this chapter suggest, murderers and capital offenders appear not to be distinctive in their prison violence proclivity; and thus findings generated from broader inmate samples are likely to generalize to them as well. Among these predictive factors from broader inmate samples, increasing age is associated with decreases in inmate misconduct of all severities.[30–32] Inmates who have earned a high school diploma or G.E.D. certificate have lower rates of disciplinary violations in general as well as assaultive misconduct in prison.[33] A prior prison term has been associated with an increased likelihood of assaultive institutional misconduct in some studies but not others.[4,34] Membership in a prison gang is a significant risk factor for prison violence.[35] Convicted murderers with a contemporaneous robbery or burglary demonstrate an increased prevalence rate of prison assault.

Two studies have examined the correlates of prison violence among samples that include capital offenders.[4,6] These first investigations on the correlates of prison violence among capital offenders in the general prison populations have been consistent with the general trends emerging from research on broader inmate samples. Mainstreamed death-sentenced inmates were included, if only constituting a small minority of the Missouri high security inmates (132 of 2,595 prisoners) studied, in developing an actuarial instrument measuring risk of prison violence. Predictive factors for violent misconduct included age, type and length of sentence, education, prior prison terms, prior probated sentences, and years served.

In the only predictive study restricted to capital offenders, Cunningham and Sorensen examined correlates of assaultive prison misconduct during the initial phase of incarceration ($M = 2.37$ years) among 136 Texas capital murderers sentenced to life terms.[21] A simplified scale was developed (i.e., RASP-Cap), utilizing weightings for age, contemporaneous robbery or burglary, and prior prison term to identify three levels of risk. No inmate scoring at the lowest point totals (i.e., level of risk) had engaged in an assault, as compared to inmates at the highest score level where 25% had been disciplined for an assault and 11.5% had committed an assault with serious injury. Though promising at varying severities of inmate violence (AUC = .715 to .766), this instrument remains experimental. Further, though higher scores reflected a comparatively higher risk, even at the highest risk classification there remained an overwhelming *improbability* of violent misconduct.

Correlates or predictive factors for prison violence among capital offenders appear to be consistent with those identified with other inmate groups. These are useful for classification, security, programming, and resource allocation. None however, identify a "more likely than not" probability of violent misconduct. Though knowledge of the rates and correlates of prison conduct among capital offenders and other convicted murderers is rapidly expanding, these emerging trends require confirmation and elaboration with samples from diverse jurisdictions. The role of arrest history as a predictive factor for institutional misconduct among these offenders remains largely unexplored. There is also a need to go beyond "importation" factors in explaining the occurrence of prison violence among convicted murderers.[36–38] This should include examining the contribution of situational and deprivation factors, as well.

■ Conclusion

Research findings regarding the comparative prison conduct of murderers and capital murderers, even when sentenced to death or life-without-parole, demonstrate the importance of obtaining and relying on data rather than intuitive expectations. Despite the severity of their offenses and the bleakness of their institutional futures, the majority of these offenders do not continue on a trajectory of serious violence following their admission to prison. These findings suggest a reexamination of longstanding public policies and correctional proce-dures directed toward these offenders. For example, data regarding rates and cor-relates of prison violence among capital offenders raises grave concerns with whether "future dangerousness" can be reliably applied at capital sentencing to determine who lives and who dies.[39] Equally notable, over a decade of data from the Missouri Department of Corrections, as well as other studies of death row and former death row inmates, challenges assumptions that death-sentenced in-mates require the segregated, super-maximum units that typify the confinement of these offenders in American prisons. Much of the public policy and correc-tional mores regarding capital murderers was conceived in an era that did not have the benefit of studies examining the prison behavior of these offenders. This provides an unparalleled opportunity for criminal justice research and the asso-ciated illumination of science to prompt more enlightened perspectives.

References

1. Sorensen, J. R., Cunningham, M. D. (2007). Conviction offense and prison violence: A comparative study of murderers and other offenders. Manuscript under review.
2. Sorensen, J. R., Cunningham, M. D. (2007). Operationalizing risk: The in-fluence of measurement choice on the prevalence and correlates of violence among incarcerated murderers. *J Crim Just*, in press.
3. Sorensen, J. R., Pilgrim, R. L. (2000). An actuarial risk assessment of vio-lence posed by capital murder defendants. *J Crim Law Criminol* 90:1251–1270.
4. Cunningham, M. D., Sorensen, J. R., Reidy, T. J. (2005). An actuarial model for assessment of prison violence risk among maximum security inmates. *Assessment* 12:40–49.
5. Cunningham, M. D., Sorensen, J. R. (2006). Nothing to lose? A compara-tive examination of prison misconduct rates among life-without-parole and other long-term high security inmates. *Crim Justice Behav* 33:683–705.
6. Sorensen, J. R., Wrinkle, R. D. (1996). No hope for parole: Disciplinary in-fractions among death-sentenced and life-without-parole inmates. *Crim Jus-tice Behav* 23:542–552.
7. Cunningham, M. D., Sorensen, J. R. (2007). Predictive factors for violent misconduct in close custody. *Prison J* 87:241–253.

References

8. Marquart, J. W., Ekland-Olson, S., Sorensen, J. R. (1989). Gazing into the crystal ball: Can jurors accurately predict dangerousness in capital cases? *Law Society Rev* 23:449–468.

9. Akman, D. D. (1966). Homicides and assaults in Canadian penitentiaries. *Can J Corrections* 8:284–299.

10. Bedau, H. A. (1964). Death sentences in New Jersey, 1907–1960. *Rutg Law Rev* 19:1–64.

11. Edens, J. F., Buffington-Vollum, J. K., Keilen, A., et al. (2005). Predictions of future dangerousness in capital murder trials: Is it time to "disinvent the wheel"? *Law Human Behav* 29:55–86.

12. Marquart, J. W., Sorensen, J. R. (1988). Institutional and post release behavior of Furman-commuted inmates in Texas. *Criminology* 26:677–693.

13. Reidy, T. J., Cunningham, M. D., Sorensen, J. R. (2001). From death to life: Prison behavior of former death row inmates. *Crim Justice Behav* 28:67–82.

14. Wagner, A. (1988). *A Commutation Study of Ex-Capital Offenders in Texas, 1924–1971.* Unpublished dissertation, Sam Houston State University, Huntsville, TX.

15. Cunningham, M. D., Sorensen, J. R., Reidy, T. J. (2004). Revisiting future dangerousness revisited: Response to DeLisi and Munoz. *Crim Justice Policy Rev* 15:365–376.

16. Marquart, J. W., Ekland-Olson, S., Sorensen, J. R. (1994). *The Rope, the Chair, the Needle: Capital Punishment in Texas, 1923–1990.* Austin: University of Texas Press.

17. Cunningham, M. D., Reidy, T. J. (1998). Integrating base rate data in violence risk assessments at capital sentencing. *Behav Sci Law* 16:71–95.

18. Cunningham, M. D., Reidy, T. J. (2002). Violence risk assessment at federal capital sentencing: Individualization, generalization, relevance, and scientific standards. *Crim Justice Behav* 29:512–537.

19. Gendreau, P., Goggin, C. E., Law, M. A. (1997). Predicting prison misconducts. *Crim Justice Behav* 24:414–431.

20. Harer, M. D., Langan, N. P. (2001). Gender differences in predictors of prison violence: Assessing the predictive validity of a risk classification system. *Crime Delinq* 47:513–536.

21. Cunningham, M. D., Sorensen, J. R. (2006). Actuarial models for assessment of prison violence risk: Revisions and extensions of the Risk Assessment Scale for Prison (RASP). *Assessment* 13:253–265.

22. McInnis, J. (2003). Senate panel pushes no-parole sentencing option. *Houston Chronicle,* April 2, 2003, page A-19.

23. *State of Texas v. Rodriquez,* Texas, Tex. Crim. App., 597 S.W.2nd 917 (1980).

24. Texas Code of Criminal Procedure. Article 37.071 Procedure in capital case. This special issue was affirmed by the U.S. Supreme Court in *Jurek v. Texas* (1976).

25. Marquart, J. W., Sorensen, J. R. (1989). A national study of the Furman-commuted inmates: Assessing the threat to society from capital offenders. *Loyola Los Angeles Law Rev* 23:5–28.

26. Lombardi, G., Sluder, R. D., Wallace, D. (1997). Mainstreaming death-sentenced inmates: The Missouri experience and its legal significance. *Fed Prob* 61:3–11.

27. *Turner v. Safley*, 482 U.S. 89 (1987).

28. Lyon, A. D., Cunningham, M. D. (2006). Reason not the need: Does the lack of compelling state interest in maintaining a separate death row make it unlawful? *Am J Crim Law* 33:1–30.

29. Cunningham, M. D. (2006). Dangerousness and death: A nexus in search of science and reason. *Am Psychol* 61:828–839.

30. DeLisi, M., Berg, M. T., Hochstetler, A. (2004). Gang members, career criminals and prison violence: Further specification of the importation model of inmate behavior. *Crim Justice Stud* 17:369–383.

31. Harer, M. D., Steffensmeier, D. J. (1996). Race and prison violence. *Criminology* 34:323–350.

32. Lemieux, C. M., Dyeson, T. B., Castiglione, B. (2002). Revisiting the literature on prisoners who are older: Are we wiser? *Prison J* 82:440–458.

33. Cooper, R., Werner, P. (1990). Predicting violence in newly admitted inmates. *Crim Justice Behav* 17:431–477.

34. Cao, L., Zhoa, J., Van Dine, S. (1997). Prison disciplinary tickets: A test of the deprivation and importation models. *J Crim Justice* 25:103–113.

35. Gaes, G. G., Wallace, S., Gilman, E., Klein-Saffran, J., Suppa, S. (2002). The influence of prison gang affiliation on violence and other prison misconduct. *Prison J* 82:359–385.

36. Jiang, S., Fisher-Giorlando, M. (2002). Inmate misconduct: A test of the deprivation, importation, and situational models. *Prison J* 82:335–358.

37. McCorkle, R. C., Miethe, T. D., Drass, K. A. (1995). The roots of prison violence: A test of the deprivation, management, and "not so total" institution models. *Crime Delinq* 41:317–331.

38. Patrick, S. (1998). Differences in inmate-inmate and inmate-staff altercations: Examples from a medium security prison. *Social Sci J* 35:253–263.

39. American Psychological Association (2005). Brief of *amicus curie* in support of defendant-appellant, *U.S. v. Sherman Lamont Fields*, in the United States Court of Appeals for the Fifth Circuit.

Sex Offenders on the Internet: Cyber-Struggles for the Protection of Children

16

Frank Kardasz

Arizona Internet Crimes Against Children Task Force and the Phoenix, Arizona Police Department

The Internet provides resources that facilitate communication, education, commerce and unfortunately, crime. Research from the University of Southern California indicated that 78% of Americans, including children, visit cyberspace.[1] Other researchers who specifically examined children's use of the Internet found that young people are frequently being exposed to sexually-related material and are also encountering predators who solicit them for sex.[2] Some criminals use cyberspace to traffic images depicting the sexual abuse of children. Some offenders use the Internet for the purpose of luring and enticing minors towards sex. The quiet collision of young people and sex offenders on the Internet has resulted in a cyber-struggle for the protection of children. This chapter explores topics related to the sex offenders who use the Internet to victimize youth.

There are many sex offenders, both registered and unregistered, in every U.S. state. The Family Watchdog group reports that there are 344,362 registered sex offenders in the United States. Many of them offended against minors.[3] According to the U.S. Justice Department, two-thirds of the victims of reported sexual assault are minors, and one out of every three victims of a sex offense is under age 12.[4] Among the most disturbing sex crimes being facilitated via the Internet are those that involve child and teen victims. In 2002, President George W. Bush said, "in the hands of incredibly wicked people, the Internet is a tool that lures children into real danger."[5] One study found that 34% of children using the Internet were exposed to unwanted sexually explicit material. The same study showed that one in seven youngsters received unwanted sexual solicitations and that 4% received aggressive solicitations involving a stranger who wanted to meet in person.[6]

It is difficult to calculate the true number of Internet crimes against children. Unlike spectacular and conspicuous crimes involving crashes, explosions, fires, shootings and public bloodletting, sex crimes against children are committed in quiet and private places. Internet predators may use chat rooms, web-cams and social networking sites to find and befriend victims. Offenders may use cyberspace to slowly groom, psychologically control, humiliate or intimidate their young victims: first into compliance and then into lifelong silence. Sometimes the crimes against children are never reported.

Offenders use Internet resources in deviously creative ways. They may construct on-line identities portraying themselves as amiable adult mentors. They may pose as other children of the same age as their intended victims. They may anonymously browse web pages for many hours until they find a preferred target and then work to gather enough information to facilitate an offense. The cyber-deviants who lure children and those who traffic child pornography sometimes find hobbies and occupations that facilitate their crimes. Some are professional photographers, computer technicians, or information technology specialists. Some find occupations in positions of trust where they can constantly be near children. Internet sexual criminals may be found in occupations including teachers, priests, day-care workers, police officers, doctors or nurses. There is no single profile of an Internet sex offender. They come from all walks of life and work in various occupations. Most offenders are males, but occasionally females are also involved in Internet crimes against children.

■ Children as the Marginalized Ideal Victims

Offenders worldwide are targeting children for pornography as the international trade in unlawful images expands across the globe. Sex offenders everywhere consider children to be the perfect victims for several reasons. In some places, including Russia, children have become a commodity. There are five reasons for this phenomenon: children are plentiful and easily accessed, child pornography is easy and inexpensive to produce, there is a huge consumer market for it, it is enormously profitable, and there is far less risk than traditional commodities like drugs, guns, and tobacco.[4]

Helpless child victims cannot summon the assistance of law enforcement. Some victims of child pornography are too young to know how to use a telephone. The evidence of a child's victimization is invisible to the general public, and the crimes are often unreported. Because crimes against children are not publicly apparent, law enforcement agencies may marginalize the problems and give the crimes lower priority than other offenses. Consequently there are fewer law enforcement resources devoted to the problems of children. Most police departments have many more traffic cops than crimes against children investigators. Abominations against children are mostly committed in private locations. The offenses do not create the conspicuous noise of gunfire or a car crash. The crimes do not have the noticeable smell of smoke from a fire and cannot be seen from the street like graffiti or broken windows, so there is little public attention drawn to the crimes. Offenders know that children can be easily intimidated into silence and often cannot communicate well enough to be understood by authorities. For offenders, children are ideal victims.

■ The Scope of the Problem

The luring and enticement of minors via the Internet is a widespread problem that is difficult to measure. Crimes involving minors who are lured or enticed are probably under-reported. Researchers who conducted telephone interviews with teens were discouraged to find that very few youths ever told authorities about episodes involving on-line misconduct. In more than half the cases, youths did not tell parents or any others about solicitations from possible Internet sexual predators.[6] The true extent of the Internet luring and enticement problem is unknown.

Internet crimes involving pornographic images of the sexual abuse of children are also widespread and probably immeasurable. A Congressional study in 2006 identified several key factors which have contributed to the proliferation of child pornography on the Internet. First, and perhaps most problematic according to the study, is the sheer number of child abuse images on the Internet. United States law enforcement sources estimated that there are approximately 3.5 million known child pornography images on-line.[7] The exact number of child pornography web sites is also difficult to determine. In 2001, the National Center for Missing and Exploited Children's CyberTipline received more than 24,400 reports of child pornography. Five years later, at the beginning of 2006, that number had climbed to more than 340,000.[8] The Internet has fueled a tremendous and immeasurable increase in the amount of child pornography being produced, trafficked, and possessed worldwide.

■ Internet Luring and Enticement of Minors

Curious, unsuspecting youngsters visit the Internet each day seeking friendship and information, but sometimes instead encountering sexual deviance and predators. The law enforcement investigators who assume on-line undercover identities for the purpose of apprehending predators know that there are many offenders lurking in chat rooms, appearing on web cams, and placing false profiles at social networking sites. Internet social networking sites are places in cyberspace where subscribers may post personal information and share it with others. Children and adults use social networking sites to communicate and to make friends. A study in 2006 estimated that 55% of young people have established on-line profiles in one or more of the dozens of social networking sites.[9]

Most social networking sites are free and permit users to register without providing information about their true identity and whereabouts. The sites are well suited for molesters who can pose as harmless mentors while disguising their true intent. There have been many incidents of registered sex offenders who have created on-line profiles portraying themselves as inoffensive individuals seeking romance without any reference to their malevolent pasts.[10] Although proactive undercover "sting" investigations often lead to the apprehension of Internet sexual predators, few of the actual teens who are victimized ever report the crimes. Victimized teens are often too embarrassed to report and fearful of their parents' wrath for disobeying rules against communicating with strangers on-line. Sometimes a teen returns home after secretly meeting an Internet stranger without his or her parents ever discovering the illicit tryst. In 2002, for example, an Arizona Internet Crimes Against Children (ICAC) Task Force undercover officer posing on-line as a young girl was contacted by a man who requested a meeting for sex. When the man went to a location where he believed that he would be meeting a minor for sex, he was arrested. Investigators learned that the offender had previously met two girls whom he had victimized and to whom he had given sexually transmitted diseases. In their shame, the girls had never notified their parents of the crimes. The girls' distraught parents only learned of the offenses when detectives informed them of the suspect's confessions.[11]

In some cases, a child's natural curiosity leads them to Internet places where they do not belong, and with unintended results. Beginning at the age of 13, a California boy was repeatedly victimized by offenders who met him via the Internet after first seeing his image on a web cam. The boy suffered sexual abuses at the hands of the men who had first contacted him on-line. Some of the boy's Internet acquaintances had assisted him in operating commercial pornography web sites featuring sexual images and videos of himself.[12] In many cases, the teens who are lured by sexual predators will never come forward due to fear or a misplaced sense of guilt. A few of them are forever silenced by Internet sexual predators that lured them via the Internet, sexually victimized them, and killed them.

Child prostitution is also being facilitated via the Internet. Pimps use message boards and social networking sites to find customers seeking to engage in paid sex acts with minors. In January 2007, Cook County, Illinois police arrested three adults who used Craigslist, a free Internet advertising site, to offer the sexual services of girls as young as 14 years old. The illegal prostitution business resulted in profits of tens of thousands of dollars for the pimps. Undercover officers investigated and solved the case by responding to postings on Craigslist.[13]

In the past, child molesters were characterized as often lurking near school yards. Folklore held that child molesters frequented school yards because that is where the children were. The Internet is the new proverbial school yard. Cyberspace provides a ready hunting-ground for those who seek children.

■ Images of the Sexual Abuse of Minors

The Internet facilitates various crimes involving images and videos depicting the sexual abuse of minors. According to Wolak, Finkelhor and Mitchell, the Internet supports the child pornography market by making images and videos easily accessible. The Internet also contributes to the problem in other ways. Researchers believe that the on-line child pornography market may motivate offenders to produce images for trade and that the potential for child pornography distribution exists whenever an image is created. Images can be easily scanned or uploaded to the Internet so that production and trafficking can be easily accomplished. In the past, film had to go through third parties for development before it could be distributed. Now, images can be produced without risk of the developer revealing the offenders' identity. The production of child pornography is also facilitated by the fact that images can be captured by hidden cameras and victims can be secretly filmed without their knowledge.[14]

Over twenty years ago, in 1986, a U.S. Attorney General's Commission found "substantial evidence" that child pornography is often used as a tool for molesting children. The report stated that pedophiles sometimes show their intended victims pictures of children engaging in sexual activity in order to persuade them that it is not wrong because other children are doing it. The Commission also said, "child pornography is extraordinarily harmful both to the children involved and to society" and recommended that combating all forms of child pornography should be "a governmental priority of the greatest urgency."[15]

The use of the Internet has contributed to an immeasurable increase in the trafficking of images of the sexual abuse of children. Digital images and videos depicting the victimization of children are easily traded by Internet users who also derive sexual gratification from viewing child sexual abuse. Some videos are accompanied by the audio sounds of the victim crying or begging the offender to stop. New images are being created and reproduced each day while the stories accompanying the images become more and more disturbing. In 2002, an alert computer information technology professional working for an electronics manufacturing firm in Arizona found child pornography on the computer of an engineer employed by the firm. Investigators learned that the engineer had viewed live web-cam molestations being performed at another location by a man whose wife operated an in-home day-care facility. Both men were subsequently arrested.[16]

Because cyberspace is without borders, it permits the rapid global distribution of child pornography. Nefarious entrepreneurs have turned the illegal trade into big business while partnering with others around the world. In April 2000, Thomas and Janice Reedy of Fort Worth, Texas were indicted for commercial distribution of child pornography. Investigators from the U.S. Postal Inspection Service and the Dallas ICAC Task Force learned that the Reedys' illegal business had 70,000 customers worldwide. In one month, the business earned over one million dollars, which was shared with Internet webmasters in Russia and Indonesia. The business employed a dozen U.S. workers and trafficked child pornography to subscribers across the globe.[5] The global connectivity of the Internet demands coordinated efforts between nations of the world so that the problem of child pornography can be stopped. The monetary profits from the trafficking of unlawful images must be curtailed so that children can be protected from the threat of those who would exploit them.

■ Child Pornography: Gateway to Danger

Some apologists for possessors of child pornography argue that possessors are simply harmless observers of images. Although it may be true that not all possessors can be assumed to be "hands-on" or "contact" offenders, recent research indicated that child pornography possession is a strong indicator of pedophilia.[18] Some of the possessors of child pornography who are also pedophiles struggle psychologically with their tendencies. In 2006, a 27-year-old Phoenix man was arrested at a residence where he lived with his wife, mother and brother. The arrest was for the crime of trafficking images of child pornography via Internet file-sharing systems. No "contact" offenses involving actual children were uncovered. The man admitted to possessing child pornography and expressed deep remorse. He lamented about the inner psychological struggles he had because of his intense sexual attractions to children. He said that he had once attempted suicide by hanging because of his self-loathing. The man said that he had to avoid being near his brother's children because of his attraction to them. His pattern of child pornography possession included a repeating cycle. He would download images from the Internet, view them, and then delete them because of his shame. He would later reacquire images by again downloading them and then again deleting them. This pattern continued repeatedly because he could not overcome his obsession with the images that fed his sexual fantasies.[19]

Some pedophiles can suppress their urges to offend against children; others cannot. A study of 1,713 child pornography possessors arrested in Internet-related crimes showed that 40% of those arrested for child pornography were "dual offenders" who both sexually victimized children and possessed child pornography, with both crimes discovered in the same investigation. In some cases, the pornography drove the offender to violent crimes.[14] There are those who argue that there is no definite proof that a link exists between possessors and "hands-on" offenders, but a study of 54 prisoners incarcerated for possession of child pornography showed that 79% had molested significant numbers of children without ever being detected. On average, each offender had over 26 child sex victims and overall the group admitted to over 1,400 contact sexual crimes. Of the over 1,400 contact sex offenses, only 53 were detected or known at the time that the offender was sentenced for the child pornography offense.[20]

In 2006, Dr. Anna Salter, a psychologist who treats sex offenders testified before a Congressional Subcommittee that was investigating Internet child pornography. Dr. Salter confirmed that a "considerable percentage" of individuals convicted for child pornography crimes had also committed contact offenses. She also suggested that the number of contact offenders may be underestimated, as one report found that only 3% of individuals who have committed contact offenses are ever caught. In addition to finding a link between possessing child pornography and committing contact offenses, Dr. Salter testified that she believes there is a link between viewing on-line pornography and committing contact offenses. With regard to reducing the number of contact offenses against children, she said that reducing on-line child pornography would also reduce contact crimes, especially among those offenders who are emboldened to act on their sexual desires or urges by viewing child pornography. According to Dr. Salter, "child pornography increases the arousal to kids and is throwing gasoline on the fire."[7]

In some cases the possessor of child pornography is not a contact molester. In other cases, actual molestation accompanies the suspect's collection of pornography. In either case the possibility that a child molester is collecting child pornography or the possibility that a child pornography collector is molesting children should always be aggressively investigated. Collecting child pornography should be viewed as significant criminal behavior by itself.[21]

■ Data Collection Efforts

The true scope of the Internet child pornography problem is difficult to measure. Among the dilemmas in trying to determine the actual number of offenses are the systemic failings of the national crime reporting methods that should capture the data but do not. Data collection methods for Internet crimes against children need improvement. Under the Uniform Crime Reporting (UCR) definitions, there are neither specific crime analysis categories for either child pornography nor for the crime of luring minors via the Internet. Such crimes might be tabulated under the catch-all category of forcible rape, but only when an actual victim is subsequently identified. Offenses against children are truly marginalized under the UCR processes.

Newly devised national data collection methods are not much better. One research study suggested that the highly-touted National Incident-Based Reporting System (NIBRS) does not accurately portray the scope of the child pornography problem. The collection methods and processes meant to provide an accurate picture of crimes were deemed unreliable by the researchers and unable to delineate juvenile victims' exact connection in pornography crimes—as subjects in images or as victims in sex crimes in which pornography was used. The research called for increased training of law enforcement officials so that information about pornography involving juveniles can be accurately and uniformly recorded in NIBRS. Nationally, the true number of Internet crimes against children is undoubtedly under-reported.[22]

Other agencies have collected data that indicates a burgeoning problem involving Internet crimes against children. Between 1996 and 2005, the number of child exploitation cases investigated by the FBI increased 2,026% from 113 investigations to 2,402. The Immigration and Customs Enforcement Service and the U.S. Postal Service have each also investigated thousands of cases. In 2005, the 46 Internet Crimes Against Children Task Forces nationwide conducted thousands of investigations resulting in over 1,600 arrests and 6,000 computer forensics examinations.[5]

One organization that collects and reports accurate statistics is the National Center for Missing and Exploited Children (NCMEC). Since 1984, it has compiled data on reported crimes against children and also now operates a CyberTipline that permits Internet users to report misconduct either on-line or via telephone. Since it began in March 1998, and as of January 2007, the CyberTipline received 444,084 complaints of child pornography, child prostitution, sex tourism, on-line enticement, and other child-related Internet crimes. In 2006, the 46 ICAC Task Forces throughout the U.S. received 17,346 cybertips. The number of offenses reported to NCMEC is intriguing considering that the organization is not as well known to most citizens as their local police department and that only a fraction of the actual number of Internet crimes against children are likely reported to NCMEC.

NCMEC also maintains a database of the child victims of pornography whose identities are known to investigators. The Child Victim Identification Program began in 2002. As of January 2007, over 6.3 million images had been reviewed with over 880 victims identified. These numbers probably represent only a fraction of the actual number of images being trafficked via the Internet and only a small number of the child victims of sex abuse.[23]

The scope of the Internet child pornography problem is large beyond measure. Accurate accounting of the number of Internet crimes against children is needed.

■ The Muted Community-Oriented Policing Response

Traditional community-oriented policing approaches are ineffectual in evaluating the child pornography problem. Internet sex crimes against minors place substantial burdens on law enforcement. The crimes are widespread, occurring throughout the criminal justice system; they are multi-jurisdictional so that they require extensive collaboration; they involve constantly changing technology; and they require specialized investigation methods. Former FBI Agent Ken Lanning studied the problem of child molestation extensively. He described the unique systemic challenges of enforcing crimes against children:

> *Law-enforcement investigators must deal with the fact that the identification, investigation, and prosecution of child molesters may not be welcomed by their communities—especially if the molester is a prominent person. Individuals may protest, and community organizations may rally to the support of the offender and even attack the victims. City officials may apply pressure to halt or cover up the investigation. Many law-enforcement supervisors, prosecutors, judges, and juries cannot or do not want to deal with the details of deviant sexual behavior. They will do almost anything to avoid these cases.[21]*

Traditional approaches based on community-oriented policing theories are not applicable in the area of Internet crimes against children. Many Internet crimes against children are only discovered as the result of undercover proactive investigations. Many more crimes are not reported and will never be reflected in crime statistics. Because few police agencies have investigators who work on-line in undercover assignments, the number of offenses reported will naturally be small. Anyone using an analysis based on the number of crimes reported may reach the wrongful conclusion that because there are few reports, no problem exists.

An administrator who follows the community-oriented policing services guidebook for child pornography by examining the recommended statistics will observe that there are a low number of reported crimes. If few crimes are reported the assumption is that there is no problem and consequently, no police resources will be devoted to the issue. The approach suggested in the guidebook provides an easy way for police administrators to dismiss the problem and to deny that it exists. Some proponents of community-oriented policing recommend surveys of the citizenry as a way to measure problems and evaluate police effectiveness. Such surveys are intended to gauge police performance and to identify community needs. The results from such surveys are often used to guide the allocation of resources towards those issues identified by respondents as needing attention. Sadly, child victims of Internet sexual predators and child pornographers cannot or do not respond to surveys. If they were capable of completing customer satisfaction surveys, child victims would likely rate police services as nonexistent. Citizen surveys are another poor way to measure crimes against children. Traditional community-oriented policing approaches are not designed to accurately evaluate Internet crimes against children. Administrators should consider re-evaluating their responses to the crimes of child pornography and the luring of minors in cyberspace.

■ Law Enforcement Spending

The Internet crime problem requires increased resources for law enforcement services, training, and equipment. Unfortunately, resources for law enforcement functions of any kind are sometimes scarce. The competition for the limited available funds occurs in environments where agencies contend with one another for each slice of the budget. Knowledgeable advocates for children continually hope that more government dollars will be devoted to the enforcement of Internet crimes against children. In testimony to Congress, Grier Weeks, Executive Director of the National Association to Protect Children, said:

> *The federal government must get serious. We are losing this war [against child pornography], and we are not supporting our troops on the front lines. Recent estimates of the size of the exploding global criminal market in child pornography are in the multi-billion dollar range. Yet, by no objective measure can we claim to be serious or prepared as a nation about stopping what is being done to these children. The FBI's Innocent Images National Initiative is funded at $10 million annually. By comparison, the Department of Housing and Urban Development just announced it was awarding more money than the entire Innocent Images budget to build 86 elderly apartment units in Connecticut and almost 7 times their budget on the homeless in Ohio. The administration has proposed 20 times the entire Innocent Images budget for abstinence-only education programs through the Department of Health and Human Services. The Department of Justice's Internet Crimes Against Children (ICAC) Task Force program received about $14.5 million in fiscal year 2006. That is less than one-*

fifth the amount proposed for a new initiative to help former prisoners reintegrate into society. Last year's budget included $211 million for the Department of the Interior for "high-priority brush removal" and related projects. $14.5 million doesn't clear much brush.[24]

In recent years federal resources have gravitated towards anti-terrorism efforts, drug enforcement, and border control, all of which have legitimate nationwide importance. Local resources are drawn to homicides, sex assaults, gangs, drugs, burglaries, property crimes, and other offenses of great and legitimate local importance. Consequently, those who fight Internet crimes against children are often underfunded and understaffed. Advocates for children agree that more funding for the enforcement of cyber-crime is needed. As the issues become more apparent to the public and to lawmakers, it is hoped that funding will increase.

■ Where is the Internet Crime Problem?

Internet crimes involving sex offenses are not confined to individual homes. Libraries, schools, businesses, and wireless free-access points are all part of the Internet crime domain. Many public libraries have resisted placing the restrictions and filters on computers that would make it tougher for offenders to commit crimes. Many incidents involving pornography at library computers have occurred nationwide. In 2004, an Arizona man, while on parole for child molestation, repeatedly used unrestricted and unfiltered computers and printers at the City of Phoenix public library to download and copy child pornography. His crimes were only discovered during a routine search of his residence by parole officers following up on his earlier child molestation conviction.[25] In 2005, a homeless man in Phoenix was apprehended while on-line at a library computer attempting to sell child pornography to an on-line undercover investigator from the Arizona ICAC Task Force. The offender was observed using open-access City of Phoenix public library computers that did not require identification or library card to operate. Investigators found computer storage media in his possession containing dozens of illegal images.[26]

Private businesses and large corporations are not immune from the threat of Internet crime. Wherever there is Internet connectivity, predators may try to exploit the service for the purpose of finding victims. In 2005, an information technology specialist employed by an Arizona health care provider reported that an employee, a prominent neuropsychologist, had used his office workplace computer to contact young men for sex. The misconduct was reported to the Arizona ICAC Task Force and a proactive investigation began. A detective posing on-line as a minor was subsequently solicited for sex by the man and he was arrested. Follow-up investigators then learned of a Phoenix boy who had been molested by the man. The neuropsychologist was later sentenced to 17 years in prison.[27] Cyber-crimes against children occur from homes, businesses and public places. Widespread unrestricted wireless access to computers means that criminals are increasingly elusive. Law enforcement must combine advanced technology with old fashioned police work in order to apprehend the offenders.

Internet crimes cannot occur without an Internet service provider (ISP) allowing the offender access to the Internet. In most cases the ISP is an unwitting facilitator to the offense. Other unwitting parties who benefit from Internet services include those retailers who advertise on web sites for the purpose of drawing buyers to their products. Some businesses have been surprised to learn that their advertising banners have appeared on web pages featuring child pornography. Most ISPs charge a fee for service, and individual subscribers often pay with a credit card. The subscription and payment process provides a path for law enforcement to use subpoenas or search warrants to trace back to a subscriber by following the money trail. The subpoena and search warrant response process can be time-consuming for both law enforcement and the ISPs. Delays in the response process can stall law enforcement investigative efforts.

In 1998, a federal law was passed requiring ISPs to report child pornography to the National Center for Missing and Exploited Children (NCMEC). By 2002, thousands of reports were flooding into NCMEC from the ISPs that chose to comply with the law. Those reports were subsequently sent to federal, state and local agencies for investigation. The large number of reports quickly overwhelmed the small staffs of those few agencies that employed investigators who had the technical expertise needed to investigate Internet crimes. Investigators began to complain that ISPs were sometimes failing to respond in a timely manner to subpoenas or search warrants requesting subscriber information. Investigators noted that in some cases, ISPs retained no information whatsoever, leaving investigations at a dead end.[28]

The need for ISP's to retain data and to subsequently respond with alacrity to legal process from law enforcement is a critical need for investigators of Internet crimes. Lack of response to law enforcement subpoenas and search warrants can have dire consequences for victims and stall or end law enforcement investigations before an offender can be identified. Internet service providers, credit card companies, social networking sites, gaming sites, providers of chat rooms, e-mail services, and those who advertise in Cyberspace are all among the facilitators who are caught in the middle of the Internet crime problem. The providers tacitly assent to Internet crime while profiting from subscribers and advertisers. Providers should logically bear some of the responsibility for correcting the problems. In the same way that automobile manufacturers begrudgingly gave way, after thousands of roadway deaths, to regulations mandating vehicle safety, ISPs must provide improved Internet safety before the annual number of Internet crimes matches the annual number of vehicular accidents.

For Internet service providers, preserving information and providing it to law enforcement in response to legal process is an unwanted and unprofitable chore. As the tragedies associated with some ISPs' reluctance to preserve and provide information gain increased attention, public pressure and legislative action may dictate that ISPs work harder to help law enforcement officers identify the suspects associated with Internet crimes. Eventually, the reluctant ISPs will be unable to turn a blind eye to the crimes and might be forced to become partners in justice instead of facilitators of injustice.

■ Sex Offenders and the Internet

Offenders befriend victims through a process that has come to be called "grooming." Grooming may be defined as the way in which an adult predator patronizes and gains the trust of a child or teen. It sometimes involves a long series of carefully planned steps that may occur over an extended period of time—or, it may proceed rapidly. When grooming a child, an Internet predator may exchange chat messages with the child and then request a phone number in order to engage in a personal voice conversation. The offender might then gradually escalate to sending money or gifts to the child. These acts not only advance the bonding process but also help the offender to gain additional information such as a phone number and address. Luring victim Katie Tarbox, who met and was victimized by an Internet predator when she was 13 years old, described the grooming process:

> He took the time to understand me, and that is why these predators are so successful. He talked about the things I was interested in, however mundane they may have been. More importantly, he told me the things that I needed to hear as a vulnerable teenager: That I was intelligent, mature, and beautiful. So he bolstered my confidence which won my trust as well.[29]

That many teens are curious about their own sexuality and seeking their own sense of identity helps the predators who wish to victimize them. Young people often share private personal information with strangers on the Internet because they feel a sense of security there. They may establish relationships based upon interests they have in common with Internet strangers.

Some offenders appear to be upstanding members of the community. Many have spent their lives trying to gain the trust of others for the purpose of being entrusted with access to children. Often the neighbors, friends and colleagues of offenders are shocked at their misdeeds and come to the defense of the offender. Former FBI agent Ken Lanning describes the tactics that offenders sometimes use:

> *At sentencing some offenders play the "sick and sympathy" game in which the offender expresses deep regret and attempts to show he is a pillar of the community, a devoted family man, a military veteran, a churchgoer/leader, nonviolent, without prior arrests, and a victim of abuse with many personal problems. They get the courts to feel sorry for them by claiming they are hard-working "nice guys" or decorated career military men who have been humiliated and lost everything. In view of the fact that many people still believe in the myth that child molesters are evil weirdos or social misfits, this tactic can unfortunately be effective, especially at sentencing.[21]*

The offenders who commit Internet crimes sometimes use the latest technologies to conceal their identities. Wireless networking now provides a means for offenders to try to hide themselves. Investigators must sometimes combine their technical knowledge with old-fashioned police work to apprehend Internet criminals. In August 2005, a 13-year-old Wisconsin boy was reported missing by his mother. Milwaukee detectives checked his computer and traced his last Internet contact to an address in Phoenix. Arizona ICAC Task Force detectives went to the address and learned that the resident there was unwittingly providing unencrypted wireless Internet access to the surrounding neighborhood. Detectives conducted surveillance and began diligently canvassing the area for the boy until they found him in the company of a wanted sex offender who had a history of abuse. The offender had surreptitiously used his unwitting neighbors' wireless Internet service to lure the boy. Investigators learned that the boy had been molested by the offender.[30] Law enforcement investigators must stay abreast of the latest techniques and equipment in use by the computer industry and subsequently by sex offenders. Training is the only way for investigators to keep abreast of the many ways in which offenders will misuse technology for criminal purposes.

Although many offenders against children are not outwardly aggressive and do not have violent criminal records of assaults against other adults, law enforcement officers should not let down their guard. There are a disproportionate number of offenders who contemplate, attempt or complete the act of suicide after being identified. There have also been cases of offenders with vendettas against the police who have attacked officers. Some offenders may be dangerous. In 2004, a Broward County, Florida Sheriff's Deputy was assisting in the service of a search warrant at the home of an offender who possessed child pornography. Using a high-powered rifle, the offender killed one deputy and wounded another before being apprehended.[31] Investigators must remain vigilant to the possibility that Internet offenders may be dangerous. Many of the crimes against children are felony offenses and officers should consider using appropriate safety tactics during confrontations with offenders.

1. U.S.C. Annenberg School. (December 7, 2005). *Fifth Study of the Internet by the Digital Future Project*. Center for the Digital Future. University of Southern California, Annenberg School. Accessed June 25, 2007 from http://www.digitalcenter.org/pdf/Center-for-the-Digital-Future-2005-Highlights.pdf

2. Wolak, J., Finkelhor, D., Mitchell, K. J. (2005). Child pornography possessors arrested in Internet-related crimes. Findings from the National Juvenile Online Victimization Study. National Center for Missing and Exploited Children. Accessed June 25, 2007 from www.missingkids.com/en_US/publications/NC144.pdf

3. Family Watchdog, LLC. (2006). *Registered Sex Offenders Counts by State*. Family Watchdog Web site. Accessed June 25, 2007 from http://www.familywatchdog.us/OffenderCountByState.asp

4. Allen, E. (December 6, 2006). Closing speech: Project safe childhood conference. Washington, D.C. Retrieved January 15, 2007 from http://www.missingkids.com/missingkids/servlet/PublicHomeServlet?LanguageCountry=en_US

5. U.S. Department of Justice. (May 2006). Project safe childhood: Protecting children from online exploitation and abuse. Accessed June 25, 2007 from http://www.projectsafechildhood.gov/guide.htm, p. 1.

6. Wolak, J., Mitchell, K., Finkelhor, D. (2006). Online victimization of youth: Five years later. National Center for Missing and Exploited Children Bulletin. Accessed June 25, 2007 from http://www.missingkids.com/en_US/publications/NC167.pdf

7. U.S. House of Representatives, Committee on Energy and Commerce. (2007). Sexual exploitation of children on the Internet: Bipartisan staff report for the use of the Committee on Energy and Commerce, 109th Congress.

8. National Center for Missing and Exploited Children. (2006). Financial and Internet industries to combat Internet child pornography: Child pornography fact sheet. NCMEC Web site. Retrieved January 15, 2007 from http://www.ncmec.org/.missingkids/servlet/NewsEventServlet?LanguageCountry=en_US&PageId=2314

9. PEW, Internet & American Life Project. (2007). Social networking web sites and teens: An overview. Reports: Family, Friends & Community. Retrieved June 28, 2007 from http://www.pewinternet.org/PPF/r/198/report_display.asp

10. Kardasz, F. (2007). Internet social networking sites. Retrieved June 28, 2007 from http://www.kardasz.org/Case_Studies.html

11. Phoenix, Arizona Police Department. (2002). Phoenix Police Report no. 2002-2233604. Available from the Phoenix, Arizona Police Department Records and Identification Bureau. http://phoenix.gov/POLICE/pub1.html

References

12. Eichenwald, K. (December 19, 2005). Through his webcam, a boy joins a sordid online world. The New York Times.com. Retrieved June 28, 2007 from http://www.nytimes.com/2005/12/19/national/19kids.ready.html?ex=1292648400&en=aea51b3919b2361a&ei=5090

13. Gutierrez, T. (January 11, 2007). On-line probe uncovers underage prostitution. ABC7chicago.cnews.com Web site. Retrieved June 28, 2007 from http://abclocal.go.com/wls/story?section=local&id=4928094

14. Wolak, J., Finkelhor, D., Mitchell, K. J. (2005). The varieties of child pornography production. In Quayle, E., Taylor, M. (Eds.), Viewing child pornography on the Internet: Understanding the offense, managing the offender, helping the victims (pp. 31–48). Dorset, UK: Russell House Publishing. Retrieved June 28, 2007 from http://www.unh.edu/ccrc/pdf/jvq/CV100.pdf

15. National Law Center for Children and Families. (2006). Child Pornography Investigation and Prosecution Manual.

16. National Law Center for Children and Families. (2006). The NLC manual on child pornography law: Cases and analysis. National Law Center for Children and Families. Alexandria, VA, pp. 42–43.

17. Phoenix, Arizona Police Department. (2003). Phoenix Police Report no. 2003-31701542. Available from the Phoenix, Arizona Police Department Records and Identification Bureau. http://phoenix.gov/POLICE/pub1.html

18. Blanchard, R., Cantor, J. M., Seto, M. C. (2006). Child pornography offenses are a valid diagnostic indicator of pedophilia. *J Abnorm Psychol* 115:610–615.

19. Phoenix Police Department. (2006). Phoenix Police Report no. 2006-62346540. Available from the Phoenix, Arizona Police Department Records and Identification Bureau. http://phoenix.gov/POLICE/pub1.html

20. Hernandez, A. E. (November 2000). Self-Reported Contact Sexual Offenses by Participants in the Federal Bureau of Prison's Sex Offender Treatment Program: Implications for Internet Sex Offenders. Paper presented at the 19th Annual Research and Treatment Conference of the Association for the Treatment of Sexual Abusers.

21. Lanning, K. V. (September, 2001). Child molesters: A behavioral analysis. National Center for Missing and Exploited Children. 4th Ed., p. 86. Retrieved June 28, 2007 from http://www.missingkids.com/en_US/publications/NC70.pdf

22. Finkelhor, D., Ormrod, R. (2004). *Child pornography: Patterns from NIBRS*. Washington, DC: U.S. Department of Justice, Office of Justice Programs, Office of Juvenile Justice and Delinquency Prevention.

23. Rabun, J. (January 2, 2007). CVIP Weekly Activity Report #223. E-mail to ICAC Task Force List serve.

24. Weeks, G. (2006). *Sexual Exploitation of Children Over the Internet: What Parents, Kids and Congress Need to Know About Child Predators*. U.S. House of Representatives, Committee on Energy and Commerce, Subcommittee on

Oversight and Investigations. Serial No. 109-126. Accessed June 25, 2007 from www.access.gpo.gov/congress/house.

25. Johnson, H. Man used library computers to download child pornography. *Arizona Republic*. Retrieved August 13, 2004 from http://www.azcentral.com/arizonarepublic/local/articles/0813childsex13.html

26. Phoenix, Arizona Police Department. (2005). Phoenix Police Report no. 2005-52427690. Available from the Phoenix, Arizona Police Department Records and Identification Bureau. http://phoenix.gov/POLICE/pub1.html

27. Phoenix, Arizona Police Department. (2005). Phoenix Police Report no. 2005-137156001. Available from the Phoenix, Arizona Police Department Records and Identification Bureau. http://phoenix.gov/POLICE/pub1.html.

28. U.S. Code, Title 42, Chapter 132.

29. CourtTV.com. (July 28, 2004). On line discussion with Katie Tarbox. Retrieved December 13, 2006 from http://www.courttv.com/talk/chat_transcripts/2004/0728tarbox.html

30. Hermann, W. (August 24, 2005). Parents can watch out for Net predators. AZCentral.com. Retrieved June 28, 2007 from http://azcentral.com/families/articles/0824netpredator24.html

31. Aaronson, T. (August 25, 2005). Deputy down: One year later, questions remain about Deputy Todd Fatta's tragic death. New Times, Broward-Palm Beach, Florida. Retrieved June 28, 2007 from http://www.browardpalmbeach.com/Issues/2005-08-25/news/feature_3.html

References

Sex Offender Registries and Criminal Predators

Shelley L. Reese, M.S.A.

Sex offender registries were developed to aid in tracking offenders convicted of criminal offenses against a victim who is a minor or any sexually violent offense. In 1947, California became the first state to develop a sex offender registry.[1] California ranks first in the nation with over 100,000 sex offenders registered and 81,000 on their public web site. Until the Jacob Wetterling Crimes Against Children and Sexually Violent Offenders Act in 1994, sex offender registries were not required in each state. In many states, once sex offenders were released from a correctional institution and were no longer on parole, probation, or supervision, no records were maintained as to their whereabouts. These offenders were free to move from community to community without the knowledge of law enforcement. The number of registered sex offenders in the United States changes daily due to convictions, deaths and individual state requirements on the length of registration.

■ Sex Offender Legislation

In October 1989, Jacob Wetterling, 11 years old, telephoned his father and mother at the dinner party they were attending in their hometown of St. Joseph, Minnesota. Jacob had been left at the family home in the town of 2,200 to watch over his siblings Trevor, 10, and Carmen, 8. Jacob's friend Aaron Larsen, 11, had also come to the house. Jacob telephoned Jerry Wetterling to ask permission for the three boys to ride their bikes to the local convenience store ten minutes away to rent a video. Trevor had attempted to get permission just minutes before by telephoning their mother, Patty Wetterling. Patty, concerned about the boys riding their bicycles on the dark roadway, told them no. Jacob, coming up with a revised plan, called his father stating that Trevor would carry a flashlight and Aaron was wearing a white sweatshirt. Jacob would wear his father's reflective vest, thus providing plenty of visibility while riding their bikes to the video store. A neighbor would baby-sit for Carmen until they returned. Jerry, knowing that Jacob was disappointed due to skating poorly at hockey tryouts, agreed for the first time to allow the boys to ride their bicycles after dark.

Jacob and Aaron, on bicycles, and Trevor on his push scooter were returning from their ride to the convenience store after renting "Naked Gun," when they approached a dark area of the roadway. The boys heard a male voice call out, ordering them to stop and turn off the flashlight. A stocking-masked man brandishing a gun ordered the children into the ditch. He then asked each of the boys their ages. As they replied, he told Trevor and Aaron to run away. The last thing the fleeing boys saw was the armed man grabbing Jacob by the sleeve. Jacob is still missing, and his abductor has never been identified. Unknown to local residents and law enforcement, area halfway houses were occupied by sex offenders released from prison.[2]

In 1994, as part of the Federal Violent Crime Control and Law Enforcement Act, the Jacob Wetterling Crimes Against Children and Sexually Violent Offender Registration Act was passed. Included in this law was the requirement of each state to develop and maintain a registry for sex offenders and offenders of crimes against children. The Jacob Wetterling Crimes Against Children and Sexually Violent Offenders Act defines the term "criminal offense against a victim who is a minor" as 1) kidnapping of a minor, except by a parent; 2) false imprisonment of a minor, except by a parent; 3) criminal sexual conduct toward a minor; 4) solicitation of a minor to engage in sexual conduct; 5) use of a minor in a sexual performance; 6) solicitation of a minor to practice prostitution; 7) any conduct that by its nature is a sexual offense against a minor; 8) production or distribution of child pornography; 9) an attempt to commit an offense listed above in (1) through (8), if the state makes such an attempt a criminal offense; and chooses to include such an offense in those which are criminal offenses against a victim who is a minor for the purposes of this section. The Wetterling Act went on to define a sexually violent offense to be any criminal offense in a "State law which is comparable to or which exceeds the range of offenses encompassed by aggravated sexual abuse or sexual abuse . . . or an offense that has its elements engaging in physical contact with another person with intent to commit aggravated sexual abuse or sexual abuse."[3]

Protection of children was the primary intent of this law. Of those inmates that are convicted of rape and sexual assault, two thirds of their victims are under the age of 18, and 58% of those were under the age of 12. In California, one in four sex offenders on the public web site were in violation of the registration laws. Sex offender registries are an aid to law enforcement to determine the movements of convicted sex offenders and to protect our children.[4]

Megan's Law, named after victim Megan Kanka, was implemented in 1996. Amending the Jacob Wetterling Act, this allows the state sex offender registries to provide information on specific offenders to the public. Community notification systems are developed within each state. Also during 1996, the Pam Lychner Sexual Offender Tracking and Identification Act passed. The Lychner Act created the National Sex Offender Registry. This act was developed to organize individual state registries and track the offender if he/she moves throughout the country. Minimum standards were set for state registries, and the FBI was mandated to register and substantiate sex offenders in those states not meeting the minimum standards. In addition, the Lychner Act defined "sexually violent predator" as "a person who has been convicted of a sexually violent offense and who suffers from a mental abnormality or personality disorder that makes the person likely to engage in a predatory sexually violent offense."[5]

Pam Lychner was a Houston real estate agent waiting at a vacant house for a prospective buyer. Unknown to her, a twice-convicted felon was at the home, and he brutally assaulted her. During the attack, Lychner's husband arrived and saved her life. Within two years, Lychner's attacker had his first parole hearing. Angered by his quick parole, Pam Lychner formed the "Justice for All" victim rights advocacy group and lobbied for tougher sentencing for violent criminals. In 1996, Lychner and her two daughters were killed in the explosion of TWA Flight 800. Congress passed the Pam Lychner Sexual Offender Tracking and Identification Act in her memory.

The Pam Lychner Act set forth fines and prison sentences for registered sex offenders who failed to comply with the law. Any registrant who moved and failed to notify authorities, if convicted as a misdemeanor for the first offense, can receive up to one year in prison and a fine of up to $100,000. The second offense, a felony, is punishable for up to ten years in prison and a fine not to exceed $100,000.[6] The Wetterling Act was again amended in 1998 by the Commerce, Justice, and State, the Judiciary, and Related Agencies Appropriations Act (CJSA) to include registration of federal and military offenders and nonresident students and workers. In addition, the CJSA required each state to participate in the National Sex Offender Registry.[7] The last significant change to the Jacob Wetterling Act came in 2000 with the Campus Sex Crimes Act. Under this act, registrants are required to report to area law enforcement if they are attending or working at an institution of higher learning. Sex offenders must provide this information to both the law enforcement agency where they live and also the local police where they are attending school. According to the National Sex Offender Registry in 2005, only 9 states have implemented this legislation: California, Florida, Illinois, Iowa, Kentucky, Michigan, South Carolina, Tennessee, and Utah. The intent of the law is to increase awareness on campuses and to deter those criminals from targeting employment at colleges and universities in order to have access to students.[8]

In 2006, President George W. Bush signed the Adam Walsh Child Protection and Safety Act. To encourage state compliance with these policies incentives were created. States that failed to abide by the Adam Walsh Act regarding sex offenders will receive reduced amounts of federal monies distributed to each state through the Omnibus Crime Control and Safe Streets Act, also known as the Edward Byrne grant funds. Those agencies implementing the policies prior to the three-year deadline will be eligible for additional monies under the Sex Offender Management Assistance Program.

An important change to registries is the requirement for sex offenders to be classified by tiers. The act classifies offenders into three tiers. A "tier I sex offender" is any sex offender other than a tier II or tier III sex offender; tier I represents the least dangerous class of sex offenders. A "tier II sex offender" is any sex offender (other than a tier III sex offender) whose offense is punishable by imprisonment for more than a year and is comparable to, or more severe than, the following offenses against a minor: sex trafficking; coercion and enticement; transportation with intent to engage in criminal sexual activity; abusive sexual contact; attempt or conspiracy to commit any of those offenses; involves use in a sexual performance, solicitation to practice prostitution; or production or distribution of child pornography; or one whose offense occurs after the offender has become a tier I sex offender (e.g., a tier I offender who re-offends becomes tier II). A "tier III sex offender" is any sex offender whose offense is punishable by imprisonment for more than a year and is comparable to, or more severe than, aggravated sexual abuse, sexual abuse, abusive sexual contact against an individual younger than 13, or an attempt or conspiracy to commit any of those offenses; involves kidnapping of a minor, unless committed by a parent or guardian; or occurs after the offender has become a tier II sex offender.

Tier I offenders are required to register for 15 years, tier II for 25 years, and tier III for life. A reduction in the length of required registration applies to those sex offenders in tier I who maintain a clear record for 10 years and to tier II sex offenders whose records are clean for 15 years. In addition, adjudicated delinquent juveniles are eligible for a reduction in their registration period by keeping a clear record and successful completion of any supervised release, including probation and parole and completing a sex offender treatment program certified by the Attorney General or by the state where they reside.

The Adam Walsh Act mandates that all sex offenders must appear within three days at the designated local law enforcement agency to update their registration when any of the following changes occur: name, residence, employment, or student status. In addition, each registrant must appear in person to this agency to verify information and have a new photograph taken. Tier I must appear once a year, tier II every six months, and tier III every three months. A sex offender must register prior to being released from a correctional institution.

Each registrant must now provide not only his/her address, employment, student status, and offense and conviction dates, but must also provide a set of fingerprints and palm prints, a DNA sample, and a photocopy of their driver's license or identification card. Prior to the Adam Walsh Act, most states did not collect palm prints or DNA samples.

State registries are required to provide public access to sex offender information through the Internet, and the public must be able to access this information by zip code or a geographic radius. The Attorney General will continue to maintain the National Sex Offender Registry, tracking offenders traveling from state to state or internationally. State public web sites are forbidden from listing any victim information or the offender's social security number. These sites also may not list any information about any arrest that did not result in a conviction. With respect to Tier I offenders, each state has discretion in listing information to indicate that the victim was an adult and to name the employer of the offender and/or any educational institution where he/she is a student.

According to the Adam Walsh Act, each state's public web site must carry a warning indicating that information found on the site should not be used to "unlawfully injure, harass, or commit a crime" against any of the registrants. This statement must also incorporate a warning that if such actions occur, criminal or civil penalties may apply. Public web sites must also provide for a way any errors in information to be reported. E-mail links are used for the public to contact state law enforcement to report errors, omissions, and noncompliant offenders. Increased penalties for sex offenses against children are also part of the Adam Walsh Act.

The Adam Walsh Child Protection and Safety Act of 2006 is dedicated to seventeen victims. The Declaration of Purpose in this act pays tribute to those victims. In order to protect the public from sex offenders and offenders against children, and in response to the vicious attacks by violent predators against the victims listed below, Congress in this Act establishes a comprehensive national system for the registration of those offenders:

1. Jacob Wetterling, who was 11 years old when he was was abducted in 1989 in Minnesota, and who remains missing;

2. Megan Nicole Kanka, who at 7 years old was abducted, sexually assaulted, and murdered in 1994, in New Jersey;

3. Pam Lychner, who at 31 years old was attacked by a career offender in Houston, Texas;

4. Jetseta Gage, who was 10 years old when she was kidnapped, sexually assaulted, and murdered in 2005, in Cedar Rapids, Iowa;

5. Dru Sjodin, who at 22 years old, was sexually assaulted and murdered in 2003, in North Dakota;

6. Jessica Lunsford, who was 9 years old when she was abducted, sexually assaulted, buried alive, and murdered in 2005, in Homosassa, Florida;

7. Sarah Lunde, who at 13 years old, was strangled in 2005 by a convicted sex offender in Ruskin, Florida;

8. Amie Zyla, who was sexually assaulted in 1996 at the age of 8 by a juvenile offender in Waukesha, Wisconsin, and who has become an advocate for child victims and protection of children from juvenile sex offenders;

9. Christy Ann Fornoff, who at age 13 was abducted, sexually assaulted, and murdered in 1984, in Tempe, Arizona;

10. Alexandra Nicole Zapp, 30 years old, who was brutally attacked and murdered in a public restroom by a repeat sex offender in 2002, in Bridgewater, Massachusetts;

11. Polly Klaas, who at 12 years old was abducted, sexually assaulted, and murdered in 1993 by a career offender in California;

12. Jimmy Ryce, age 9, who was kidnapped and murdered in Florida in 1995;

13. Carlie Brucia, 11 years old, who was abducted and murdered in Florida in February, 2004;

14. Amanda Brown, 7 years old, abducted and murdered in Florida in 1998;

15. Elizabeth Smart, who at 14 years old, was abducted and sexually assaulted in Salt Lake City, Utah in June 2002;

16. Molly Bish, 16 years old, abducted in 2000 while working as a lifeguard in Warren, Massachusetts, where her remains were found 3 years later;

17. Samantha Runnion, 5 years old, was abducted, sexually assaulted, and murdered in California in July, 2002.[9]

■ National Sex Offender Registry

The National Sex Offender Registry (NSOR) was developed in 1997 as a result of the Pam Lychner Sexual Offender Tracking and Identification Act signed into effect in 1996. This mandated the Attorney General to establish a national database with the Federal Bureau of Investigation with two goals: 1) Develop and maintain a national database to track the location and movements of all persons convicted of a criminal offense against a minor or convicted of a sexually violent offense or is determined to be a sexually violent predator; and 2) To maintain a registry and verify the addresses of these offenders in those states that does not have a "minimally sufficient" sex offender registry program. With the exception of sexually violent predators, address verification occurs once every year. For sexually violent predators, address verification is once every 90 days. Crimes Against Children (CAC) is the division of the Federal Bureau of Investigation that oversees the National Sex Offender Registry. Using the National Crime Information Center the National Sex Offender Registry is able to maintain a database of registered sex offenders, their offenses and addresses. The Lychner Act strictly prohibits the FBI from releasing the identity of victims of a registered sex offender.

State Sex Offender Registries

Due to funding from the Jacob Wetterling Act, all 50 states and the District of Columbia have a sex offender registry. Initial registration is completed upon release from any correctional facility, placement on parole, probation, or supervision for offenses stipulated by law. Most states require that the offender report any address changes to local law enforcement within one to ten days of moving. Federal guidelines also require offenders to register in any state they are a student or have employment if different from their residence.

Currently registration forms vary from state to state but all include address, date of birth, social security number, place of employment and conviction information. Most states also require parent's names and addresses, vehicle descriptions and physical identifiers such as tattoos, scars and marks. After completing the registration form the offender must sign and date and acknowledge the requirements of registration for this state. At the time of registering, the offender must be fingerprinted and photographed.

Each state sex offender registry is required to maintain its own database and participate in the national database. State registries forward information to the National Sex Offender Registry. All offenders will have their addresses verified annually by his state of residence. Many states conduct this verification through the mail by sending a letter to the registrant that must be signed and returned. If no response is received the state will follow up on the verification, either in person or by contacting the local police for verification.

The length of registration was initially also set forth in the Wetterling Act, although states may invoke stricter registration requirements. Under the Wetterling Act all offenders meeting the requirements of this law must register for a minimum of 10 years from release from prison, probation, parole, or supervision, or register for life if the offender has more than one conviction, has been convicted of an aggravated offense, or has been determined to be a sexually violent predator. A sexually violent predator, as defined in the Wetterling Act, is a "person who has been convicted of a sexually violent offense and who suffers from a mental abnormality or personality disorder that make the person likely to engage in predatory sexually violent offenses." Megan's law allows each state sex offender registry program to determine what information will be given to the public. Some states will not release such information, including addresses or photographs. Other states have most or all registrants available for public view on their web sites.[10] The Dru Sjodin National Sex Offender Public Web site is maintained by the Attorney General and provides for access to information by zip code. Named after college coed Dru Sjodin, a kidnap and murder victim, this web site is the first national online listing providing the public with information on sex offenders and a link to each state's web site. Supporters of Dru's Voice, an independent Web site, state the development of this database "will aid police officers in finding more than 100,000 unaccounted for sex offenders."[11]

By accessing the National Sex Offender Registry web site at http://www.nsopr .gov, anyone can review and access individual state registries. Some states may provide limited information or provide information on offenders they have determined to be high risk. Each state has specific parameters in regards to the public notification program.

■ Problems with Public Notification

Critics of public notification and Internet web sites listing information on registered sex offenders cite many problems. Not all states are consistent with what information is posted. Some web sites for state registries post all of their registered sex offenders, while others list only the offenders that are determined to be high risk. This creates a situation in which for some states, a sex offender registered in that state may not be identified as such to the public.

Another problem is that not all sex offenders have been caught and convicted. Many offenders are still in the community but have not been apprehended. Critics say that the state registries that do not list all offenders promote a false sense of security for the community. Individuals searching the Internet may not find the registered sex offender living next door because he does not meet the criteria for the states' web site. The majority of sexual offenders knows their victims, and many times are a family member or a friend. Only 14% of offenders were unknown to their minor victims. The use and promotion of the availability of locating sex offenders using the Internet or public notification furthers the misconception of what constitutes a safe environment. A different problem is that web sites listing sex offenders may not distinguish sex offenders based on the nature of the offense. Registries may list both the serial rapist that murders his child victims—clearly a dangerous person in the community—alongside the 19-year-old who had sex with his willing, but underage, girlfriend two weeks before her 16th birthday and was convicted of statutory rape. Unless the type of offense is made clear, the 19-year-old "rapist" may face social ostracism as a sex offender, when in reality his wrongdoing consists primarily of bad judgment and he is unlikely to harm anyone else in the community.

Sex offender registration occasionally has serious unintended consequences. Incidents of violence have also been recorded when sex offenders' home addresses have been listed on registries' web sites. In Maine, a 20-year-old dishwasher located the addresses of two registered sex offenders using the state web site. He then drove to their homes, in two different cities, and shot and killed the two men before committing suicide himself. Many other cases of harassment and discrimination have been reported due to public web sites listing employment addresses and photographs of registrants despite the fact that such actions are clearly listed as illegal on the web sites.[12] Finally, as published on most state web sites, confirmation of a registered sex offender's identity can only be determined through fingerprint examination and not by a description or photo on a web site. Inaccurate identification of a person as a sex offender is possible due to similar names or appearance.

■ Residency Restriction Law

Residency restriction laws stipulate the minimum distance a registered sex offender may live from facilities where children are cared for or educated. The restriction stipulates a radius of a specific number of feet from a facility, usually a school, library, or daycare center, within which a sex offender is prohibited from living. In Iowa, the law applies to those sex offenders who had victims who were under the age of 18 and limits the offender from living within 2,000 feet of "property comprising a public or nonpublic elementary or secondary school or a child care facility." Aside from state laws, cities have passed additional local ordinances banning offenders from living close to public libraries, parks, and youth athletic fields.[13] For instance, Dyersville, Iowa has created a city ordinance that bans sex offenders from living anywhere within the city limits, although the constitutionality of this ordinance has not been determined, as no one has yet challenged the law. Does this law really protect the citizens? Or do sex offenders just go underground, registering with an address at a rest area and living next door without law enforcement and community knowledge?[14]

These types of laws are difficult to enforce and may force sex offenders into noncompliance with the law. For the offender, residency restrictions eliminate many towns and cities as an option to live due to the presence of schools and child care facilities. Larger metropolitan areas in particular have few housing options due to the high frequency of child care centers and schools. Even smaller towns that have several day cares and a school become off limits altogether to offenders. This limitation means that offenders who require public transit may not have access to a community with bus lines, subways, or taxi services. Attempting to abide by the law, sex offenders end up living miles away from choice employment opportunities, their families, and treatment opportunities which isolates the offender from a normal support structure. Feelings of isolation or estrangement from society can serve as a precondition to reoffend.

■ Enforcement Issues

Although the residency restriction laws have good intentions, they are difficult to enforce. Most states define residence as where a person sleeps. This means that a sex offender who perpetrated his crime on a minor can only be convicted if law enforcement can prove he is sleeping at a location where he is not registered. Since most residency laws do not stipulate when a person must sleep, a sex offender can spend unlimited time at an unregistered home so long as law enforcement cannot prove he was asleep.

In an effort to comply with the law, sex offenders are now registering at rest areas or commuter parking areas and are seeking out other offenders to rent a room or apartment together in a location acceptable under the law. Many times, the offender is simply using the address and is not actually living at this location. Prior to the residency restriction law, many police agencies conducted home checks on offenders and were able to determine with whom they were living and at what location they were spending the majority of their free time. Law enforcement would note if children were living in the home and investigate to determine if this was a violation of their probation or parole. Under the current law, investigations are limited to where the offender is sleeping. If the offender is registered at a rest area, parking lot, or other public place, law enforcement must monitor this location twenty-four hours per day for several days to determine if the offender is violating the law. This type of surveillance takes a multitude of manpower, hours and expensive equipment that local police may not have.

Another problem for law enforcement is the ability to find the offender on short notice. If the offender is registering at a public location, law enforcement cannot leave a message or note for him/her to contact the probation officer or police department. Arguments against the current residency restrictions include:

1. there is no research showing a correlation between residency restrictions and improving the safety of children;
2. research does not support the belief that children are more likely to be victimized by strangers at the locations listed in the residency laws;

3. residency restrictions are intended to reduce sex crimes committed against children at places such as schools and child care centers, but statistics show that 80 to 90% of these crimes are committed by either a relative or someone known to the child;

4. law enforcement is finding that the residency laws are causing offenders to be homeless, register incorrect addresses, or simply fail to register. In all of these situations, both law enforcement and the community do not know where this offender actually lives; and

5. residency restrictions have failed to demonstrate any type of protection intended but have caused a huge drain on law enforcement resources attempting to enforce these laws.

Many offenders are back living with or are married to their victims, causing the law to penalize the victims. Offenders that have families are forced to move their families, uprooting children from school, friends, and any type of current community support system.[15]

Many offenders have physical or mental disabilities but cannot live with family for assistance. Due to the residency restrictions, attempting to find affordable housing may be difficult. Prosecutors are seeing more cases going to trial because the offender is unwilling to plea to a charge that would require residency restrictions. States without residency restrictions are seeing an increase of sex offenders coming to their states. Wyoming is considering adopting residency laws similar to other states. Currently they have no laws restricting where a registered sex offender can live, but 56% of the state's 1,200 registered sex offenders moved to Wyoming after they were convicted. Wyoming also only publishes information on high risk offenders, another reason the state appeals to registered sex offenders.[16]

◼ Paramour Law and Safe Zones

Paramour laws are common in many states. These laws are designed to protect children from being victims of registered sex offenders in their own homes. Paramour laws are usually part of the state code directed at child endangerment. Although each state may differ slightly in the approach, most paramour laws make it illegal for a person to knowingly allow a registered sex offender to live in their home where children also reside. This does not apply if the sex offender is married to the parent of the child, or if the child is his or her own offspring. Under this law it is not the sex offender that breaks the law: it is the parent who allows the sex offender to live at the residence who is guilty of the crime.

The intention of this law is to prohibit sex offenders from selecting a partner based on the availability of children in the home. Punishment is not sanctioned against the sex offender, but against the partner who allows the offender to move into the home. Prosecution of this law depends on proving first that the sex offender resides in the home, and second that the partner knows he/she is a registered sex offender. Law enforcement may find this difficult to prove, especially if the living arrangements are not constant but the offender is staying overnight occasionally.

Safe zones are another type of restriction placed on registered sex offenders. These are designated areas specified by law as to the footage surrounding a location frequented by children where a sex offender must have prior permission to enter. Among areas that can be designated as safety zones are schools, parks, and child care facilities. The locations and restrictions are determined by the state law.

■ Other Criminal Justice Responses

Ankle or wrist electronic monitoring has been used for years by correctional officers to monitor all types of offenders. These units coordinate with a unit inside the home and monitor when the offender is within a specified distance to the unit. In addition, this type of monitoring can be programmed to require the offender to maintain that distance during certain hours of the day. If the wearer violates that home curfew, the device will notify the proper correctional authorities through the phone system.

Some states require high risk sex offenders to carry a GPS monitoring device that allows constant tracking of the offender. Although it is accurate, GPS tracking is expensive due to the equipment and labor costs. Using this type of tracking system requires the registrant to wear an ankle band and also to carry the GPS device when further than a predetermined distance from the receiver unit located in the offender's home. When the offender moves farther away from the receiver than the allocated amount without carrying the GPS device, a notification will be sent to the monitoring system. This type of tracking also allows law enforcement to check the movements of an offender in regards to a crime that occurred.

Voice verification is a tracking system that uses little equipment and requires the least amount of manpower. This is generally used on sex offenders who are restricted to being at their residences at particular times. An example would be a registered sex offender who is required to be at his home between 6:00 pm and 6:00 am. The voice verification system makes automated, random telephone calls during these hours to the residence asking questions that only the offender could answer. If the answers are incorrect or the voice template does not match, the system notifies the appropriate law enforcement agency.

New technology in tracking and identifying sex offenders has been introduced in North Carolina. The Sex Offender Registry and Identification System (SORIS) is a biometric database that will record and document images of the sex offender's irises. For instance, Mecklenburg County Sheriff's Office is using the technology in the tracking of registered sex offenders. All sex offenders have their irises scanned; these scans are placed in a database, enabling law enforcement to identify them using a device the size of a palm pilot. The technology allows officers to scan an iris and immediately know if the person is a registered sex offender. Law officers hope that the technology will spread across the United States placing all sex offenders into the iris database.[17]

References

1. California Department of Justice, Office of the Attorney General. (2003). *Public access to information about sex offenders expires at end of 2003.* Retrieved March 19, 2007, www.ag.ca.gov/newsalerts/release.php?id=1137&year=2003&month=9

2. Irsay, S. (2002). *The search for Jacob.* Retrieved June 29, 2007, http://archives.cnn.com/2002/LAW/11/19/ctv.wetterling/index.html

3. The Jacob Wetterling Crimes Against Children and Sexually Violent Offenders Act, 42 U.S.C. §14071 (1994).

4. Bureau of Justice Statistics. (2000). *Sexual Assault of Young Children as Reported to Law Enforcement: Victim, Incident, and Offender Characteristics.* Washington, DC: U.S. Department of Justice.

5. The Pam Lychner Sexual Offender Tracking and Identification Act, 42 U.S.C. §14072 (1996).

6. Federal Bureau of Investigation. (no date). *Investigative Programs: Crimes Against Children.* Retrieved June 29, 2007, from http://www.fbi.gov/hq/cid/cac/registry.htm

7. Bureau of Justice Assistance. (no date). *Overview and history of the Jacob Wetterling Act.* Retrieved June 29, 2007, from http://www.ojp.usdoj.gov/BJA/what/2a1jwacthistory.html

8. The Campus Sex Crimes Prevention Act, 20 U.S.C. §1092 (2000).

9. The Adam Walsh Child Protection and Safety Act of 2006, 42 U.S.C. §16901. Retrieved on June 29, 2007, www.govtrack.us/data/us/bills.text/109/h/h4472.pdf

References

10. National Sex Offender Registry. (2005). Megan's Law. Retrieved on June 29, 2007, http://www.registeredoffenderslist.org/megans-law.htm
11. Dru's Voice. (2006, August). *Dru's Law*. Retrieved March 4, 2007, www.drusvoice.com/law
12. Cavanaugh, T. (2006). Deadly sex offender registries. *Reason* 38:6–7.
13. Iowa Code §692A.2A (2007). Residency restrictions-child care facilities and schools.
14. Rood, L. (2007). Keep Iowa's sex offender laws strict, one city says. *Des Moines Register,* February, 13, 2007, 1A, 12A.
15. Iowa County Attorneys Association (2006). *Statement on sex offender residency restrictions in Iowa*. Des Moines, IA: Iowa County Attorneys Association.
16. Miller, K. (2007, February 21). Wyoming worries loose rules luring out-of-state sex offenders. *Des Moines Register*, February 21, 2007, 16A.
17. Waddell, L., & Campo-Flores, A., (2006). Iris scans keeping an eye on sex offenders. *Newsweek*, 148:8.

Domestic Abuse Program-Generated Risks of Battered Women

18

Kirsten Faisal and Laurie Schipper
Iowa Coalition Against Domestic Violence

There is an exercise that we often use in training for domestic abuse advocates adapted from a presentation by Lydia Walker, one of the battered women's movement's grandmothers. First, the group is asked to list the clients that they dread having to work with, the ones that are difficult and cause problems in the shelter. The list always looks something like this: the clients who won't do their chores, the dirty clients, the clients who are always having conflicts with other residents, the clients that steal, clients that move from shelter to shelter (often called shelter-hoppers), angry clients, manipulative clients, the clients who lie, needy clients, and irresponsible mothers. Next, the training group is asked to list the clients they like working with. First on the list is always clients who are appreciative and say thank you, clients who clean and watch other women's children, clients who get their chores done, clients with resources, good mothers, and women without any complicating issues such as substance abuse, incest, or lack of English-speaking skills. These are the conversations advocates have behind closed doors, and the participants are encouraged to be honest. There is usually laughter, and a palpable relief that other advocates have the same responses as they vent the day-to-day difficulty of the work.

Then we ask for a third list. This time, the focus is on the general symptoms of trauma. This list can get rather long, with items such as depression, fear, anger, sleep and eating disturbances, compromised social skills, difficulty concentrating or remembering, exhaustion, anxiety, isolation, physical symptoms, and desperation. The final step is to determine whether the list of good clients or bad clients bears the closest resemblance to the trauma symptoms, followed by a declaration that if you are in this field to work with the easy clients, then it's time to start hunting for another job! Laughter follows as the group takes this step back. Battered women come from all kinds of backgrounds and have all kinds of personalities, needs, and resources, but the experience of violence itself is likely to create the symptoms that we tag as "difficult" among our clients. In doing so, advocates fall into the same stereotyping that has long plagued the majority of battered women, who do not fit the mold of being meek, weak, and mild. Similarly, it logically follows that the harder a woman may be to work with, or advocate for, the greater in need of services she is likely to be.

Here we want to go one step further to examine what happens when battered women are "institutionalized" by domestic abuse service providers. Research on people living in institutional settings has documented numerous impacts, such as isolation, the development of an "us vs. them" stance between staff and clients, sleep disruptions, aggression, defiance, passivity, helplessness, depression, physical complaints, withdrawal, depersonalization, and manipulation. Again, this list has a familiar cast to it. We would suggest that trauma alone may not account for the behavior of battered women experienced by domestic abuse advocates: some of it may be iatrogenic in origin.

◼ History Repeats Itself

At the beginning of our country's history, mental health concerns were largely blamed on the individual: the result of sin, lack of moral character, or perhaps even demonic possession. Having such a person in the family was a private matter, an embarrassment best kept out of public scrutiny and handled in the home. A similar view was taken toward people with physical disabilities. There were some early lunatic asylums established to at least house, if not treat, people with mental illnesses from as early as 1247 in England (Bethlehem Royal Hospital or Bedlam) but widespread concerted and public care did not take off until the 19th century in America, perhaps in response to the urbanization brought on by the Industrial Revolution, when cities were challenged by populations burgeoning beyond the capacity of community infrastructures. These mental institutions provided cost-effective care and safety for people with mental illnesses. However, they also served the purpose of providing emotional and physical security for neurotypical society by removing community members unable or unwilling to behave in socially acceptable ways.

The human cost of two world wars—veterans left with physical disabilities, post-traumatic stress disorder, and other emotional traumas—challenged our methods and capacity to provide for and rehabilitate former community members. Advances in psychotherapeutic medicines, the emergence of self-help groups, identity reclaiming and political activism among numerous socially disadvantaged groups, and significant paradigm shifts in the ways mental illness was viewed all converged to open the door to the deinstitutionalization movement of the 1960s and 1970s. The Community Mental Health Centers Act of 1963 was a watershed in establishing a national system of community-based care for mentally ill people, emptying the chronic-care hospitals established in remote areas well away from "normal" citizens. Unfortunately, the emptying of hospitals gained a lot of its momentum over the next few decades, not only from advances in practice, but from federal and state budget cuts to social services of all kinds, including mental health. This had the impact of "freeing" some chronically and pervasive mentally ill people to "make the choice" of adding to the homeless population of our nation's streets.

If we trace its history, we can see the same pattern of response to battered women as we see to people with mental illness. Prior to the 1960s, domestic abuse, like mental illness, was regarded as a private matter largely due to individual moral or educational failings. The 1970s saw the beginning of the battered women's movement, arising out of the women's movement and the anti-sexual assault movements particularly. Shelter was offered in people's homes and in "safe houses," but soon the need for safety led to the rise of shelters across the country. Initially these were small agencies, often housed in older homes, with few beds, but a growing push for more efficiency and increased demand for beds has led to the building of large new facilities housing upwards of 30, 50, 100, or more residents.

One of the driving forces behind the change to community-based mental health services was the realization that, when it comes to humans, bigger does not necessarily mean better. The larger the institution, the greater the need for social controls that were, ironically, generative of even greater management issues and individual psychopathology. In our own community, the county mental hospital, safely tucked away from society in a corn field, was abandoned in the early 1980s for smaller group-living sites around town and a drop-in community center. What the mental health system learned the hard way is that, for the majority of people living with mental health issues, living in as "normal" and home-like an environment as possible and having access to the social, employment, and supportive services in their communities are the keys to stability, recovery, and quality of life. Also, because of its success, it is also the most cost-effective method of service delivery in the long run.

Some women with mental illness are battered, and many battered women experience post-traumatic stress disorder and other psychiatric problems from being battered. However, this comparison of issues facing battered women and those facing people with mental illnesses throughout this essay should not be misinterpreted as a belief on the authors' part that battered women are mentally ill; rather, we have a duty as advocates for battered women to provide the best services possible and that often means drawing on the experiences and knowledge of other professionals. We would be negligent if we did not examine the history and practice of other systems engaged in sheltering vulnerable members of our communities.

And if those systems have, over time, learned that their own practices could lead to negative behaviors and have unsafe impacts on those they serve, isn't it reasonable to assume the same of domestic abuse programs? Are the women we are working with really as manipulative, angry, aggressive, lying, thieving, etc. as we might suppose, or do we encourage such behavior by the way we treat them?

Take, for example, the case of a woman calling a hotline to know if she can come to a shelter. There is usually some kind of initial brief screening that happens to determine whether she is appropriate for services. In many places in the country, the screening includes determining if she has a substance abuse problem and if she uses currently. If the answer is yes to those questions, she is denied shelter services until she has completed a treatment program. This means that only women without substance abuse problems and women who lie about their issues will be sheltered. As a consequence of this program practice, a battered woman with substance abuse problems will not feel safe disclosing to her advocate that she has a need or barrier in that area, because honesty will mean she has nowhere to go but back to her abusive situation. However, if she is dishonest about her substance use, the program will not be able to adequately address her needs, and she may leave the program or return to her abuser anyway; she will either be seen as "not being ready" to leave her abuse situation if her substance issues remain secret, or if they become known, she will be viewed as a bad client and a liar.

As staff at a state domestic abuse coalition, we are often privy to the backstage conversations, arguments, and frustrations domestic abuse advocates are engaged in, not only locally, but across the country. It's not unusual to hear advocates complain about the time-consuming nature of tasks like shelter room checks. The room checks are said to be necessary for a variety of reasons, from making sure beds are made to looking for contraband such as alcohol or drugs. These practices must be examined by asking questions such as: why are you concerned if someone is making her bed? What kind of enforcement are you willing to do on an infraction? If she leaves or is asked to leave because of bed-making, how comfortable would you be in the courtroom on the stand defending that policy if her batterer kills her? One program director who refuses to have her staff perform room checks, says, "I figure that addicts are always going to better at hiding their drugs than we are at finding them, and it's just not the way to open a conversation about wanting to help." In the end, we need to ask ourselves, if women keep breaking a rule, are the women the problem, or is it the rule itself?

■ Battered Women's Risks

As it stands today, there are several, sometimes contradictory, streams within the battered women's movement. One set of streams frequently goes under the rubric of "professionalizing." There is no cohesive agreement on the meaning of this word or on whether it is a good thing. The term "professionalizing" is applied to situations in which domestic abuse advocates become embedded in the infrastructure of other systems so that they cannot operate effectively, or at least cannot get grant money without collaboration from domestic abuse advocacy programs. Depending on one's point of view, this is proof of having the power to create systemic change or of being co-opted by the very systems that create barriers for battered women.

"Professionalizing" is also used to describe the development of service standards or accreditation for domestic abuse programs and certification programs for domestic abuse advocates. The positive view on these developments notes the increased accountability for how and what services are provided, more knowledgeable staff, consistency of service, grievance procedures, and drive to improvement by the delineation of best practices. On the negative side, critics highlight the move toward more one-size-fits-all models, an increased "us vs. them" mentality that separates advocates from the women receiving services, and a paradigm shift from a social movement with a primary goal of social change to a social institution with a primary goal of helping individual clients.

Jill Davies focuses attention on battered women's analysis of their risks by breaking them down into batterer-generated and life-generated risks.[1] *Batterer-generated risks* are those physical and non-physical risks to a woman directly caused by her batterer's use of force and coercion, factors such as isolation, injuries, the undermining of her parental authority, or post-traumatic stress disorder. *Life-generated risks* are those barriers battered women face that their batterers didn't cause (but often benefit from), such as a lack of living-wage jobs or housing, language barriers, social status, disabilities, or rural isolation and lack of services. These risks are often created and sustained by racism, heterosexism, sexism, and other oppressive ideologies. This framework for analyzing battered women's risks has been expanded to include *intervention-generated risks*, which arise from institutional actions or failure to act, such as deportation of battered immigrant women or the removal of children by child protective services.[1] The battered women's movement has a well-earned reputation for critiquing other systems and service providers; we must be no less fearless or ruthless in examining our own. In doing so, we must open the discussion of battered women's domestic abuse program-generated risks. The term may make advocates cringe but demanding transparency and accountability from ourselves can help raise the respect we receive from other systems.

■ Hoops and Fences

Battered women who kill have as varied of personality types, histories, and skills as anyone else. Some of them are easy to empathize with, but some of them are a challenge to advocate for, and some of them may be downright frightening. As an individual setting about to work on behalf of these women, you must do some fundamental soul searching about what people deserve, what constitutes self-defense, and what behavior is beyond what you are personally capable of dealing with or getting past so that you can serve someone to the best of your ability.

When individuals seek help from institutions, they are always faced with a set of criteria that they must meet in order to receive services. These criteria are both formal, such as financial resources, age, residency, etc. and informal, such as "good client"/"bad client" lists. These are "hoops" that clients have to jump through and "fences" set up to keep certain people out of receiving services. The informal and formal criteria are not static. A woman who resembles the "bad client" list might find that the criteria are higher for her. For an illustration of this in practice, consider: infractions, such as leaving her children unattended, may be overlooked for a woman who cleans all the time and is skilled at expressing her appreciation, but will result in a written warning being given to a woman who instigates conflict among the shelter residents.

Advocates should begin at a personal level exploring and naming their hoops and fences. It is all right to have personal boundaries. A battered woman who was also a sexual perpetrator would probably not get through an advocate's hoops, and she would not be the best advocate for that person. Another would be challenged by an angry aggressive woman she found personally intimidating. This self-assessment is a step toward uncovering, rather than masking, limitations and ensuring that all women are treated fairly when they seek domestic abuse services.

Advocates can back one another up, knowing where each other's strengths and weaknesses are to ensure that women are matched to the right person, or hold one another accountable. In our staff meetings, this has the appearance of a sudden attack of calisthenics as someone raises her arms to make a big circle over her head, saying, "I'm sensing a hoop-fence issue here, is there something about this situation that's hitting too close to home?" or, "I've got a hoop-fence thing I need to talk through." The next step requires a similar assessment at the agency level, constantly asking the question: how can we lower the hoops? How can we eliminate as many fences as possible? Rather than assuming we know best, we need to critically audit our own programs for philosophy and practice that are about agency needs rather than the needs of battered women.

■ Problematic Features of Institutions of Social Management

The community audit work spearheaded by Ellen Pence is based on an analysis of the impact of public and private agency systems on individuals.[2] This analysis begins with the following model of individuals and institutions: in everyday life, an individual is surrounded by public and private agencies such as schools, courts, welfare authorities, mental and physical health care providers, law enforcement, and housing authorities. Informed by regulatory bodies, ideology, and discourse, these agencies regulate and address social concerns, usually by processing individual "cases." Cases are assessed and channeled to receive services deemed appropriate or available.[2]

Based on this relationship between individuals, communities, and agencies, the Praxis model for community audits delineates twelve problematic features of these institutions of social management:

- They fragment lives. Different aspects being dealt with by different agencies that may or may not coordinate services. A battered woman may have a criminal case, civil dissolution, and juvenile court case all going on within just the legal system, simultaneous with a social service case(s).
- They are coordinated by texts (regulations, reports, policies) that define concepts, embody philosophy, and standardize responses. They are so strongly textually driven that text is sometimes held at a higher level of reality than the persons involved, such as when a report stating that an alleged incident of child abuse is unfounded is read as proof that no child abuse is actually occurring.
- They must rely on categories to sort and channel people through service systems. These categories are unlikely to capture the complexity of an individual's needs and experience, especially for marginalized groups who were unlikely to have even been considered when the categories were being defined.
- Their time lines that have little to do with the realities of people's lives. It is typical for a domestic abuse case in Iowa to take six to nine months from the incident to the trial.
- They give priority to institutional needs over those of individuals. Clients may have access to their caseworkers only during standard business hours that conflict with their work schedule. People with a variety of needs may be lumped into receiving the same standard service, such as a class, because the agency cannot afford to provide specialized services.

- They generate a great deal of communication, but often little dialogue. For example, victims may be "notified" about the status of a criminal case—and sometimes not even that—but have little opportunity for meaningful input in how the case is handled.
- They engage in conceptual practices that organize how workers think and act. Establishing a collective philosophy and approach may be helpful to those working within institutions, but philosophy can negatively impact clients if it is based on misunderstanding, lack of awareness, or negative interpretations of clients' real experiences and barriers.
- They create a fictitious universal person as a standard. One size doesn't fit all in the physical sphere of life, much less the more complex social and emotional sphere.
- Their funding and public opinion often depends on an appearance of success and infallibility. This creates an institutional stance of defensiveness in which hiding inadequacies, problems, and failures take precedence over acknowledging and rectifying them.
- They are not very accountable to the people being managed. Not only do the individuals receiving services have little decision-making capacity in those services, they may not have access to grievance processes or opportunities to provide feedback. They rarely have meaningful input in policy and agency development.
- They use coercion to gain compliance. In Iowa, for example, victims who refuse to cooperate with prosecution have been charged with false reporting.
- Finally, rather than conceptualizing social concerns as negative features and consequences of the larger social structure, they focus on individuals as the source of troublesome issues, e.g., focusing on batterers as the cause of domestic violence and treating those individuals convicted of the crime to solve the problem, as opposed to viewing domestic abuse as a predictable and intrinsic feature of a hierarchical social system and engaging in social change activities.[3]

■ Domestic Abuse Program-Generated Risks

We can use these twelve problematic features to begin identifying the framework that gives rise to battered women's domestic-abuse program-generated risks.

Fragmented Lives

No agency staff person has the ability to be everything to all clients, and the current trend is for program staff to be divided into more and more specialized roles: child advocate, legal advocate, shelter advocate, economic justice advocate. This means that a woman may not only have multiple caseworkers in systems outside of shelter, she may also have dealings with three or four specialized advocates as well. She must juggle the information and approaches of each, and often must tell her story and work to establish rapport with each, at a time when her emotional resources and social skills capacity are likely to be taxed to their limit.

Textual Coordination

Domestic abuse advocates do not typically keep the kind of extensive reports and case files required by many institutions, but our work doesn't escape being corralled along specific parameters by agency policies, state laws, training manuals, schedules, etc. The Iowa Coalition Against Domestic Violence has standards for member programs that set out requirements for service provision to battered women. Occasionally, a battered woman or agency staff person will contact us with a grievance about a particular program. The Coalition can only respond if it is a violation of one of these written standards. Sometimes we have been unable to address very legitimate concerns because there was no textual foundation to act.

Categorization

Almost all of the domestic abuse programs in our state are also sexual assault victim service providers. One of the first category splits encountered by a woman seeking services is whether or not she is a battered woman or a sexual assault survivor. The service she receives from that point on largely depends on which form of violence she is tagged with. There are also the informal tags encountered in our opening exercise: a "cleaner," "a shelter hopper," a "bad mom."

Institutional Time

While many programs will negotiate with a woman who meets certain criteria (such as being able to show progress on specific identified goals), most programs around the country have limits on the length of time clients may stay in shelter. Shelters may have schedules that delineate meal times, when chores are to be done, when children must be in bed, and even curfews. A woman's job schedule, cultural differences, or trauma reactions can easily conflict with such arbitrary scheduling.

Institutional Needs Over Individual Ones

Kitchens may be kept locked at certain times, to both control food supplies and limit unsupervised use. Curfews may be established for "safety" but in reality are based on limited nighttime staff. Most domestic abuse programs have a rule for residents that mothers must supervise their children at all times—yet everyone who has been a parent knows that you must rely at times on other people, or your children's ability to self-supervise, in order to work, cook meals, or even shower. The emphasis on parental responsibility is often due to a lack of staff to look after children, lack of child-care licensing, and liability concerns. A program that truly focused on parenting needs would likely provide on site daycare and/or respite care for exhausted and traumatized mothers.[4]

Communication Without Dialogue

Programs frequently inform residents of shelter rules and guidelines without providing the opportunity for women living there to have meaningful input in the development of those rules. As programs develop, they may make many plans for outreach or developing new projects without asking the women targeted by those activities what would actually be helpful. The importance of getting that feedback is best illustrated by what happened here in Iowa when economic justice efforts began to get off the ground. Wisely, efforts began with a series of focus groups with women receiving services. The assumption was that if programs could help women to be safer, that would improve their economic self-sufficiency; but the answer that came back from the women themselves was a resounding: "help us to be economically self-sufficient, and we will be safer." This message requires an entirely different approach to advocacy, where building job skills, English language classes, and housing programs become primary program components to helping battered women.

Conceptual Practices

There are many conceptual practices in need of scrutiny: one is a widespread belief among domestic abuse program staff that women who abuse substances are going to be violent in shelter and must achieve sobriety before being housed. Programs are also uneasy about providing services to women used in prostitution because they are absent from the conceptual framework of "battered woman" or "sexual assault victim." Transgender women encounter similar barriers. Another conceptual practice that we frequently hear about has to do with child abuse reporting. Programs frequently have a policy that staff will follow mandatory reporter child abuse guidelines, but in the state of Iowa, domestic abuse advocates are not under any such statutory obligation. In conjunction with this practice is the concept that any use of violence toward a child is "child abuse" and should be reported. This is not in fact the case: while we would certainly not argue that a mother slapping her child across the face constitutes good parenting, unless it leaves a significant mark that lasts at least twenty-four hours, it is extremely unlikely that such an action would meet the definition of child abuse that governs the response of child protective services. Consequently, the impact of a report to child protective services is likely to sever the program's rapport with that mother, perhaps even to the extent that she leaves all services, without engaging her in any real assistance to support her parenting.

Fictitious Universal Person

Deaf women using a TTY may be hung up on when they call a crisis line because it does not cross the advocate's mind that the beeping sound they hear could be anything but a fax. The universal battered woman is conceptualized as white, English-speaking, lower income, about 20 to 50 years old, heterosexual, able-bodied, hearing, with children. This is the segment of battered women that programs have historically reached and, because of familiarity, are most comfortable serving. When financial crises force programs to cut services, outreach to underserved communities is frequently the first to go. This is, ipso facto, a decision to focus on the fictitious "universal" battered woman and therefore to reduce services to women of color and others the program finds more challenging to serve.

Masking Limits and Failures

More than once, we have heard bad policy defended on the basis that it is a battered woman's choice whether or not to use the agency (the "like it or lump it" defense), but there is no abundance of alternative competitive choices available in communities. A great deal is made in the movement about battered women having choices—about choice being the key to regain personal control over your life and destiny. This language is subverted when used by programs to describe a woman's "choice" to leave a shelter rather than cope with curfews, room searches, etc., or her "choice" to continuing using drugs rather than going to treatment so that she can receive advocacy.

Lack of Accountability

Do agencies prioritize the hiring and use of formerly battered women as volunteers as staff and board? Are focus groups of current or formerly battered women who have received services convened to discuss programmatic or policy changes? And ultimately, what advocacy groups do battered women turn to to give them voice?

Coercion to Gain Compliance

Universally, all programs have at least one rule for which the consequence of violation is to be refused services, usually in the form of being asked to leave shelter. Lesser rules may have consequences such as written warnings, the accumulation of which at some point may lead to expulsion. Asking about consequences is a test we suggest to analyze rules. How will you handle the situation if this rule is violated? Will you really throw a woman out after five warnings because she never does her dishes? Will you only implement the consequence on a case-by-case basis? How do the bad client vs. good client lists we started with come into play in determining who receives the consequence and whose transgressions are overlooked? How useful is that rule then?

Individualizing the Social

The story of women being rescued from a river one after the other until someone decides to go upstream to stop whomever is throwing them in has become canon in this movement, and yet, just like outreach to underserved communities, social change activities are the first to be cut from program budgets—if they receive any budgetary consideration whatsoever. The money is there to help women one by one—so many nights in a shelter bed, so many restraining orders, so many counseling hours—but not to improve women's safety by changing society. A number of women within the battered women's movement have warned against the transformation from a focus on social justice to social work. Yet that is one of the most significant changes that has taken place within the movement.

■ Conclusion

This chapter presents just a taste of how critical skills need to be applied to our own work. The focus in the above is primarily on shelter-based services, but similar analysis can and must be applied to out-client services. Domestic abuse programs, as institutions of social management, cannot help but fall prey to these problematic features. They are the requirements of being a service provider. Programs cannot function without organizing principles and practices. The challenge to the battered women's movement is finding ways for domestic abuse programs and staff to maintain an ongoing realistic awareness of those features and work to, at the very least, not blame battered women for them, and at best, curtail them to the maximum extent possible.

1. Davies, J. (2000). *Introduction to Policy Advocacy and Analysis: Improving How Systems Respond to Battered Women.* Washington, DC: National Resource Center on Domestic Violence.
2. Pence, E., McMahon, M. (2003). Making social change: Reflections on individual and institutional advocacy with women arrested for domestic violence. *Viol Against Women* 9:47–74.
3. Jaaber, R. A., Das Dasgupta, S. (2007). Assessing social risks of battered women. http://www.preventingviolence.org.nz/Files/G_Barnes/Graham%20 Barnes,%201.13.pdf., Accessed July 7, 2007.
4. Krane, J., Davies, L. (2002). Sisterhood is not enough: The invisibility of mothering in shelter practice with battered women. *Affilia* 17:167–190.

References